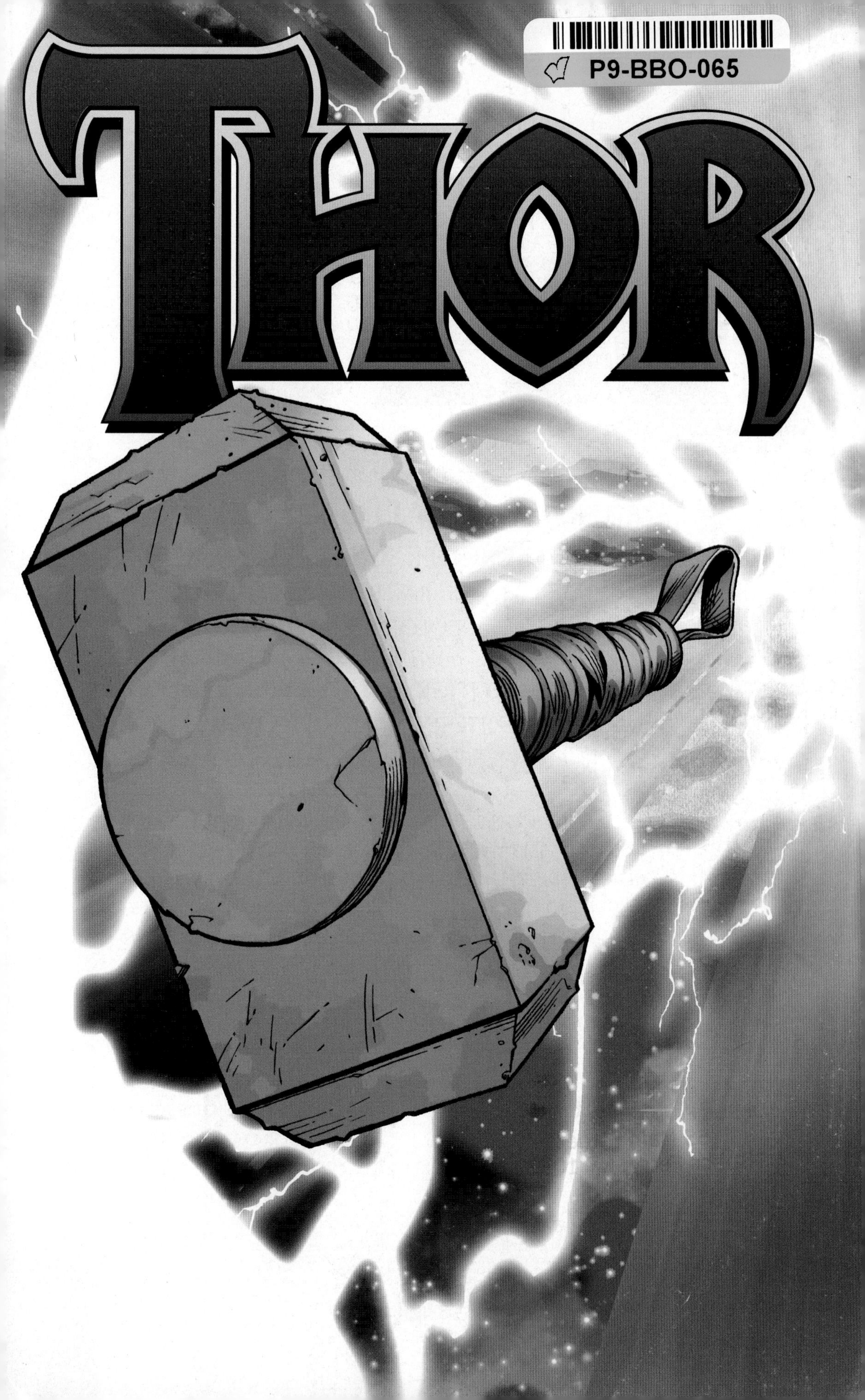
THOR

# THOR

WRITER: **J. MICHAEL STRACZYNSKI**

PENCILER: **OLIVIER COIPEL**

INKER: **MARK MORALES**

COLORIST: **LAURA MARTIN**

(WITH **PAUL MOUNTS,** ISSUE #5)

LETTERER: **CHRIS ELIOPOULOS**

ASSISTANT EDITOR: **ALEJANDRO ARBONA**

EDITOR: **WARREN SIMONS**

COLLECTION EDITOR: **JENNIFER GRÜNWALD**

EDITORIAL ASSISTANTS: **JAMES EMMETT** & **JOE HOCHSTEIN**

ASSISTANT EDITORS: **ALEX STARBUCK** & **NELSON RIBEIRO**

EDITOR, SPECIAL PROJECTS: **MARK D. BEAZLEY**

SENIOR EDITOR, SPECIAL PROJECTS: **JEFF YOUNGQUIST**

SENIOR VICE PRESIDENT OF SALES: **DAVID GABRIEL**

SVP OF BRAND PLANNING & COMMUNICATIONS: **MICHAEL PASCIULLO**

BOOK DESIGNER: **RODOLFO MURAGUCHI**

EDITOR IN CHIEF: **AXEL ALONSO**

CHIEF CREATIVE OFFICER: **JOE QUESADA**

PUBLISHER: **DAN BUCKLEY**

EXECUTIVE PRODUCER: **ALAN FINE**

THOR BY J. MICHAEL STRACZYNSKI VOL. 1. Contains material originally published in magazine form as THOR #1-6. Sixth printing 2011. ISBN# 978-0-7851-1722-3. Published by MARVEL WORLDWIDE, INC., a subsidiary of MARVEL ENTERTAINMENT, LLC. OFFICE OF PUBLICATION: 135 West 50th Street, New York, NY 10020. Copyright © 2007 and 2008 Marvel Characters, Inc. All rights reserved. $14.99 per copy in the U.S. and $16.99 in Canada (GST #R127032852); Canadian Agreement #40668537. All characters featured in this issue and the distinctive names and likenesses thereof, and all related indicia are trademarks of Marvel Characters, Inc. No similarity between any of the names, characters, persons, and/or institutions in this magazine with those of any living or dead person or institution is intended, and any such similarity which may exist is purely coincidental. **Printed in the U.S.A.** ALAN FINE, EVP - Office of the President, Marvel Worldwide, Inc. and EVP & CMO Marvel Characters B.V.; DAN BUCKLEY, Publisher & President - Print, Animation & Digital Divisions; JOE QUESADA, Chief Creative Officer; JIM SOKOLOWSKI, Chief Operating Officer; DAVID BOGART, SVP of Business Affairs & Talent Management; TOM BREVOORT, SVP of Publishing; C.B. CEBULSKI, SVP of Creator & Content Development; DAVID GABRIEL, SVP of Publishing Sales & Circulation; MICHAEL PASCIULLO, SVP of Brand Planning & Communications; JIM O'KEEFE, VP of Operations & Logistics; DAN CARR, Executive Director of Publishing Technology; JUSTIN F. GABRIE, Director of Publishing & Editorial Operations; SUSAN CRESPI, Editorial Operations Manager; ALEX MORALES, Publishing Operations Manager; STAN LEE, Chairman Emeritus. For information regarding advertising in Marvel Comics or on Marvel.com, please contact John Dokes, SVP Integrated Sales and Marketing, at jdokes@marvel.com. For Marvel subscription inquiries, please call 800-217-9158. **Manufactured between 4/11/2011 and 5/2/2011 by R.R. DONNELLEY, INC., SALEM, VA, USA.**

10 9 8 7 6

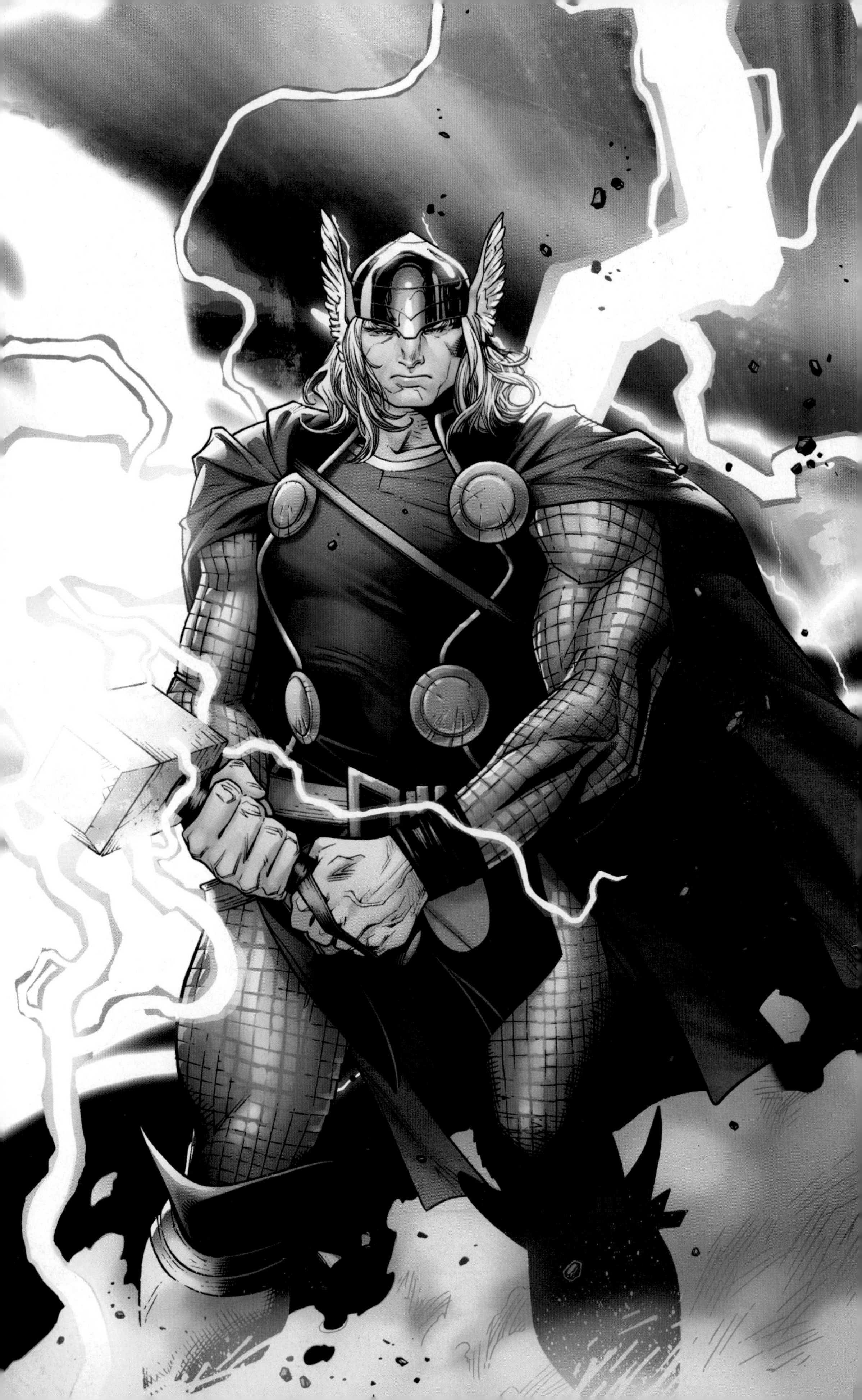

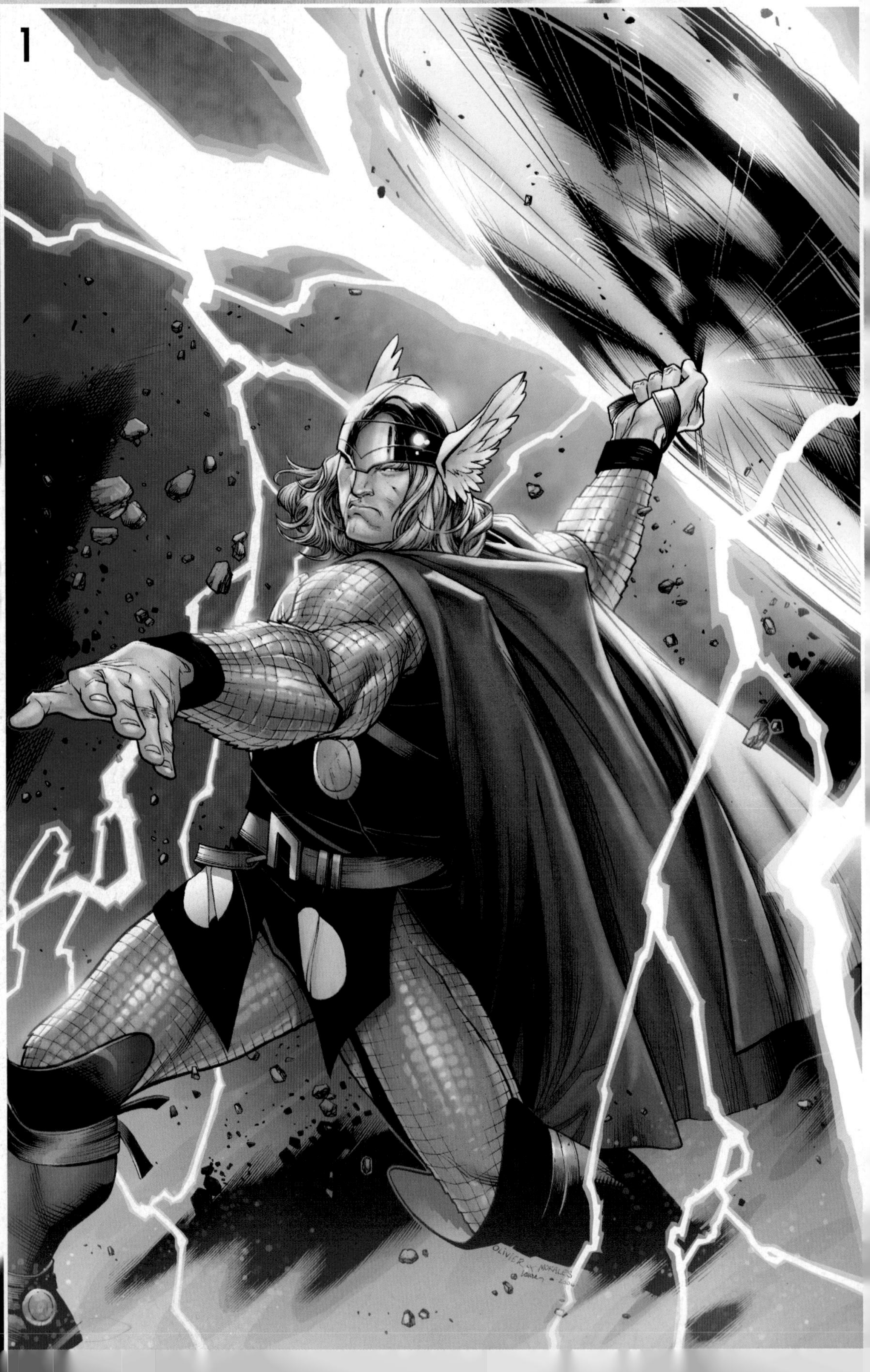
1

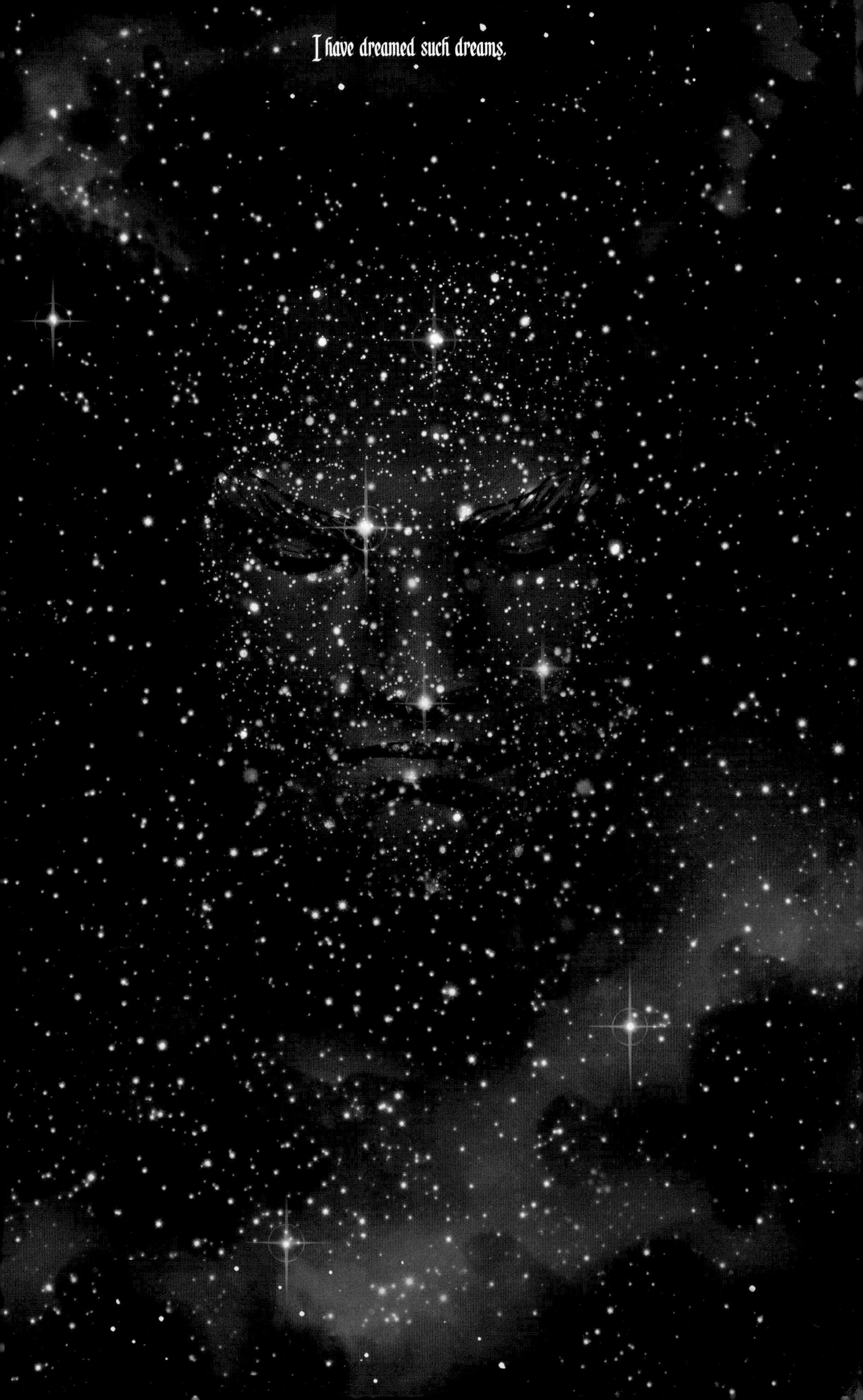
I have dreamed such dreams.

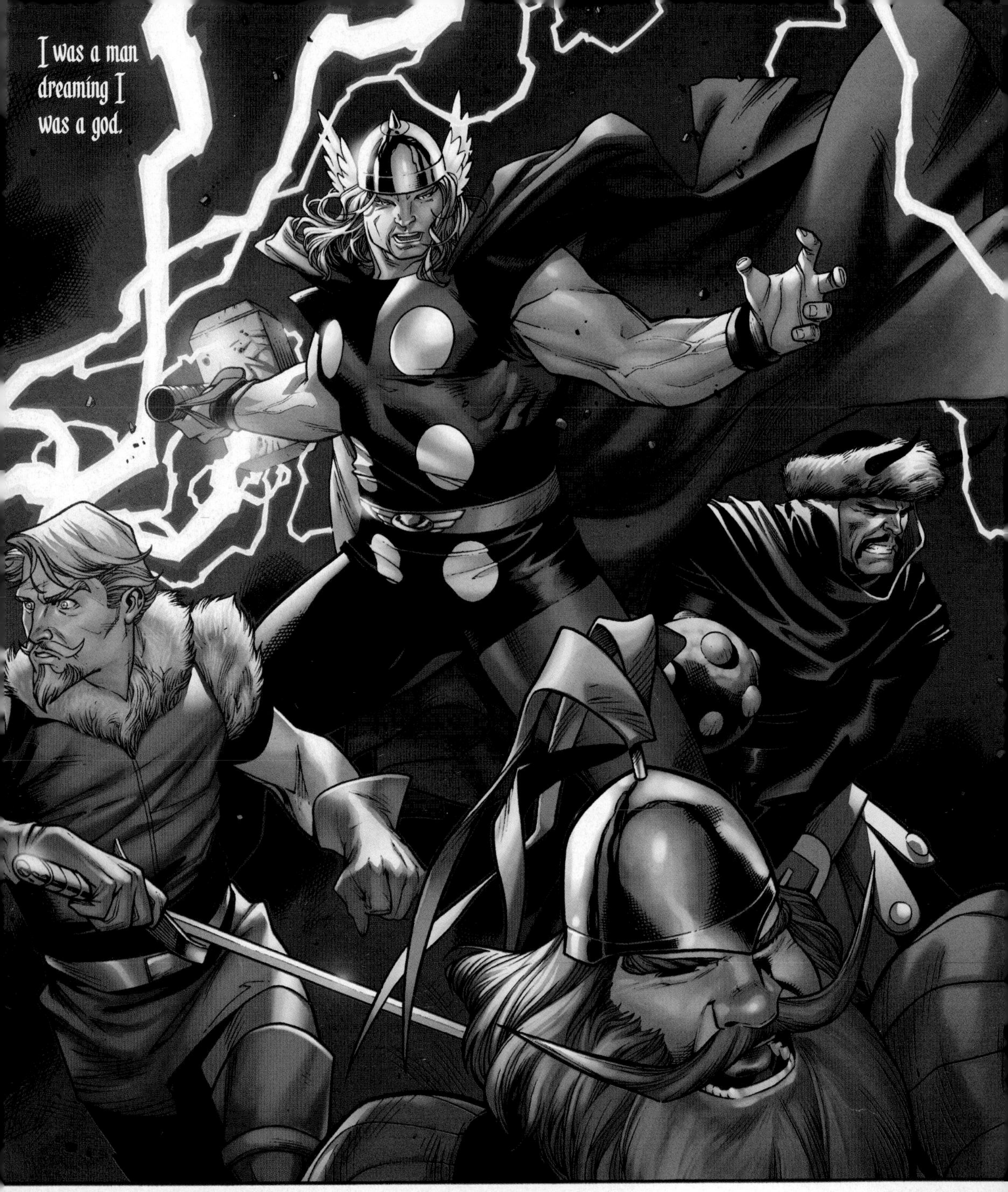
I was a man dreaming I was a god.

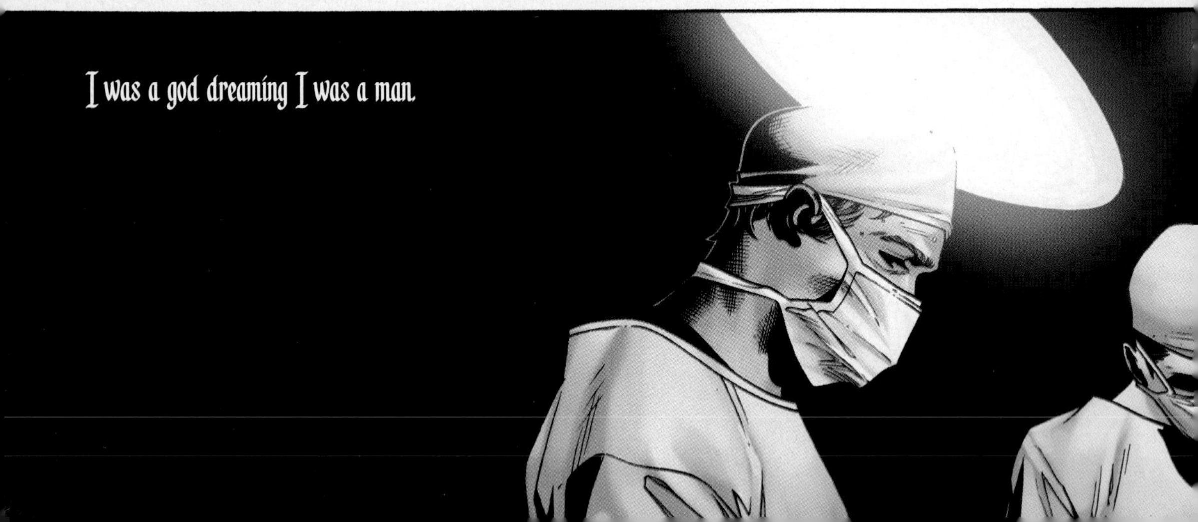
I was a god dreaming I was a man.

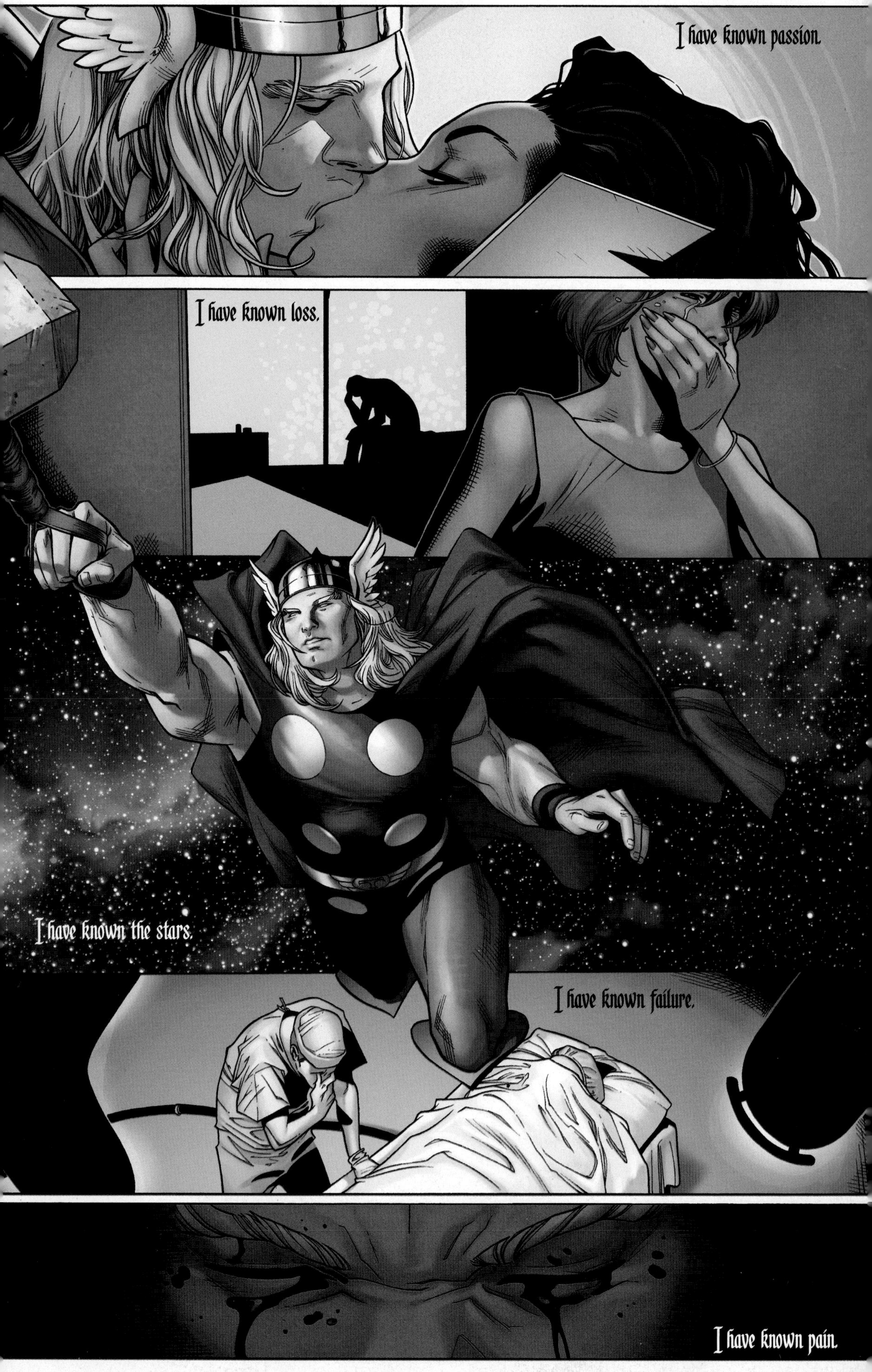

I have known passion.
I have known loss.
I have known the stars.
I have known failure.
I have known pain.

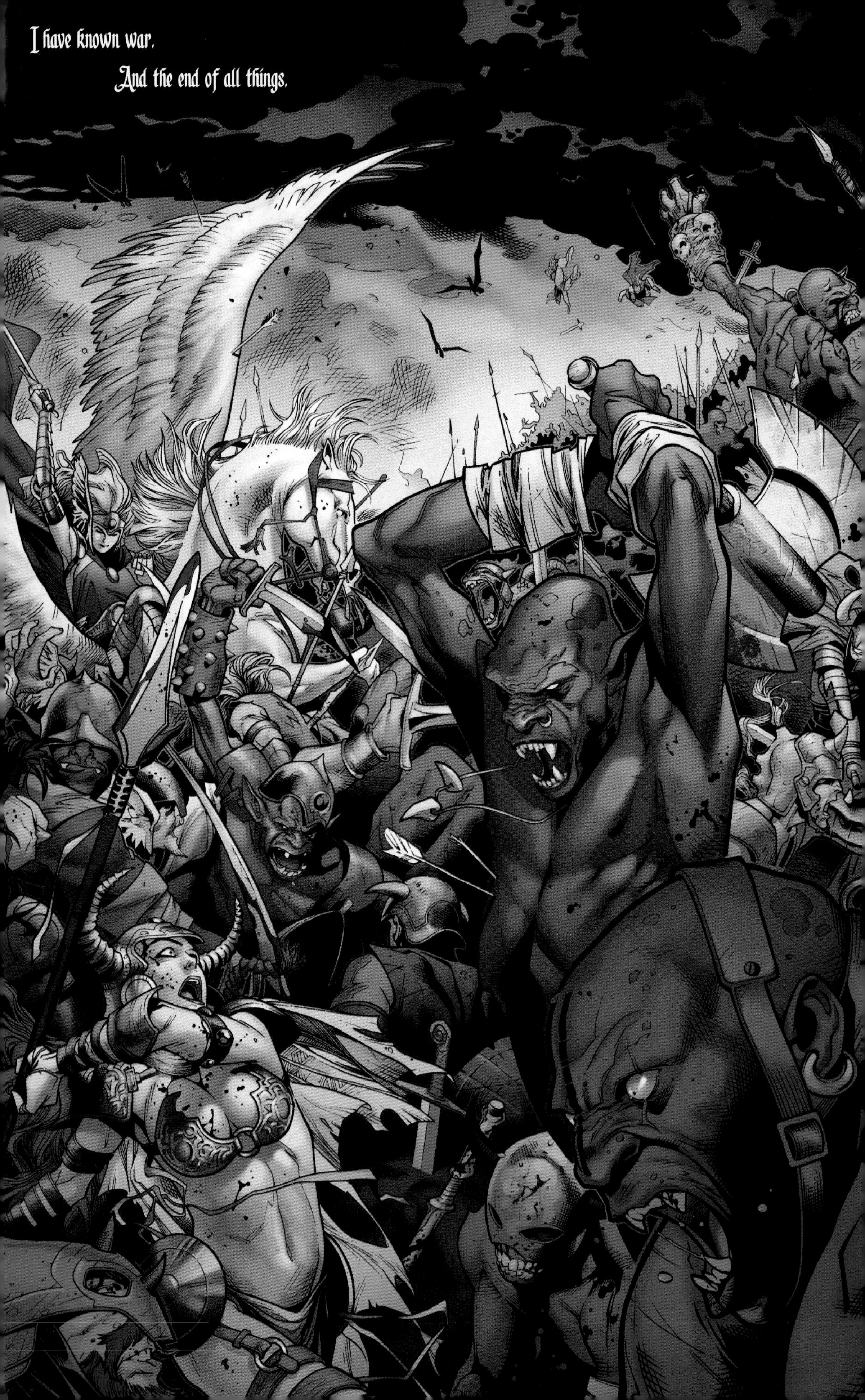
I have known war.
And the end of all things.

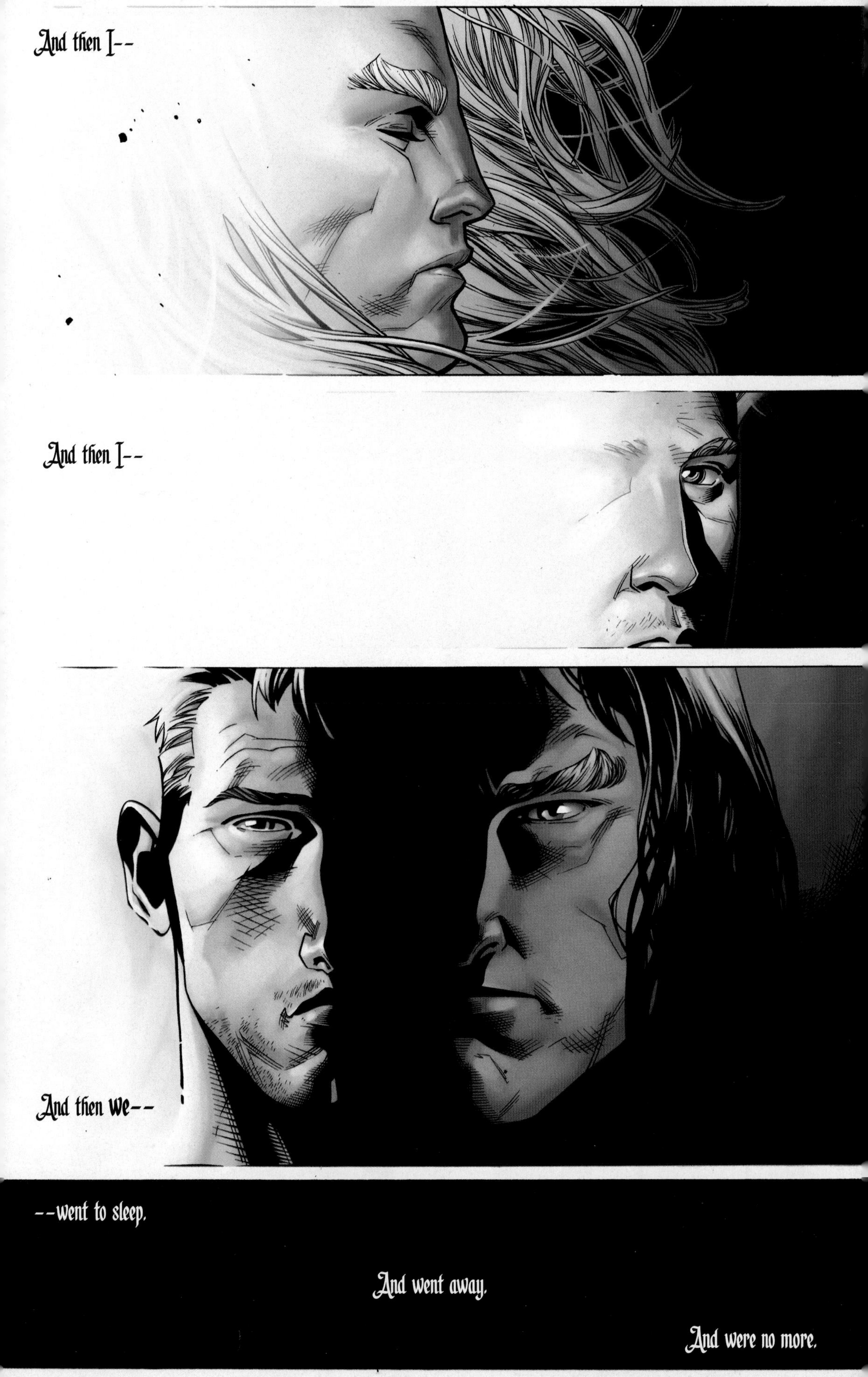
And then I--
And then I--
And then we--
--went to sleep.
And went away.
And were no more.

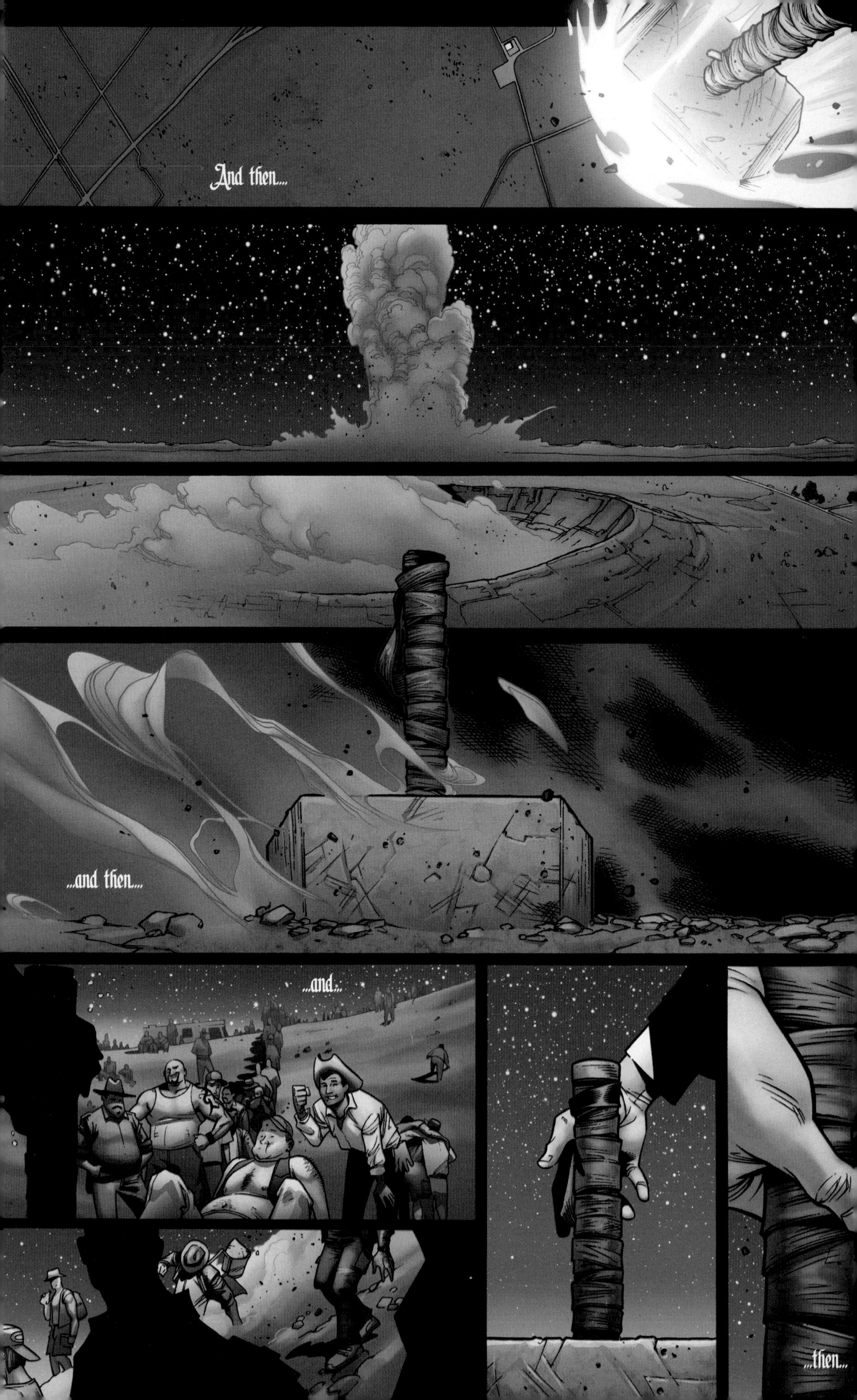
And then....
...and then....
...and...
...then...

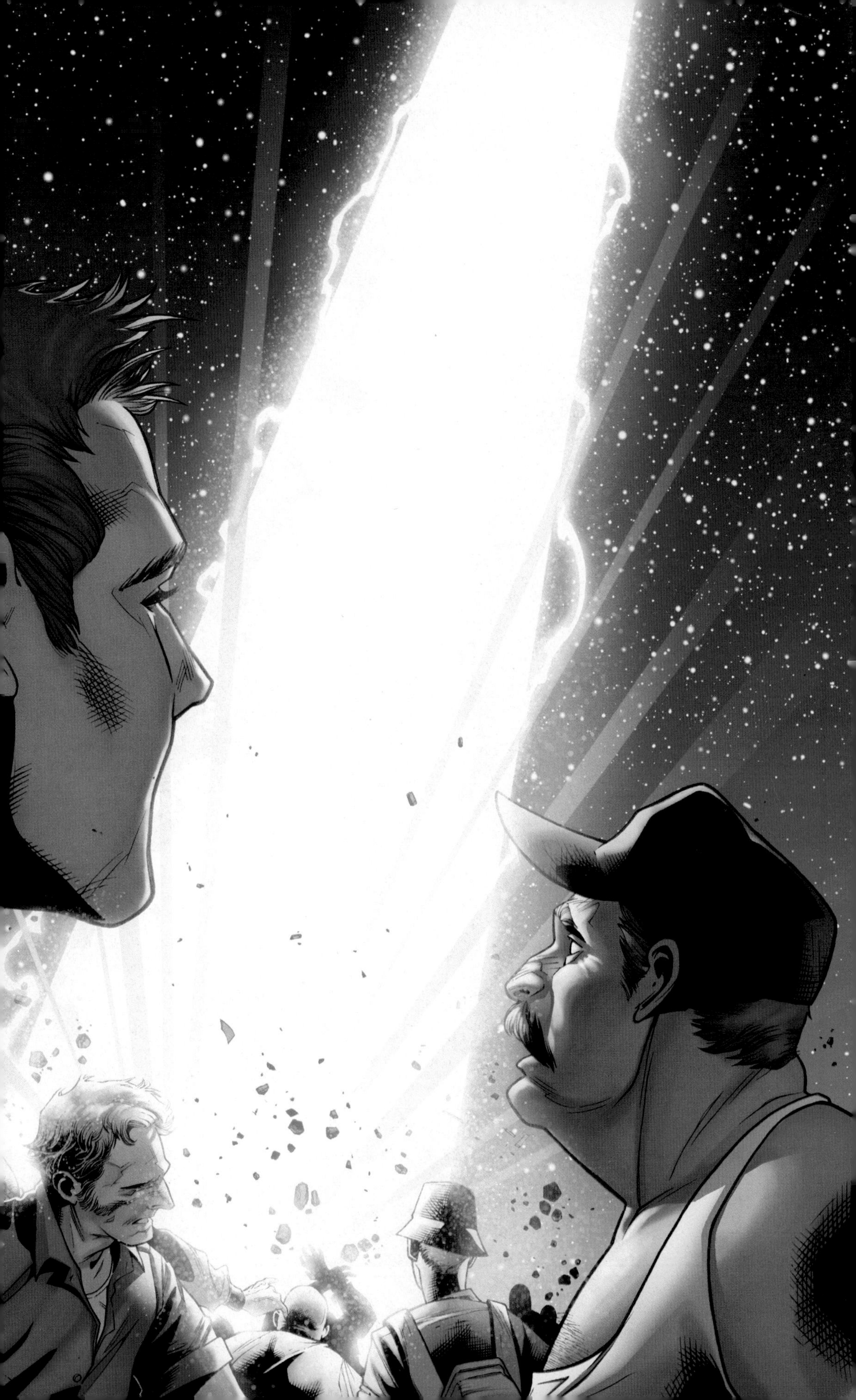

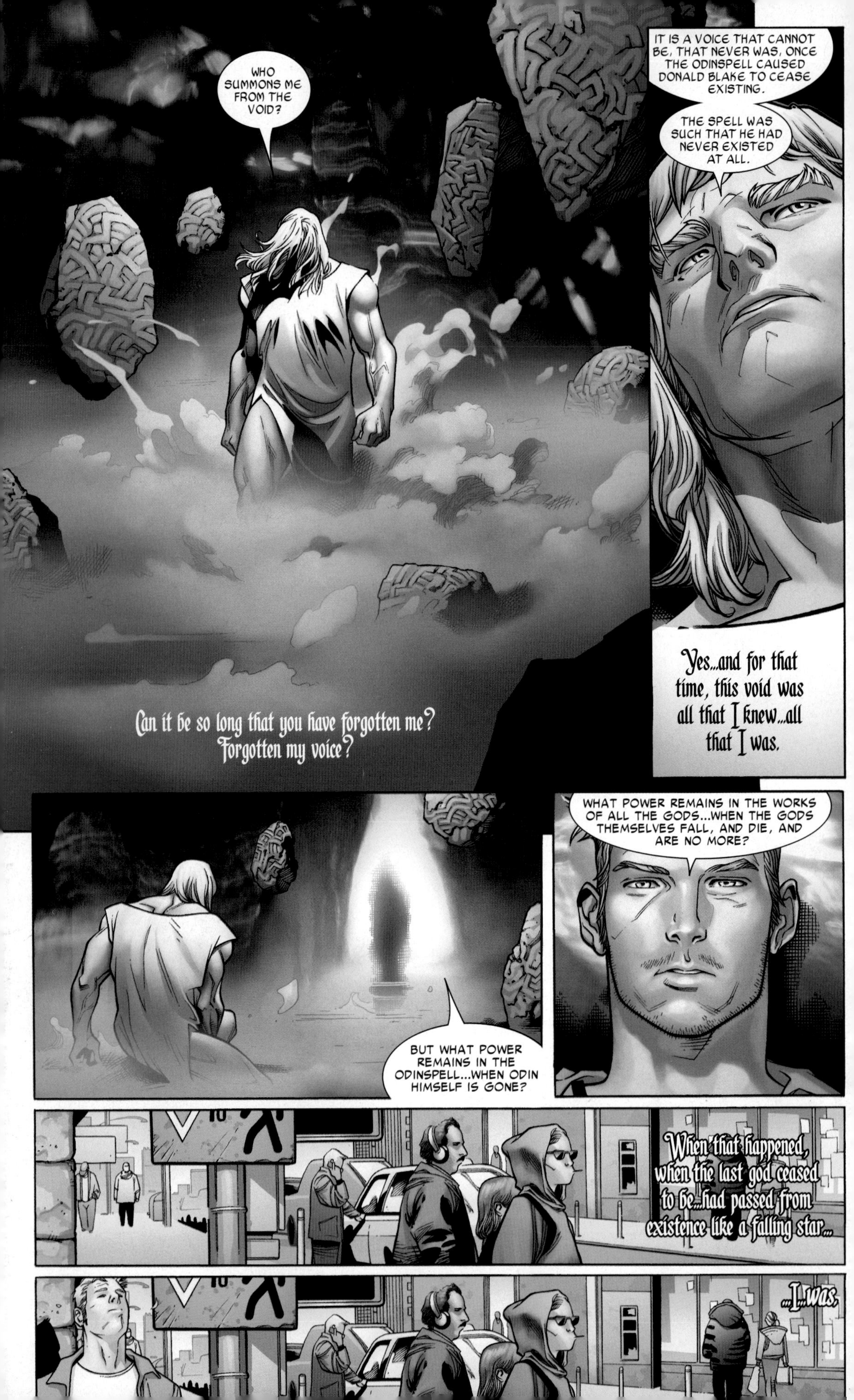
WHO SUMMONS ME FROM THE VOID?
IT IS A VOICE THAT CANNOT BE, THAT NEVER WAS, ONCE THE ODINSPELL CAUSED DONALD BLAKE TO CEASE EXISTING.
THE SPELL WAS SUCH THAT HE HAD NEVER EXISTED AT ALL.
Can it be so long that you have forgotten me? Forgotten my voice?
Yes...and for that time, this void was all that I knew...all that I was.
BUT WHAT POWER REMAINS IN THE ODINSPELL...WHEN ODIN HIMSELF IS GONE?
WHAT POWER REMAINS IN THE WORKS OF ALL THE GODS...WHEN THE GODS THEMSELVES FALL, AND DIE, AND ARE NO MORE?
When that happened, when the last god ceased to be...had passed from existence like a falling star...
...I was.

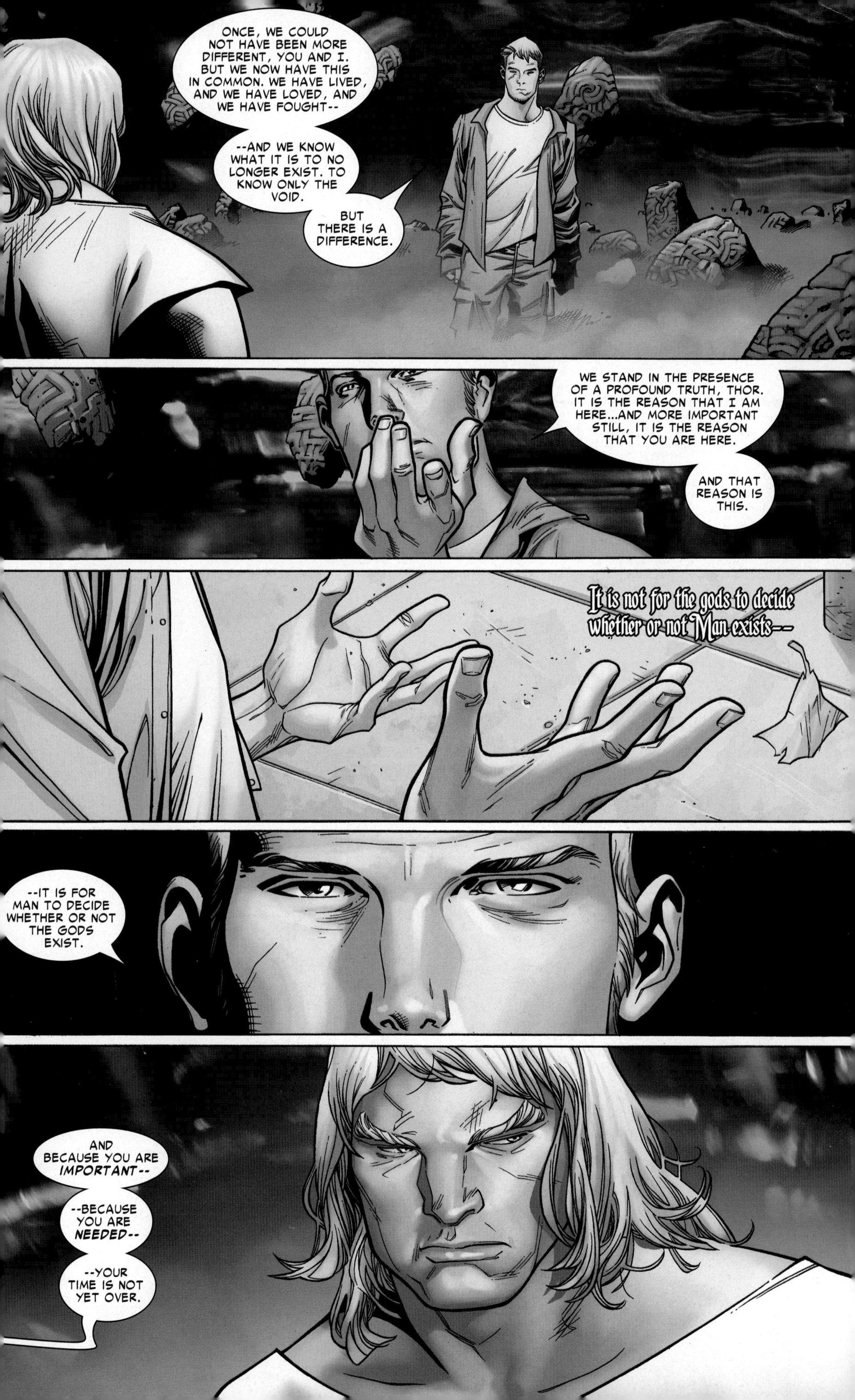
ONCE, WE COULD NOT HAVE BEEN MORE DIFFERENT, YOU AND I. BUT WE NOW HAVE THIS IN COMMON. WE HAVE LIVED, AND WE HAVE LOVED, AND WE HAVE FOUGHT--
--AND WE KNOW WHAT IT IS TO NO LONGER EXIST. TO KNOW ONLY THE VOID.
BUT THERE IS A DIFFERENCE.
WE STAND IN THE PRESENCE OF A PROFOUND TRUTH, THOR. IT IS THE REASON THAT I AM HERE...AND MORE IMPORTANT STILL, IT IS THE REASON THAT YOU ARE HERE.
AND THAT REASON IS THIS.
It is not for the gods to decide whether or not Man exists--
--IT IS FOR MAN TO DECIDE WHETHER OR NOT THE GODS EXIST.
AND BECAUSE YOU ARE *IMPORTANT*--
--BECAUSE YOU ARE *NEEDED*--
--YOUR TIME IS NOT YET OVER.

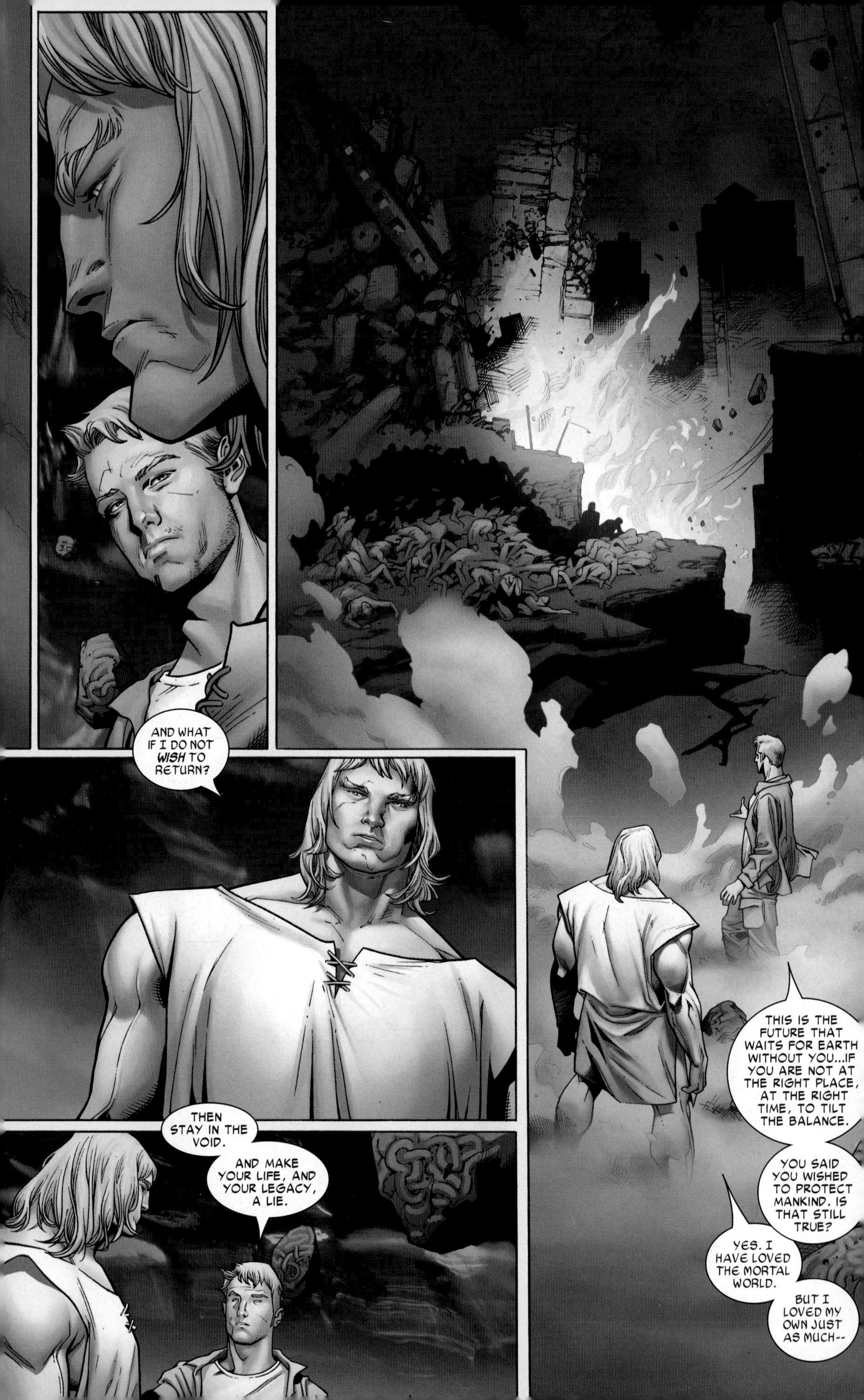
AND WHAT IF I DO NOT *WISH* TO RETURN?
THEN STAY IN THE VOID.
AND MAKE YOUR LIFE, AND YOUR LEGACY, A LIE.
THIS IS THE FUTURE THAT WAITS FOR EARTH WITHOUT YOU...IF YOU ARE NOT AT THE RIGHT PLACE, AT THE RIGHT TIME, TO TILT THE BALANCE.
YOU SAID YOU WISHED TO PROTECT MANKIND. IS THAT STILL TRUE?
YES. I HAVE LOVED THE MORTAL WORLD.
BUT I LOVED MY OWN JUST AS MUCH--

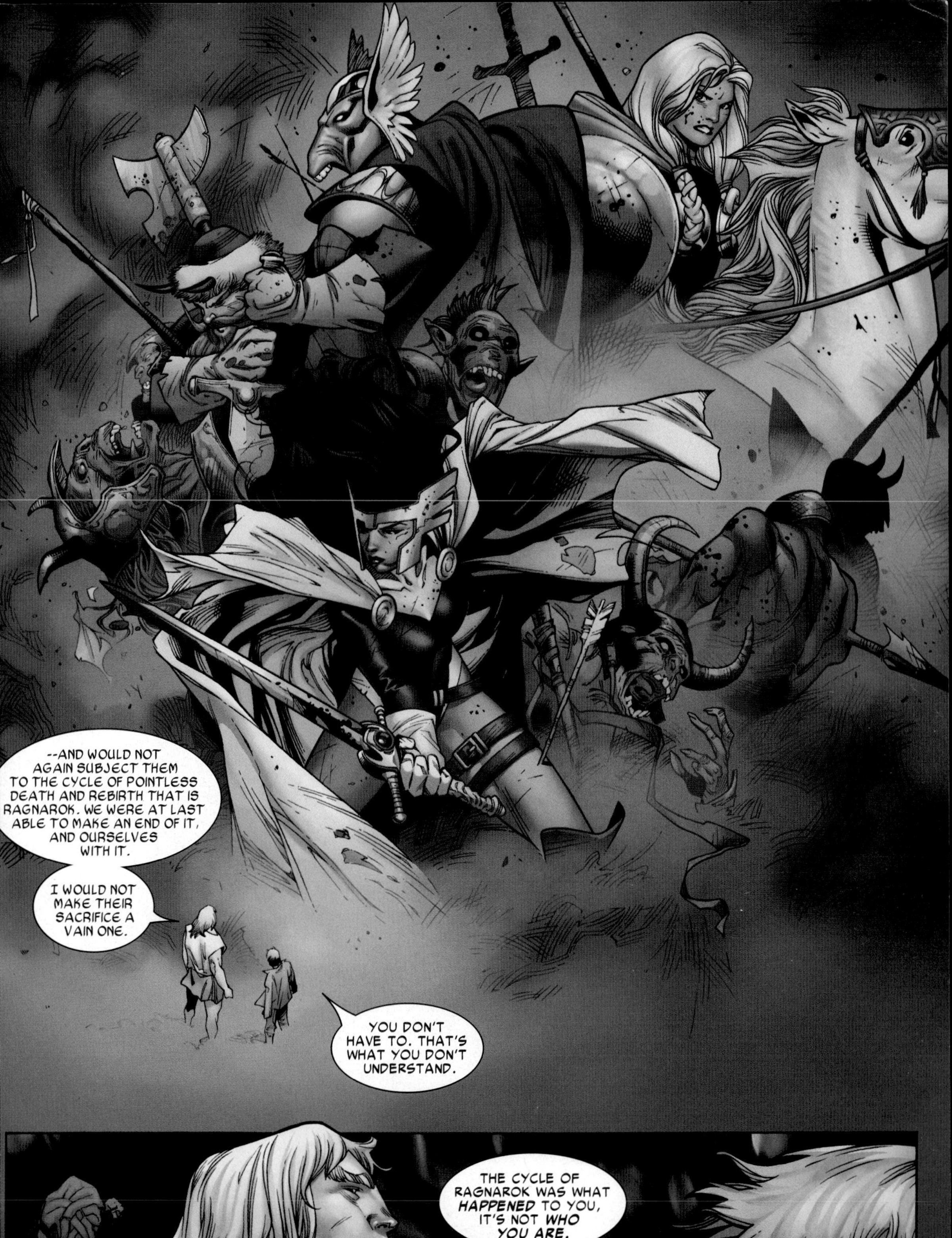
--AND WOULD NOT AGAIN SUBJECT THEM TO THE CYCLE OF POINTLESS DEATH AND REBIRTH THAT IS RAGNAROK. WE WERE AT LAST ABLE TO MAKE AN END OF IT, AND OURSELVES WITH IT.
I WOULD NOT MAKE THEIR SACRIFICE A VAIN ONE.
YOU DON'T HAVE TO. THAT'S WHAT YOU DON'T UNDERSTAND.

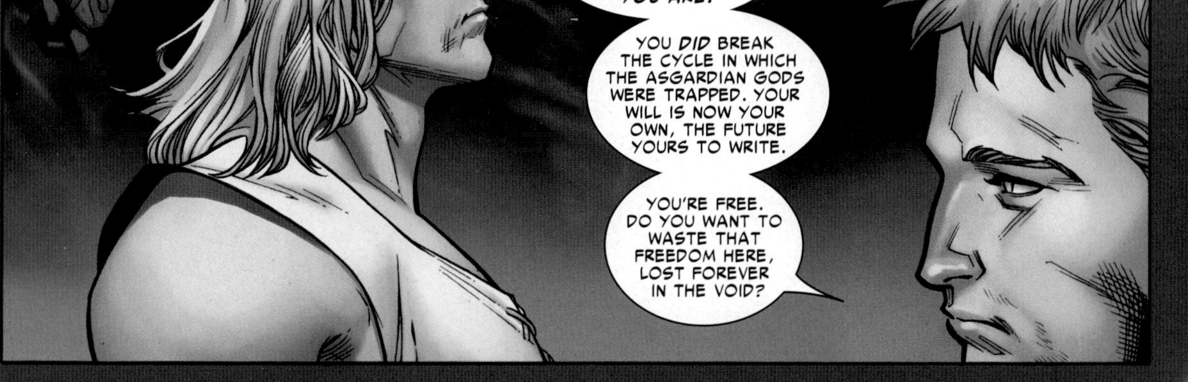
THE CYCLE OF RAGNAROK WAS WHAT *HAPPENED* TO YOU, IT'S NOT *WHO YOU ARE.*
YOU *DID* BREAK THE CYCLE IN WHICH THE ASGARDIAN GODS WERE TRAPPED. YOUR WILL IS NOW YOUR OWN, THE FUTURE YOURS TO WRITE.
YOU'RE FREE. DO YOU WANT TO WASTE THAT FREEDOM HERE, LOST FOREVER IN THE VOID?

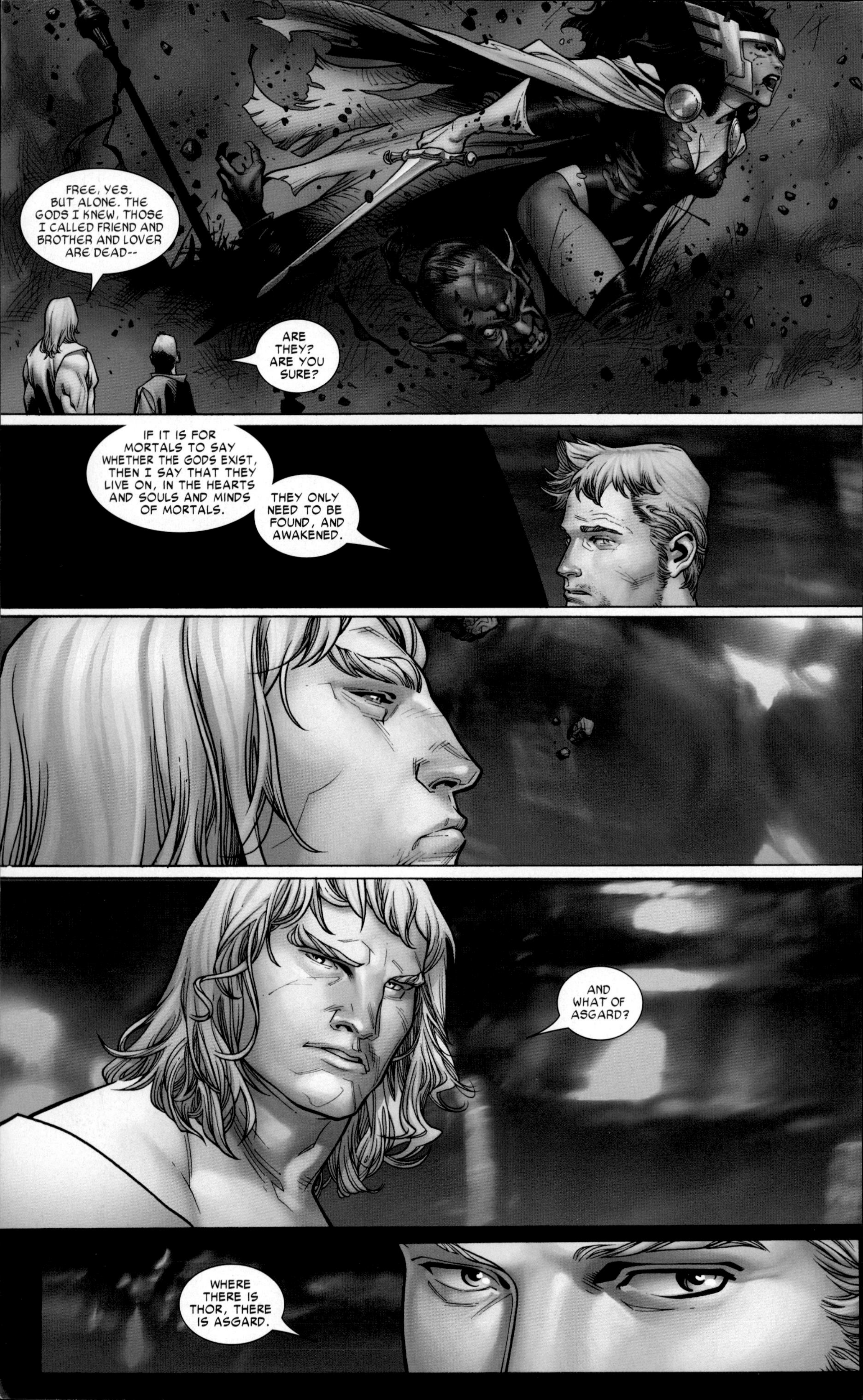

FREE, YES. BUT ALONE. THE GODS I KNEW, THOSE I CALLED FRIEND AND BROTHER AND LOVER ARE DEAD--
ARE THEY? ARE YOU SURE?
IF IT IS FOR MORTALS TO SAY WHETHER THE GODS EXIST, THEN I SAY THAT THEY LIVE ON, IN THE HEARTS AND SOULS AND MINDS OF MORTALS.
THEY ONLY NEED TO BE FOUND, AND AWAKENED.
AND WHAT OF ASGARD?
WHERE THERE IS THOR, THERE IS ASGARD.

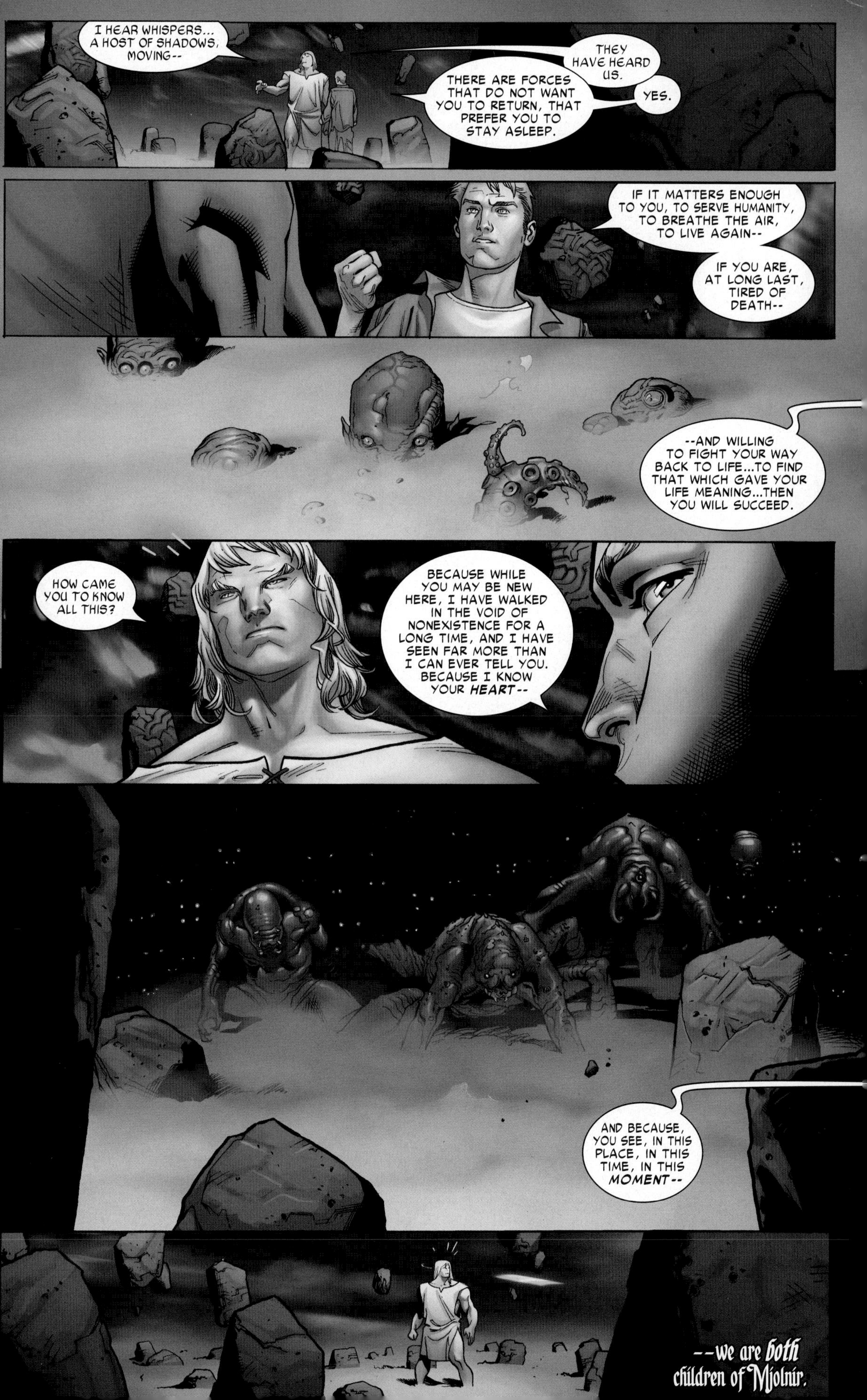
I HEAR WHISPERS... A HOST OF SHADOWS, MOVING--
THERE ARE FORCES THAT DO NOT WANT YOU TO RETURN, THAT PREFER YOU TO STAY ASLEEP.
THEY HAVE HEARD US.
YES.
IF IT MATTERS ENOUGH TO YOU, TO SERVE HUMANITY, TO BREATHE THE AIR, TO LIVE AGAIN--
IF YOU ARE, AT LONG LAST, TIRED OF DEATH--
--AND WILLING TO FIGHT YOUR WAY BACK TO LIFE...TO FIND THAT WHICH GAVE YOUR LIFE MEANING...THEN YOU WILL SUCCEED.
HOW CAME YOU TO KNOW ALL THIS?
BECAUSE WHILE YOU MAY BE NEW HERE, I HAVE WALKED IN THE VOID OF NONEXISTENCE FOR A LONG TIME, AND I HAVE SEEN FAR MORE THAN I CAN EVER TELL YOU. BECAUSE I KNOW YOUR *HEART*--
AND BECAUSE, YOU SEE, IN THIS PLACE, IN THIS TIME, IN THIS *MOMENT*--
--we are *both* children of Mjolnir.

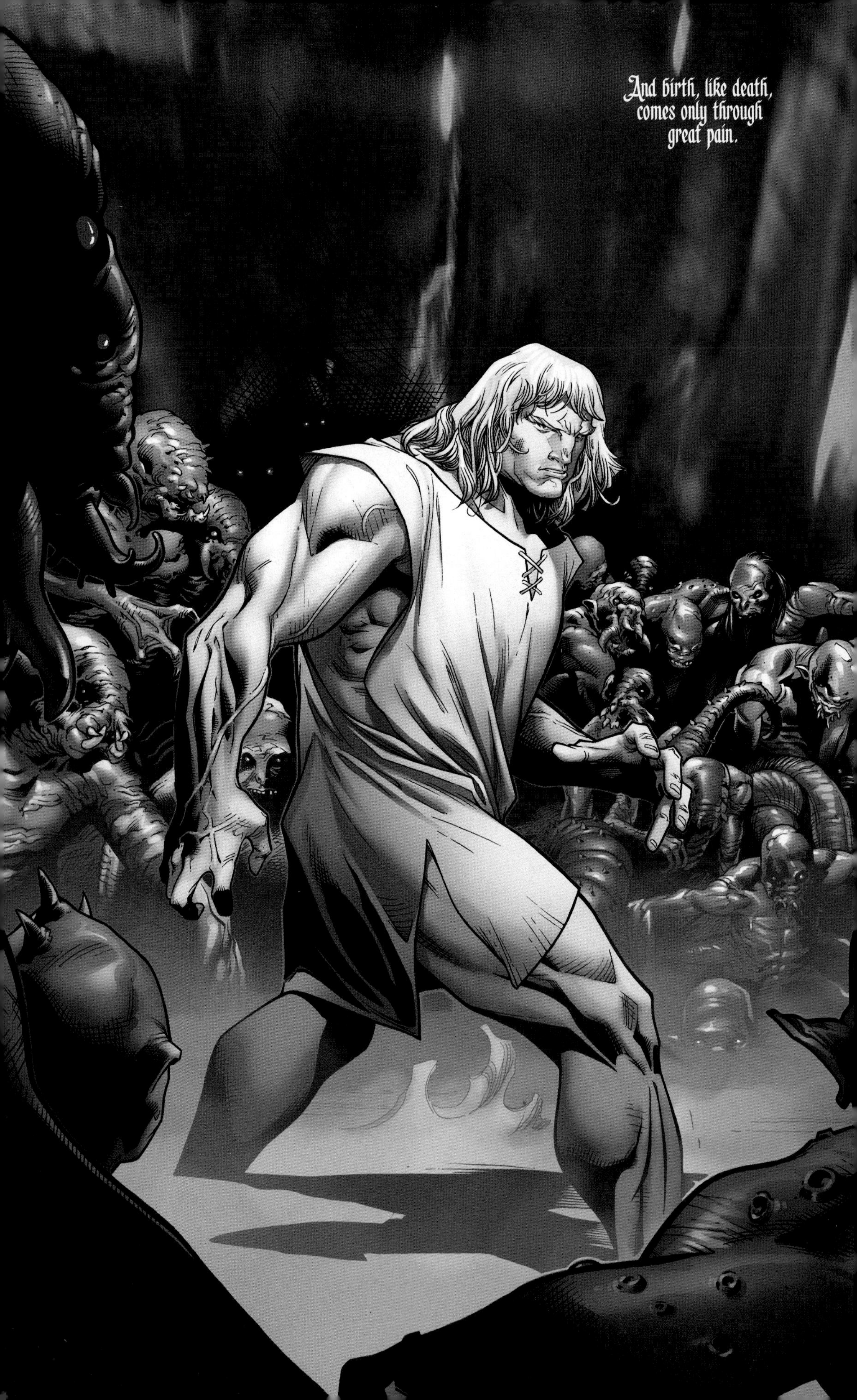
And birth, like death, comes only through great pain.

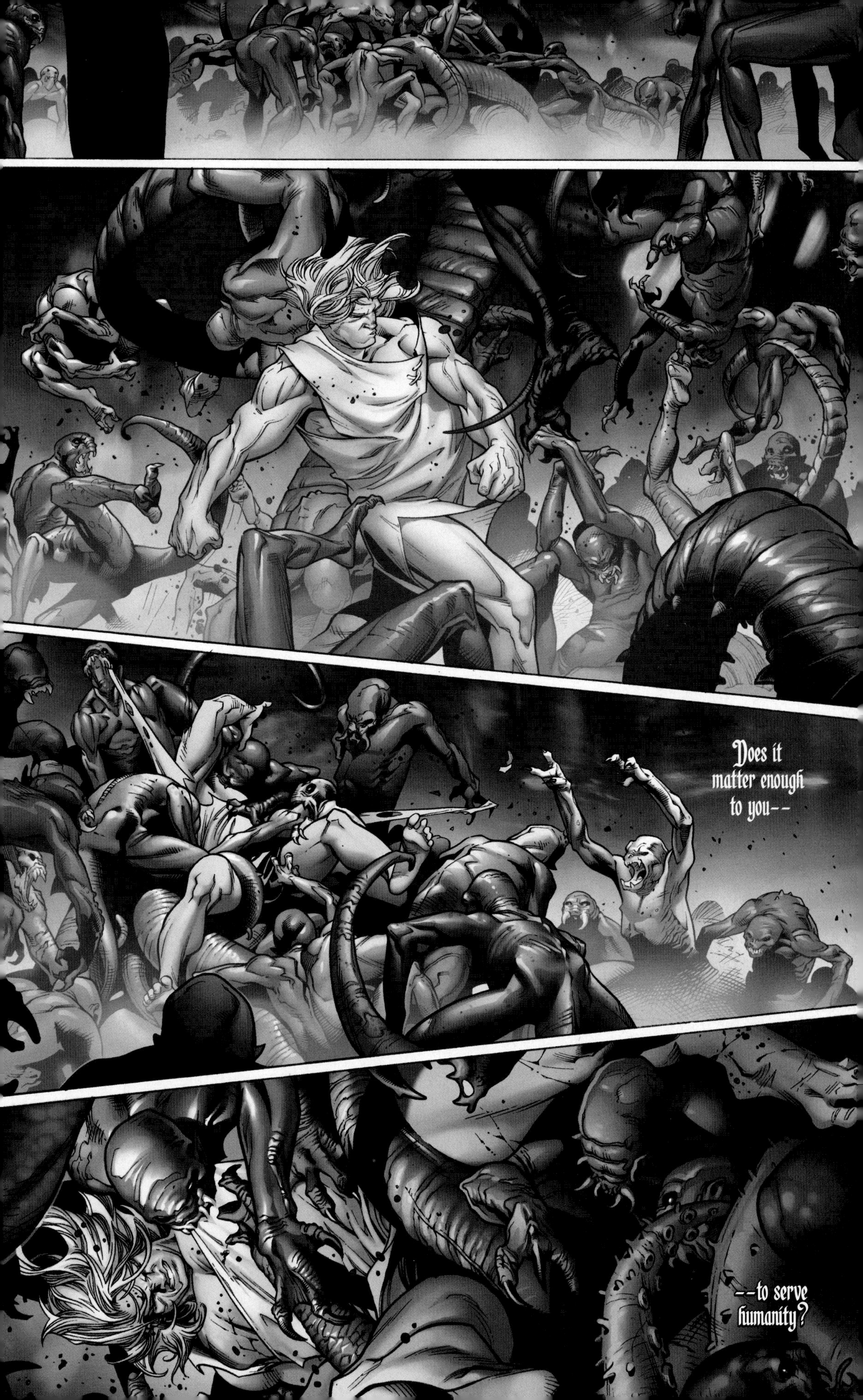
Does it matter enough to you--
--to serve humanity?

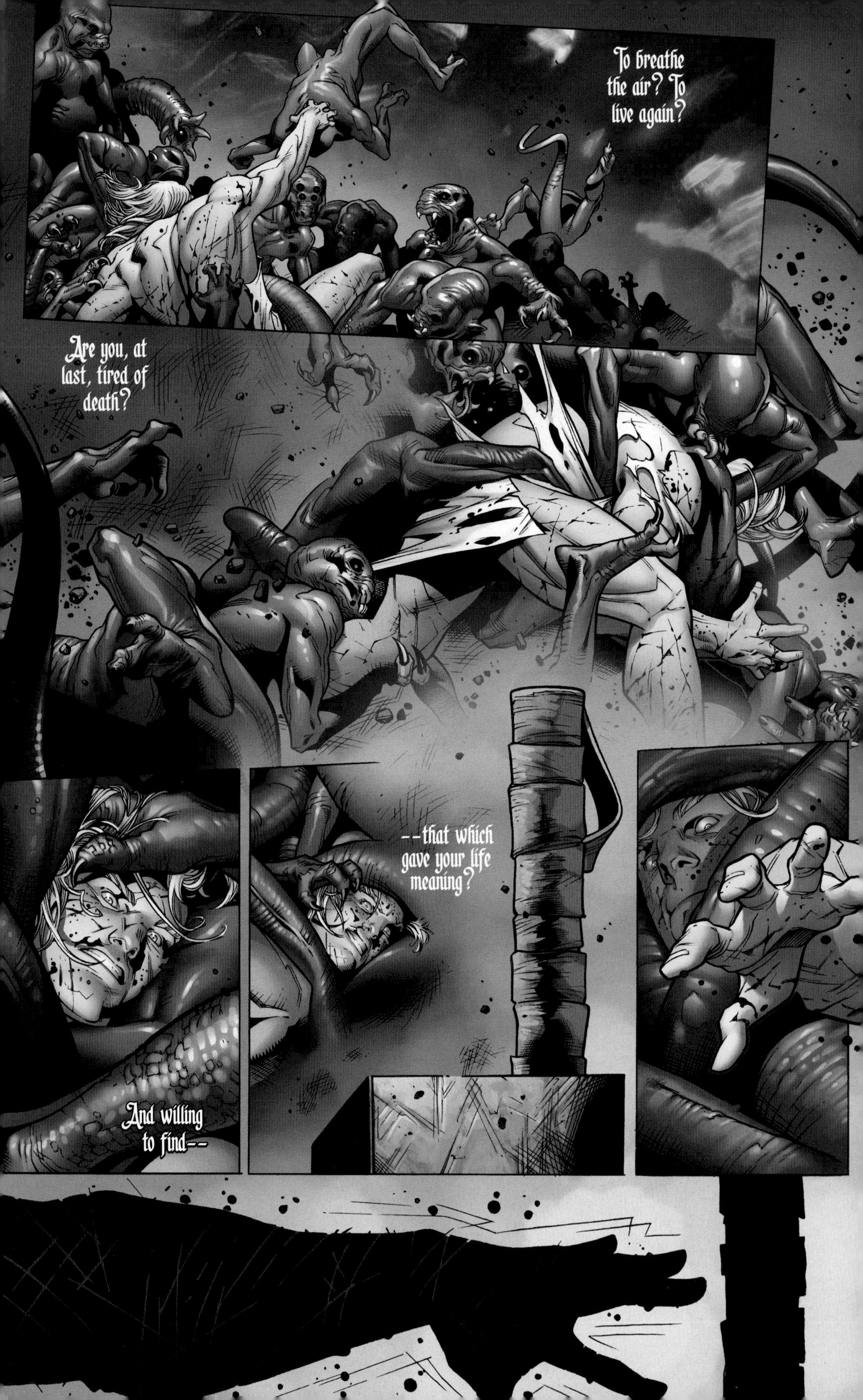
To breathe the air? To live again?
Are you, at last, tired of death?
And willing to find--
--that which gave your life meaning?

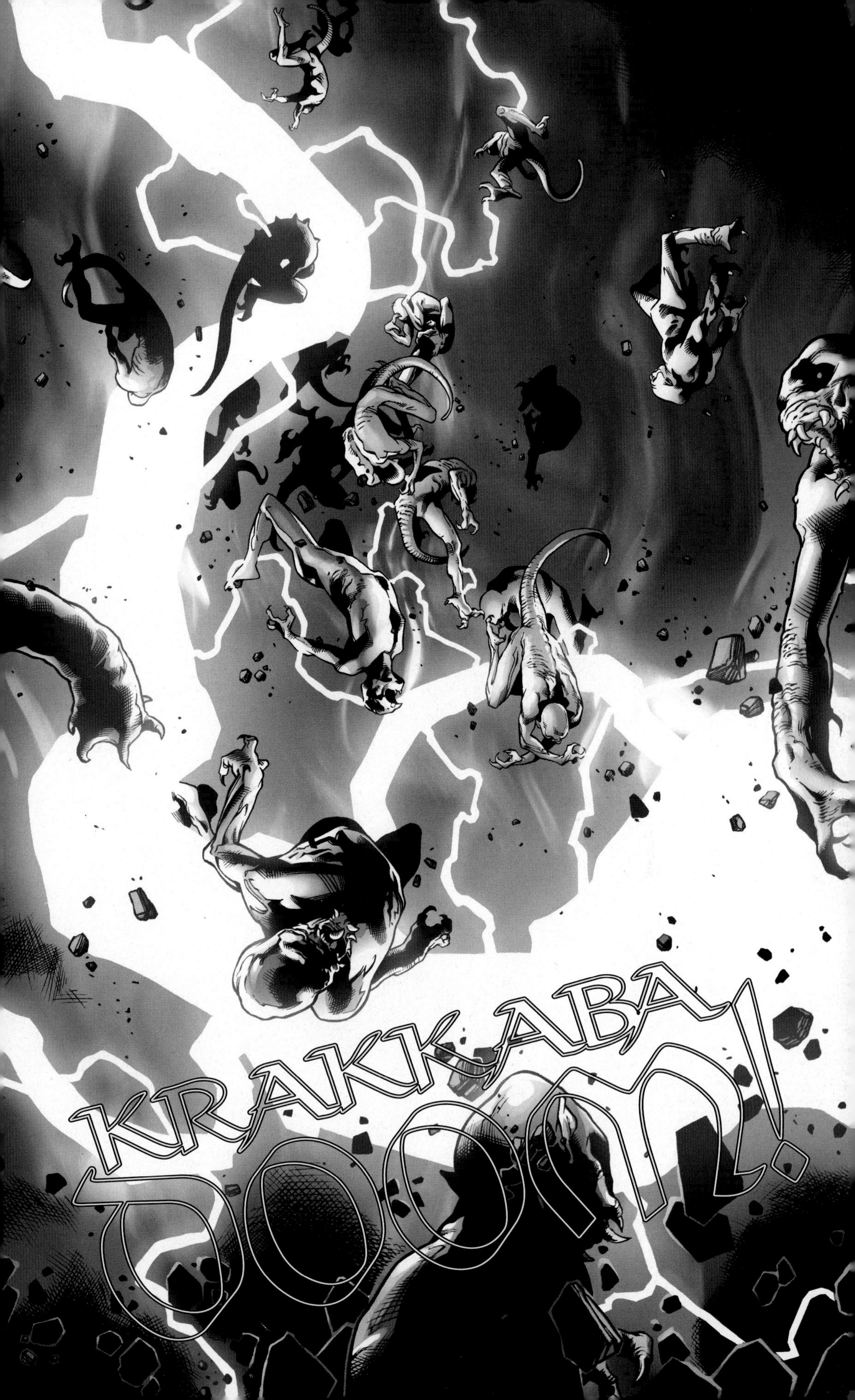
KRAKKABA
DOOOM!

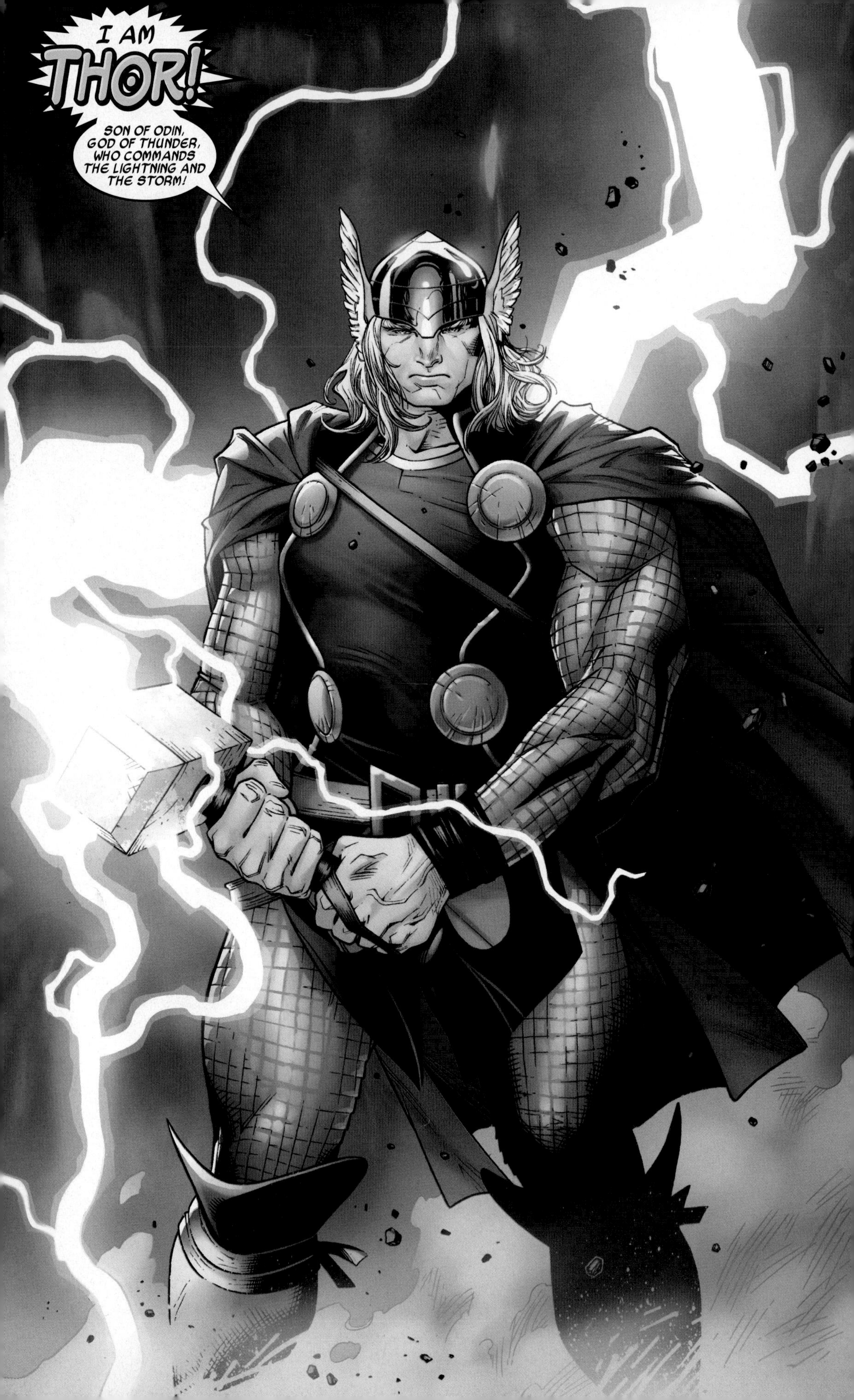
I AM THOR!
SON OF ODIN, GOD OF THUNDER, WHO COMMANDS THE LIGHTNING AND THE STORM!

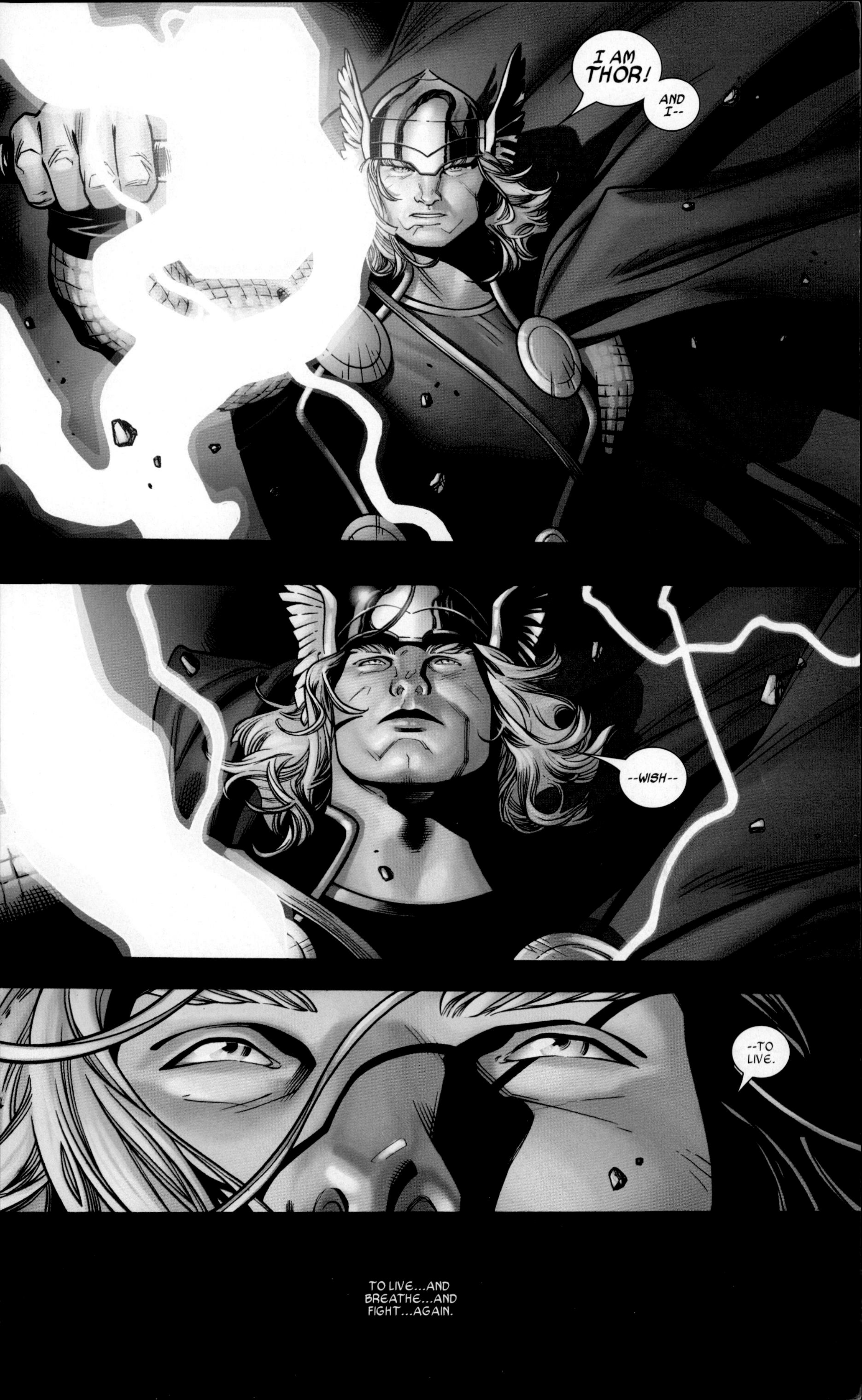
I AM THOR!
AND I--
--WISH--
--TO LIVE.
TO LIVE...AND BREATHE...AND FIGHT...AGAIN.

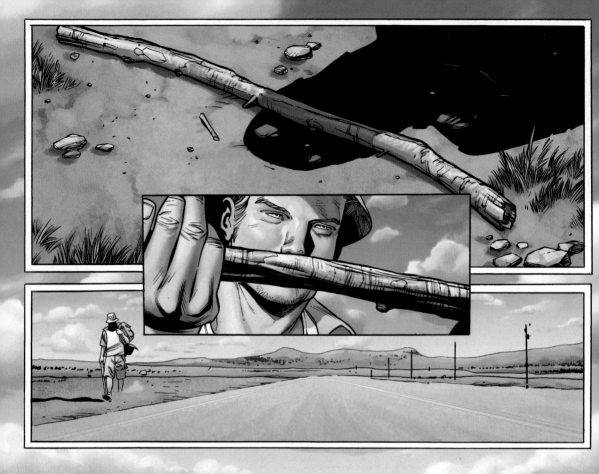

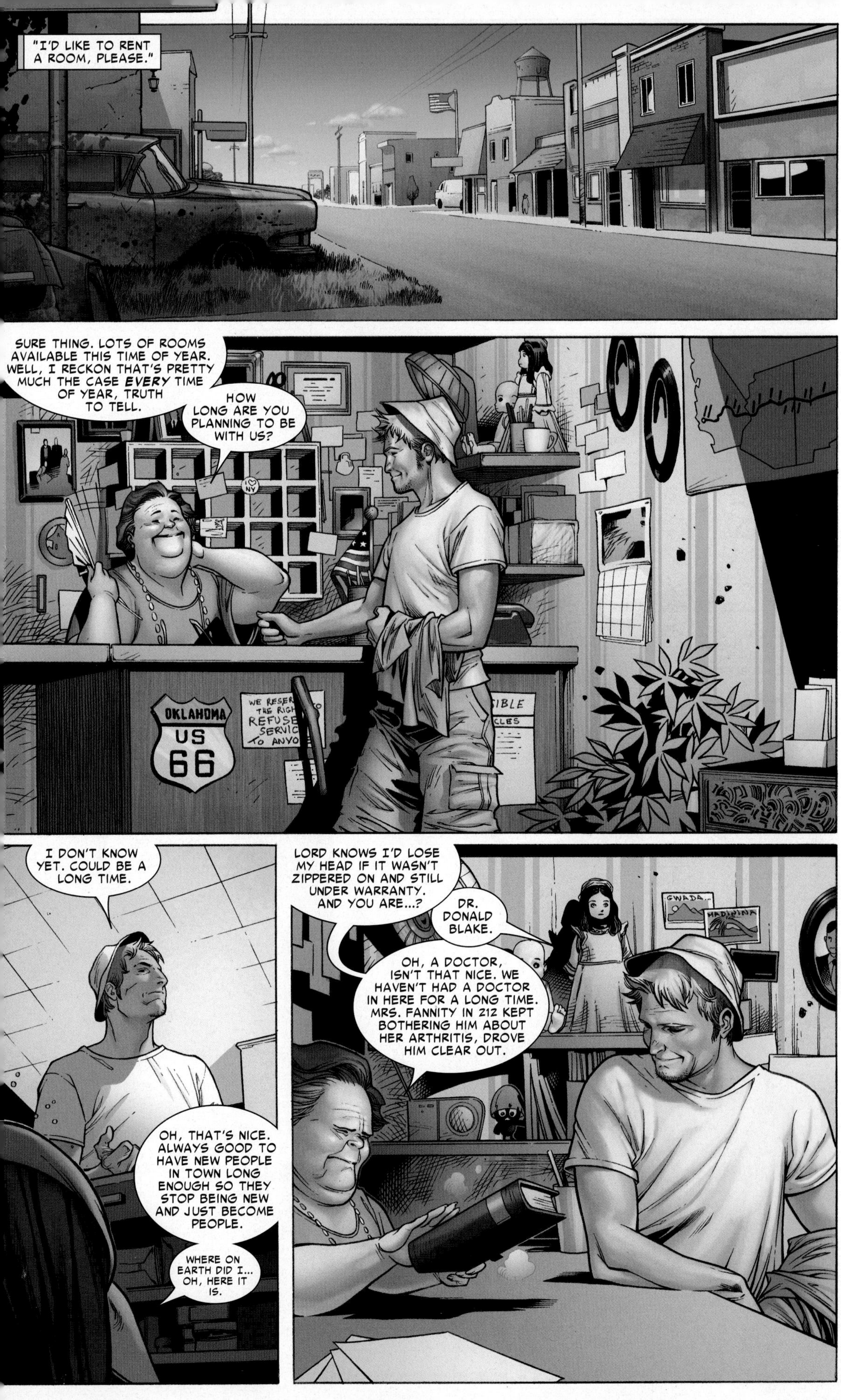
"I'D LIKE TO RENT A ROOM, PLEASE."
SURE THING. LOTS OF ROOMS AVAILABLE THIS TIME OF YEAR. WELL, I RECKON THAT'S PRETTY MUCH THE CASE *EVERY* TIME OF YEAR, TRUTH TO TELL.
HOW LONG ARE YOU PLANNING TO BE WITH US?
OKLAHOMA
US
66
I DON'T KNOW YET. COULD BE A LONG TIME.
OH, THAT'S NICE. ALWAYS GOOD TO HAVE NEW PEOPLE IN TOWN LONG ENOUGH SO THEY STOP BEING NEW AND JUST BECOME PEOPLE.
WHERE ON EARTH DID I... OH, HERE IT IS.
LORD KNOWS I'D LOSE MY HEAD IF IT WASN'T ZIPPERED ON AND STILL UNDER WARRANTY. AND YOU ARE...?
DR. DONALD BLAKE.
OH, A DOCTOR, ISN'T THAT NICE. WE HAVEN'T HAD A DOCTOR IN HERE FOR A LONG TIME. MRS. FANNITY IN 212 KEPT BOTHERING HIM ABOUT HER ARTHRITIS, DROVE HIM CLEAR OUT.

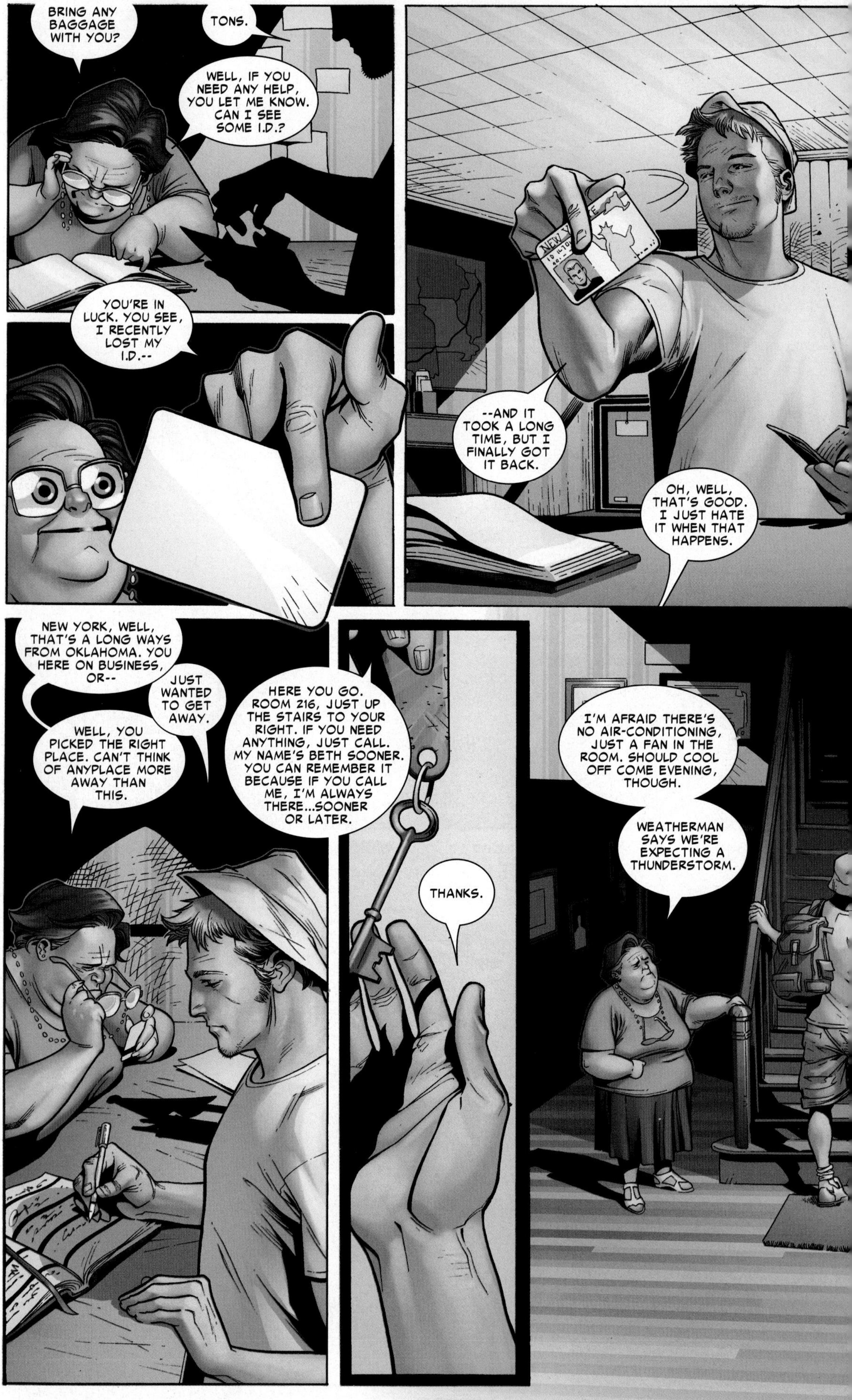
BRING ANY BAGGAGE WITH YOU?
TONS.
WELL, IF YOU NEED ANY HELP, YOU LET ME KNOW. CAN I SEE SOME I.D.?
YOU'RE IN LUCK. YOU SEE, I RECENTLY LOST MY I.D.--
--AND IT TOOK A LONG TIME, BUT I FINALLY GOT IT BACK.
OH, WELL, THAT'S GOOD. I JUST HATE IT WHEN THAT HAPPENS.
NEW YORK, WELL, THAT'S A LONG WAYS FROM OKLAHOMA. YOU HERE ON BUSINESS, OR--
JUST WANTED TO GET AWAY.
WELL, YOU PICKED THE RIGHT PLACE. CAN'T THINK OF ANYPLACE MORE AWAY THAN THIS.
HERE YOU GO. ROOM 216, JUST UP THE STAIRS TO YOUR RIGHT. IF YOU NEED ANYTHING, JUST CALL. MY NAME'S BETH SOONER. YOU CAN REMEMBER IT BECAUSE IF YOU CALL ME, I'M ALWAYS THERE...SOONER OR LATER.
THANKS.
I'M AFRAID THERE'S NO AIR-CONDITIONING, JUST A FAN IN THE ROOM. SHOULD COOL OFF COME EVENING, THOUGH.
WEATHERMAN SAYS WE'RE EXPECTING A THUNDERSTORM.

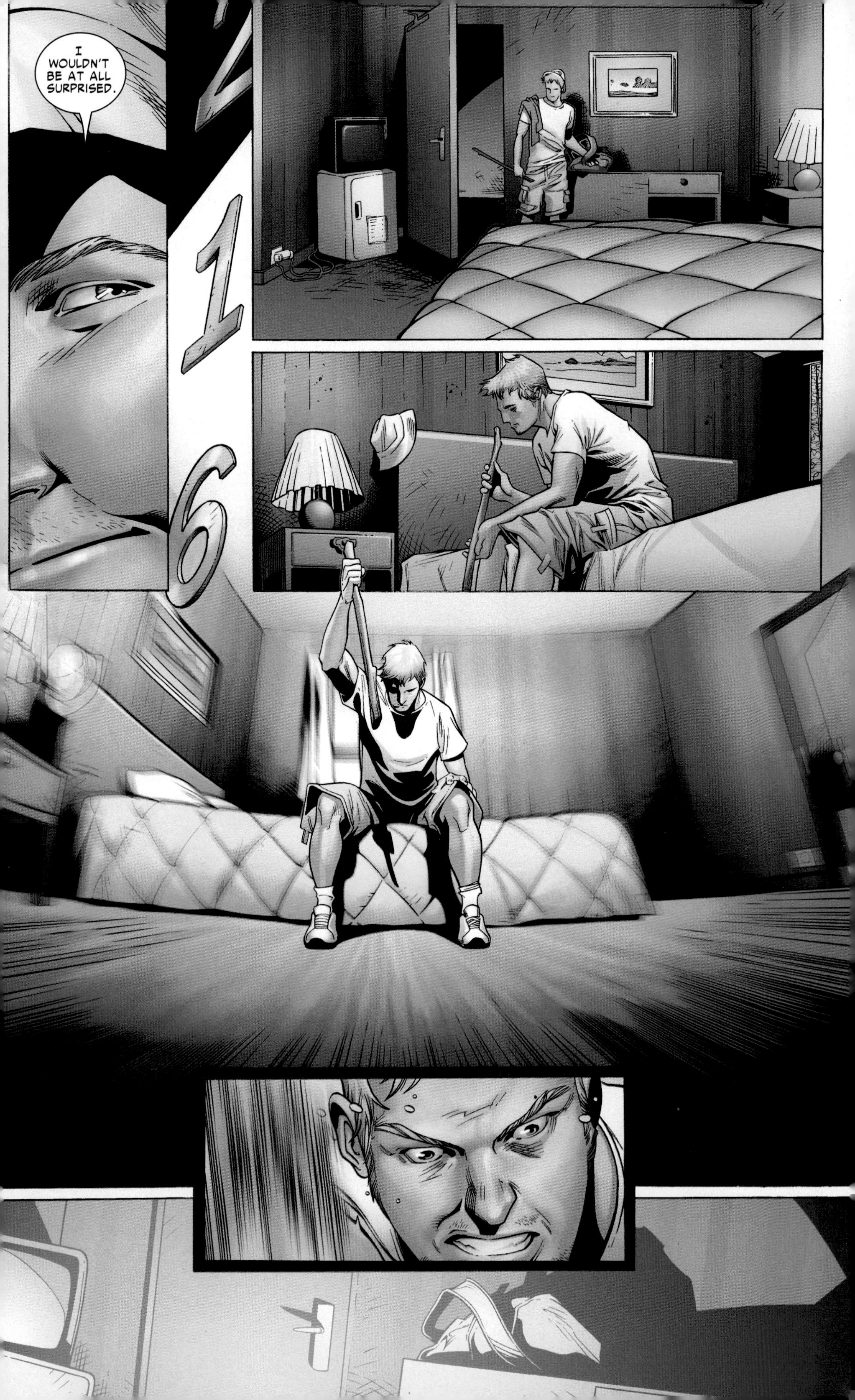
I WOULDN'T BE AT ALL SURPRISED.
1
6

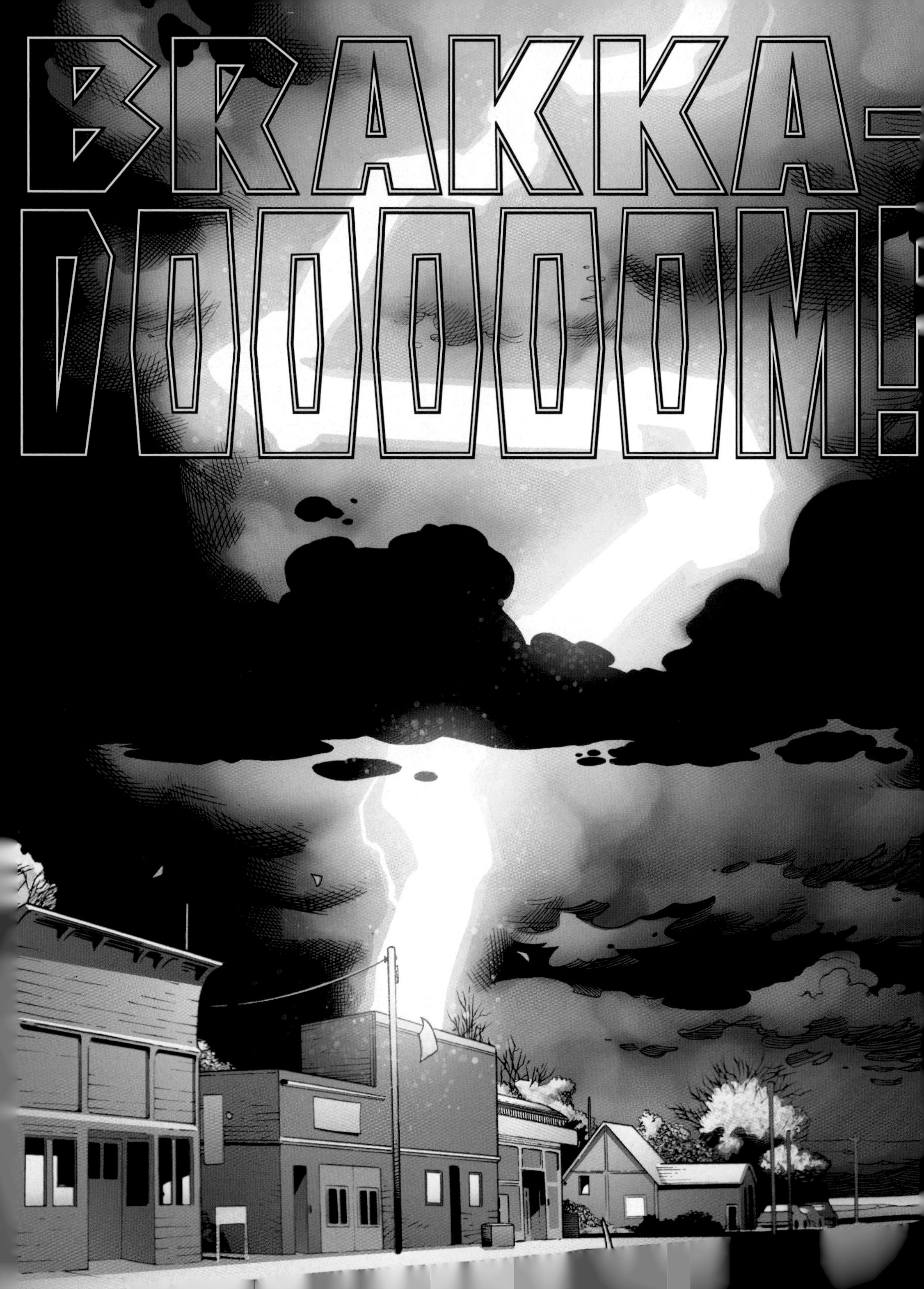
BRAKKA-DOOOOOM!

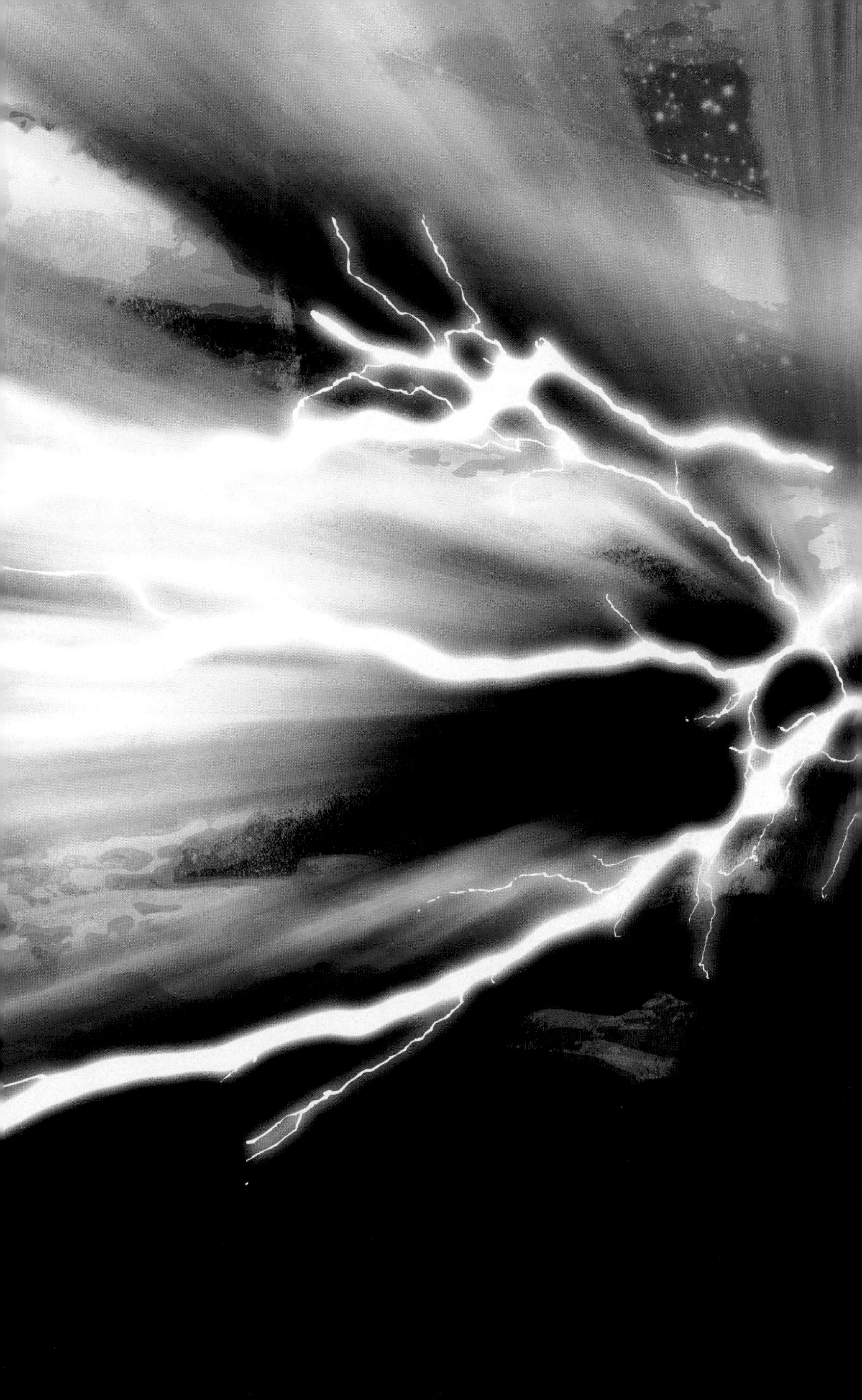

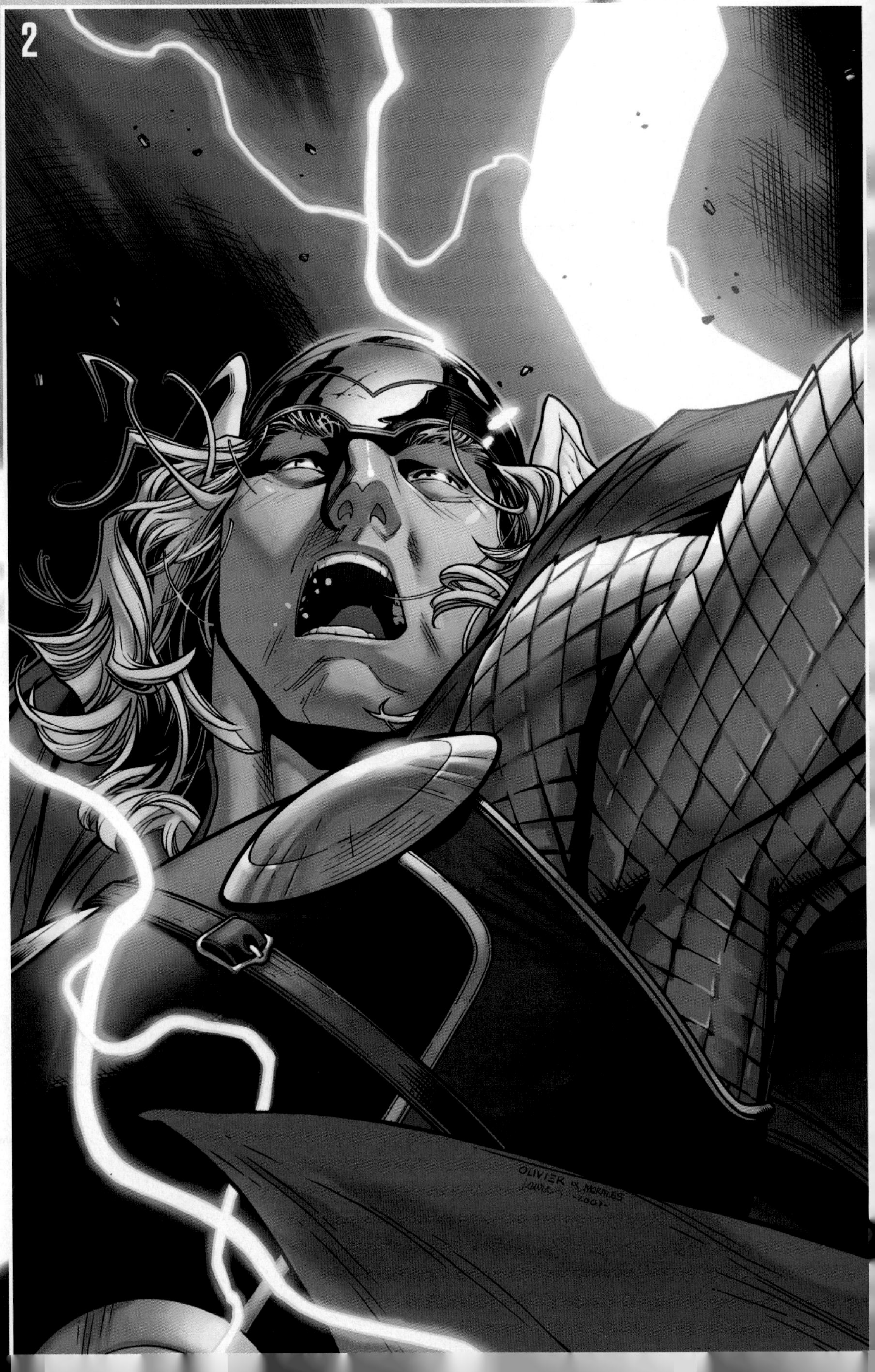
2

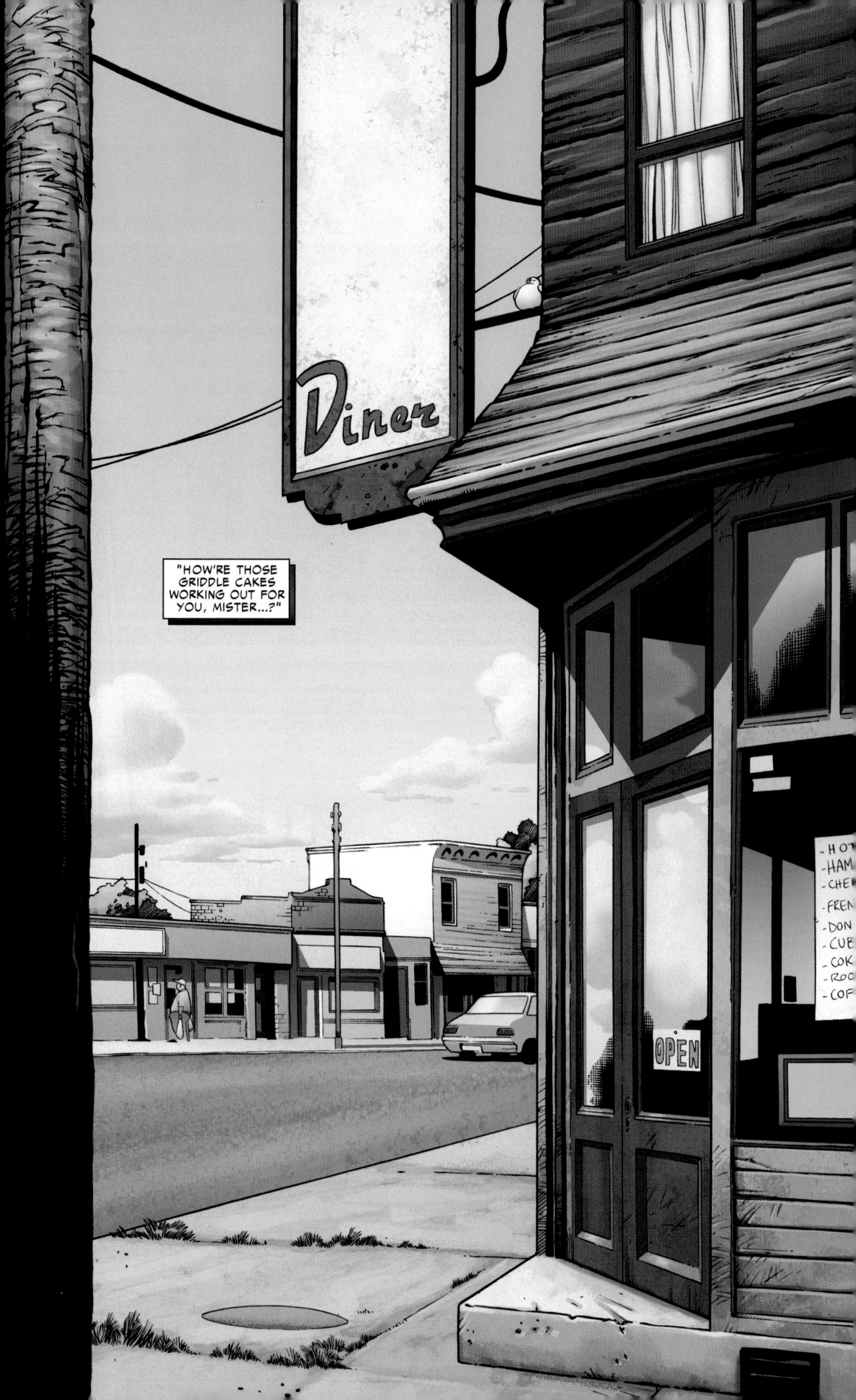
Diner
"HOW'RE THOSE GRIDDLE CAKES WORKING OUT FOR YOU, MISTER...?"
OPEN

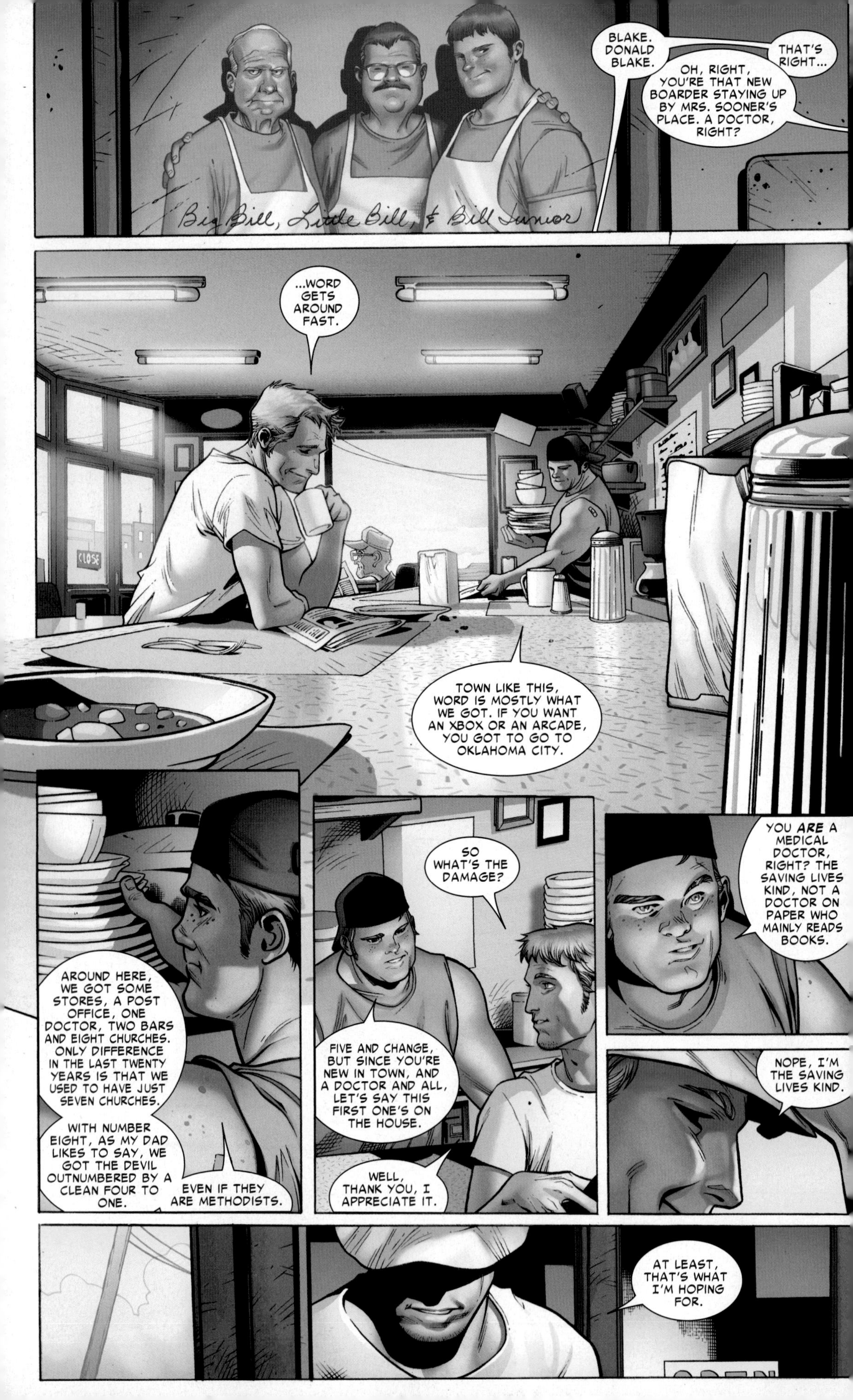

Big Bill, Little Bill, & Bill Junior
BLAKE. DONALD BLAKE.
THAT'S RIGHT...
OH, RIGHT, YOU'RE THAT NEW BOARDER STAYING UP BY MRS. SOONER'S PLACE. A DOCTOR, RIGHT?
...WORD GETS AROUND FAST.
CLOSE
TOWN LIKE THIS, WORD IS MOSTLY WHAT WE GOT. IF YOU WANT AN XBOX OR AN ARCADE, YOU GOT TO GO TO OKLAHOMA CITY.
AROUND HERE, WE GOT SOME STORES, A POST OFFICE, ONE DOCTOR, TWO BARS AND EIGHT CHURCHES. ONLY DIFFERENCE IN THE LAST TWENTY YEARS IS THAT WE USED TO HAVE JUST SEVEN CHURCHES.
WITH NUMBER EIGHT, AS MY DAD LIKES TO SAY, WE GOT THE DEVIL OUTNUMBERED BY A CLEAN FOUR TO ONE.
EVEN IF THEY ARE METHODISTS.
SO WHAT'S THE DAMAGE?
FIVE AND CHANGE, BUT SINCE YOU'RE NEW IN TOWN, AND A DOCTOR AND ALL, LET'S SAY THIS FIRST ONE'S ON THE HOUSE.
WELL, THANK YOU, I APPRECIATE IT.
YOU *ARE* A MEDICAL DOCTOR, RIGHT? THE SAVING LIVES KIND, NOT A DOCTOR ON PAPER WHO MAINLY READS BOOKS.
NOPE, I'M THE SAVING LIVES KIND.
AT LEAST, THAT'S WHAT I'M HOPING FOR.

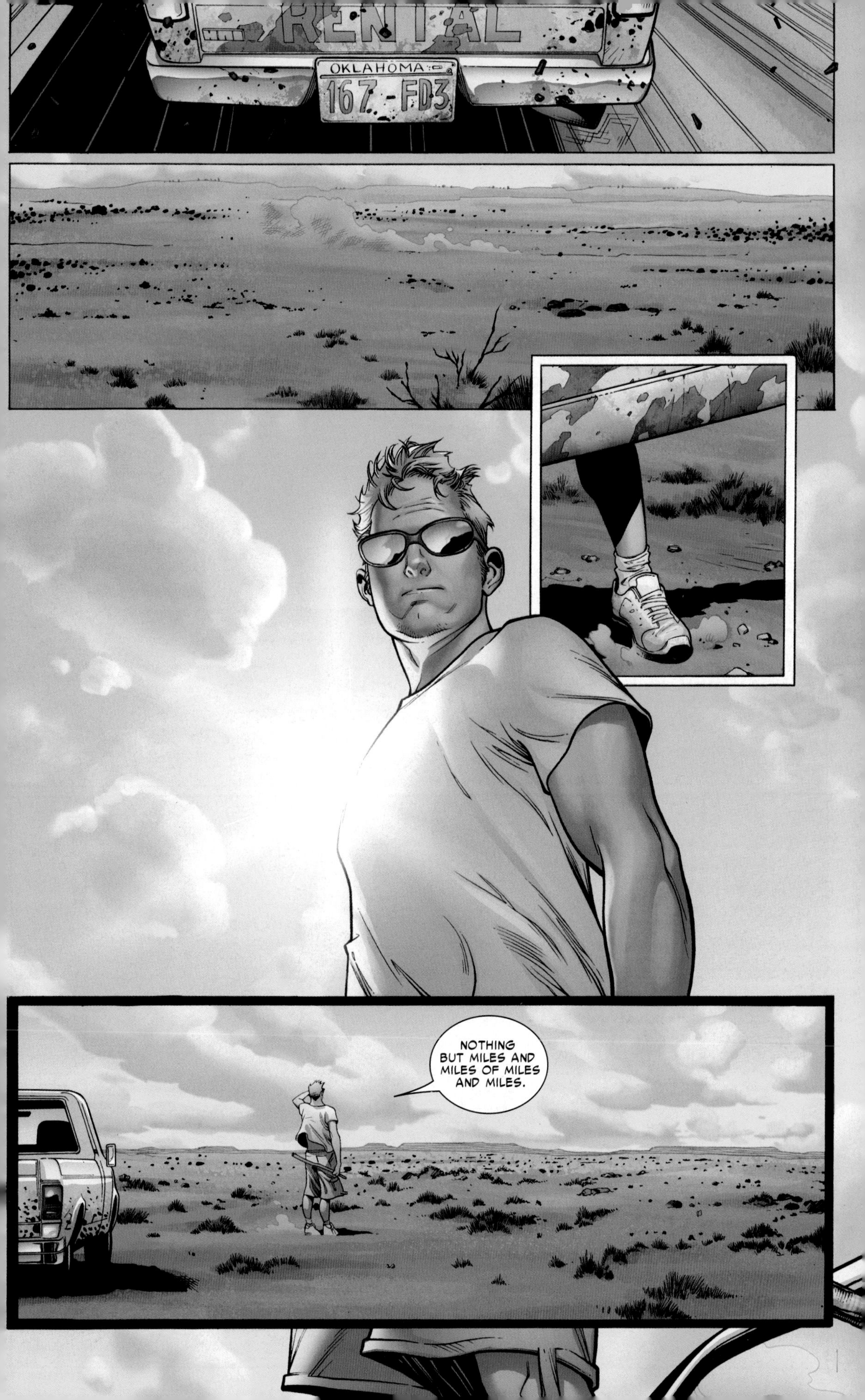
RENTAL
OKLAHOMA
167-FD3
NOTHING BUT MILES AND MILES OF MILES AND MILES.

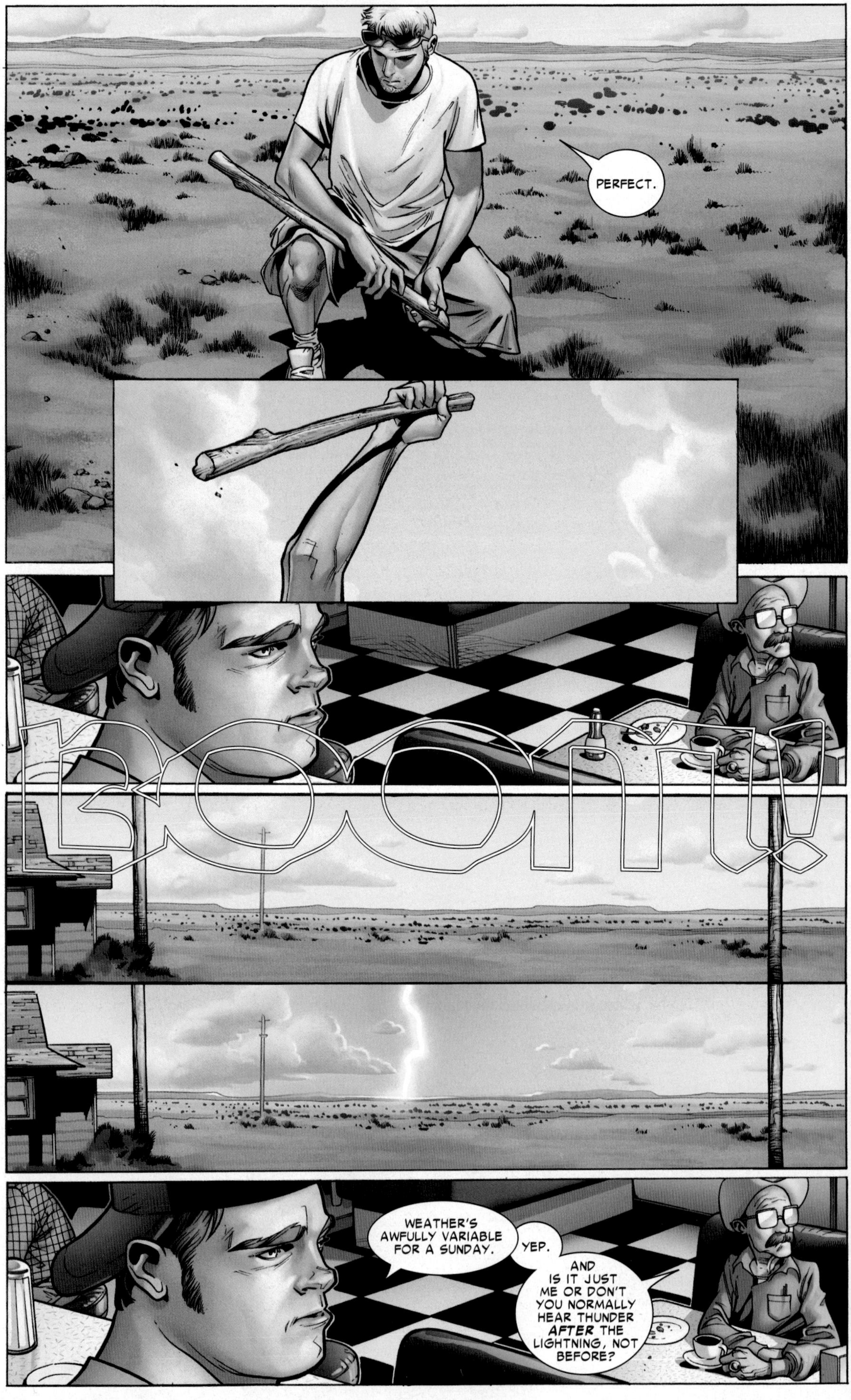
PERFECT.
BOOM!
WEATHER'S AWFULLY VARIABLE FOR A SUNDAY.
YEP.
AND IS IT JUST ME OR DON'T YOU NORMALLY HEAR THUNDER *AFTER* THE LIGHTNING, NOT BEFORE?

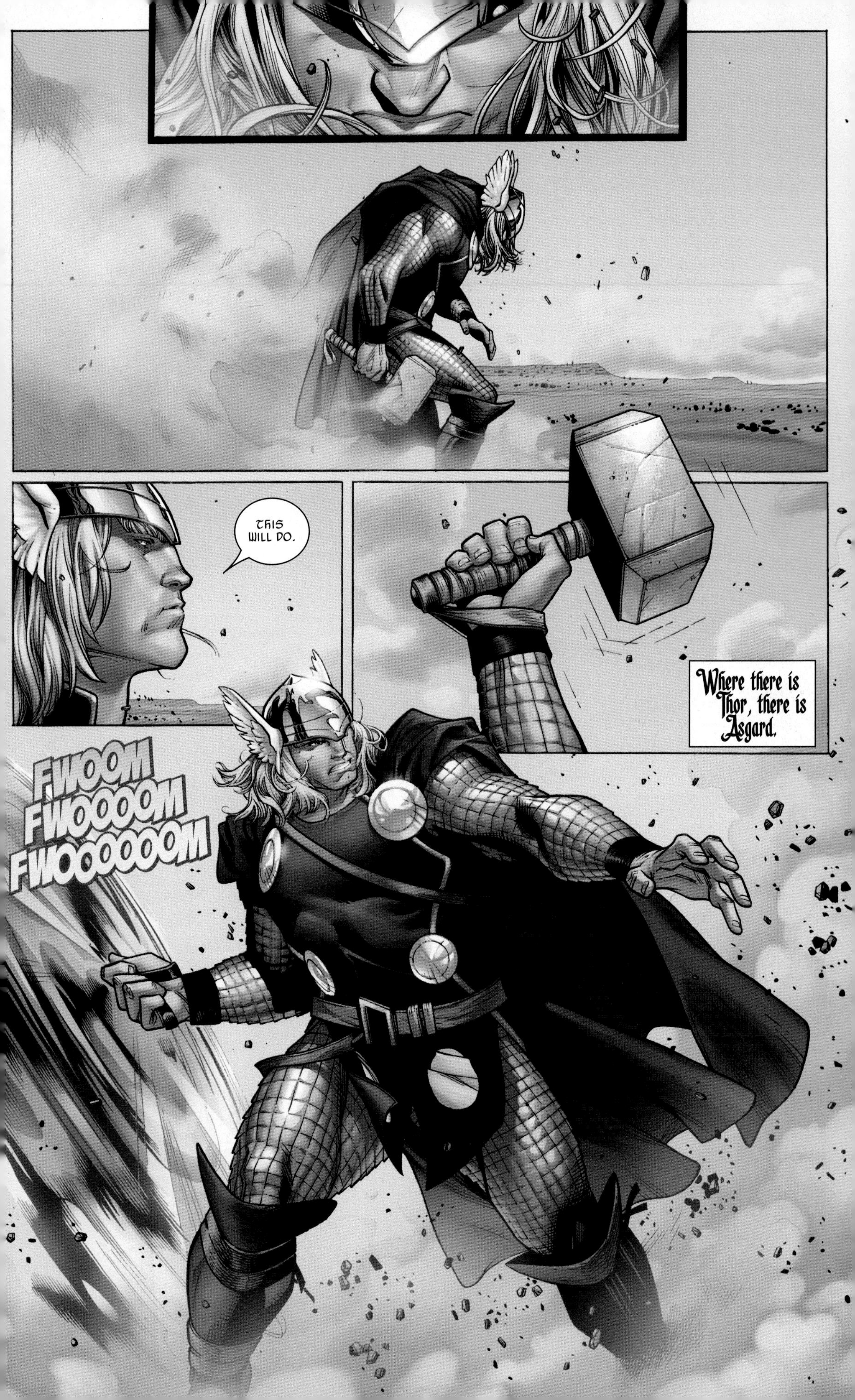
THIS WILL DO.
Where there is Thor, there is Asgard.
FWOOM
FWOOOOM
FWOOOOOOM

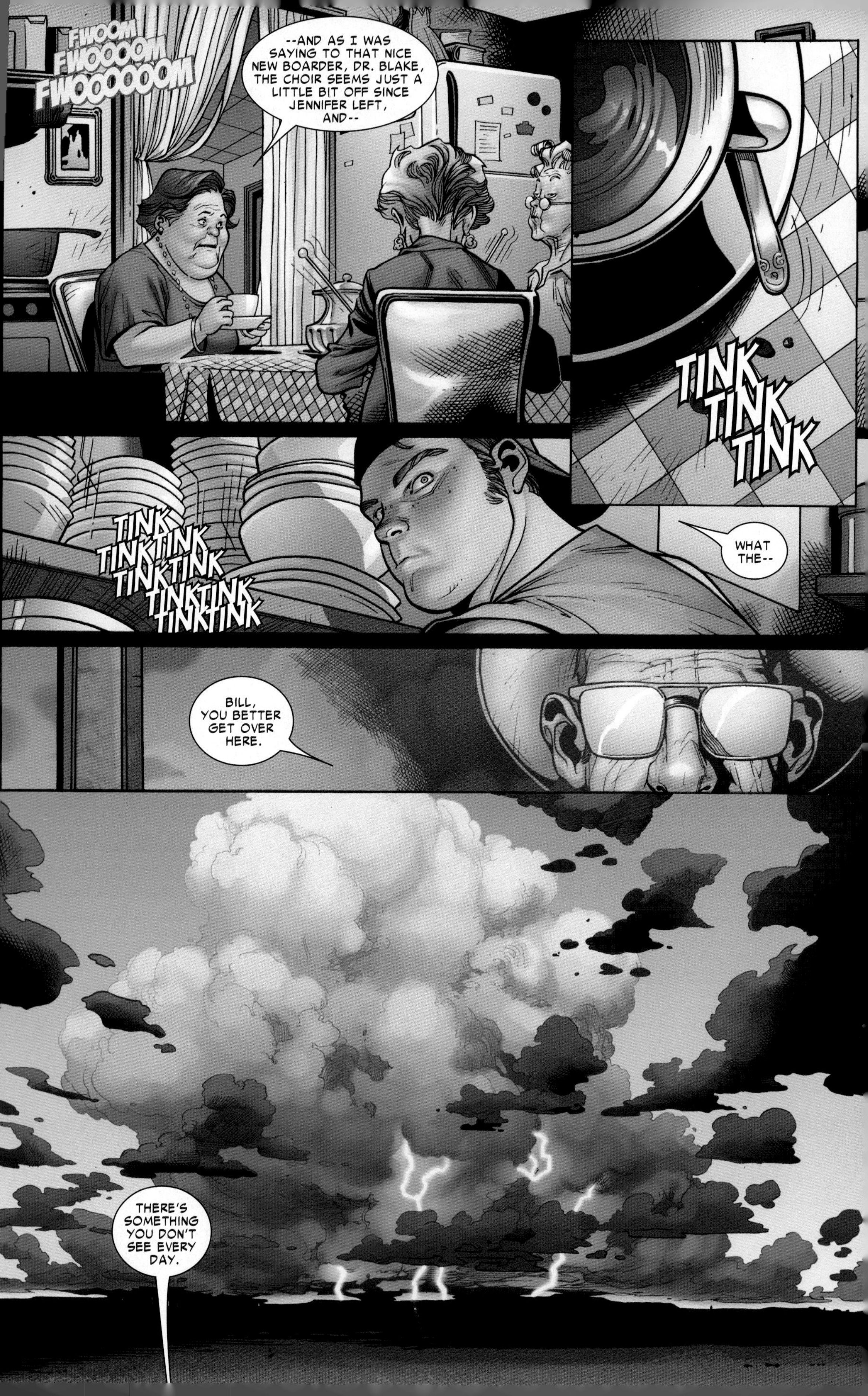
FWOOM
FWOOOOM
FWOOOOOOM
--AND AS I WAS SAYING TO THAT NICE NEW BOARDER, DR. BLAKE, THE CHOIR SEEMS JUST A LITTLE BIT OFF SINCE JENNIFER LEFT, AND--
TINK
TINK
TINK
TINK
TINKTINK
TINKTINK
TINKTINK
TINKTINK
WHAT THE--
BILL, YOU BETTER GET OVER HERE.
THERE'S SOMETHING YOU DON'T SEE EVERY DAY.

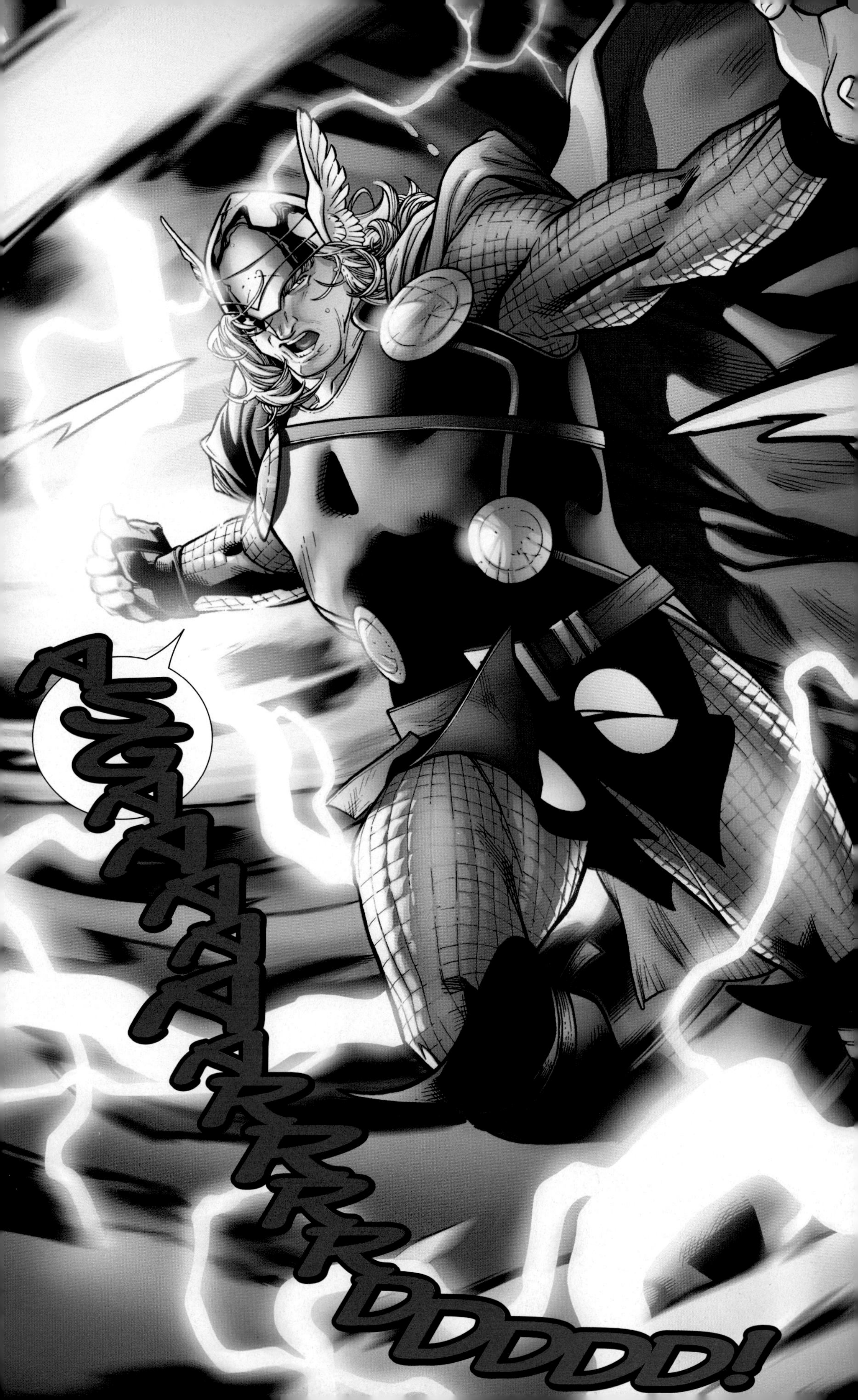
ASGAAAARRRRDDDDD!

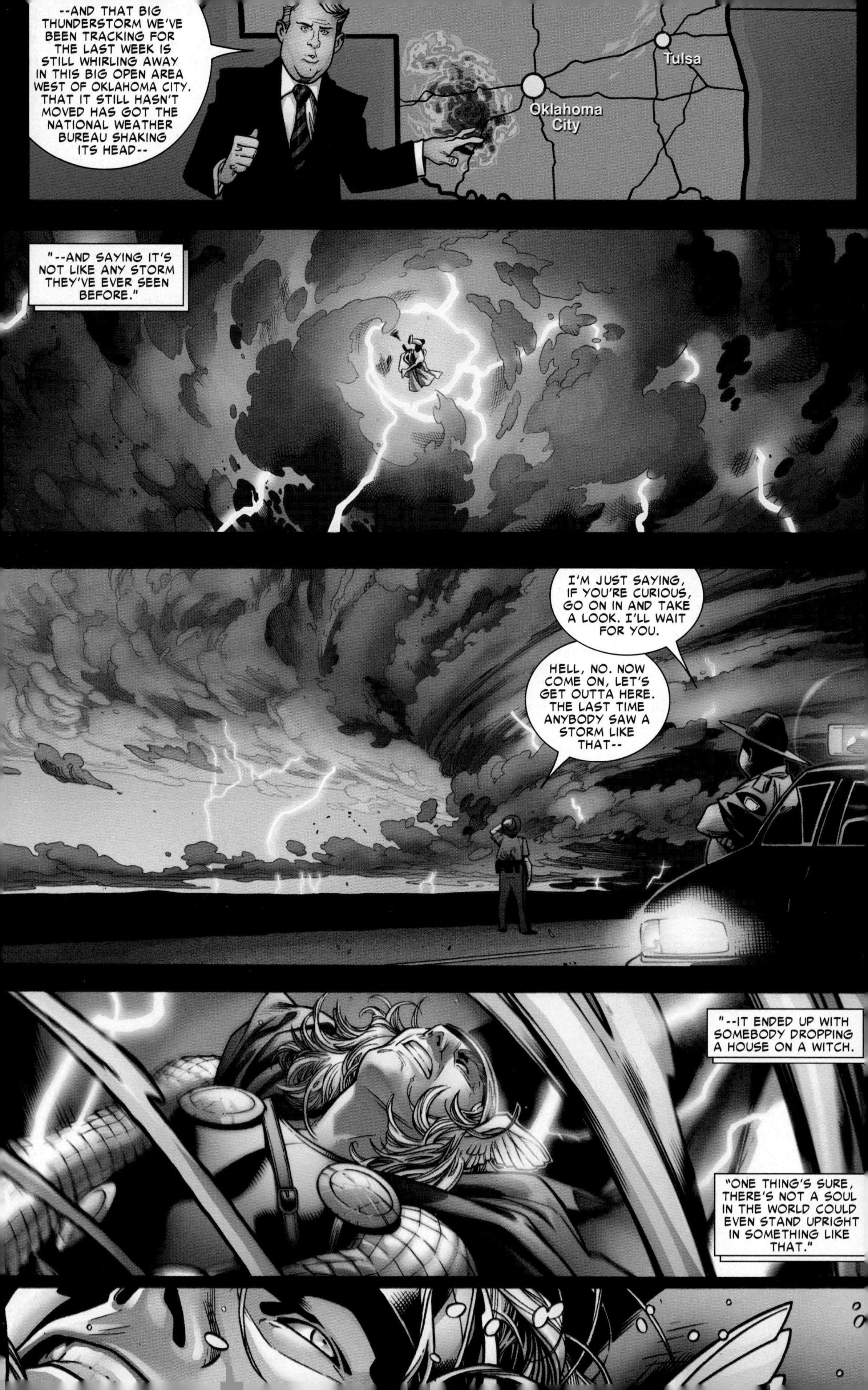
--AND THAT BIG THUNDERSTORM WE'VE BEEN TRACKING FOR THE LAST WEEK IS STILL WHIRLING AWAY IN THIS BIG OPEN AREA WEST OF OKLAHOMA CITY. THAT IT STILL HASN'T MOVED HAS GOT THE NATIONAL WEATHER BUREAU SHAKING ITS HEAD--
Tulsa
Oklahoma City
"--AND SAYING IT'S NOT LIKE ANY STORM THEY'VE EVER SEEN BEFORE."
I'M JUST SAYING, IF YOU'RE CURIOUS, GO ON IN AND TAKE A LOOK. I'LL WAIT FOR YOU.
HELL, NO. NOW COME ON, LET'S GET OUTTA HERE. THE LAST TIME ANYBODY SAW A STORM LIKE THAT--
"--IT ENDED UP WITH SOMEBODY DROPPING A HOUSE ON A WITCH.
"ONE THING'S SURE, THERE'S NOT A SOUL IN THE WORLD COULD EVEN STAND UPRIGHT IN SOMETHING LIKE THAT."

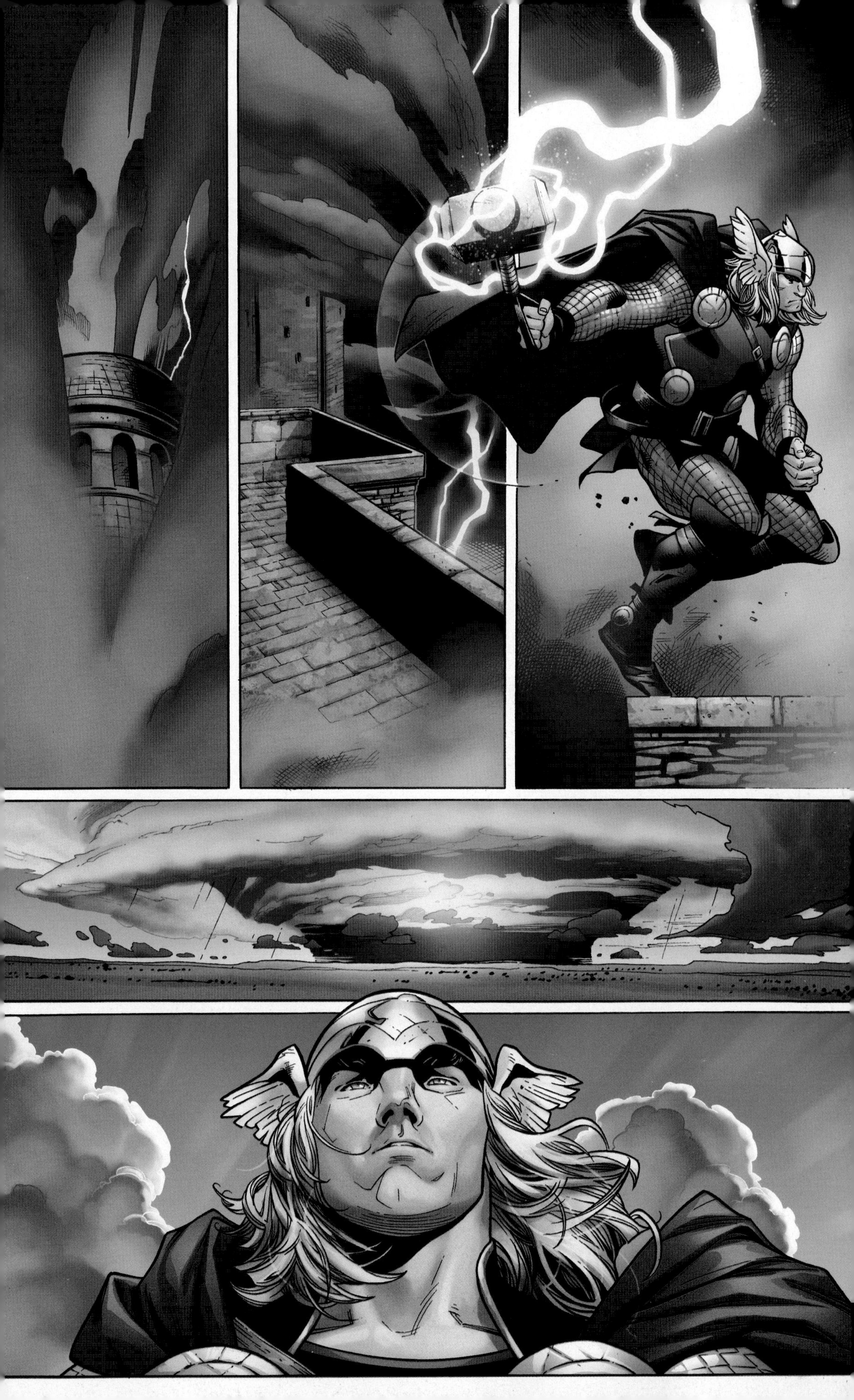

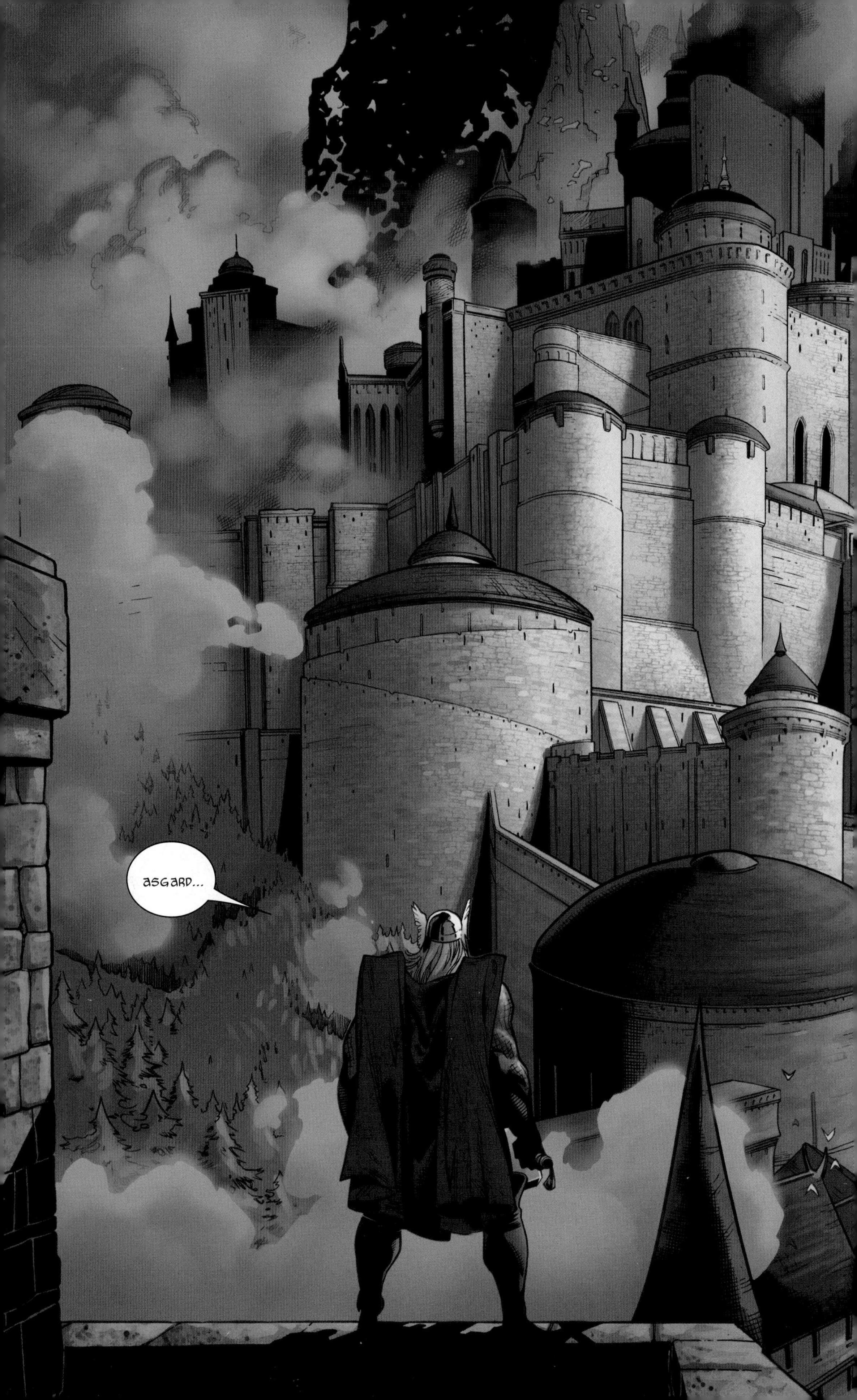
ASGARD...

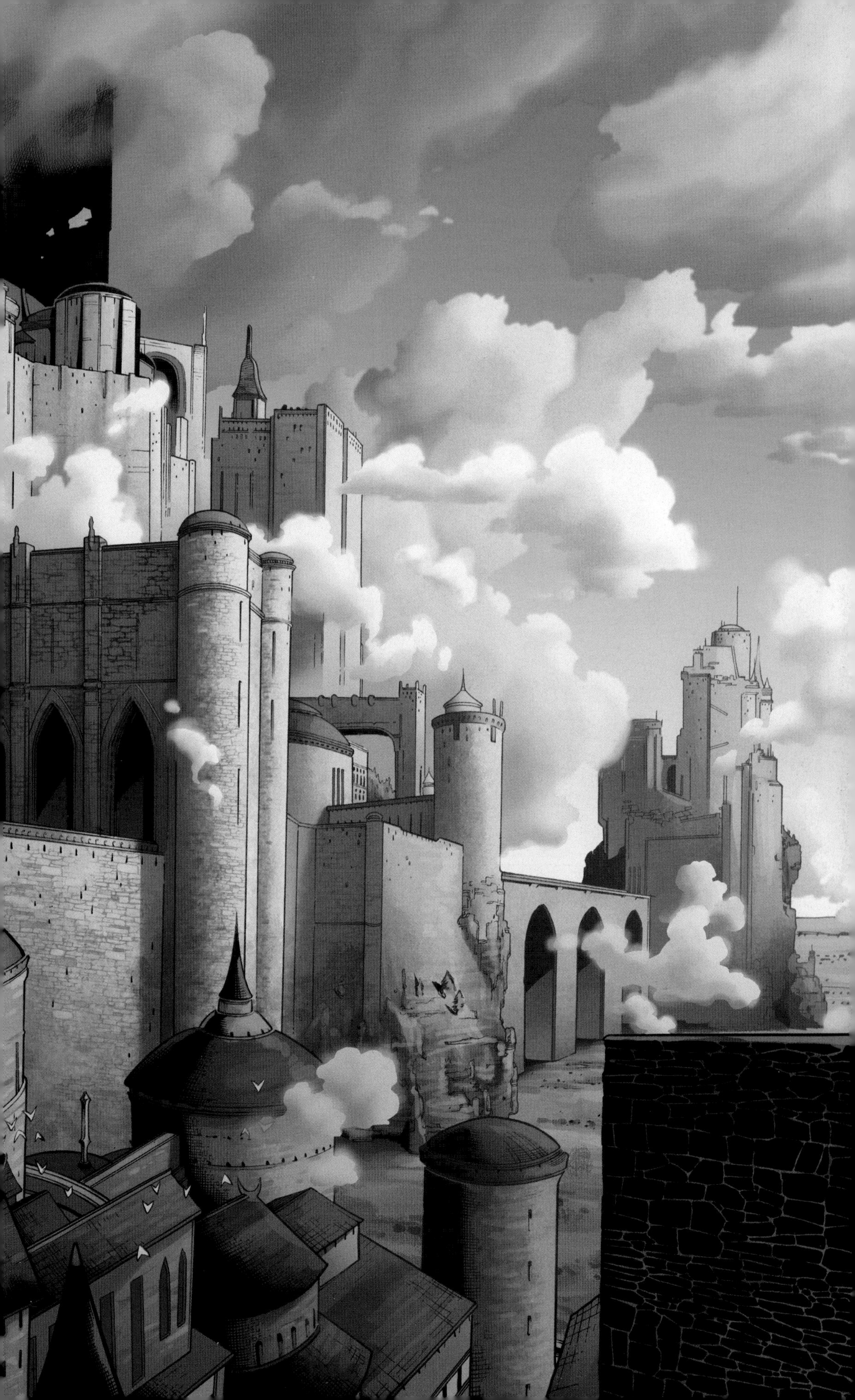

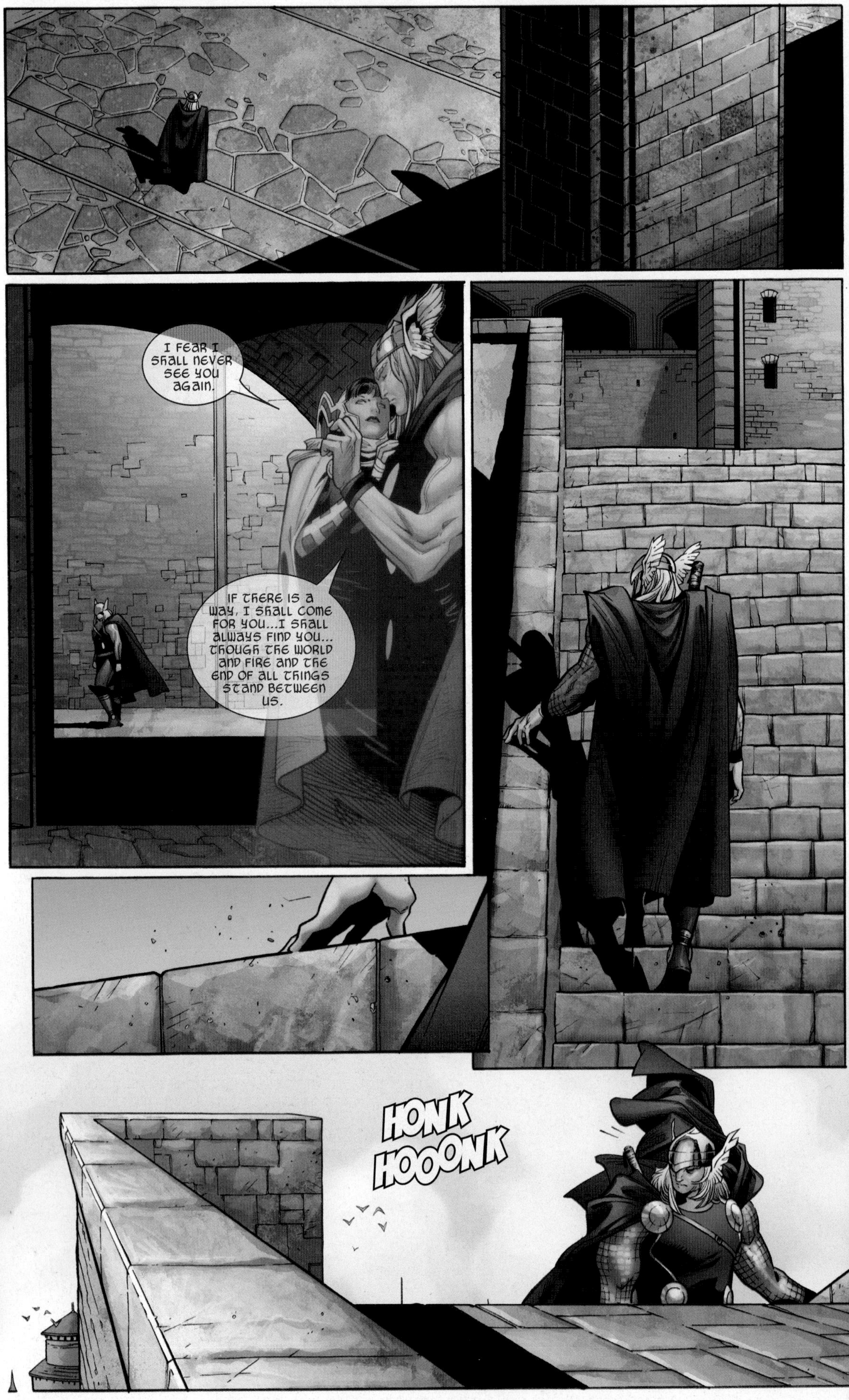
I FEAR I SHALL NEVER SEE YOU AGAIN.
IF THERE IS A WAY, I SHALL COME FOR YOU...I SHALL ALWAYS FIND YOU... THOUGH THE WORLD AND FIRE AND THE END OF ALL THINGS STAND BETWEEN US.
HONK HOOONK

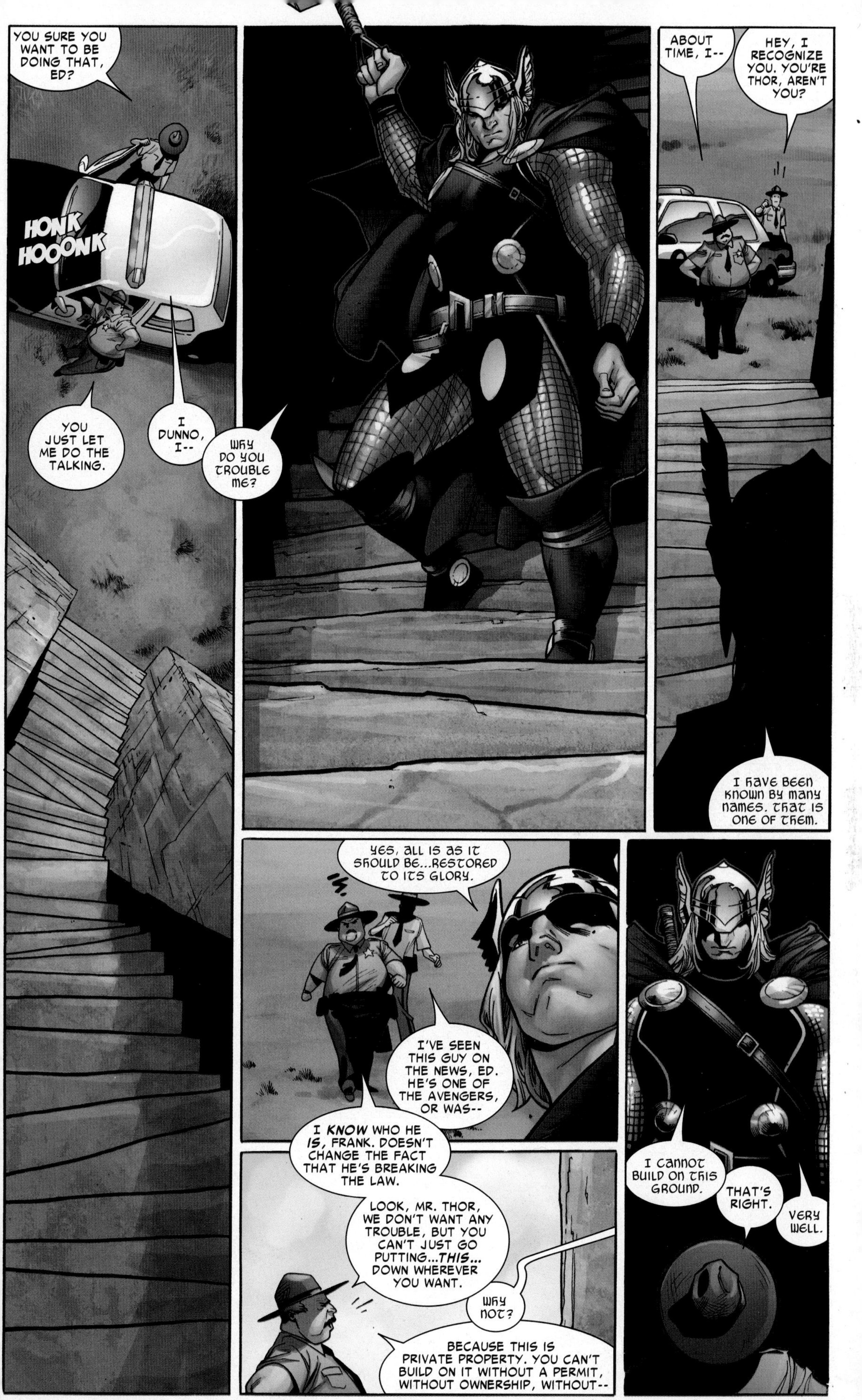
YOU SURE YOU WANT TO BE DOING THAT, ED?
HONK HOOONK
YOU JUST LET ME DO THE TALKING.
I DUNNO, I--
WHY DO YOU TROUBLE ME?
ABOUT TIME, I--
HEY, I RECOGNIZE YOU. YOU'RE THOR, AREN'T YOU?
I HAVE BEEN KNOWN BY MANY NAMES. THAT IS ONE OF THEM.
YES, ALL IS AS IT SHOULD BE...RESTORED TO ITS GLORY.
I'VE SEEN THIS GUY ON THE NEWS, ED. HE'S ONE OF THE AVENGERS, OR WAS--
I KNOW WHO HE IS, FRANK. DOESN'T CHANGE THE FACT THAT HE'S BREAKING THE LAW.
LOOK, MR. THOR, WE DON'T WANT ANY TROUBLE, BUT YOU CAN'T JUST GO PUTTING...THIS... DOWN WHEREVER YOU WANT.
WHY NOT?
BECAUSE THIS IS PRIVATE PROPERTY. YOU CAN'T BUILD ON IT WITHOUT A PERMIT, WITHOUT OWNERSHIP, WITHOUT--
I CANNOT BUILD ON THIS GROUND.
THAT'S RIGHT.
VERY WELL.

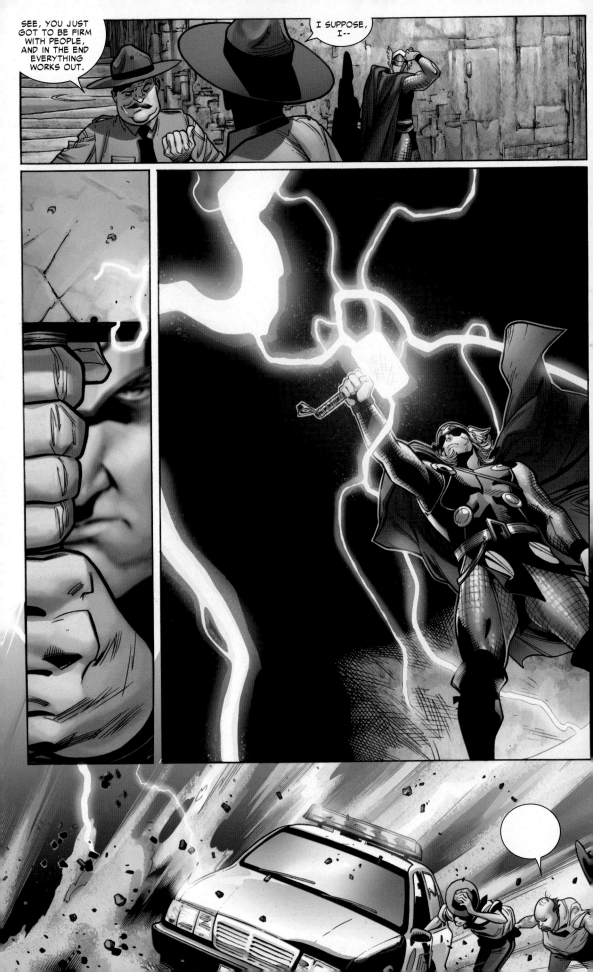

SEE, YOU JUST GOT TO BE FIRM WITH PEOPLE, AND IN THE END EVERYTHING WORKS OUT.

I SUPPOSE, I--

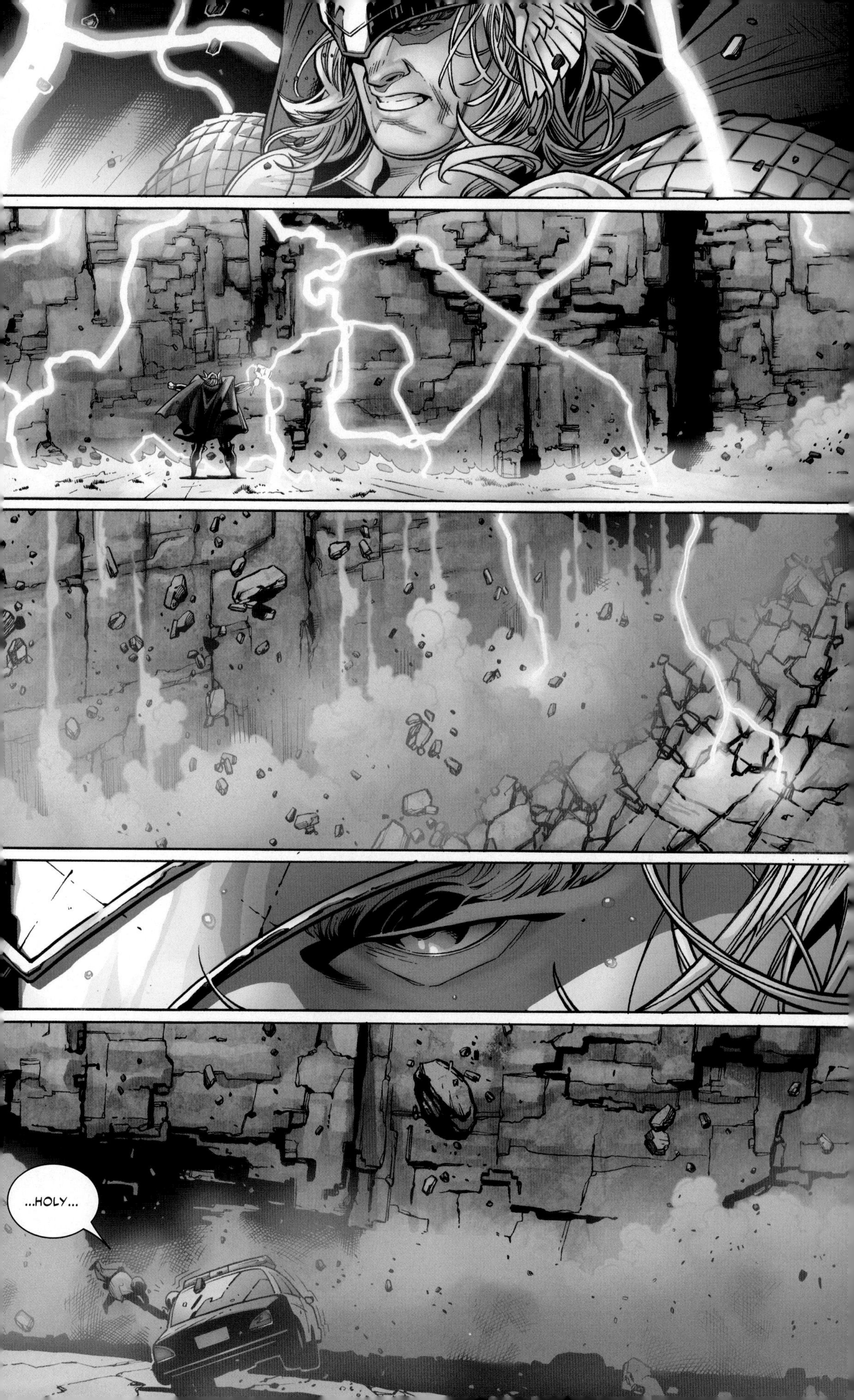
...HOLY...

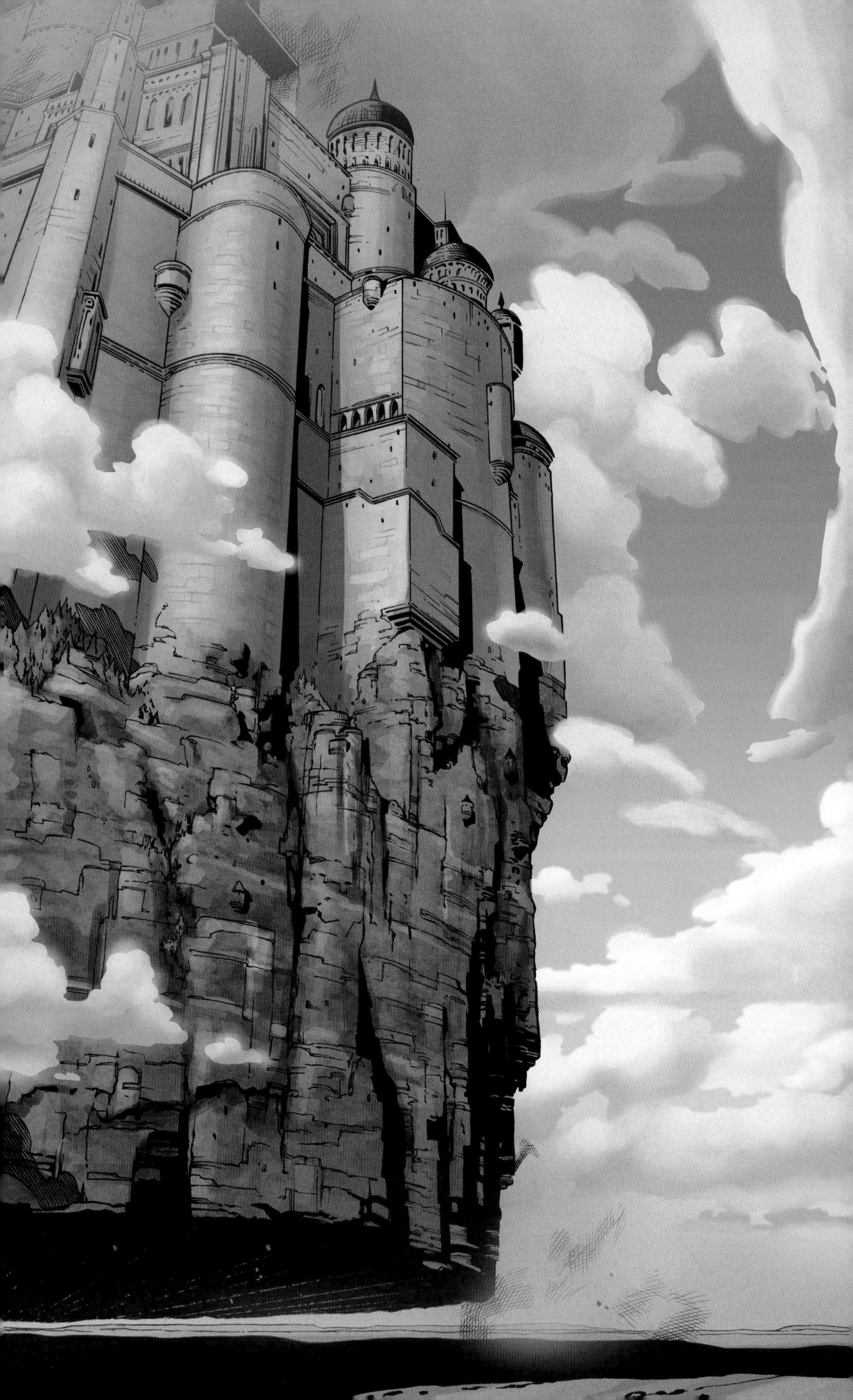

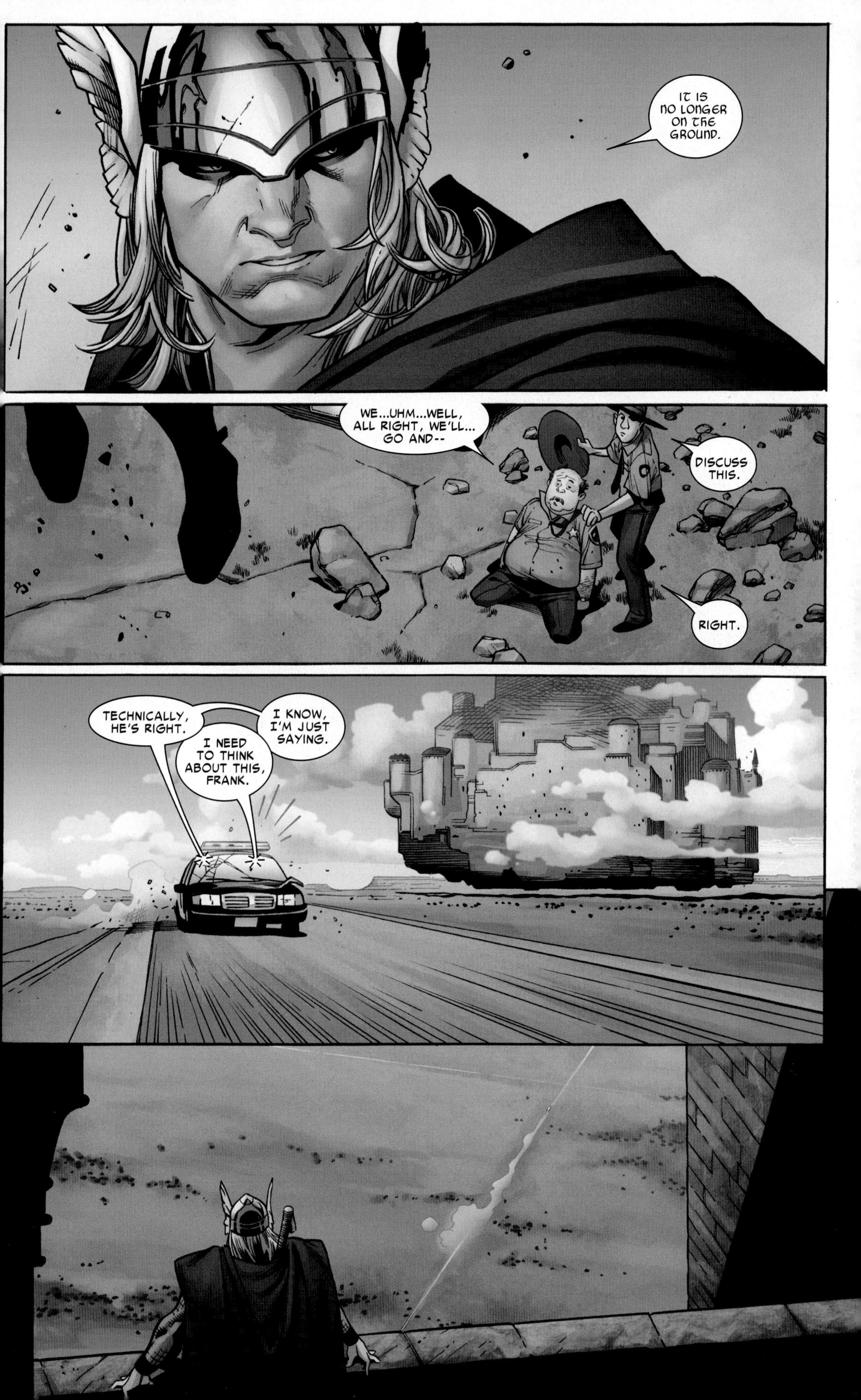
IT IS NO LONGER ON THE GROUND.
WE...UHM...WELL, ALL RIGHT, WE'LL... GO AND--
DISCUSS THIS.
RIGHT.
TECHNICALLY, HE'S RIGHT.
I KNOW, I'M JUST SAYING.
I NEED TO THINK ABOUT THIS, FRANK.

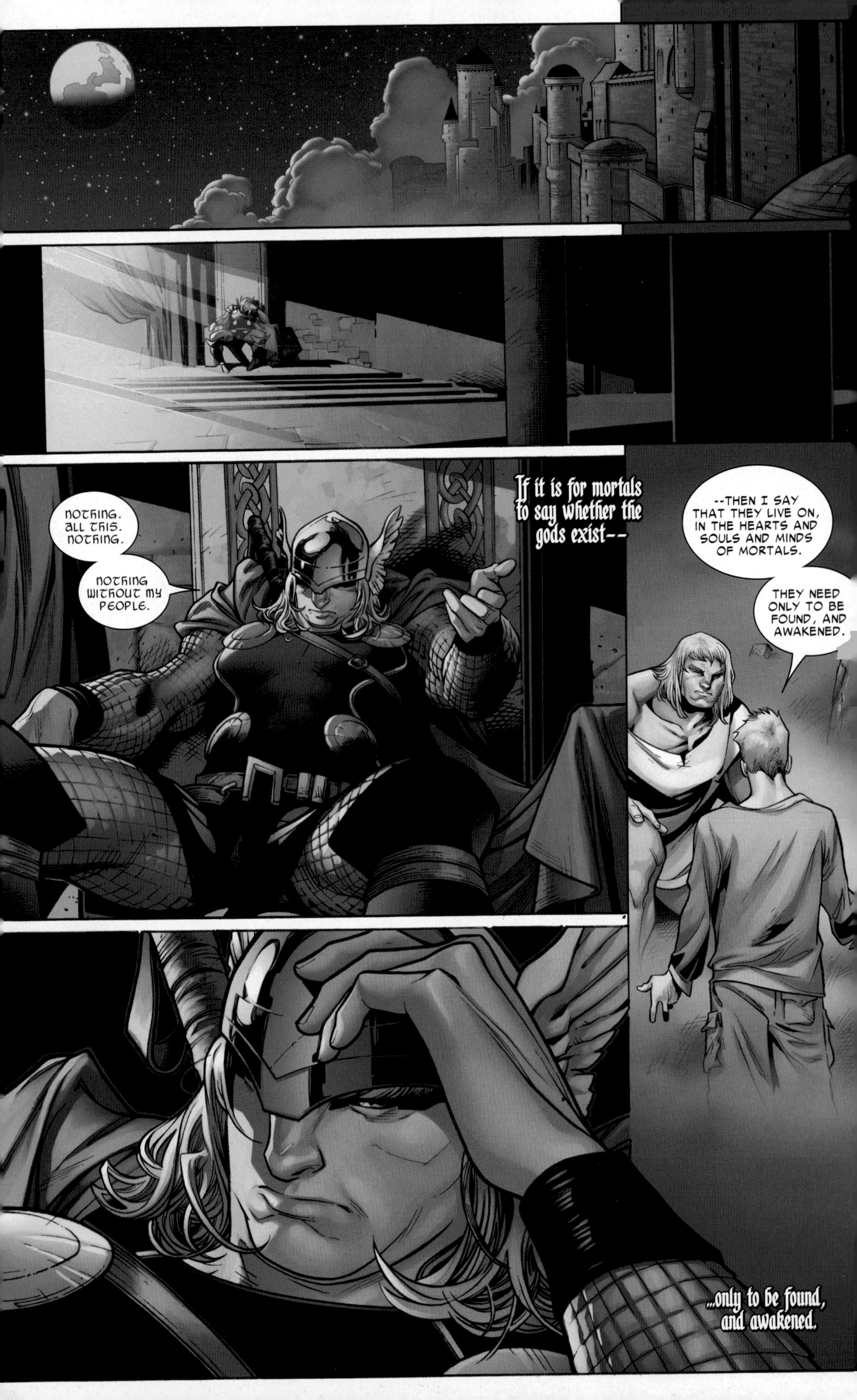

NOTHING.
ALL THIS.
NOTHING.
NOTHING WITHOUT MY PEOPLE.
If it is for mortals to say whether the gods exist--
--THEN I SAY THAT THEY LIVE ON, IN THE HEARTS AND SOULS AND MINDS OF MORTALS.
THEY NEED ONLY TO BE FOUND, AND AWAKENED.
...only to be found, and awakened.

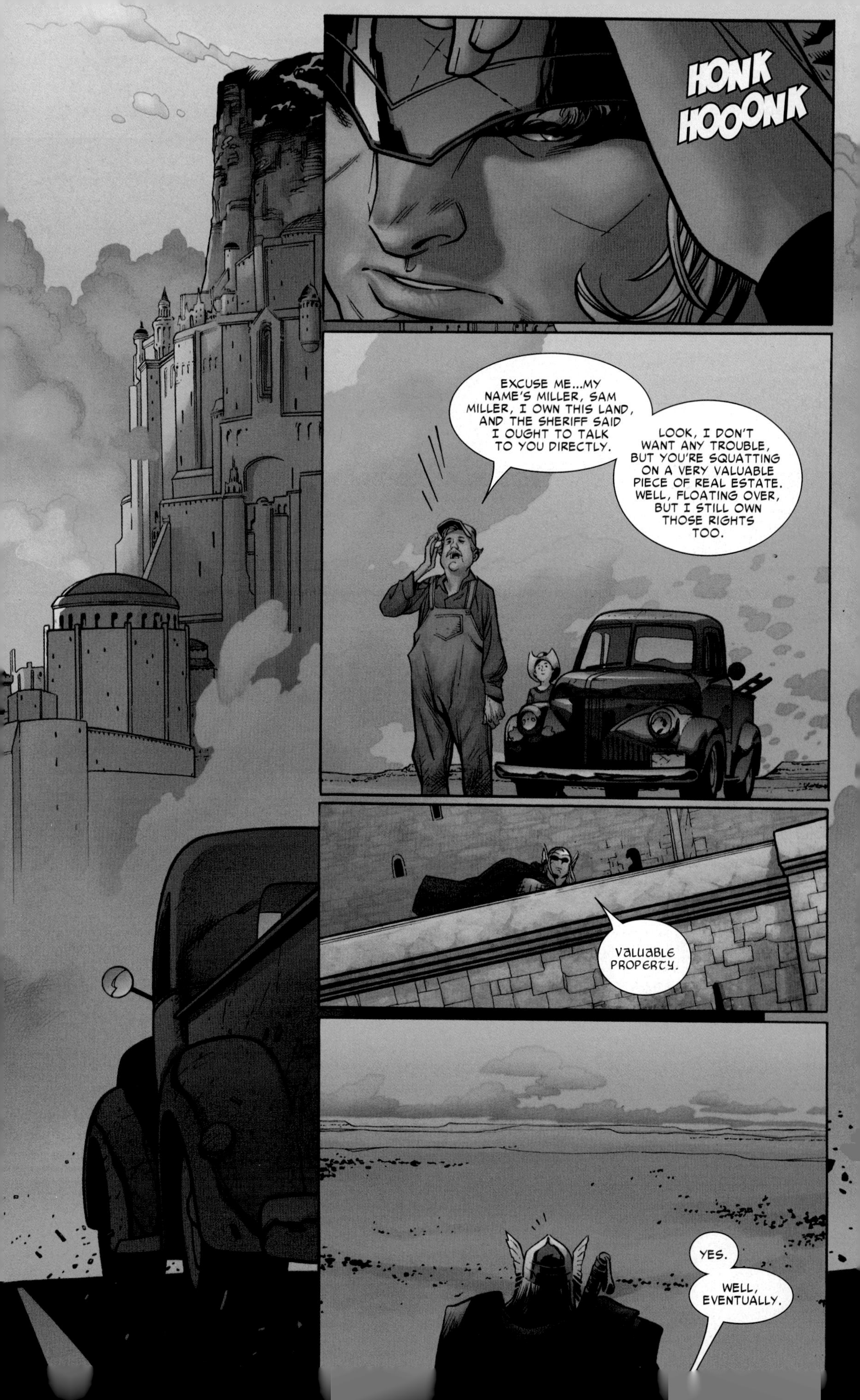
HONK
HOOONK
EXCUSE ME...MY NAME'S MILLER, SAM MILLER, I OWN THIS LAND, AND THE SHERIFF SAID I OUGHT TO TALK TO YOU DIRECTLY.
LOOK, I DON'T WANT ANY TROUBLE, BUT YOU'RE SQUATTING ON A VERY VALUABLE PIECE OF REAL ESTATE. WELL, FLOATING OVER, BUT I STILL OWN THOSE RIGHTS TOO.
VALUABLE PROPERTY.
YES.
WELL, EVENTUALLY.

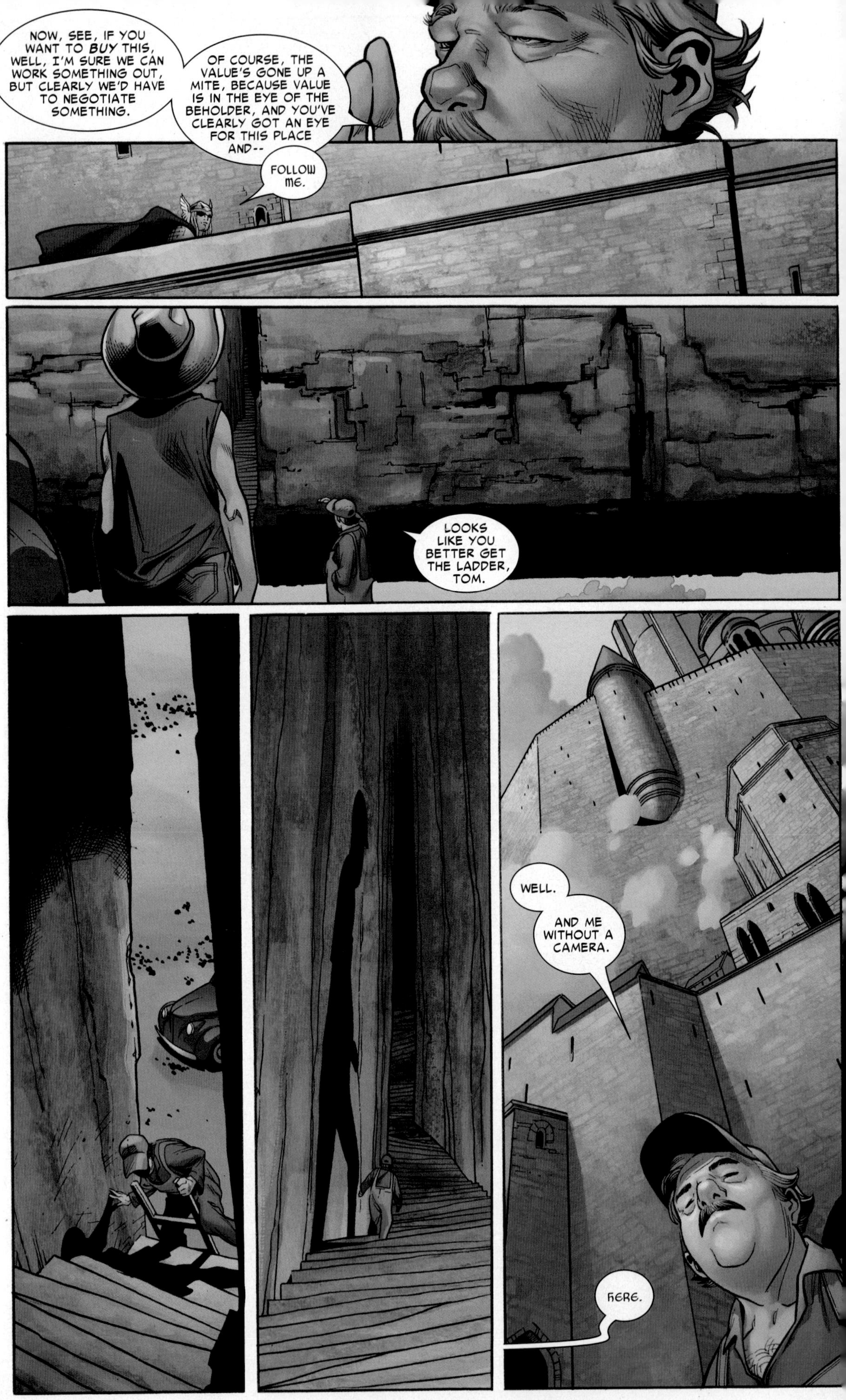
NOW, SEE, IF YOU WANT TO *BUY* THIS, WELL, I'M SURE WE CAN WORK SOMETHING OUT, BUT CLEARLY WE'D HAVE TO NEGOTIATE SOMETHING.
OF COURSE, THE VALUE'S GONE UP A MITE, BECAUSE VALUE IS IN THE EYE OF THE BEHOLDER, AND YOU'VE CLEARLY GOT AN EYE FOR THIS PLACE AND--
FOLLOW ME.
LOOKS LIKE YOU BETTER GET THE LADDER, TOM.
WELL.
AND ME WITHOUT A CAMERA.
HERE.

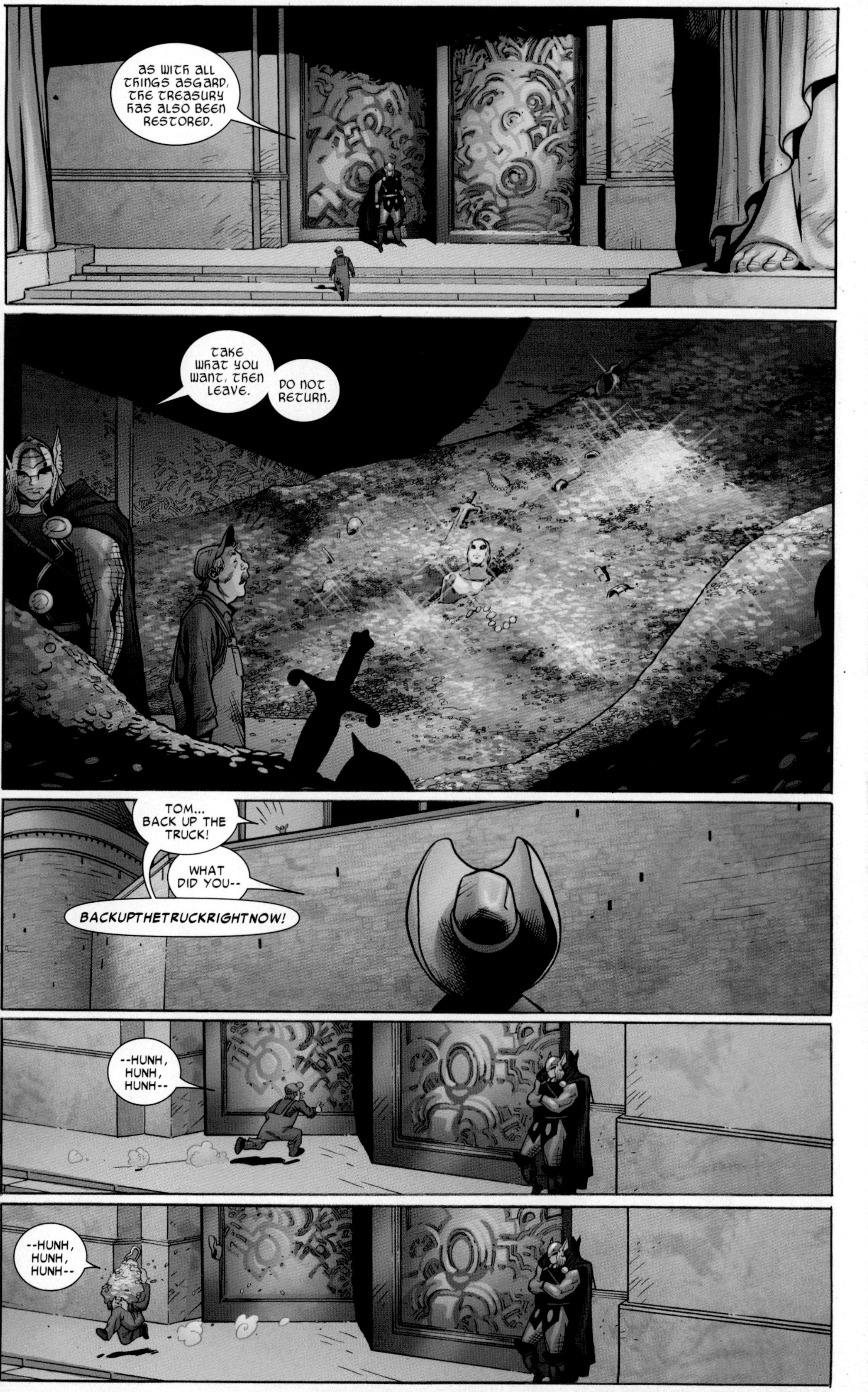

AS WITH ALL THINGS ASGARD, THE TREASURY HAS ALSO BEEN RESTORED.
TAKE WHAT YOU WANT, THEN LEAVE.
DO NOT RETURN.
TOM... BACK UP THE TRUCK!
WHAT DID YOU--
BACKUPTHETRUCKRIGHTNOW!
--HUNH, HUNH, HUNH--
--HUNH, HUNH, HUNH, HUNH--

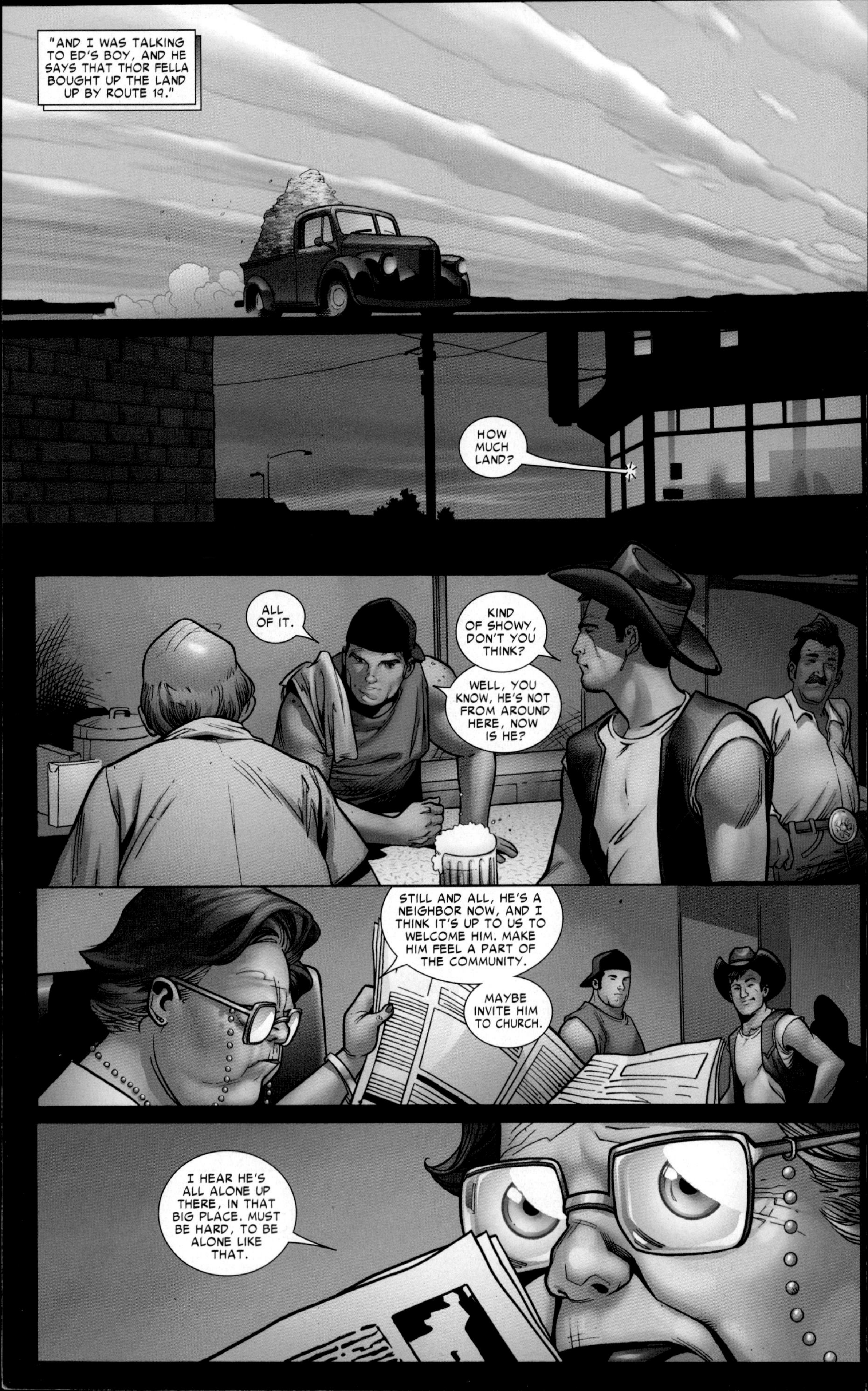
"AND I WAS TALKING TO ED'S BOY, AND HE SAYS THAT THOR FELLA BOUGHT UP THE LAND UP BY ROUTE 19."
HOW MUCH LAND?
ALL OF IT.
KIND OF SHOWY, DON'T YOU THINK?
WELL, YOU KNOW, HE'S NOT FROM AROUND HERE, NOW IS HE?
STILL AND ALL, HE'S A NEIGHBOR NOW, AND I THINK IT'S UP TO US TO WELCOME HIM. MAKE HIM FEEL A PART OF THE COMMUNITY.
MAYBE INVITE HIM TO CHURCH.
I HEAR HE'S ALL ALONE UP THERE, IN THAT BIG PLACE. MUST BE HARD, TO BE ALONE LIKE THAT.

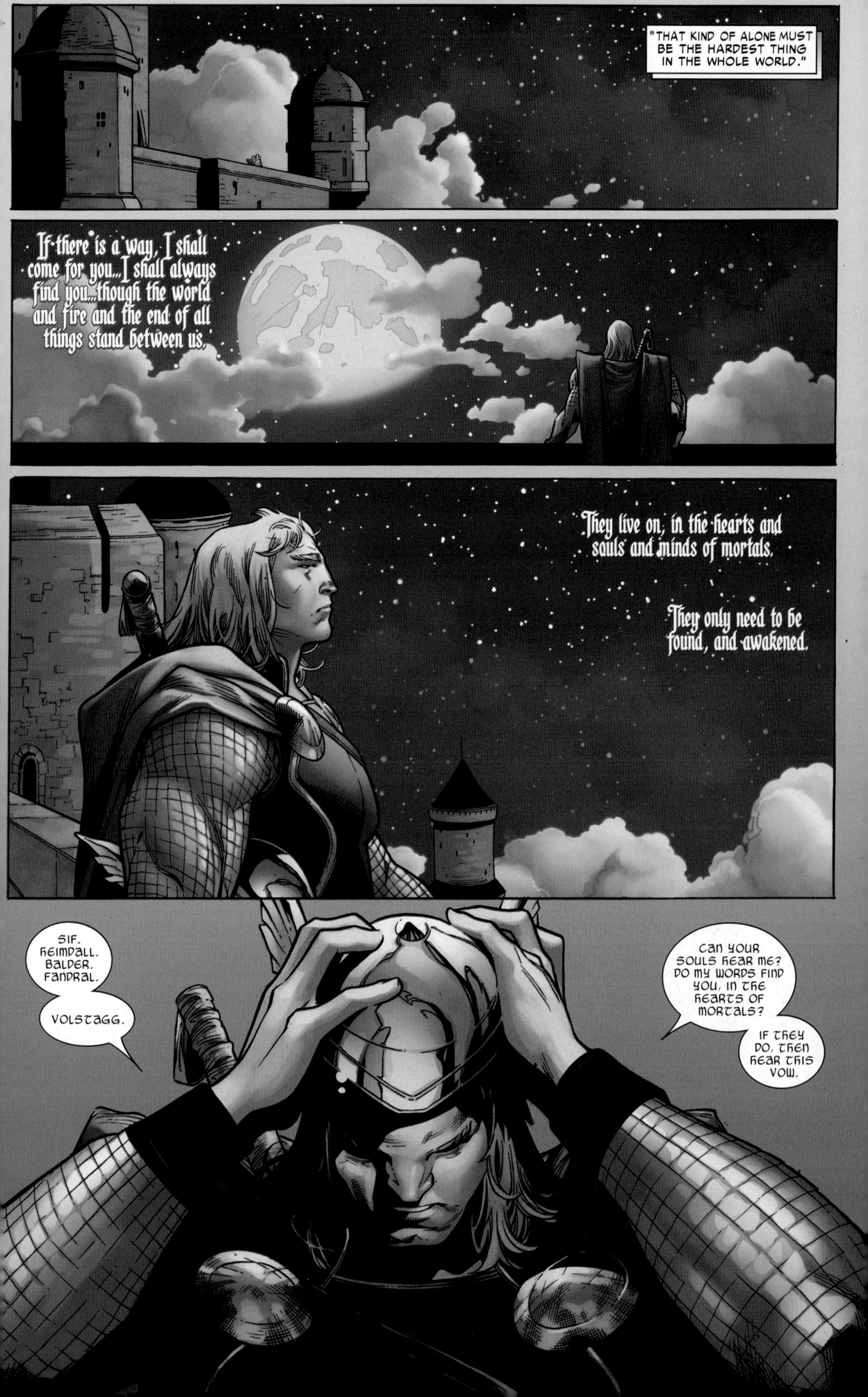
"THAT KIND OF ALONE MUST BE THE HARDEST THING IN THE WHOLE WORLD."
If there is a way, I shall come for you...I shall always find you...though the world and fire and the end of all things stand between us.
They live on, in the hearts and souls and minds of mortals.
They only need to be found, and awakened.
SIF. HEIMDALL. BALDER. FANDRAL.
VOLSTAGG.
CAN YOUR SOULS HEAR ME? DO MY WORDS FIND YOU, IN THE HEARTS OF MORTALS?
IF THEY DO, THEN HEAR THIS VOW.

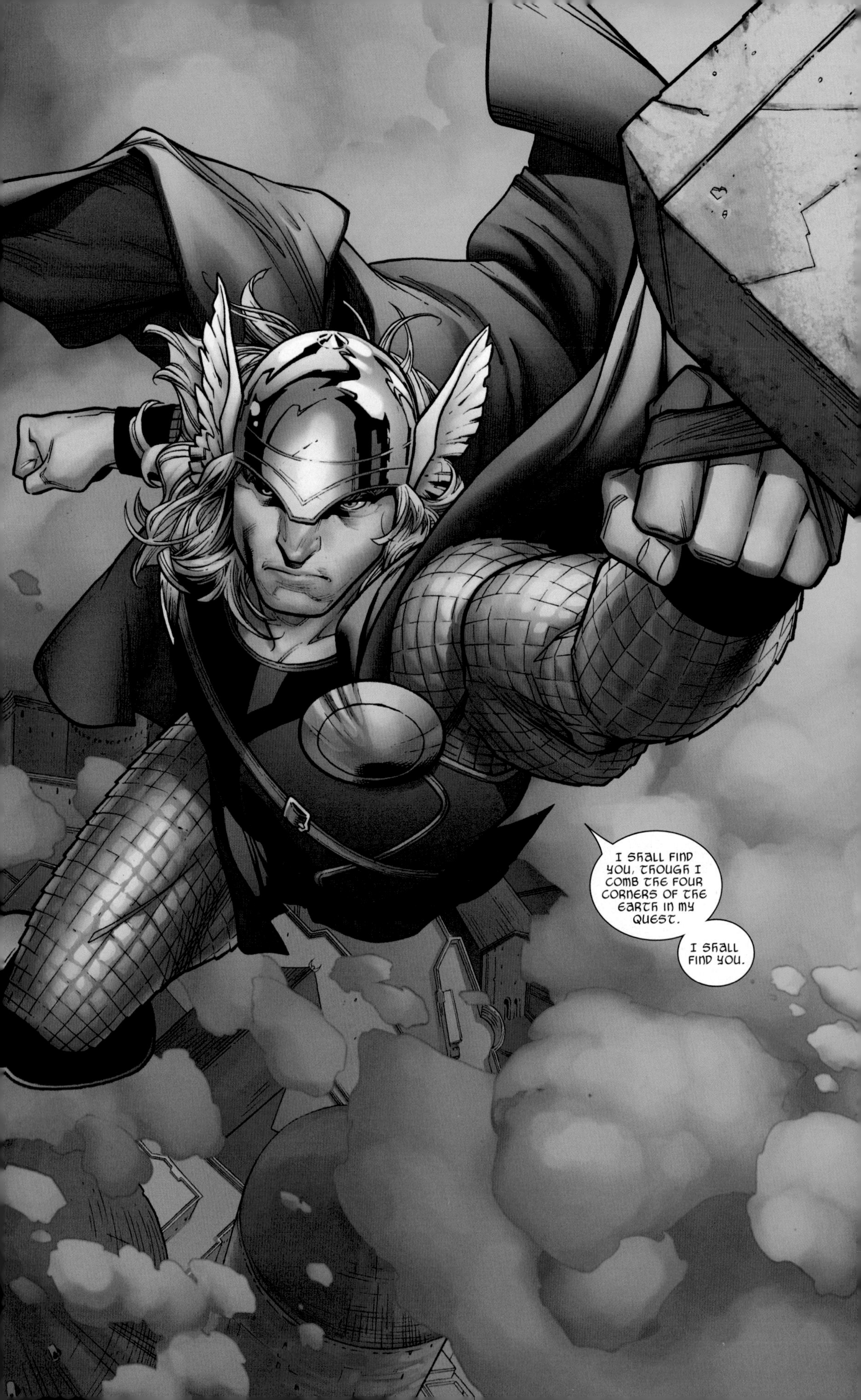
I SHALL FIND YOU, THOUGH I COMB THE FOUR CORNERS OF THE EARTH IN MY QUEST.
I SHALL FIND YOU.

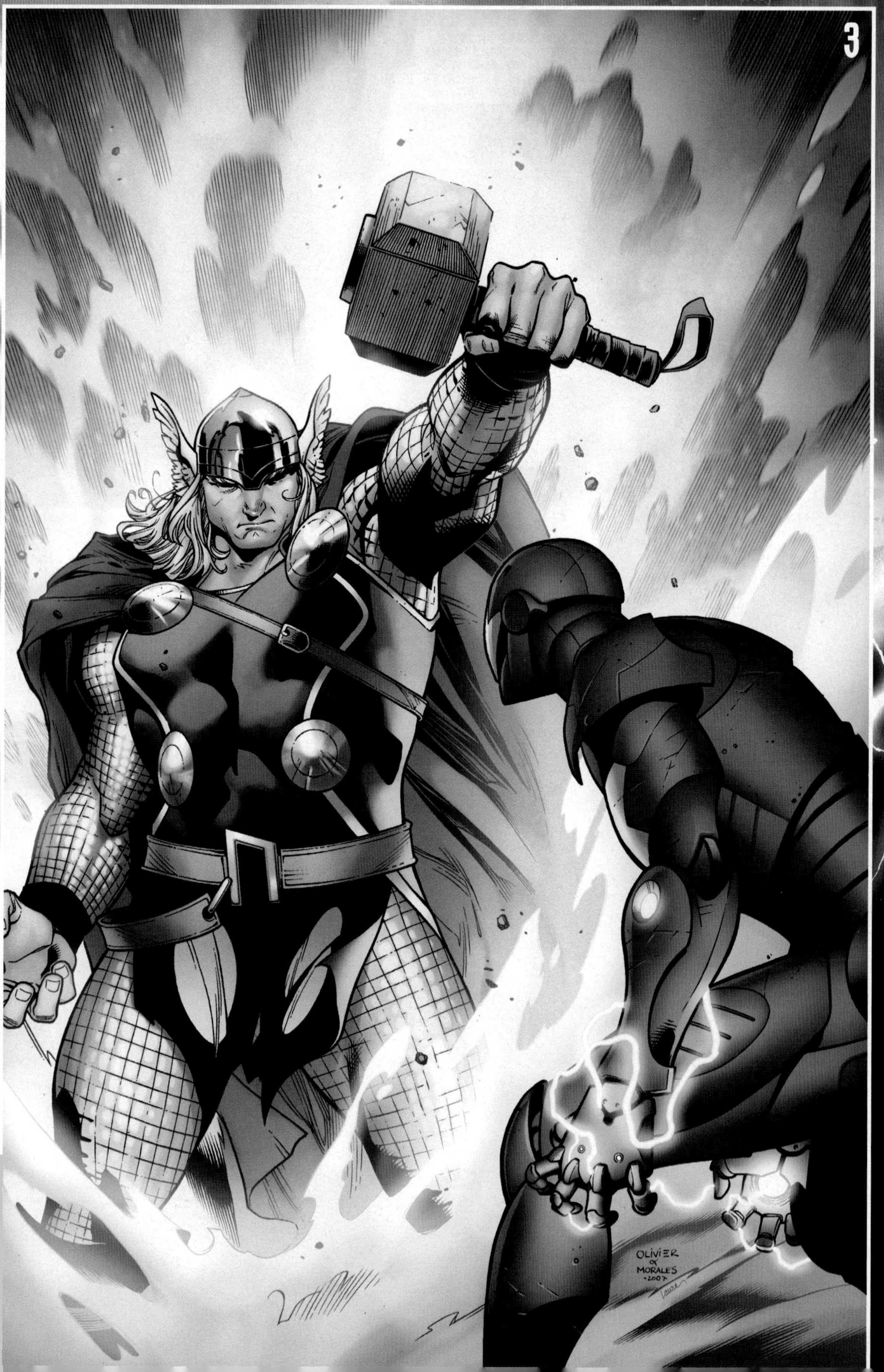
3
OLIVIER
MORALES
2007

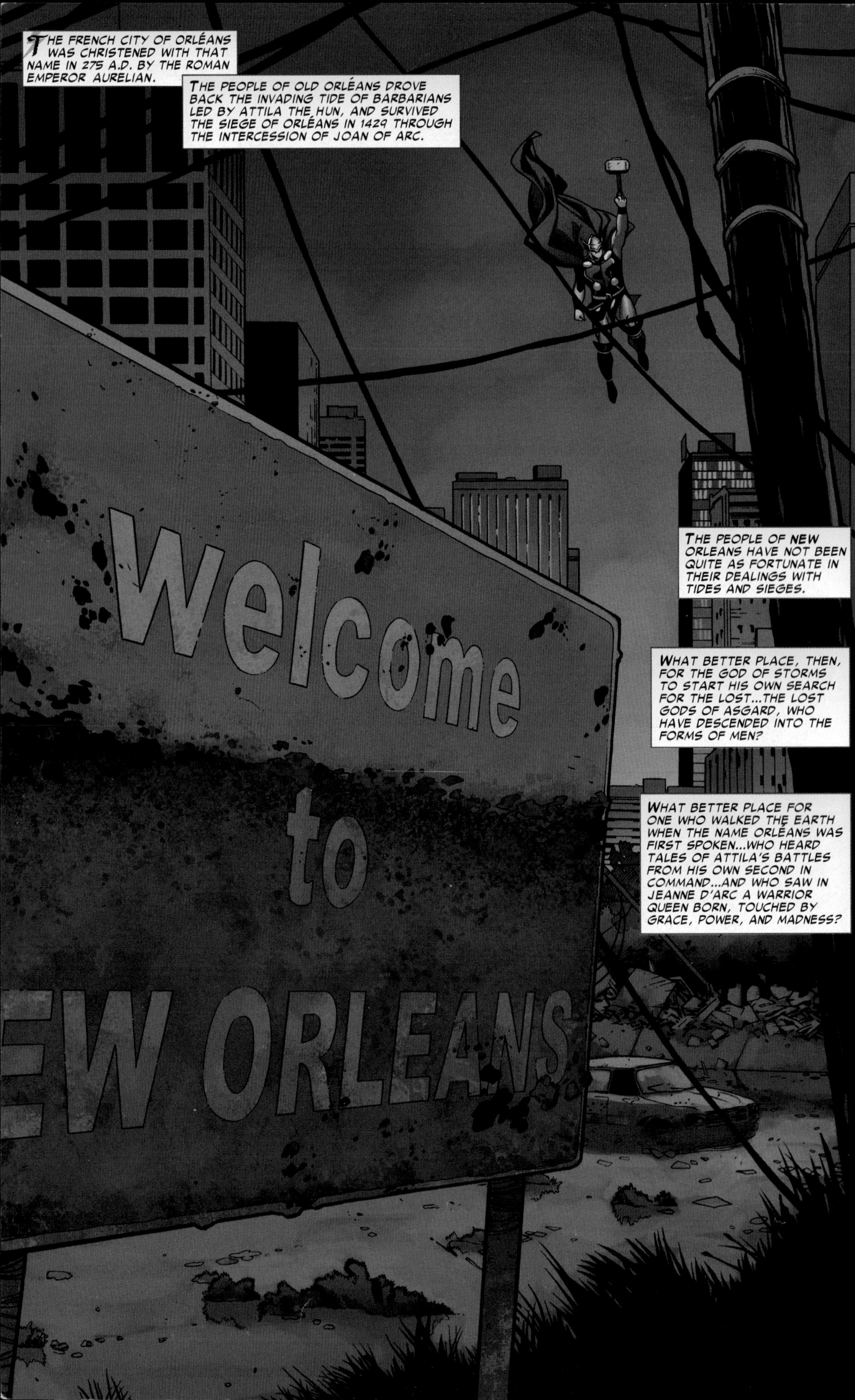
THE FRENCH CITY OF ORLÉANS WAS CHRISTENED WITH THAT NAME IN 275 A.D. BY THE ROMAN EMPEROR AURELIAN.
THE PEOPLE OF OLD ORLÉANS DROVE BACK THE INVADING TIDE OF BARBARIANS LED BY ATTILA THE HUN, AND SURVIVED THE SIEGE OF ORLÉANS IN 1429 THROUGH THE INTERCESSION OF JOAN OF ARC.
Welcome to
EW ORLEANS
THE PEOPLE OF NEW ORLEANS HAVE NOT BEEN QUITE AS FORTUNATE IN THEIR DEALINGS WITH TIDES AND SIEGES.
WHAT BETTER PLACE, THEN, FOR THE GOD OF STORMS TO START HIS OWN SEARCH FOR THE LOST...THE LOST GODS OF ASGARD, WHO HAVE DESCENDED INTO THE FORMS OF MEN?
WHAT BETTER PLACE FOR ONE WHO WALKED THE EARTH WHEN THE NAME ORLÉANS WAS FIRST SPOKEN...WHO HEARD TALES OF ATTILA'S BATTLES FROM HIS OWN SECOND IN COMMAND...AND WHO SAW IN JEANNE D'ARC A WARRIOR QUEEN BORN, TOUCHED BY GRACE, POWER, AND MADNESS?

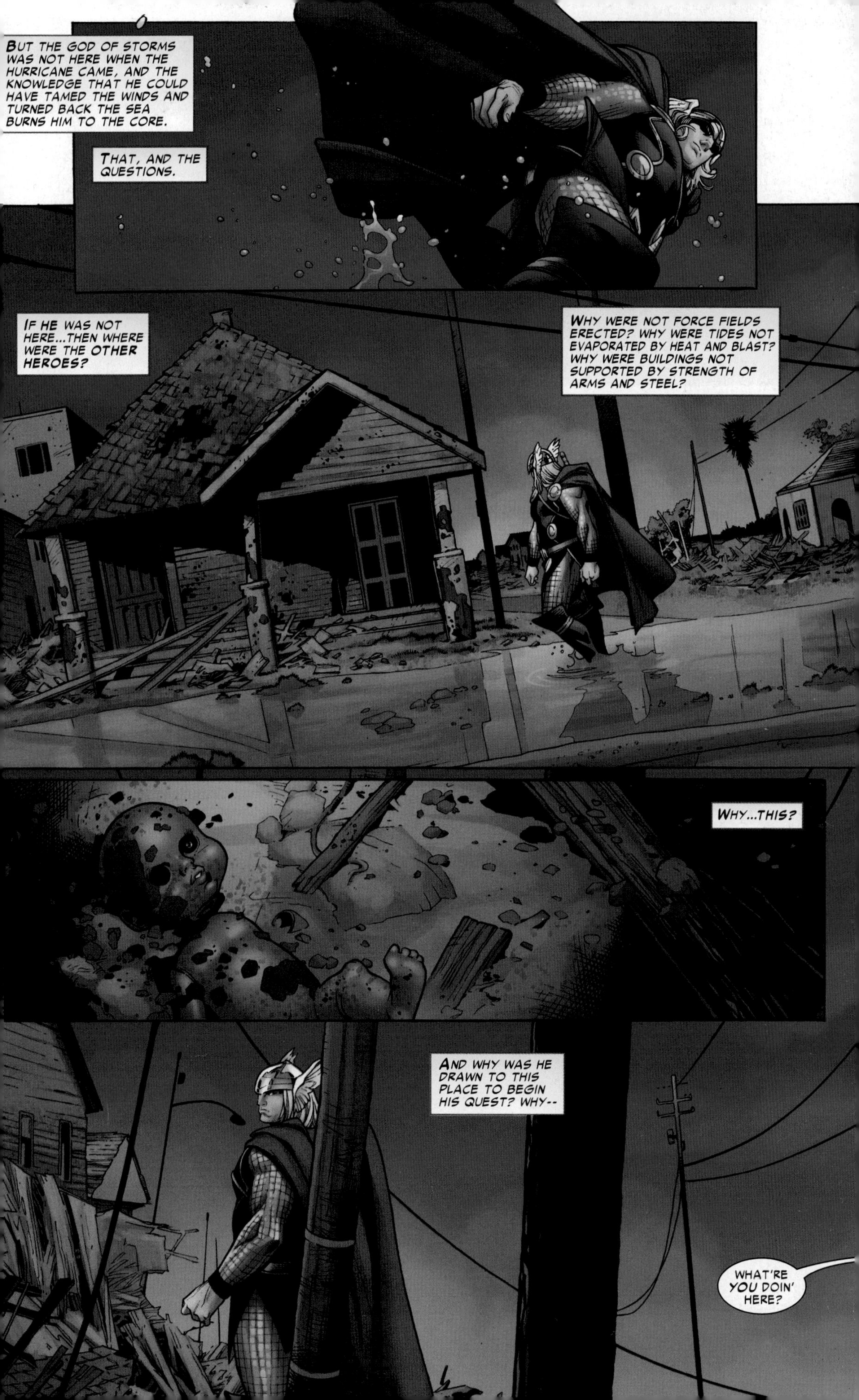
BUT THE GOD OF STORMS WAS NOT HERE WHEN THE HURRICANE CAME, AND THE KNOWLEDGE THAT HE COULD HAVE TAMED THE WINDS AND TURNED BACK THE SEA BURNS HIM TO THE CORE.
THAT, AND THE QUESTIONS.
IF HE WAS NOT HERE...THEN WHERE WERE THE OTHER HEROES?
WHY WERE NOT FORCE FIELDS ERECTED? WHY WERE TIDES NOT EVAPORATED BY HEAT AND BLAST? WHY WERE BUILDINGS NOT SUPPORTED BY STRENGTH OF ARMS AND STEEL?
WHY...THIS?
AND WHY WAS HE DRAWN TO THIS PLACE TO BEGIN HIS QUEST? WHY--
WHAT'RE YOU DOIN' HERE?

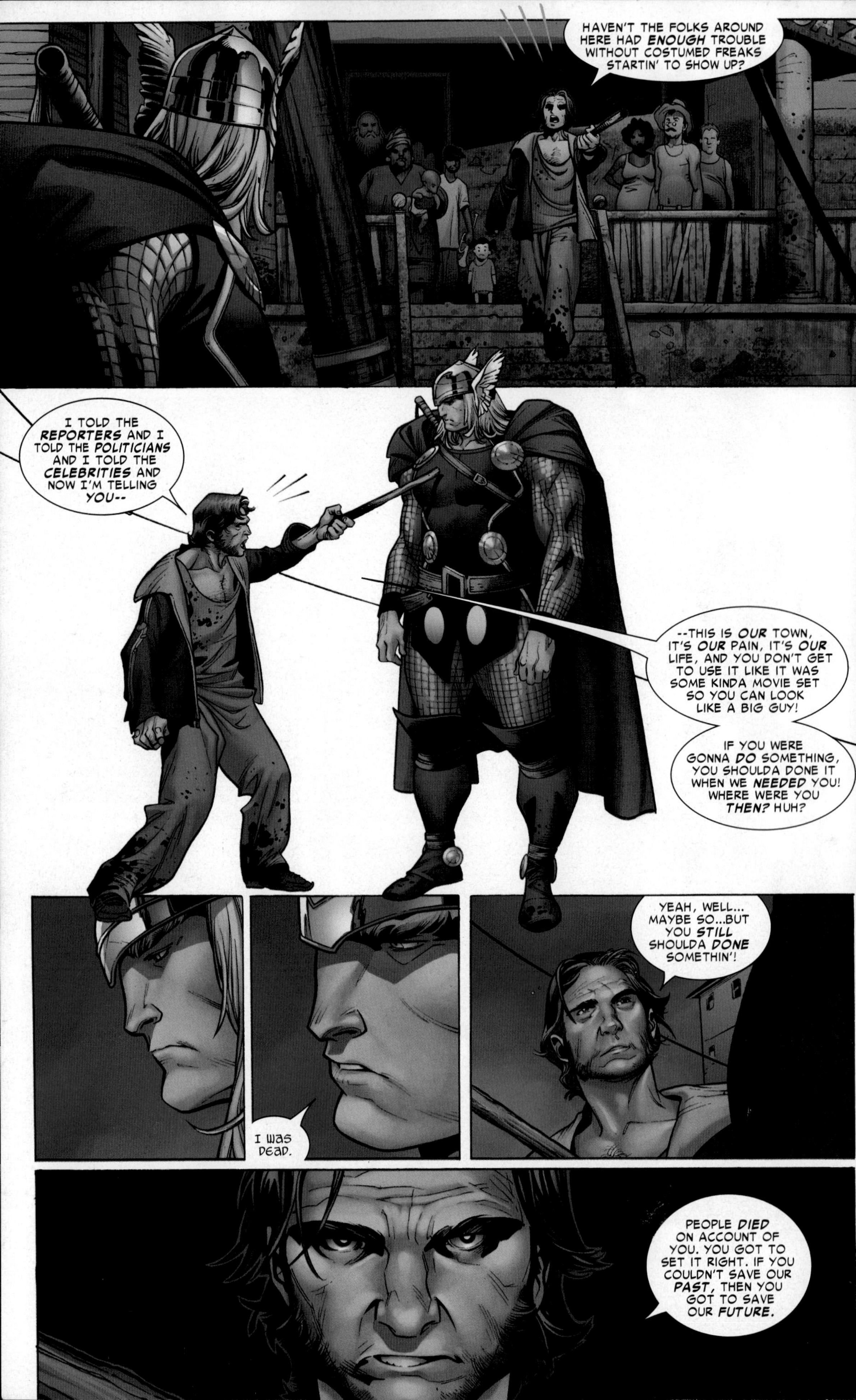
HAVEN'T THE FOLKS AROUND HERE HAD ENOUGH TROUBLE WITHOUT COSTUMED FREAKS STARTIN' TO SHOW UP?
I TOLD THE REPORTERS AND I TOLD THE POLITICIANS AND I TOLD THE CELEBRITIES AND NOW I'M TELLING YOU--
--THIS IS OUR TOWN, IT'S OUR PAIN, IT'S OUR LIFE, AND YOU DON'T GET TO USE IT LIKE IT WAS SOME KINDA MOVIE SET SO YOU CAN LOOK LIKE A BIG GUY!
IF YOU WERE GONNA DO SOMETHING, YOU SHOULDA DONE IT WHEN WE NEEDED YOU! WHERE WERE YOU THEN? HUH?
I WAS DEAD.
YEAH, WELL... MAYBE SO...BUT YOU STILL SHOULDA DONE SOMETHIN'!
PEOPLE DIED ON ACCOUNT OF YOU. YOU GOT TO SET IT RIGHT. IF YOU COULDN'T SAVE OUR PAST, THEN YOU GOT TO SAVE OUR FUTURE.

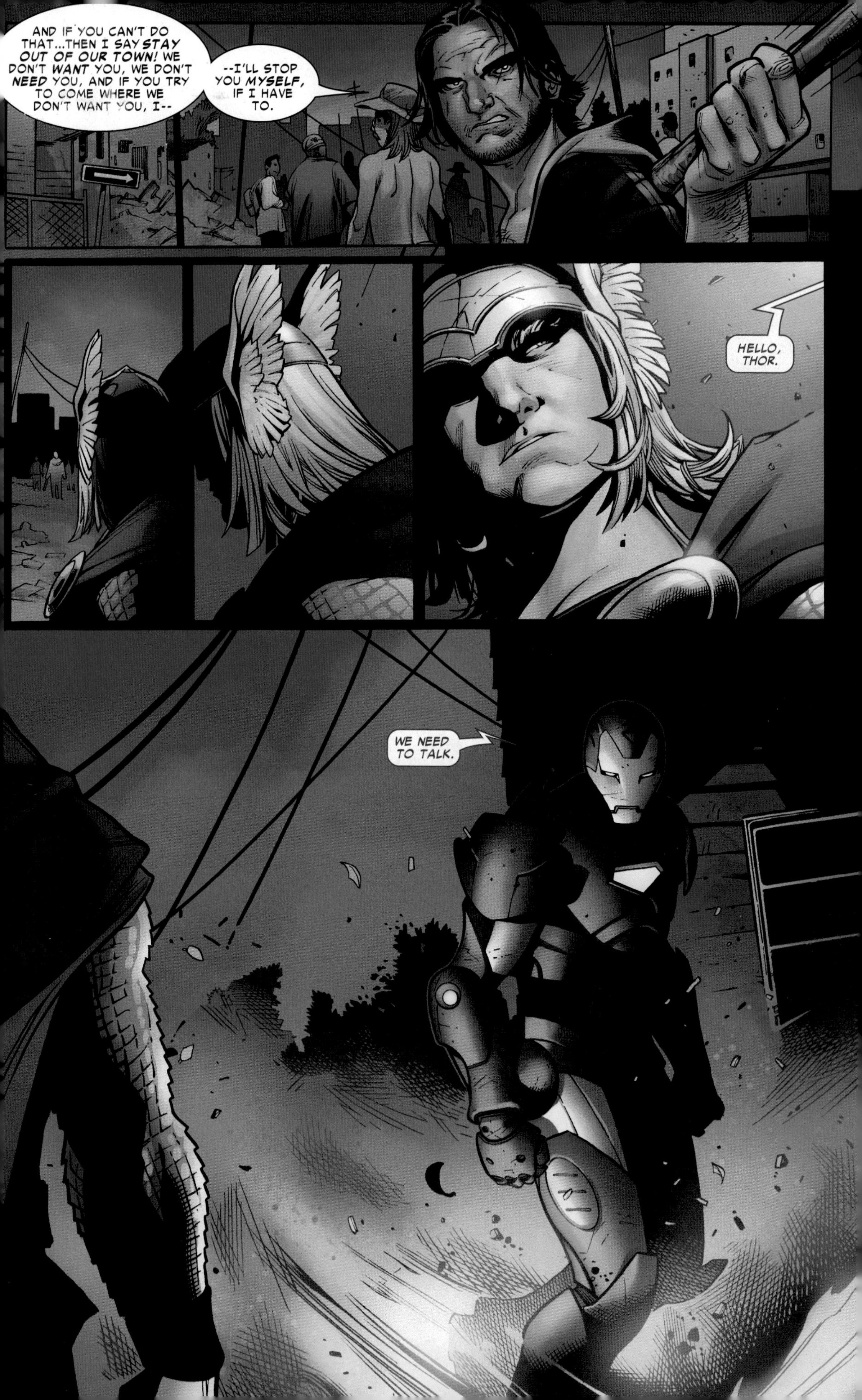
AND IF YOU CAN'T DO THAT...THEN I SAY STAY OUT OF OUR TOWN! WE DON'T WANT YOU, WE DON'T NEED YOU, AND IF YOU TRY TO COME WHERE WE DON'T WANT YOU, I--
--I'LL STOP YOU MYSELF, IF I HAVE TO.
HELLO, THOR.
WE NEED TO TALK.

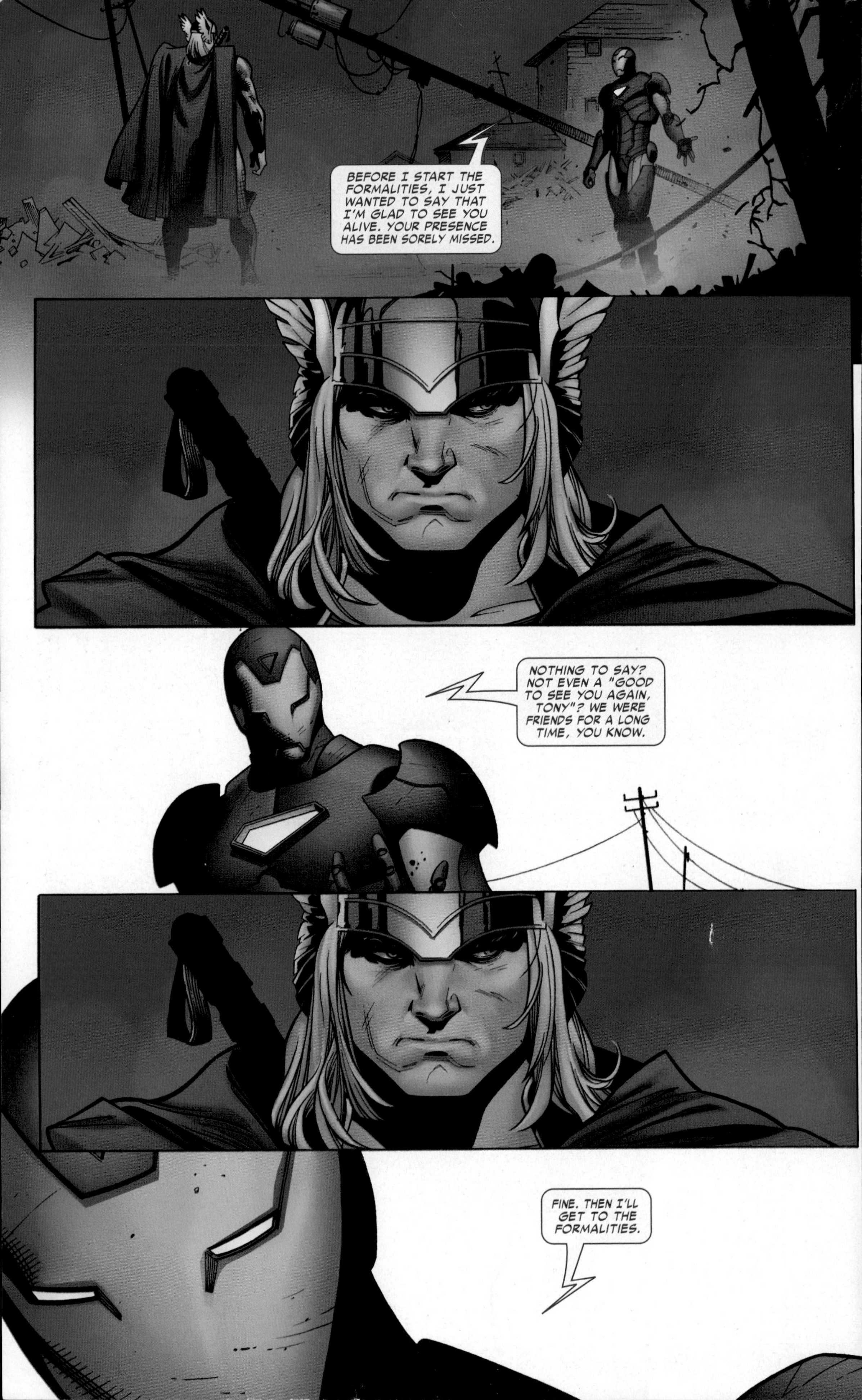
BEFORE I START THE FORMALITIES, I JUST WANTED TO SAY THAT I'M GLAD TO SEE YOU ALIVE. YOUR PRESENCE HAS BEEN SORELY MISSED.
NOTHING TO SAY? NOT EVEN A "GOOD TO SEE YOU AGAIN, TONY"? WE WERE FRIENDS FOR A LONG TIME, YOU KNOW.
FINE. THEN I'LL GET TO THE FORMALITIES.

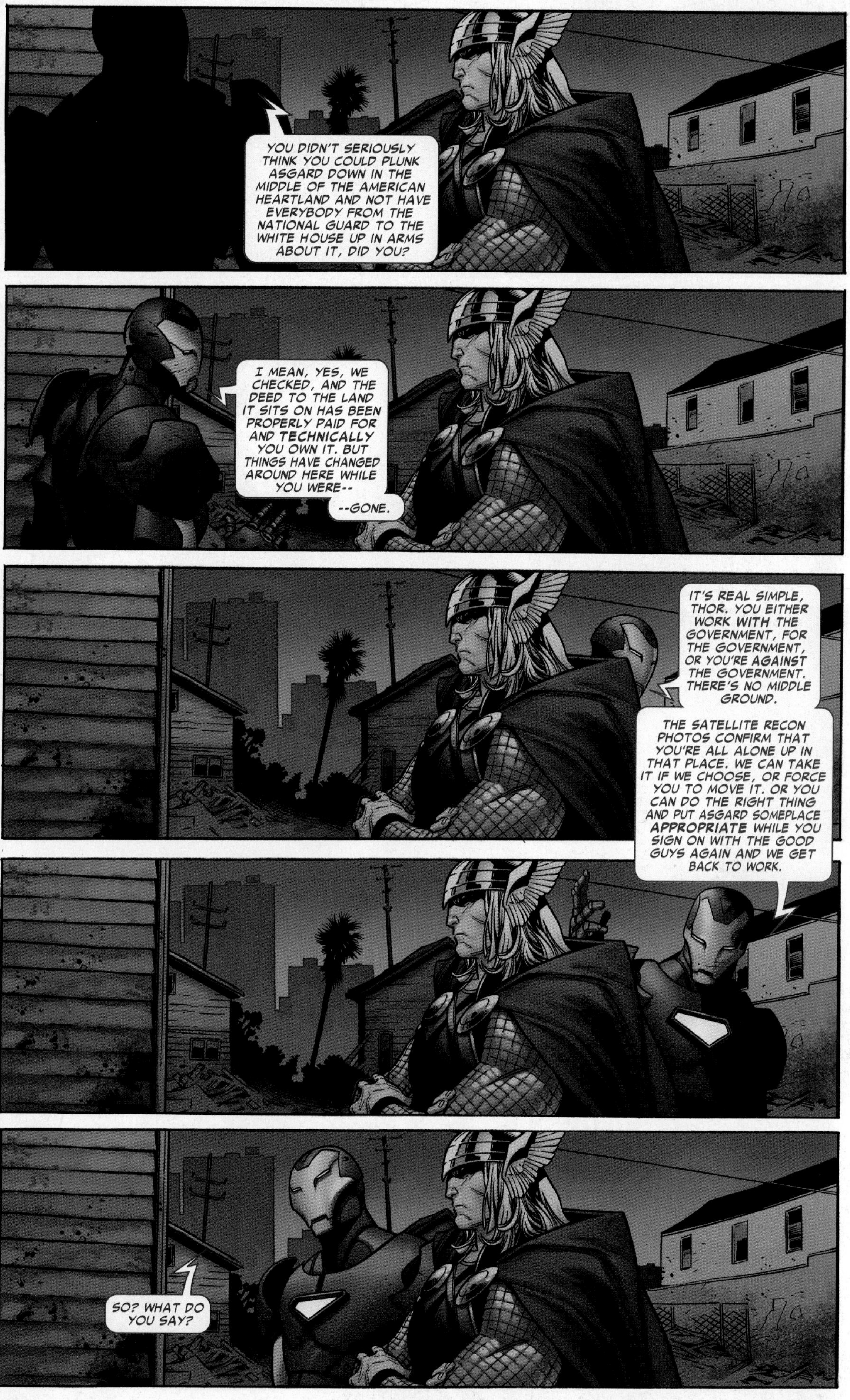
YOU DIDN'T SERIOUSLY THINK YOU COULD PLUNK ASGARD DOWN IN THE MIDDLE OF THE AMERICAN HEARTLAND AND NOT HAVE EVERYBODY FROM THE NATIONAL GUARD TO THE WHITE HOUSE UP IN ARMS ABOUT IT, DID YOU?
I MEAN, YES, WE CHECKED, AND THE DEED TO THE LAND IT SITS ON HAS BEEN PROPERLY PAID FOR AND TECHNICALLY YOU OWN IT. BUT THINGS HAVE CHANGED AROUND HERE WHILE YOU WERE--
--GONE.
IT'S REAL SIMPLE, THOR. YOU EITHER WORK WITH THE GOVERNMENT, FOR THE GOVERNMENT, OR YOU'RE AGAINST THE GOVERNMENT. THERE'S NO MIDDLE GROUND.
THE SATELLITE RECON PHOTOS CONFIRM THAT YOU'RE ALL ALONE UP IN THAT PLACE. WE CAN TAKE IT IF WE CHOOSE, OR FORCE YOU TO MOVE IT. OR YOU CAN DO THE RIGHT THING AND PUT ASGARD SOMEPLACE APPROPRIATE WHILE YOU SIGN ON WITH THE GOOD GUYS AGAIN AND WE GET BACK TO WORK.
SO? WHAT DO YOU SAY?

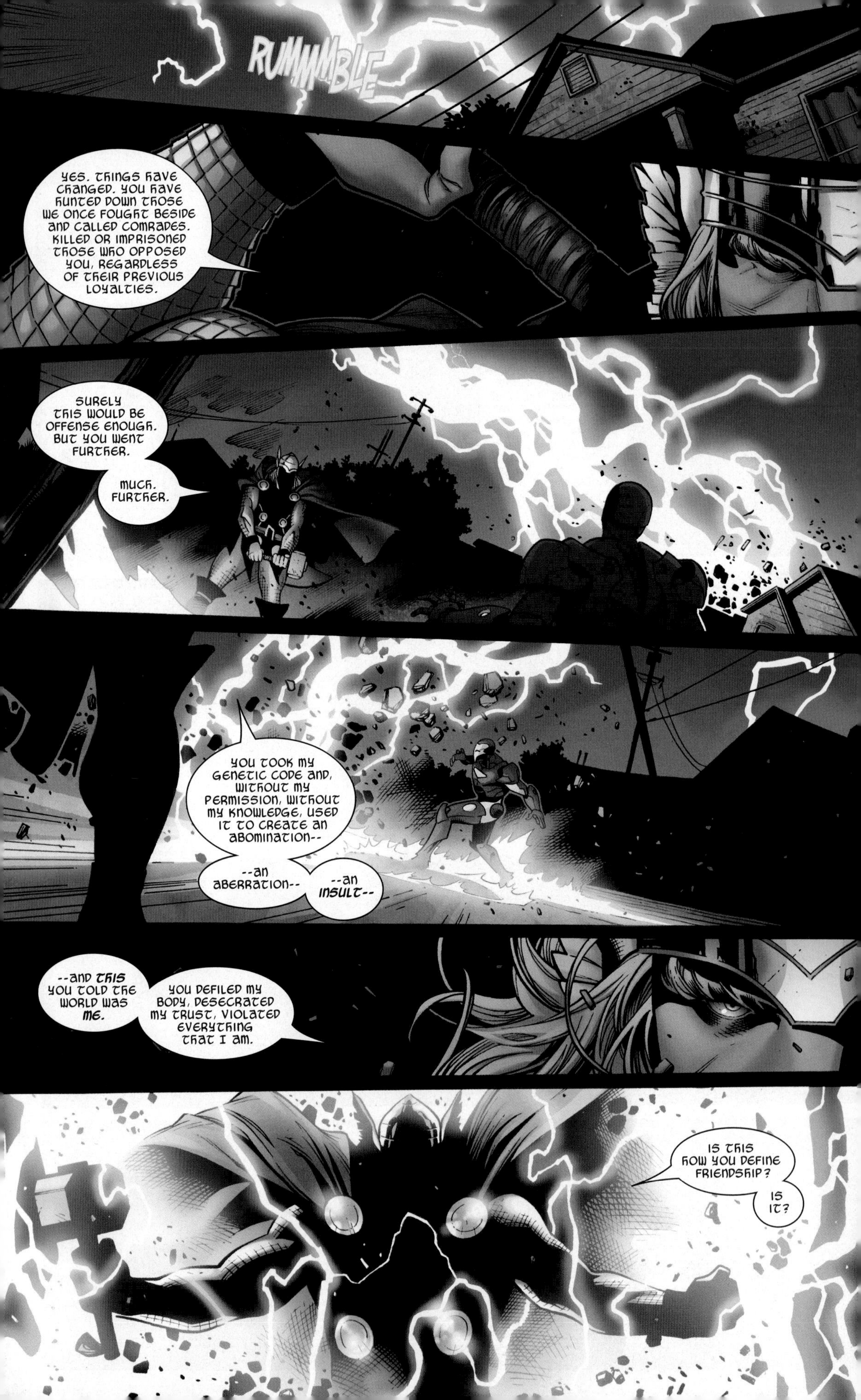
RUMMMBLE
YES. THINGS HAVE CHANGED. YOU HAVE HUNTED DOWN THOSE WE ONCE FOUGHT BESIDE AND CALLED COMRADES. KILLED OR IMPRISONED THOSE WHO OPPOSED YOU, REGARDLESS OF THEIR PREVIOUS LOYALTIES.
SURELY THIS WOULD BE OFFENSE ENOUGH. BUT YOU WENT FURTHER.
MUCH. FURTHER.
YOU TOOK MY GENETIC CODE AND, WITHOUT MY PERMISSION, WITHOUT MY KNOWLEDGE, USED IT TO CREATE AN ABOMINATION--
--AN ABERRATION--
--AN INSULT--
--AND THIS YOU TOLD THE WORLD WAS ME.
YOU DEFILED MY BODY, DESECRATED MY TRUST, VIOLATED EVERYTHING THAT I AM.
IS THIS HOW YOU DEFINE FRIENDSHIP?
IS IT?

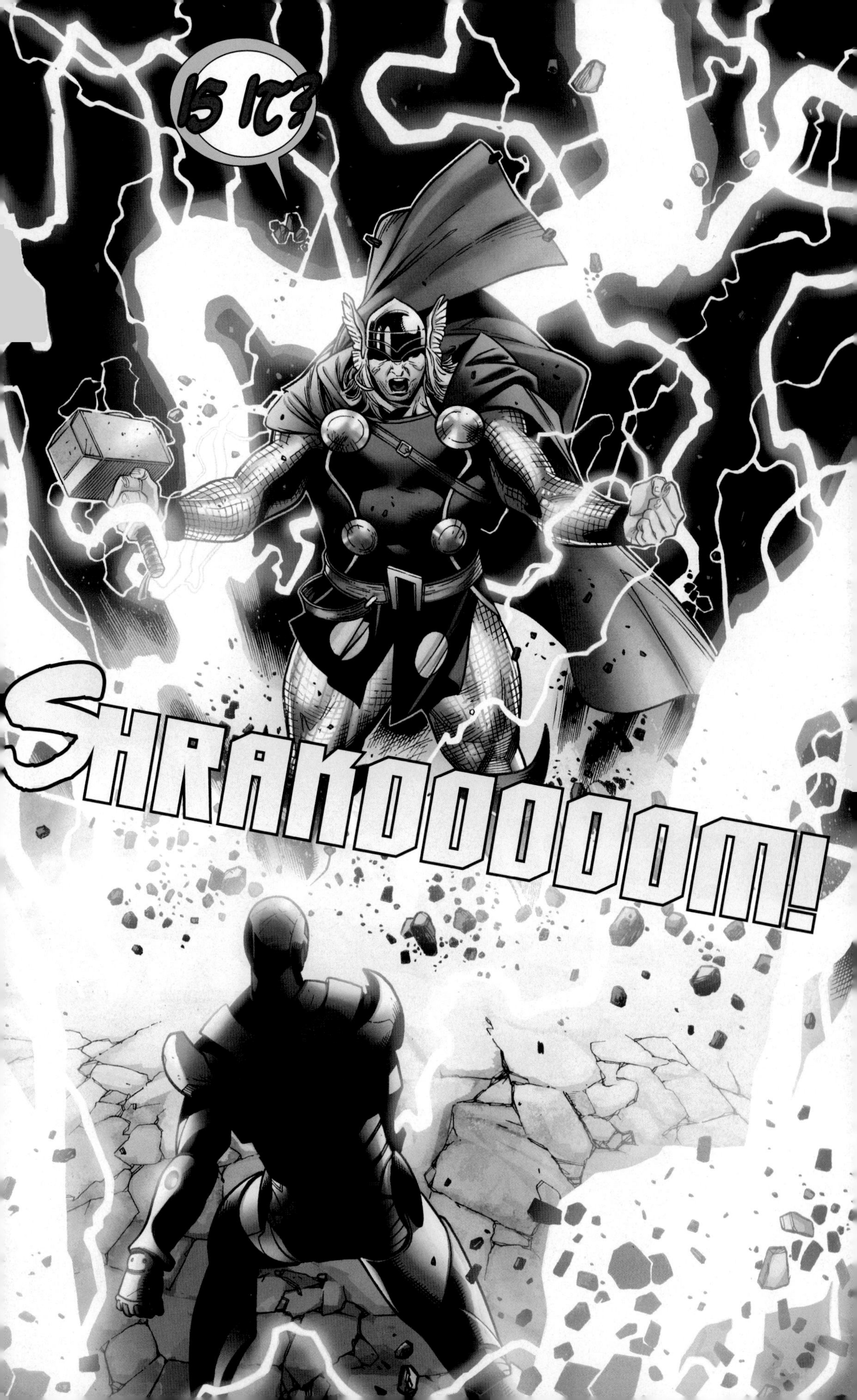
IS IT?
SHRAKOOOOOOM!

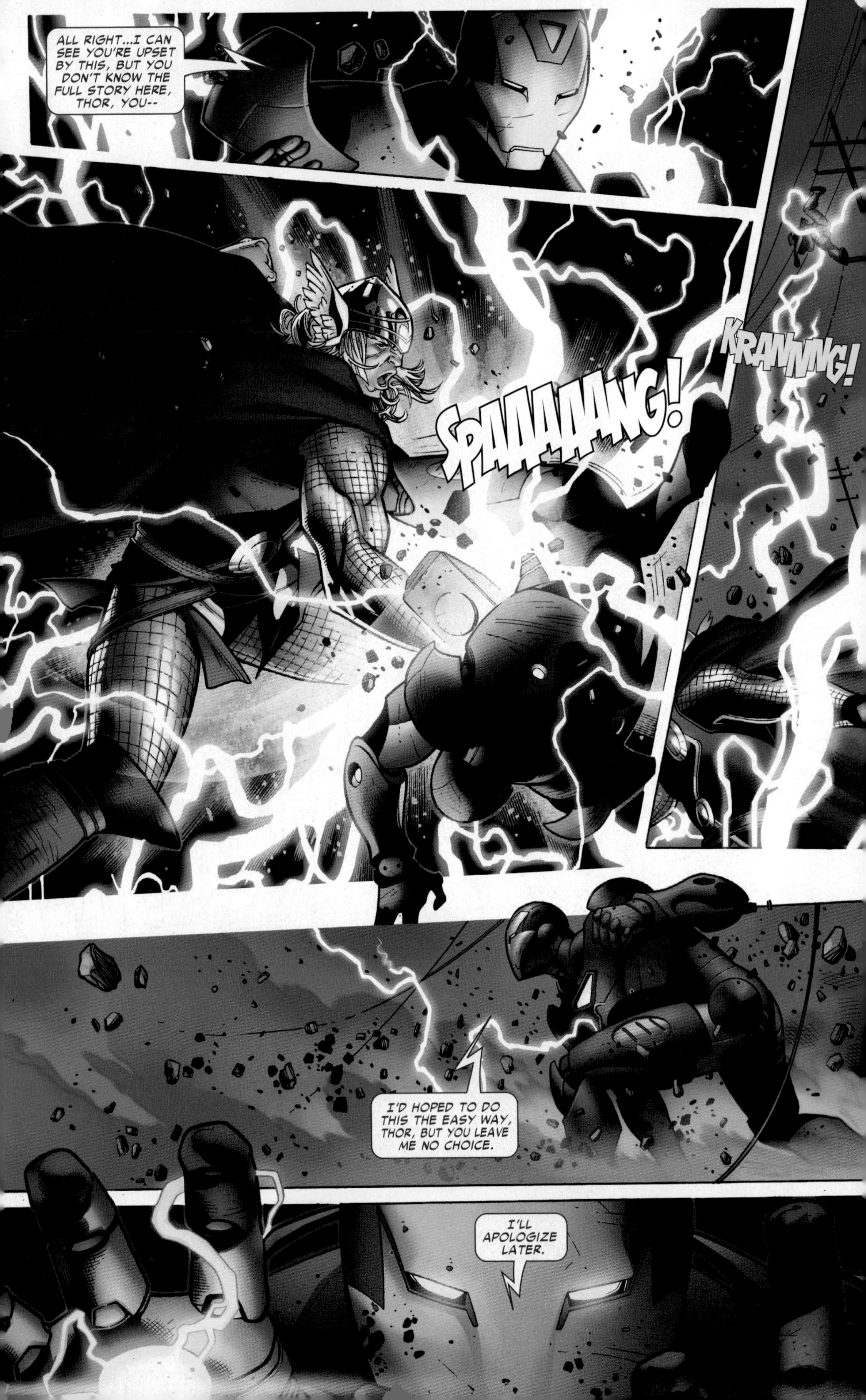
ALL RIGHT...I CAN SEE YOU'RE UPSET BY THIS, BUT YOU DON'T KNOW THE FULL STORY HERE, THOR, YOU--
SPAAAAANG!
KRANNNG!
I'D HOPED TO DO THIS THE EASY WAY, THOR, BUT YOU LEAVE ME NO CHOICE.
I'LL APOLOGIZE LATER.

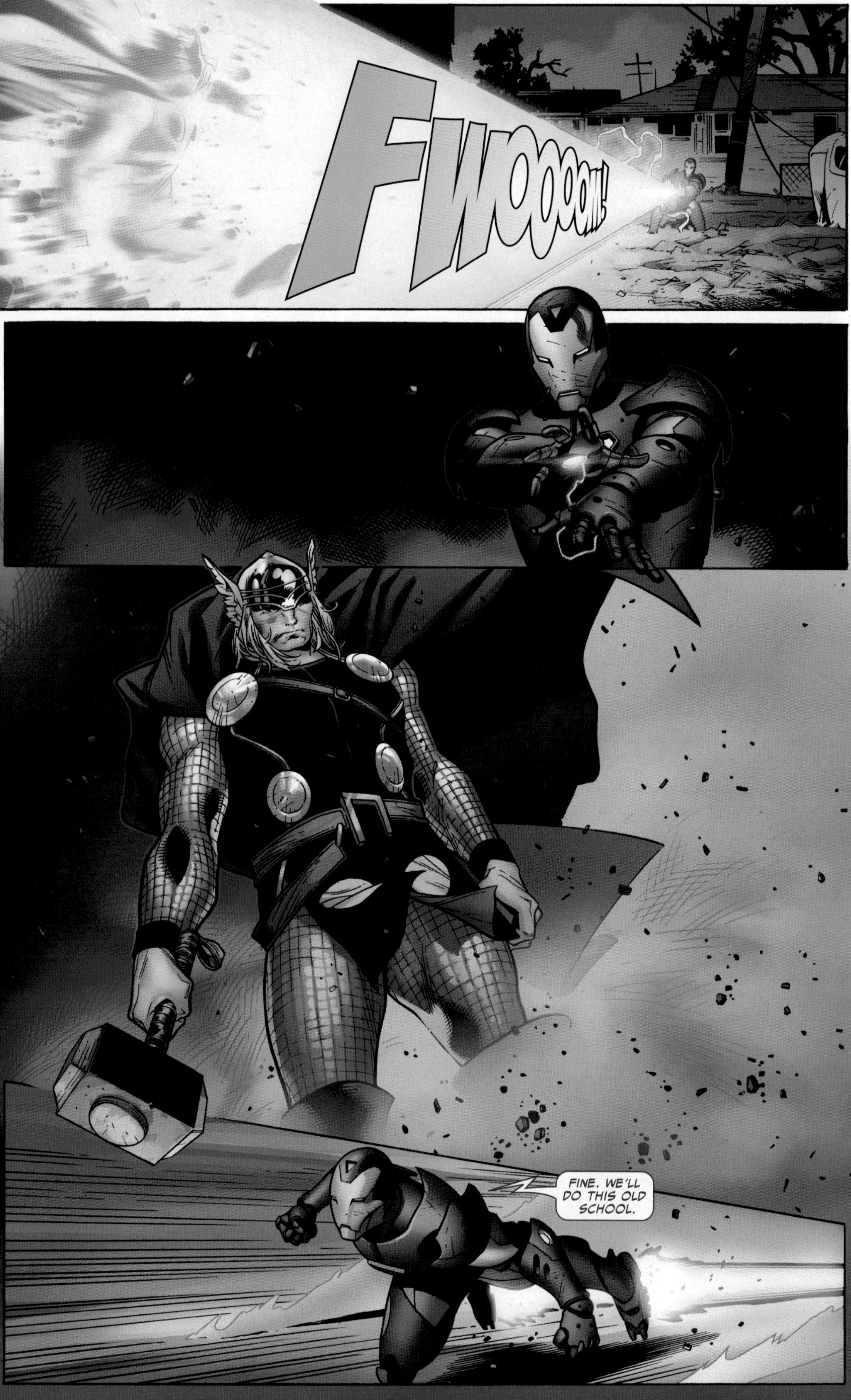
FWOOOOM!
FINE. WE'LL DO THIS OLD SCHOOL.

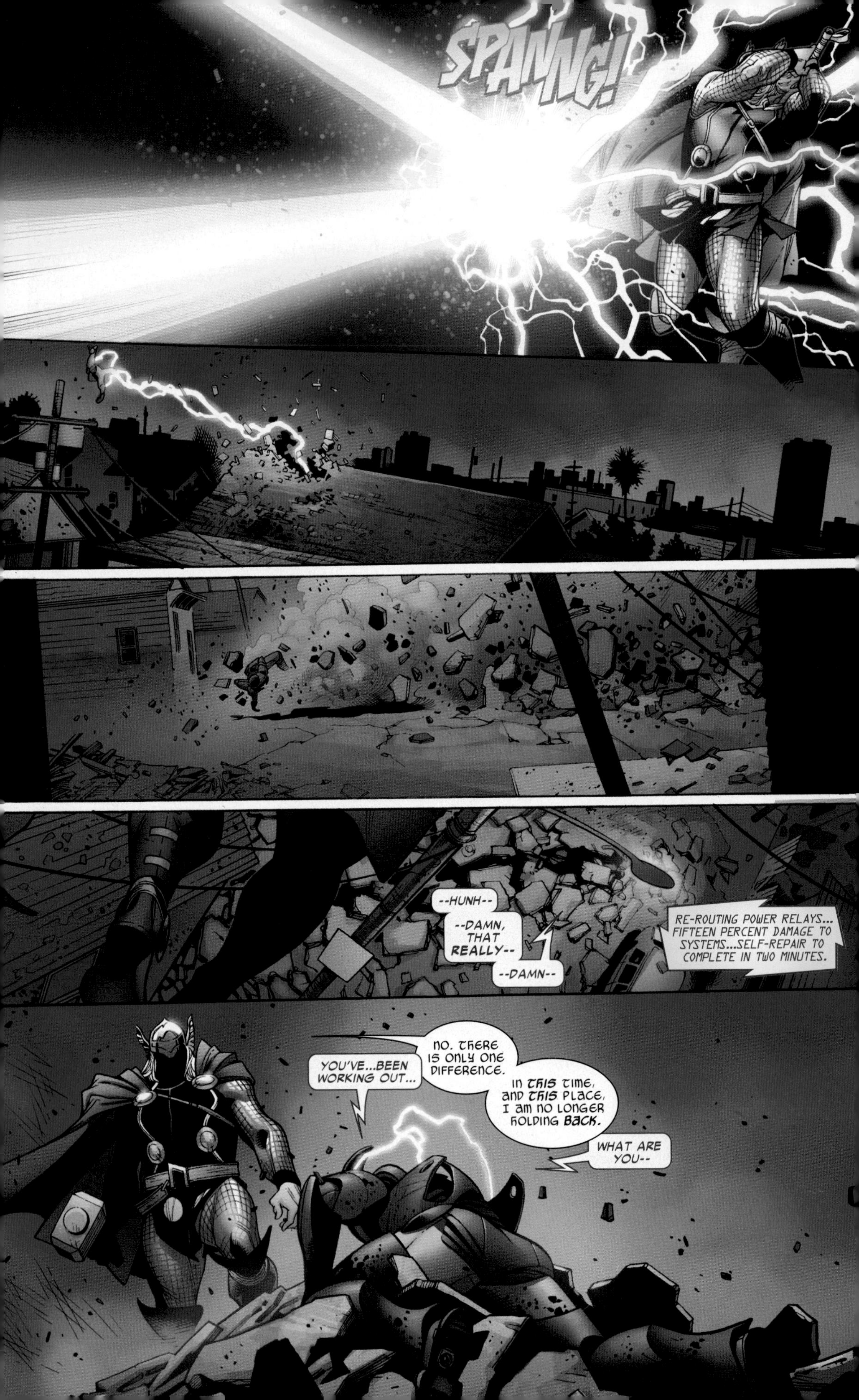

SPANNG!
--HUNH--
--DAMN, THAT REALLY--
--DAMN--
RE-ROUTING POWER RELAYS... FIFTEEN PERCENT DAMAGE TO SYSTEMS...SELF-REPAIR TO COMPLETE IN TWO MINUTES.
YOU'VE...BEEN WORKING OUT...
NO. THERE IS ONLY ONE DIFFERENCE.
IN THIS TIME, AND THIS PLACE, I AM NO LONGER HOLDING BACK.
WHAT ARE YOU--

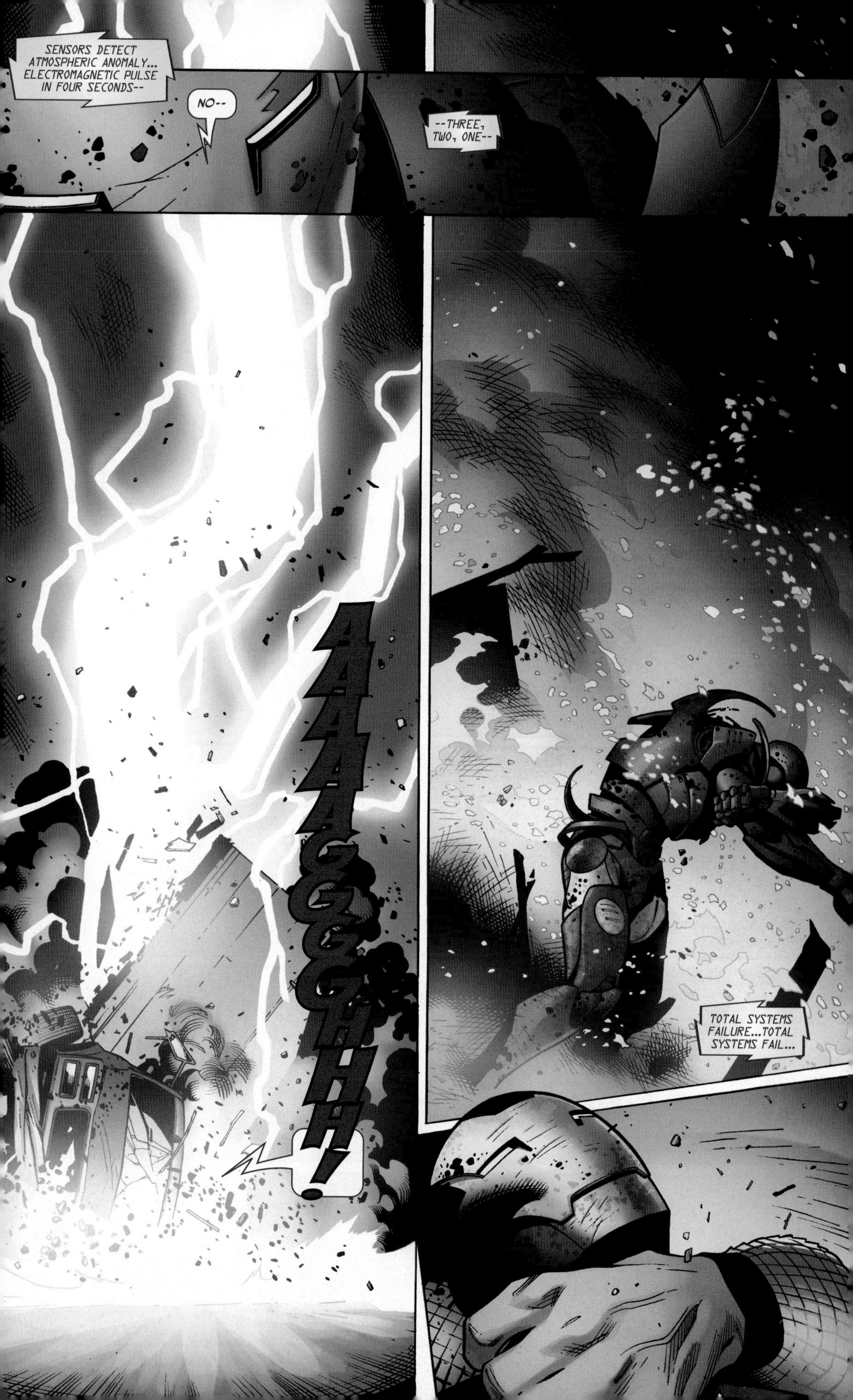
SENSORS DETECT ATMOSPHERIC ANOMALY... ELECTROMAGNETIC PULSE IN FOUR SECONDS--
NO--
--THREE, TWO, ONE--
AAAAAAGGGGHHHHH!
TOTAL SYSTEMS FAILURE...TOTAL SYSTEMS FAIL...

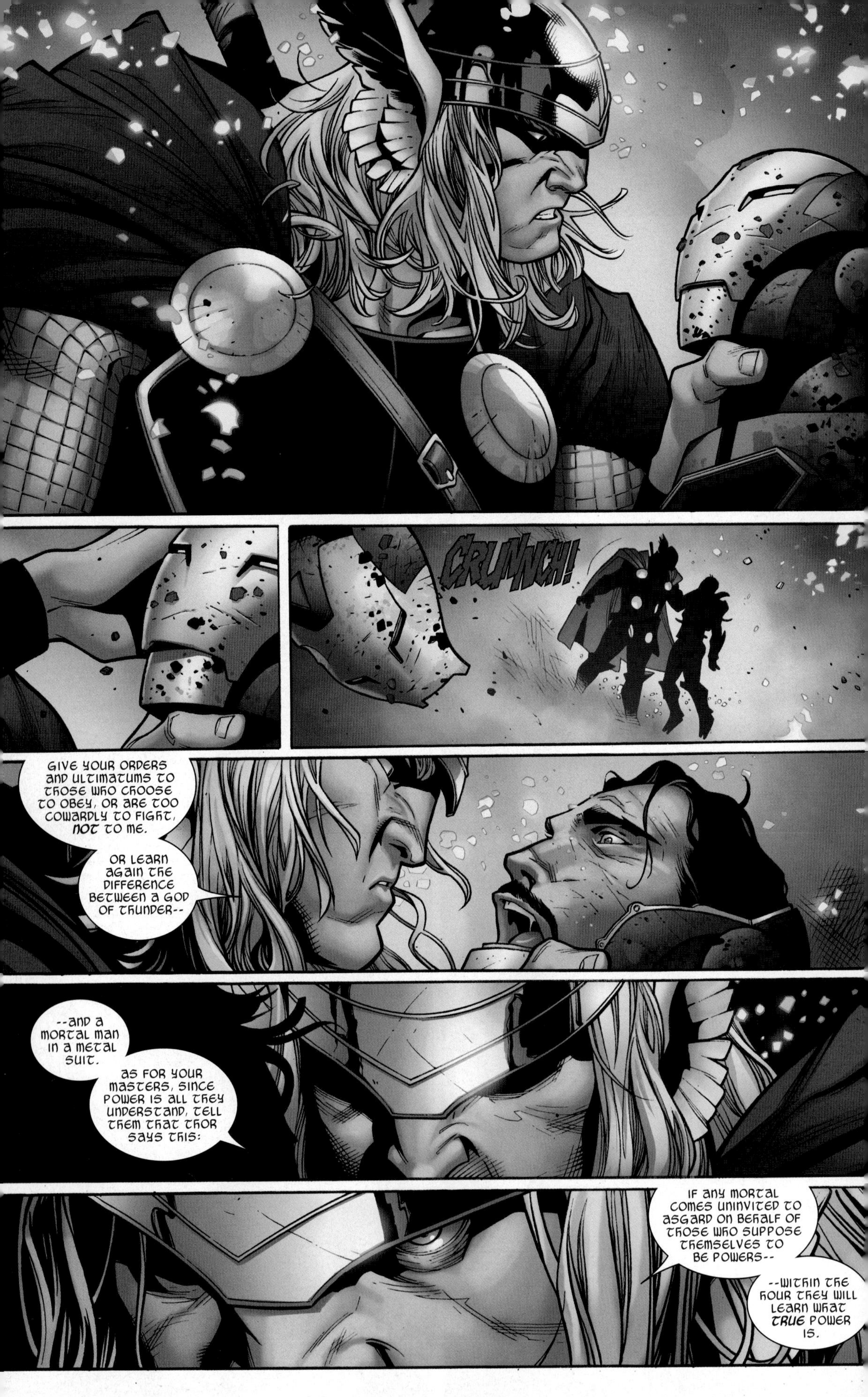
CRUNNCH!
GIVE YOUR ORDERS AND ULTIMATUMS TO THOSE WHO CHOOSE TO OBEY, OR ARE TOO COWARDLY TO FIGHT, NOT TO ME.
OR LEARN AGAIN THE DIFFERENCE BETWEEN A GOD OF THUNDER--
--AND A MORTAL MAN IN A METAL SUIT.
AS FOR YOUR MASTERS, SINCE POWER IS ALL THEY UNDERSTAND, TELL THEM THAT THOR SAYS THIS:
IF ANY MORTAL COMES UNINVITED TO ASGARD ON BEHALF OF THOSE WHO SUPPOSE THEMSELVES TO BE POWERS--
--WITHIN THE HOUR THEY WILL LEARN WHAT TRUE POWER IS.

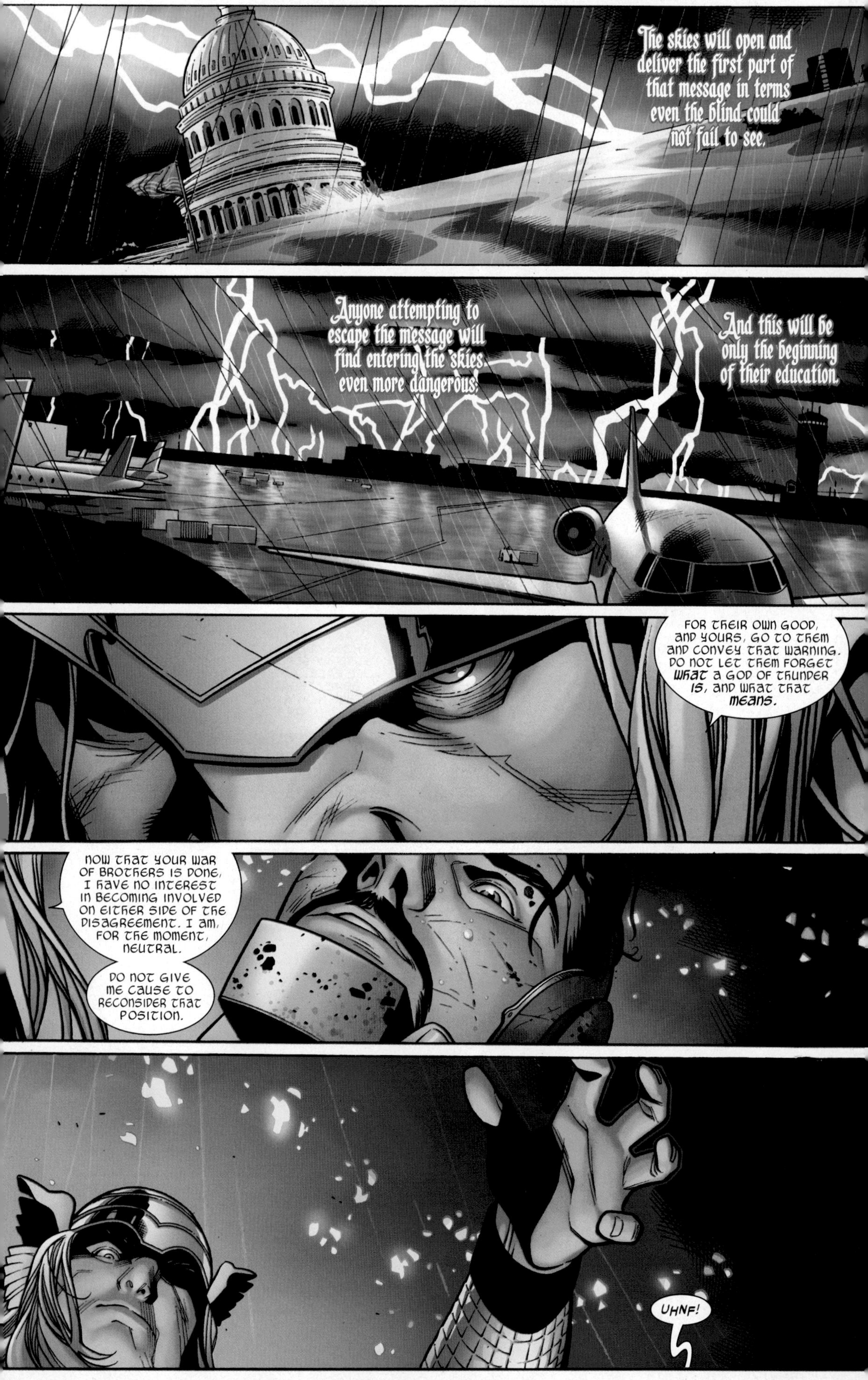
The skies will open and deliver the first part of that message in terms even the blind could not fail to see.
Anyone attempting to escape the message will find entering the skies even more dangerous.
And this will be only the beginning of their education.
FOR THEIR OWN GOOD, AND YOURS, GO TO THEM AND CONVEY THAT WARNING. DO NOT LET THEM FORGET WHAT A GOD OF THUNDER IS, AND WHAT THAT MEANS.
NOW THAT YOUR WAR OF BROTHERS IS DONE, I HAVE NO INTEREST IN BECOMING INVOLVED ON EITHER SIDE OF THE DISAGREEMENT. I AM, FOR THE MOMENT, NEUTRAL.
DO NOT GIVE ME CAUSE TO RECONSIDER THAT POSITION.
UHNF!

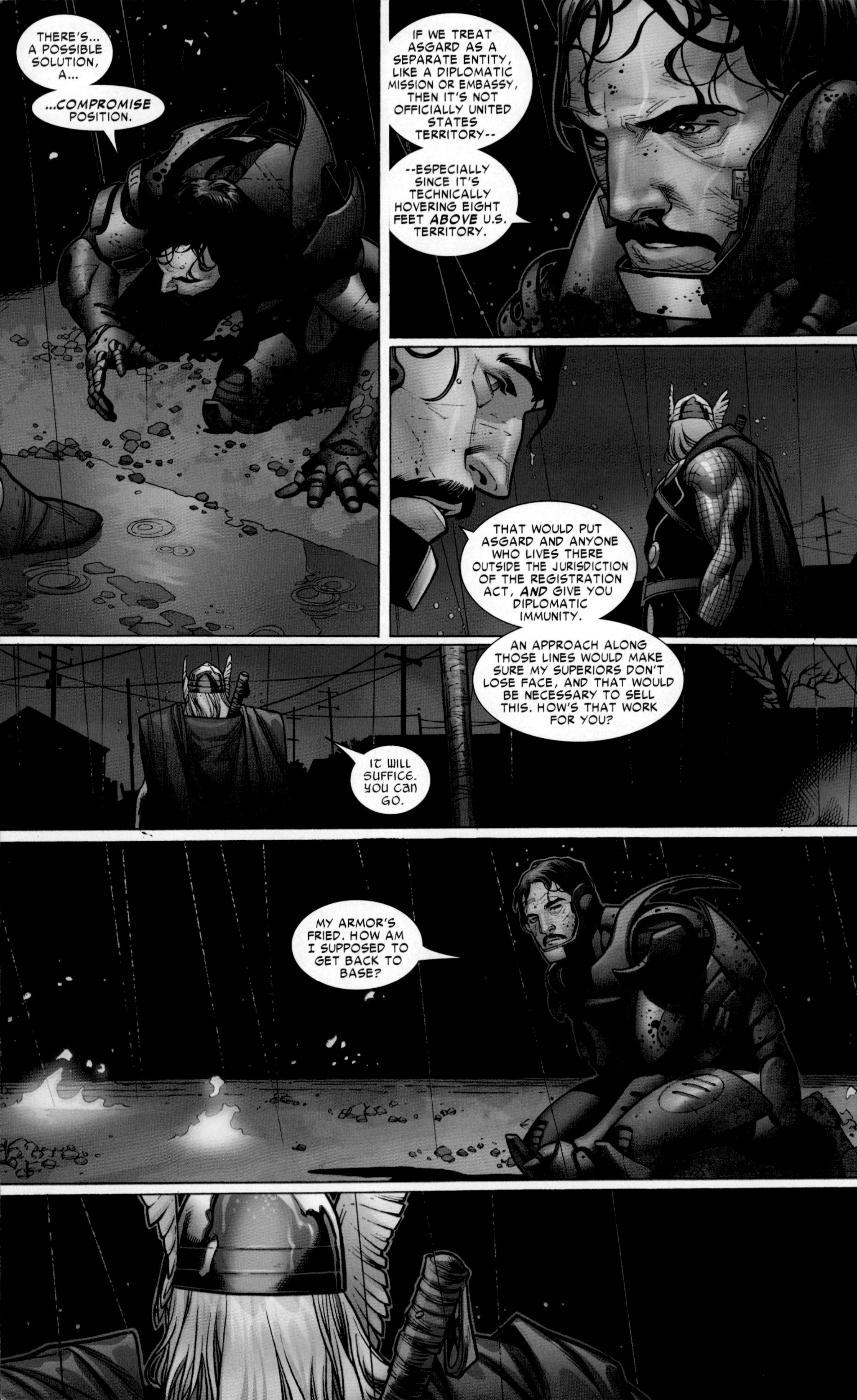
THERE'S... A POSSIBLE SOLUTION, A...
...COMPROMISE POSITION.
IF WE TREAT ASGARD AS A SEPARATE ENTITY, LIKE A DIPLOMATIC MISSION OR EMBASSY, THEN IT'S NOT OFFICIALLY UNITED STATES TERRITORY--
--ESPECIALLY SINCE IT'S TECHNICALLY HOVERING EIGHT FEET ABOVE U.S. TERRITORY.
THAT WOULD PUT ASGARD AND ANYONE WHO LIVES THERE OUTSIDE THE JURISDICTION OF THE REGISTRATION ACT, AND GIVE YOU DIPLOMATIC IMMUNITY.
AN APPROACH ALONG THOSE LINES WOULD MAKE SURE MY SUPERIORS DON'T LOSE FACE, AND THAT WOULD BE NECESSARY TO SELL THIS. HOW'S THAT WORK FOR YOU?
IT WILL SUFFICE. YOU CAN GO.
MY ARMOR'S FRIED. HOW AM I SUPPOSED TO GET BACK TO BASE?

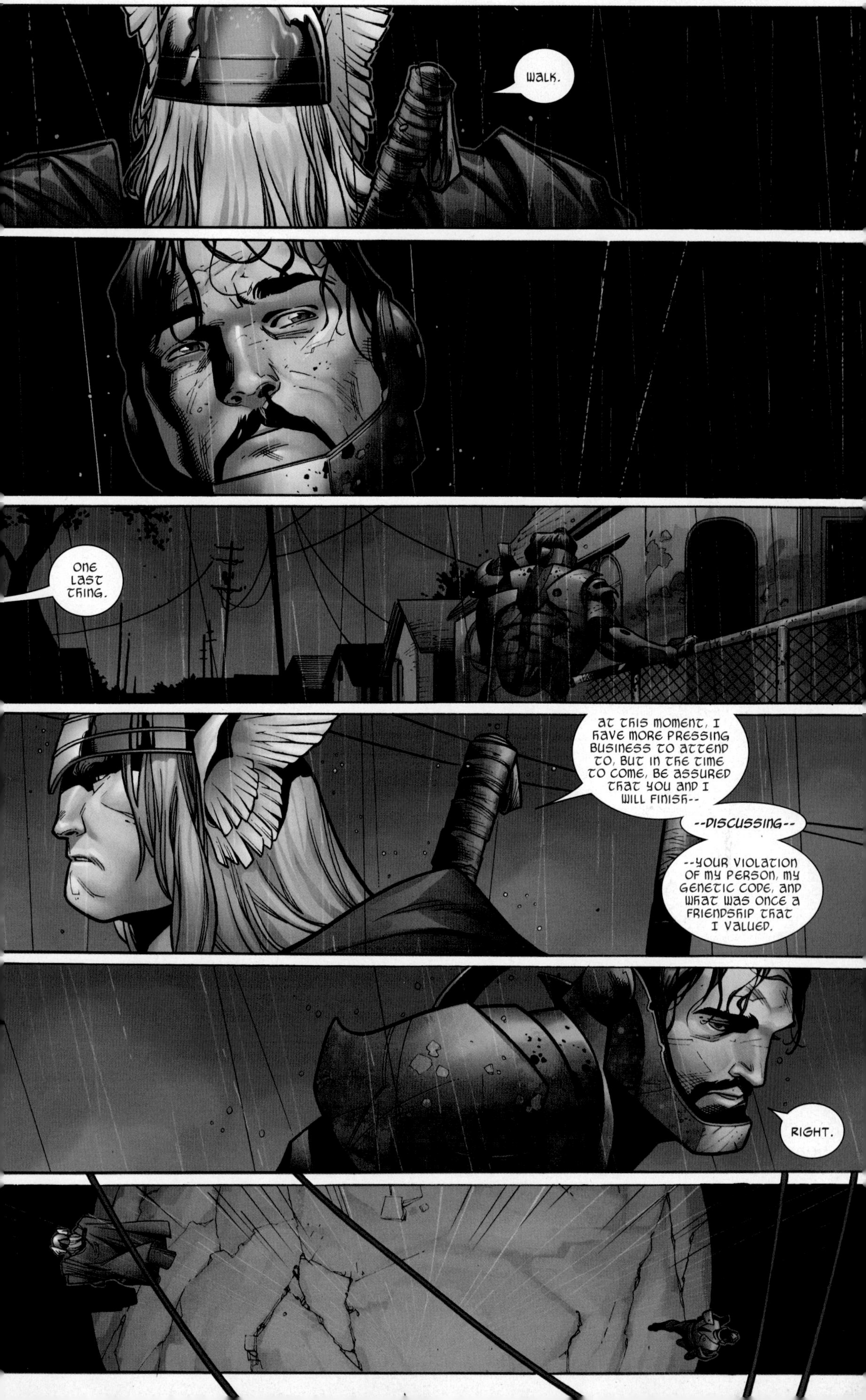
WALK.
ONE LAST THING.
AT THIS MOMENT, I HAVE MORE PRESSING BUSINESS TO ATTEND TO, BUT IN THE TIME TO COME, BE ASSURED THAT YOU AND I WILL FINISH--
--DISCUSSING--
--YOUR VIOLATION OF MY PERSON, MY GENETIC CODE, AND WHAT WAS ONCE A FRIENDSHIP THAT I VALUED.
RIGHT.

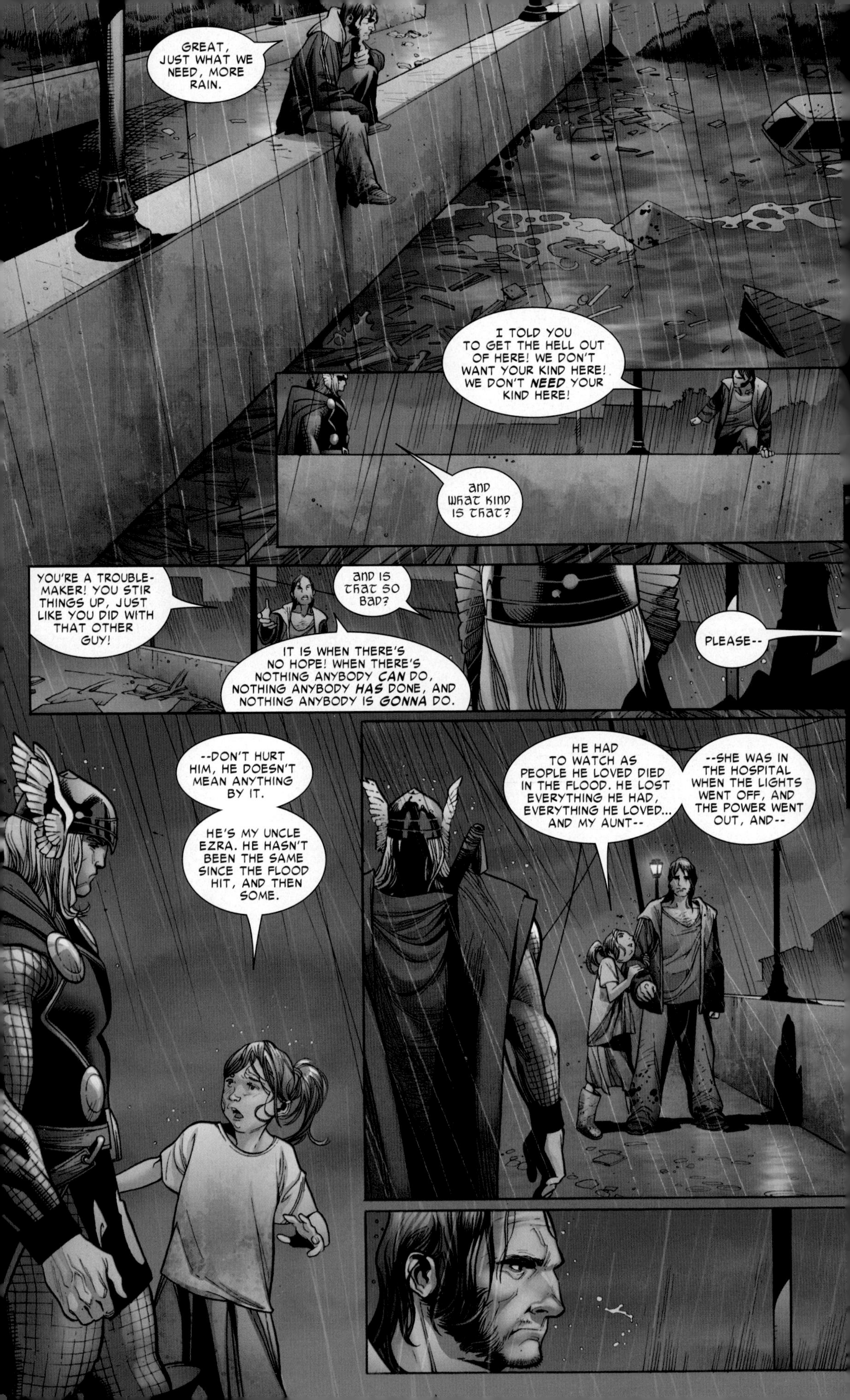
GREAT, JUST WHAT WE NEED, MORE RAIN.
I TOLD YOU TO GET THE HELL OUT OF HERE! WE DON'T WANT YOUR KIND HERE! WE DON'T NEED YOUR KIND HERE!
AND WHAT KIND IS THAT?
YOU'RE A TROUBLE-MAKER! YOU STIR THINGS UP, JUST LIKE YOU DID WITH THAT OTHER GUY!
AND IS THAT SO BAD?
IT IS WHEN THERE'S NO HOPE! WHEN THERE'S NOTHING ANYBODY CAN DO, NOTHING ANYBODY HAS DONE, AND NOTHING ANYBODY IS GONNA DO.
PLEASE--
--DON'T HURT HIM, HE DOESN'T MEAN ANYTHING BY IT.
HE'S MY UNCLE EZRA. HE HASN'T BEEN THE SAME SINCE THE FLOOD HIT, AND THEN SOME.
HE HAD TO WATCH AS PEOPLE HE LOVED DIED IN THE FLOOD. HE LOST EVERYTHING HE HAD, EVERYTHING HE LOVED... AND MY AUNT--
--SHE WAS IN THE HOSPITAL WHEN THE LIGHTS WENT OFF, AND THE POWER WENT OUT, AND--

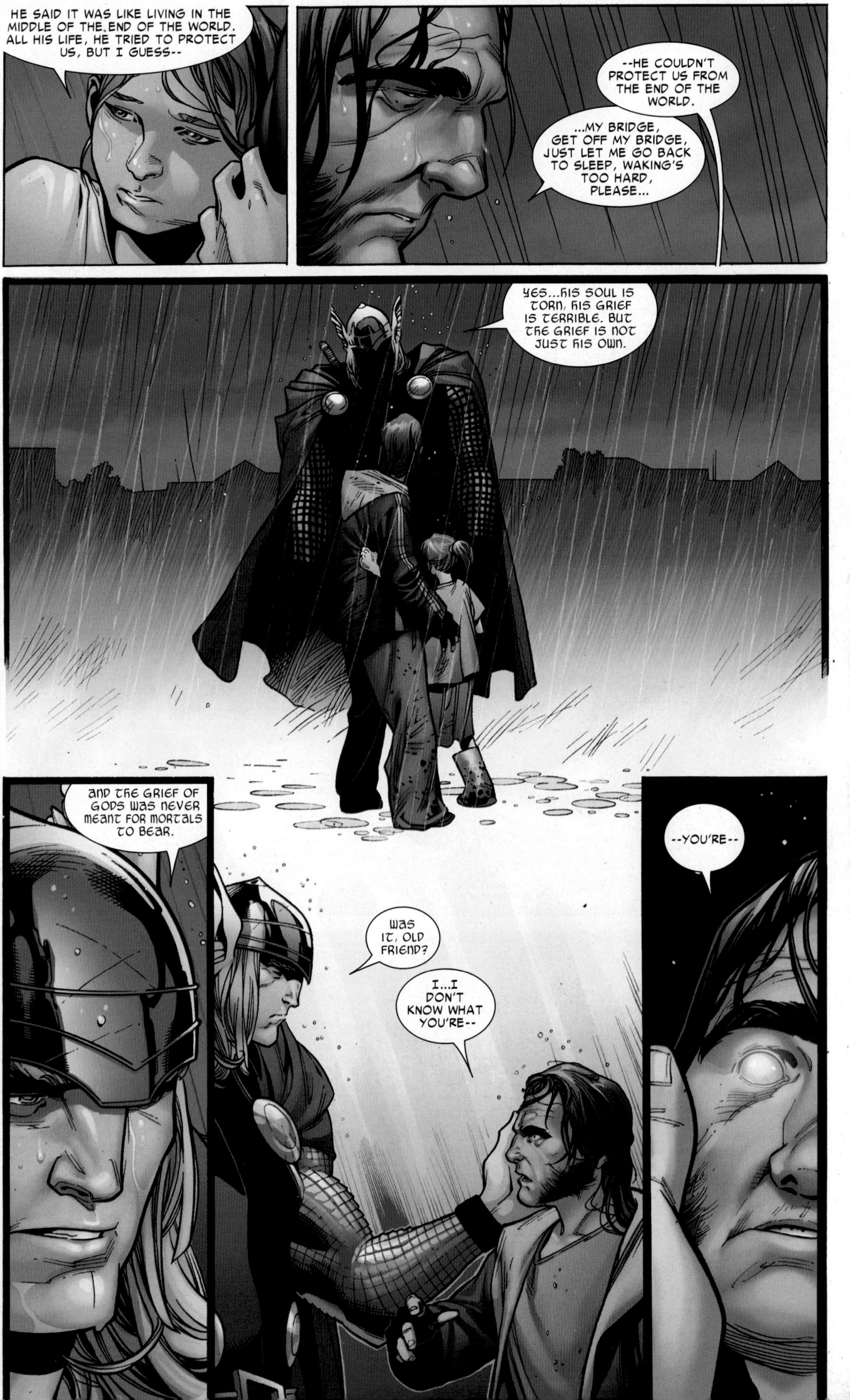
HE SAID IT WAS LIKE LIVING IN THE MIDDLE OF THE END OF THE WORLD. ALL HIS LIFE, HE TRIED TO PROTECT US, BUT I GUESS--
--HE COULDN'T PROTECT US FROM THE END OF THE WORLD.
...MY BRIDGE, GET OFF MY BRIDGE, JUST LET ME GO BACK TO SLEEP, WAKING'S TOO HARD, PLEASE...
YES...HIS SOUL IS TORN, HIS GRIEF IS TERRIBLE. BUT THE GRIEF IS NOT JUST HIS OWN.
AND THE GRIEF OF GODS WAS NEVER MEANT FOR MORTALS TO BEAR.
WAS IT, OLD FRIEND?
I...I DON'T KNOW WHAT YOU'RE--
--YOU'RE--

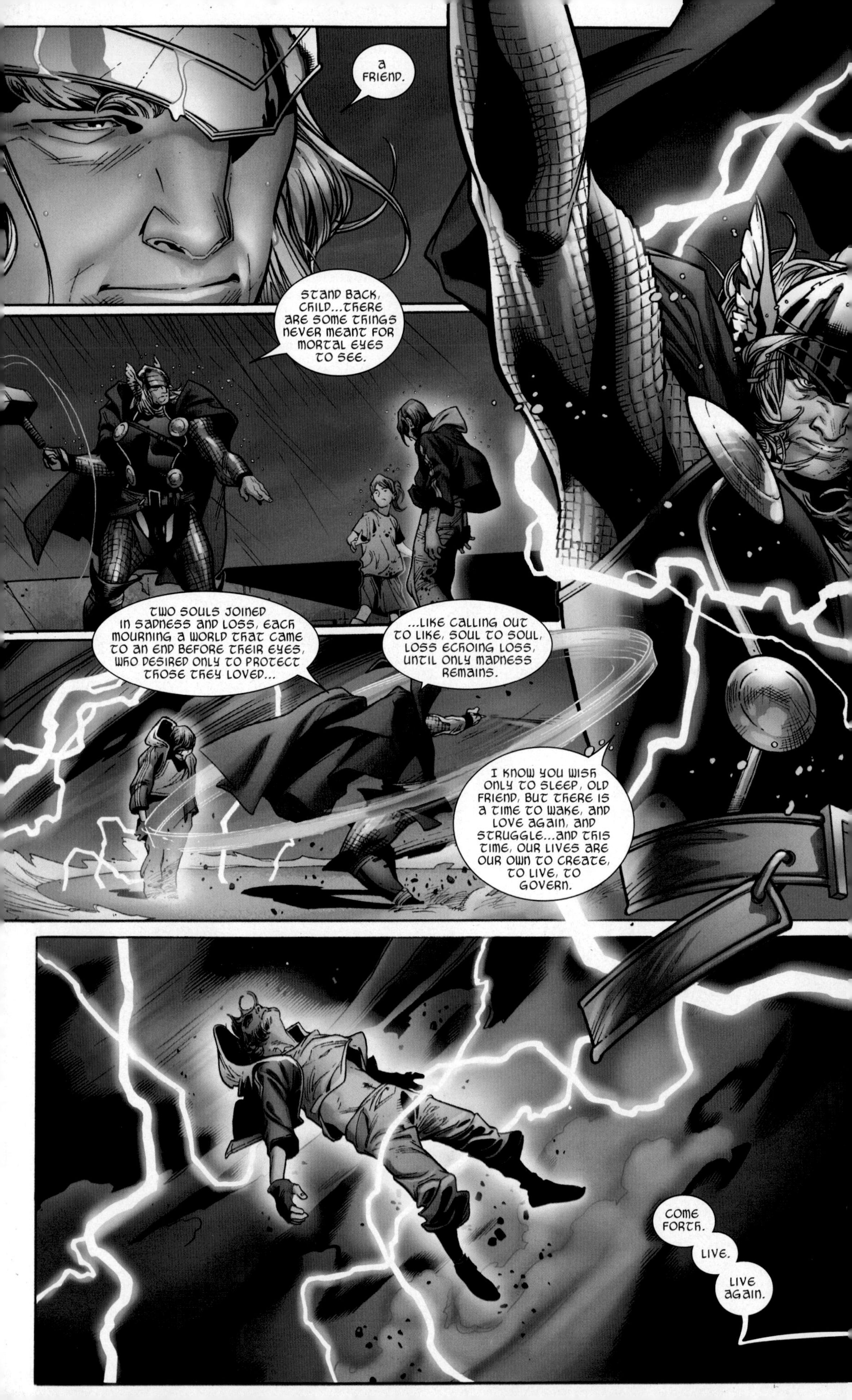
A FRIEND.
STAND BACK, CHILD...THERE ARE SOME THINGS NEVER MEANT FOR MORTAL EYES TO SEE.
TWO SOULS JOINED IN SADNESS AND LOSS, EACH MOURNING A WORLD THAT CAME TO AN END BEFORE THEIR EYES, WHO DESIRED ONLY TO PROTECT THOSE THEY LOVED...
...LIKE CALLING OUT TO LIKE, SOUL TO SOUL, LOSS ECHOING LOSS, UNTIL ONLY MADNESS REMAINS.
I KNOW YOU WISH ONLY TO SLEEP, OLD FRIEND, BUT THERE IS A TIME TO WAKE, AND LOVE AGAIN, AND STRUGGLE...AND THIS TIME, OUR LIVES ARE OUR OWN TO CREATE, TO LIVE, TO GOVERN.
COME FORTH.
LIVE.
LIVE AGAIN.

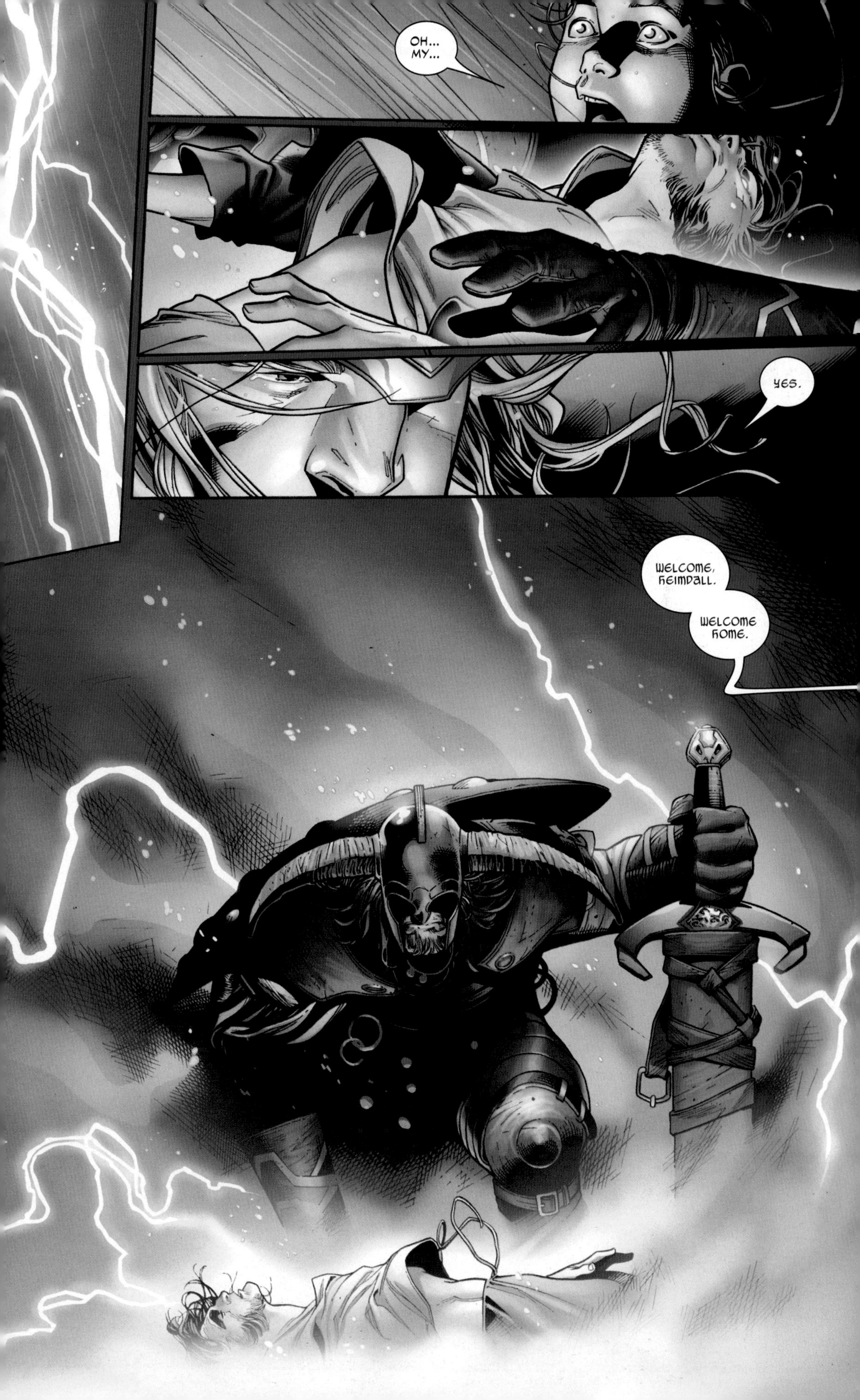
OH... MY...
YES.
WELCOME, HEIMDALL.
WELCOME HOME.

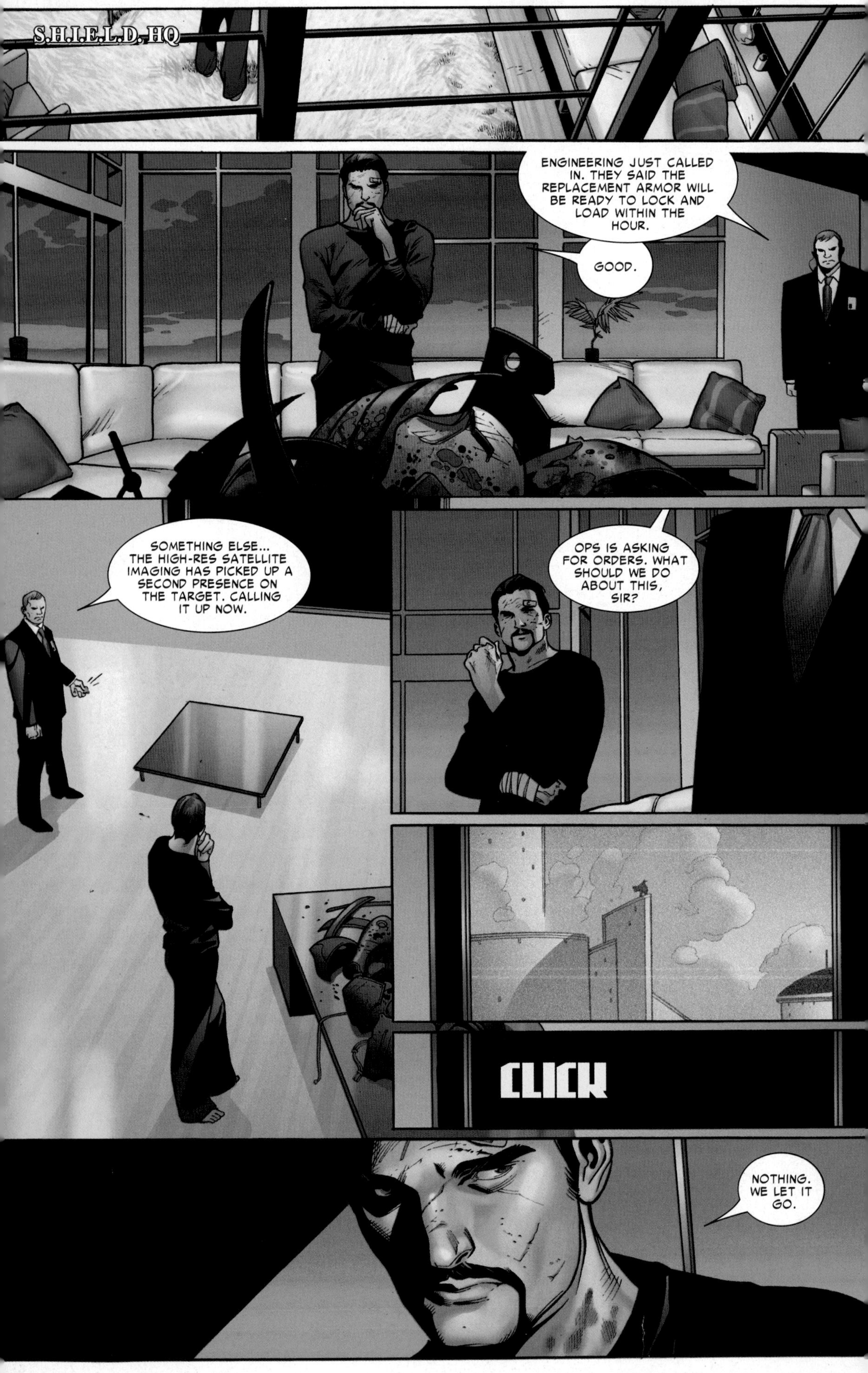
S.H.I.E.L.D. HQ
ENGINEERING JUST CALLED IN. THEY SAID THE REPLACEMENT ARMOR WILL BE READY TO LOCK AND LOAD WITHIN THE HOUR.
GOOD.
SOMETHING ELSE... THE HIGH-RES SATELLITE IMAGING HAS PICKED UP A SECOND PRESENCE ON THE TARGET. CALLING IT UP NOW.
OPS IS ASKING FOR ORDERS. WHAT SHOULD WE DO ABOUT THIS, SIR?
CLICK
NOTHING. WE LET IT GO.

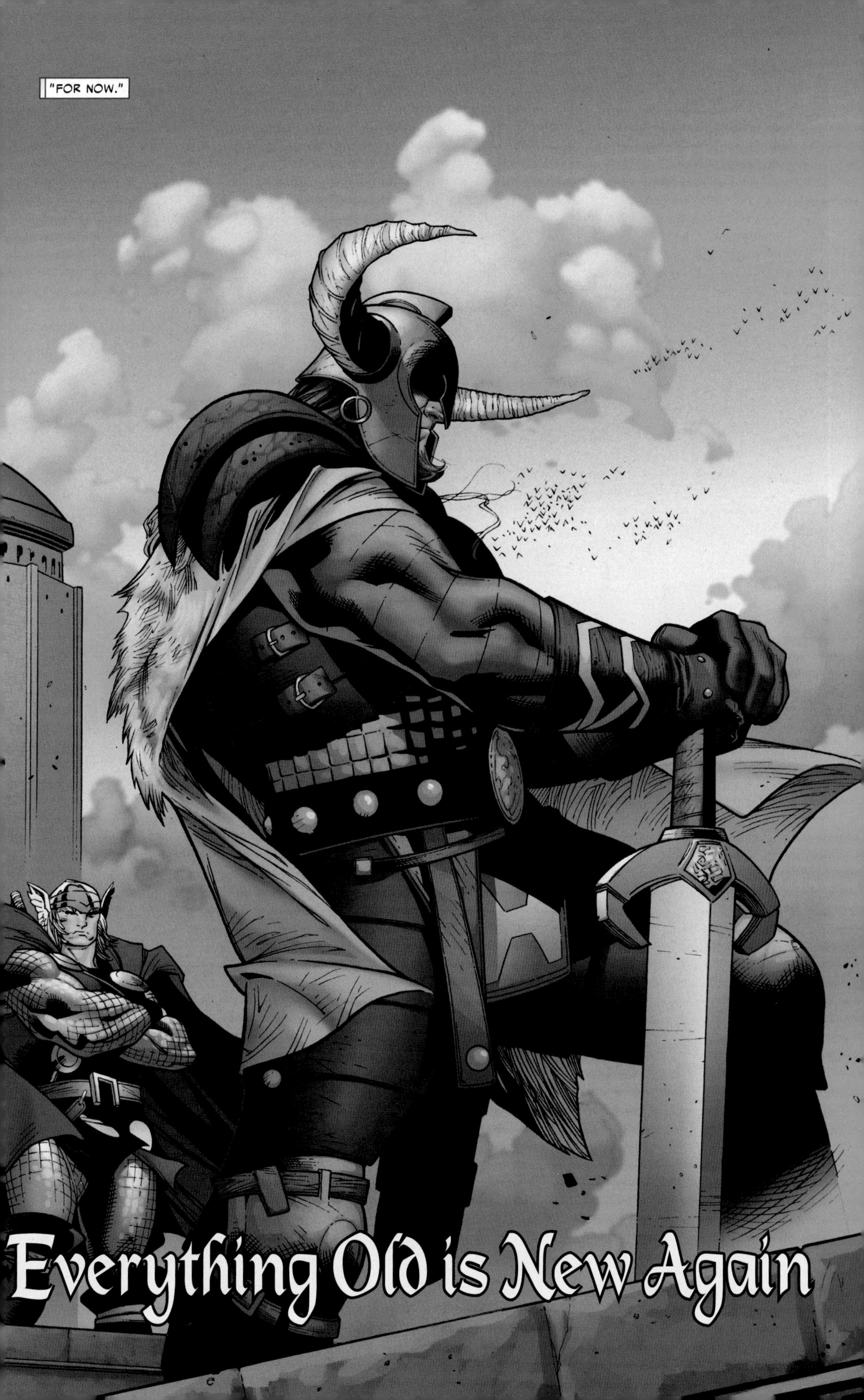
"FOR NOW."
Everything Old is New Again

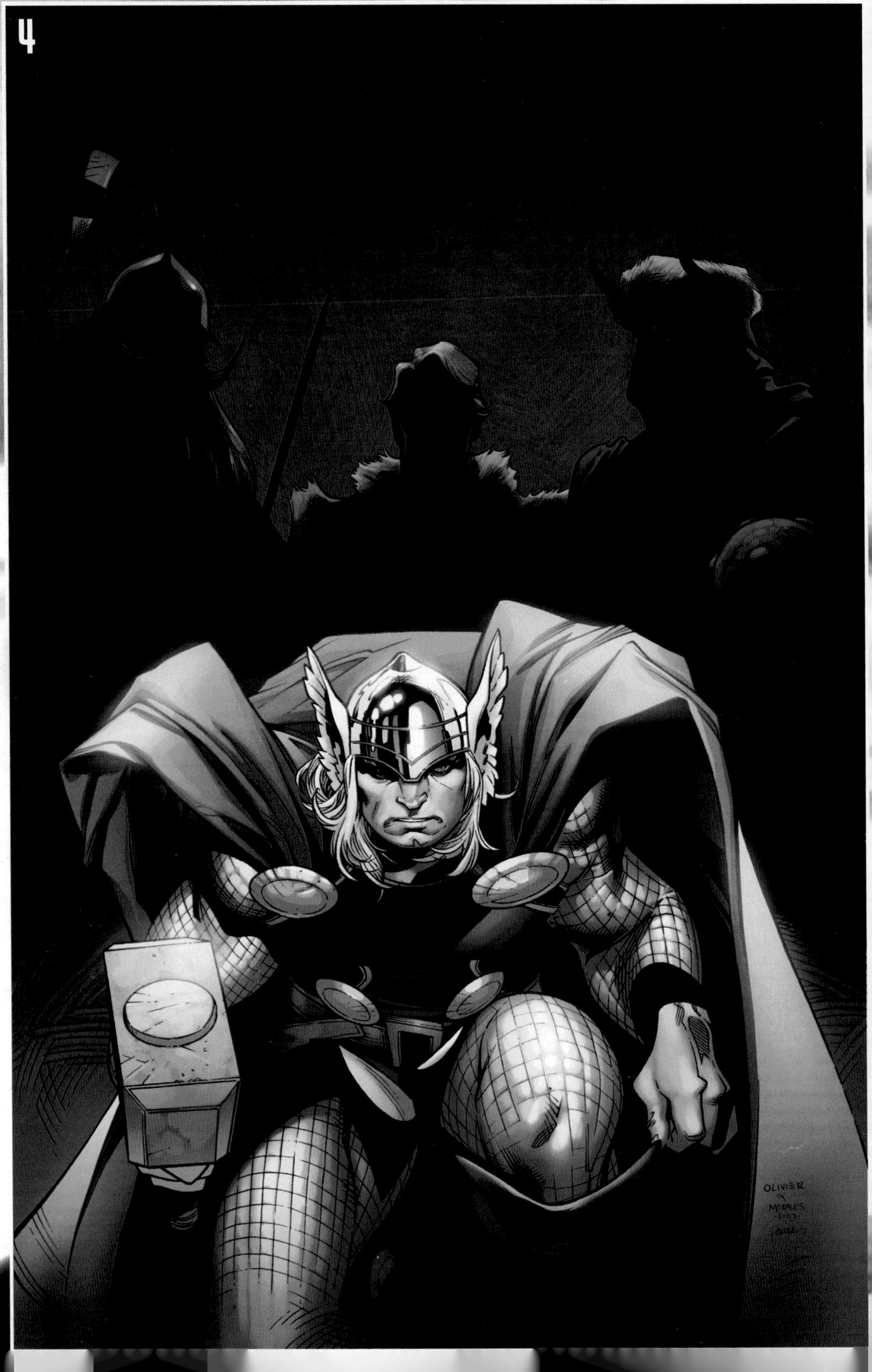
4

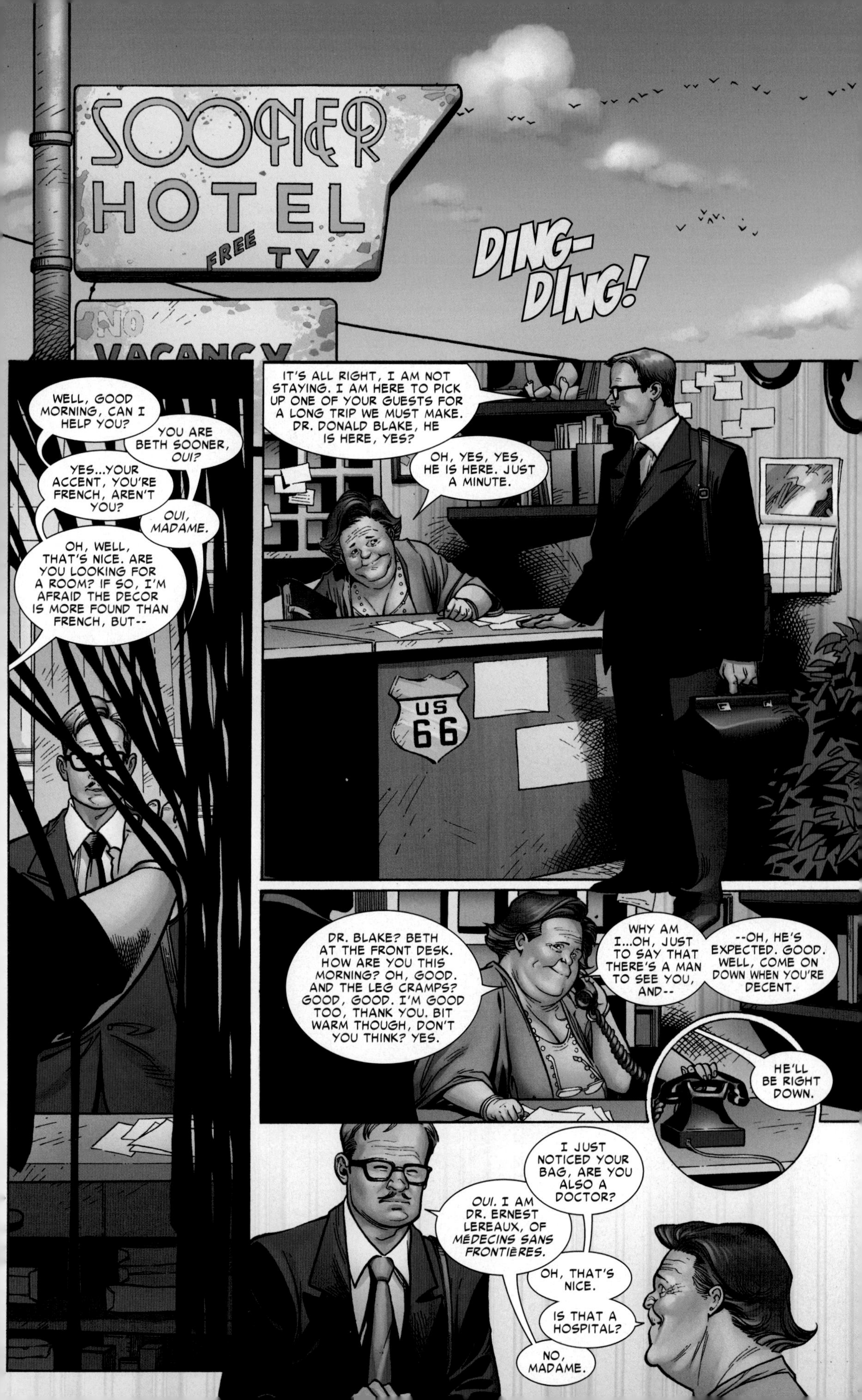
SOONER
HOTEL
FREE TV
NO
VACANCY
DING-DING!
WELL, GOOD MORNING, CAN I HELP YOU?
YOU ARE BETH SOONER, OUI?
YES...YOUR ACCENT, YOU'RE FRENCH, AREN'T YOU?
OUI, MADAME.
OH, WELL, THAT'S NICE. ARE YOU LOOKING FOR A ROOM? IF SO, I'M AFRAID THE DECOR IS MORE FOUND THAN FRENCH, BUT--
IT'S ALL RIGHT, I AM NOT STAYING. I AM HERE TO PICK UP ONE OF YOUR GUESTS FOR A LONG TRIP WE MUST MAKE. DR. DONALD BLAKE, HE IS HERE, YES?
OH, YES, YES, HE IS HERE. JUST A MINUTE.
US 66
DR. BLAKE? BETH AT THE FRONT DESK. HOW ARE YOU THIS MORNING? OH, GOOD. AND THE LEG CRAMPS? GOOD, GOOD. I'M GOOD TOO, THANK YOU. BIT WARM THOUGH, DON'T YOU THINK? YES.
WHY AM I...OH, JUST TO SAY THAT THERE'S A MAN TO SEE YOU, AND--
--OH, HE'S EXPECTED. GOOD. WELL, COME ON DOWN WHEN YOU'RE DECENT.
HE'LL BE RIGHT DOWN.
I JUST NOTICED YOUR BAG, ARE YOU ALSO A DOCTOR?
OUI. I AM DR. ERNEST LEREAUX, OF MÉDECINS SANS FRONTIÈRES.
OH, THAT'S NICE.
IS THAT A HOSPITAL?
NO, MADAME.

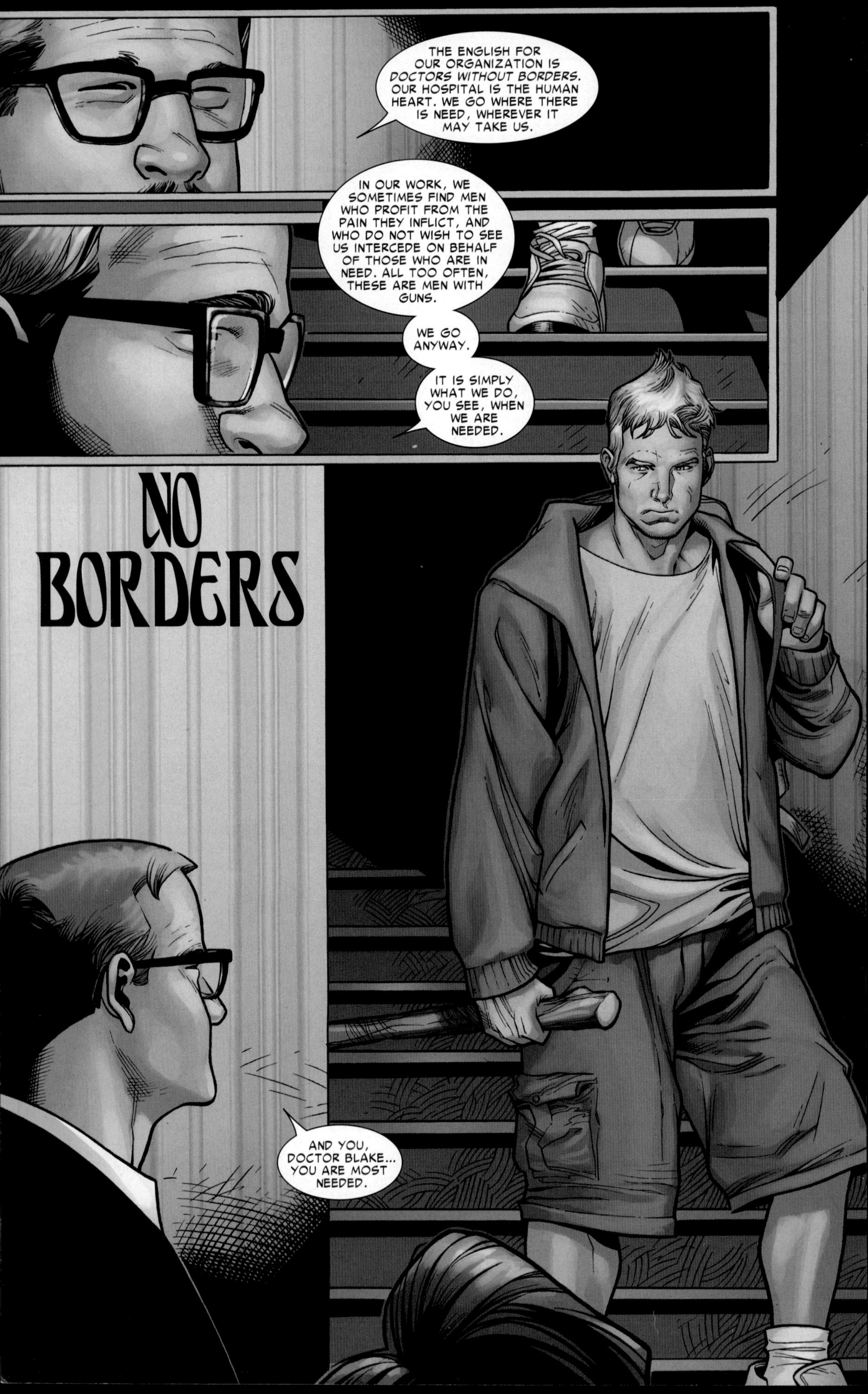
THE ENGLISH FOR OUR ORGANIZATION IS DOCTORS WITHOUT BORDERS. OUR HOSPITAL IS THE HUMAN HEART. WE GO WHERE THERE IS NEED, WHEREVER IT MAY TAKE US.
IN OUR WORK, WE SOMETIMES FIND MEN WHO PROFIT FROM THE PAIN THEY INFLICT, AND WHO DO NOT WISH TO SEE US INTERCEDE ON BEHALF OF THOSE WHO ARE IN NEED. ALL TOO OFTEN, THESE ARE MEN WITH GUNS.
WE GO ANYWAY.
IT IS SIMPLY WHAT WE DO, YOU SEE, WHEN WE ARE NEEDED.
NO BORDERS
AND YOU, DOCTOR BLAKE... YOU ARE MOST NEEDED.

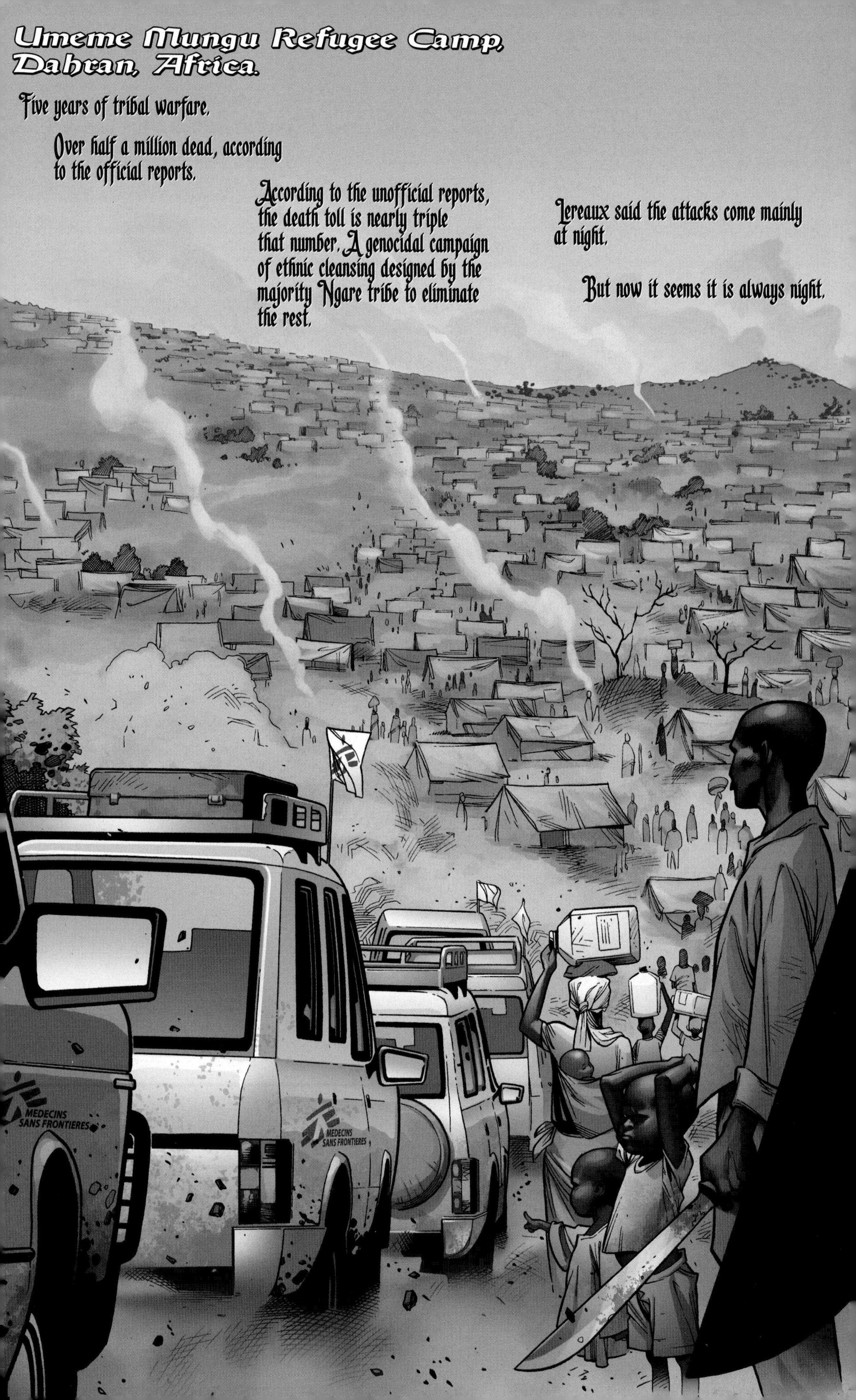
Umeme Mungu Refugee Camp, Dahran, Africa.
Five years of tribal warfare.
Over half a million dead, according to the official reports.
According to the unofficial reports, the death toll is nearly triple that number. A genocidal campaign of ethnic cleansing designed by the majority Ngare tribe to eliminate the rest.
Lereaux said the attacks come mainly at night.
But now it seems it is always night.
MEDECINS SANS FRONTIERES
MEDECINS SANS FRONTIERES

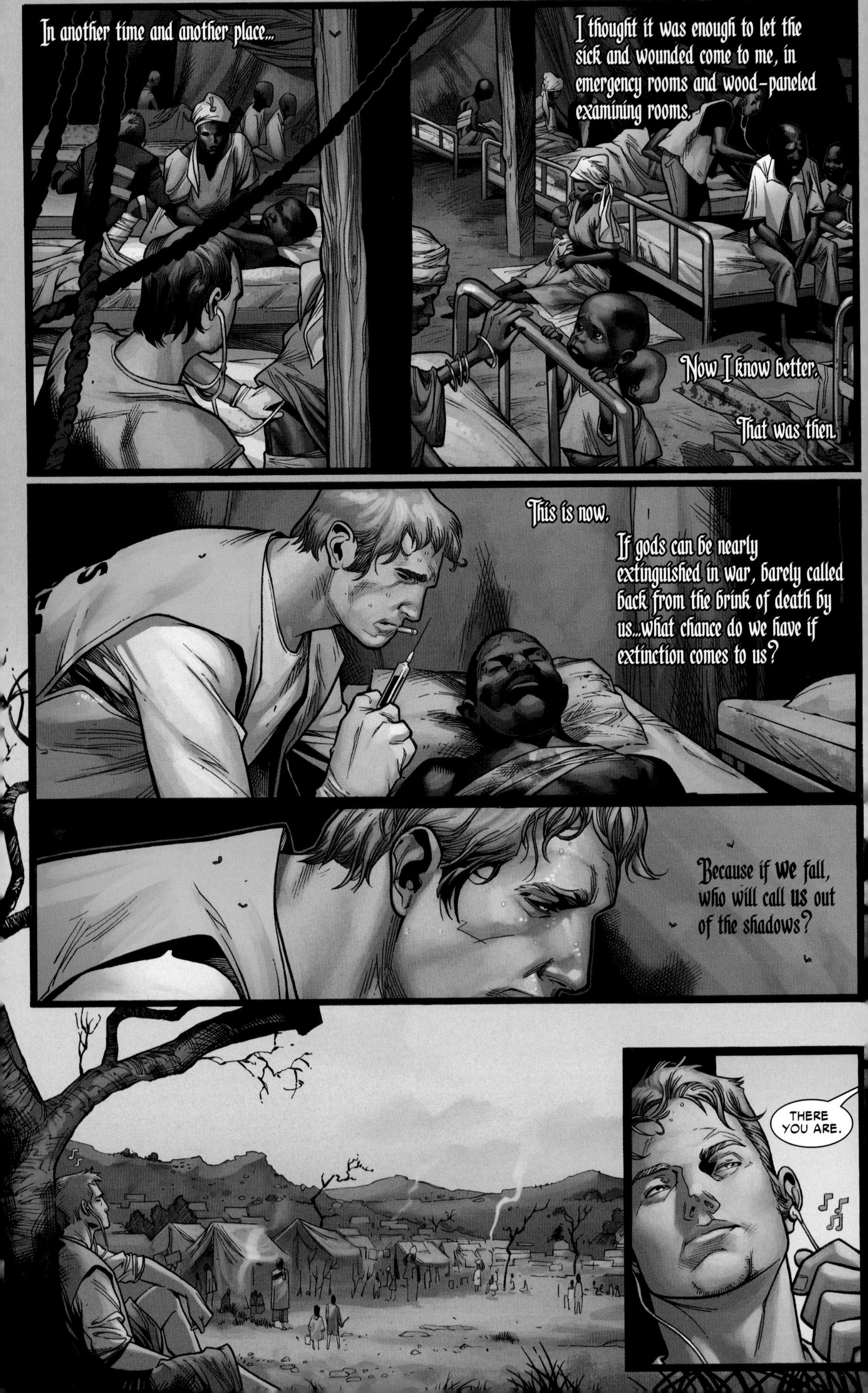
In another time and another place...
I thought it was enough to let the sick and wounded come to me, in emergency rooms and wood-paneled examining rooms.
Now I know better.
That was then.
This is now.
If gods can be nearly extinguished in war, barely called back from the brink of death by us...what chance do we have if extinction comes to us?
Because if we fall, who will call us out of the shadows?
THERE YOU ARE.

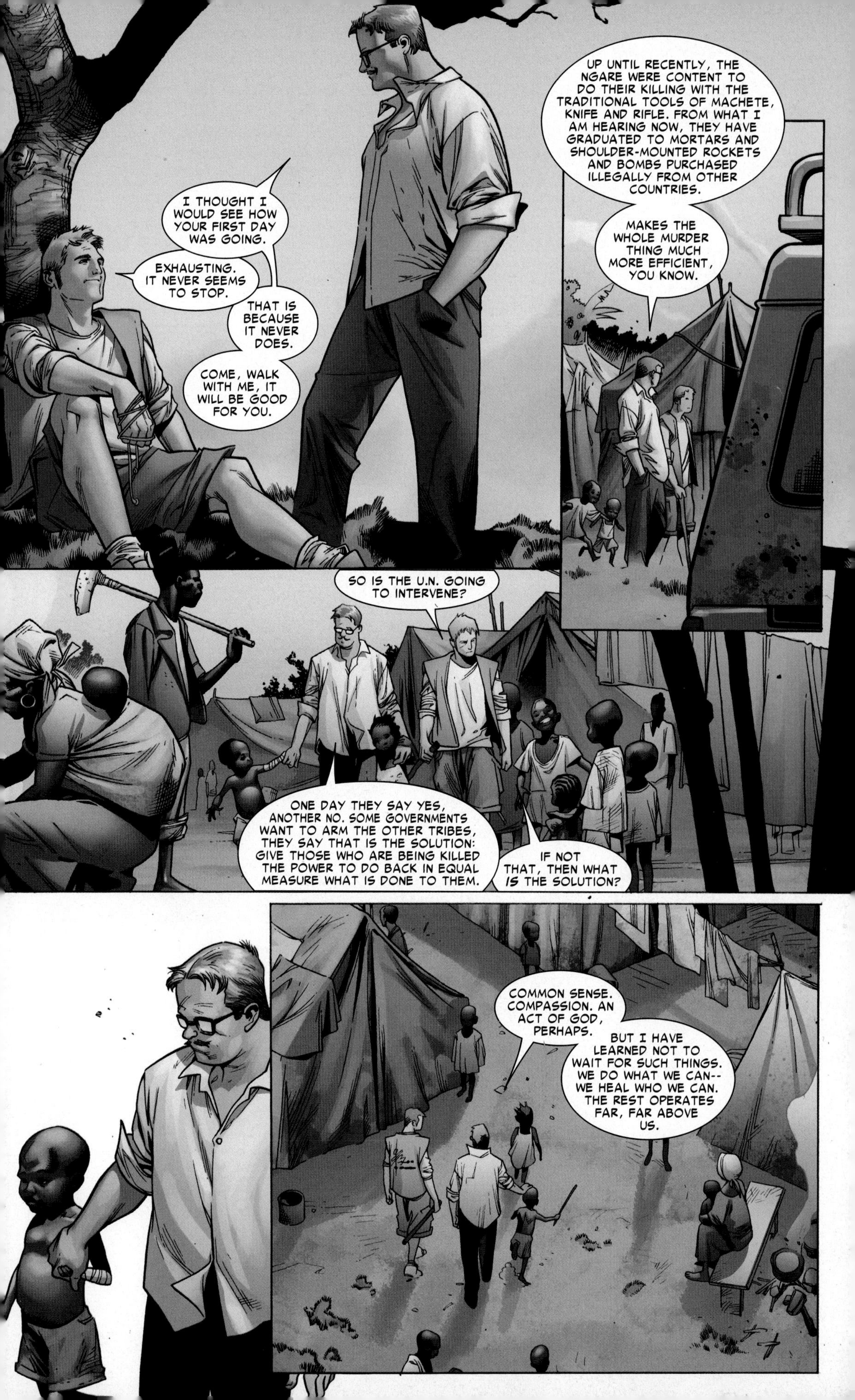
I THOUGHT I WOULD SEE HOW YOUR FIRST DAY WAS GOING.
EXHAUSTING. IT NEVER SEEMS TO STOP.
THAT IS BECAUSE IT NEVER DOES.
COME, WALK WITH ME, IT WILL BE GOOD FOR YOU.
UP UNTIL RECENTLY, THE NGARE WERE CONTENT TO DO THEIR KILLING WITH THE TRADITIONAL TOOLS OF MACHETE, KNIFE AND RIFLE. FROM WHAT I AM HEARING NOW, THEY HAVE GRADUATED TO MORTARS AND SHOULDER-MOUNTED ROCKETS AND BOMBS PURCHASED ILLEGALLY FROM OTHER COUNTRIES.
MAKES THE WHOLE MURDER THING MUCH MORE EFFICIENT, YOU KNOW.
SO IS THE U.N. GOING TO INTERVENE?
ONE DAY THEY SAY YES, ANOTHER NO. SOME GOVERNMENTS WANT TO ARM THE OTHER TRIBES, THEY SAY THAT IS THE SOLUTION: GIVE THOSE WHO ARE BEING KILLED THE POWER TO DO BACK IN EQUAL MEASURE WHAT IS DONE TO THEM.
IF NOT THAT, THEN WHAT *IS* THE SOLUTION?
COMMON SENSE. COMPASSION. AN ACT OF GOD, PERHAPS.
BUT I HAVE LEARNED NOT TO WAIT FOR SUCH THINGS. WE DO WHAT WE CAN-- WE HEAL WHO WE CAN. THE REST OPERATES FAR, FAR ABOVE US.

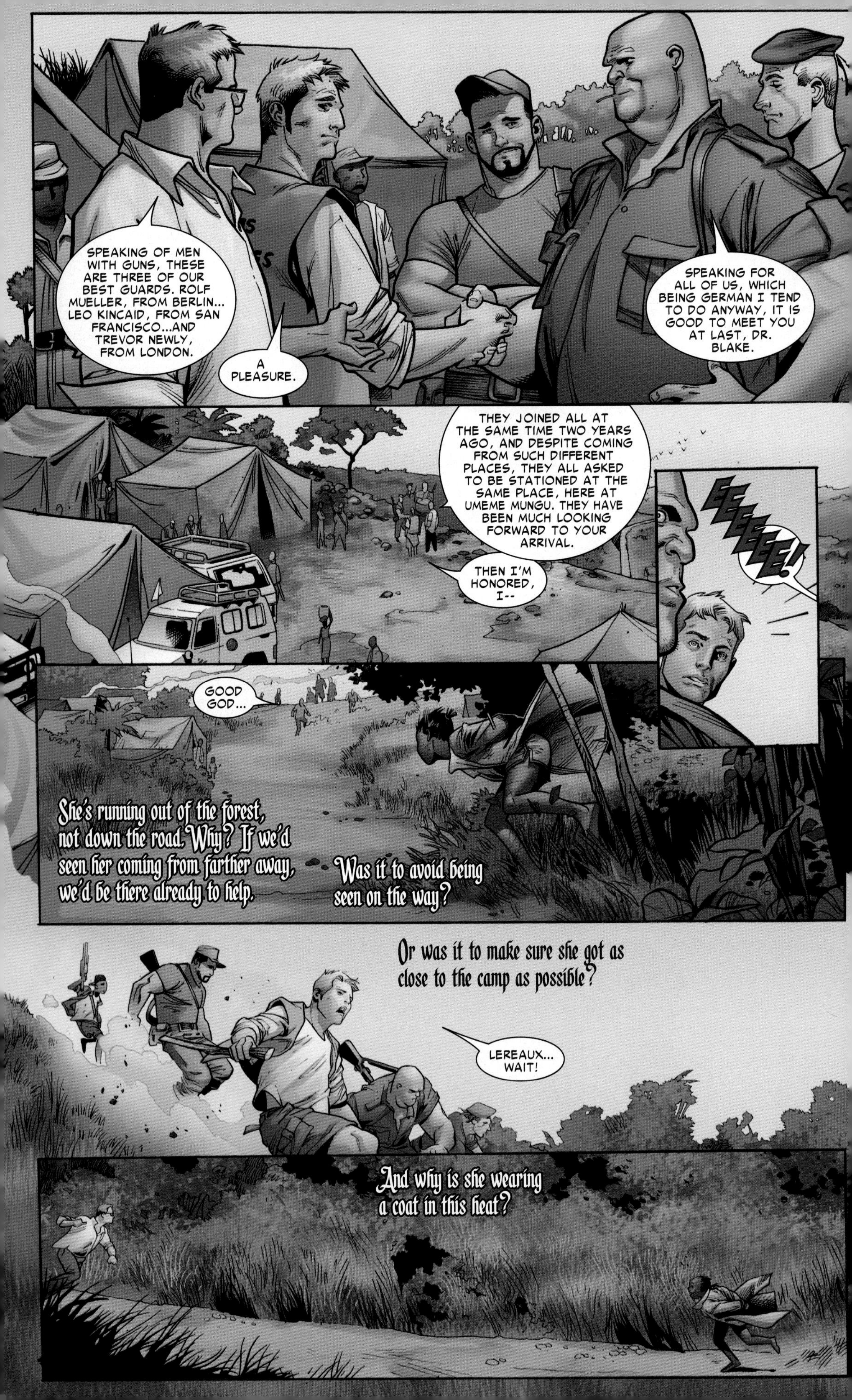
SPEAKING OF MEN WITH GUNS, THESE ARE THREE OF OUR BEST GUARDS. ROLF MUELLER, FROM BERLIN... LEO KINCAID, FROM SAN FRANCISCO...AND TREVOR NEWLY, FROM LONDON.
A PLEASURE.
SPEAKING FOR ALL OF US, WHICH BEING GERMAN I TEND TO DO ANYWAY, IT IS GOOD TO MEET YOU AT LAST, DR. BLAKE.
THEY JOINED ALL AT THE SAME TIME TWO YEARS AGO, AND DESPITE COMING FROM SUCH DIFFERENT PLACES, THEY ALL ASKED TO BE STATIONED AT THE SAME PLACE, HERE AT UMEME MUNGU. THEY HAVE BEEN MUCH LOOKING FORWARD TO YOUR ARRIVAL.
THEN I'M HONORED, I--
EEEEEE!
GOOD GOD...
She's running out of the forest, not down the road. Why? If we'd seen her coming from farther away, we'd be there already to help.
Was it to avoid being seen on the way?
Or was it to make sure she got as close to the camp as possible?
LEREAUX... WAIT!
And why is she wearing a coat in this heat?

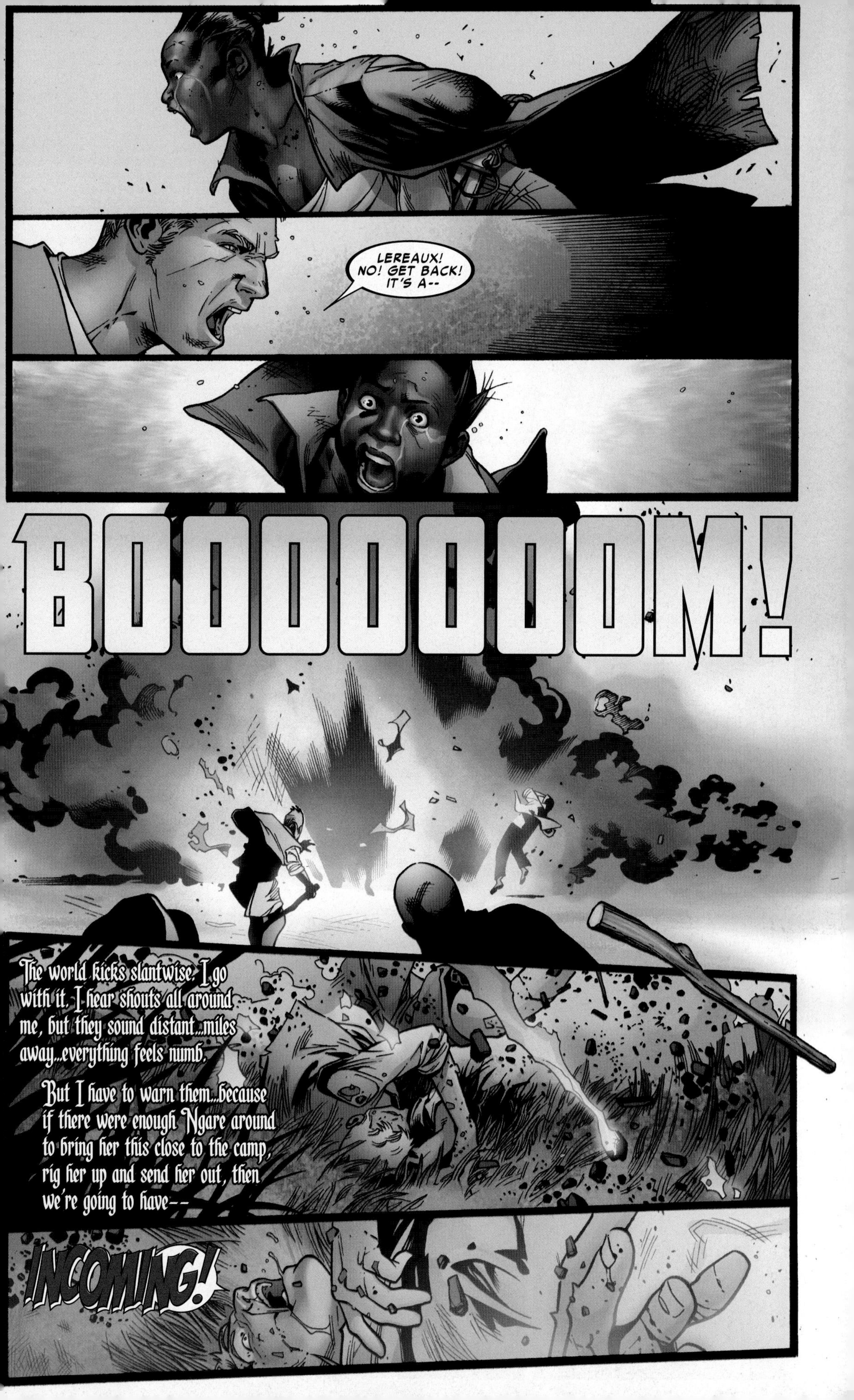
LEREAUX! NO! GET BACK! IT'S A--
BOOOOOOOM!
The world kicks slantwise. I go with it. I hear shouts all around me, but they sound distant...miles away...everything feels numb.
But I have to warn them...because if there were enough Ngare around to bring her this close to the camp, rig her up and send her out, then we're going to have--
INCOMING!

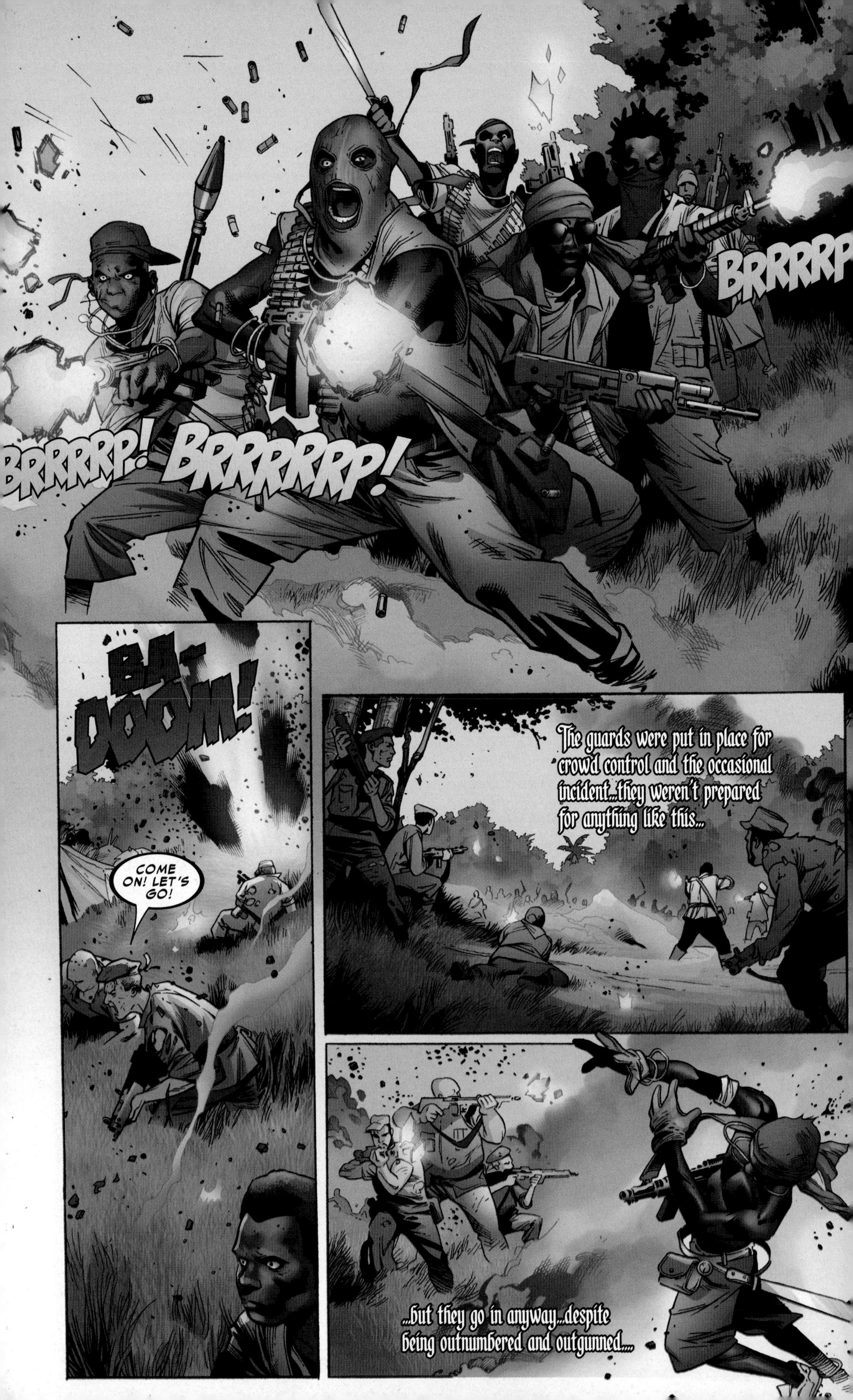
BRRRRP
BRRRRP! BRRRRRP!
BA-DOOM!
COME ON! LET'S GO!
The guards were put in place for crowd control and the occasional incident...they weren't prepared for anything like this...
...but they go in anyway...despite being outnumbered and outgunned....

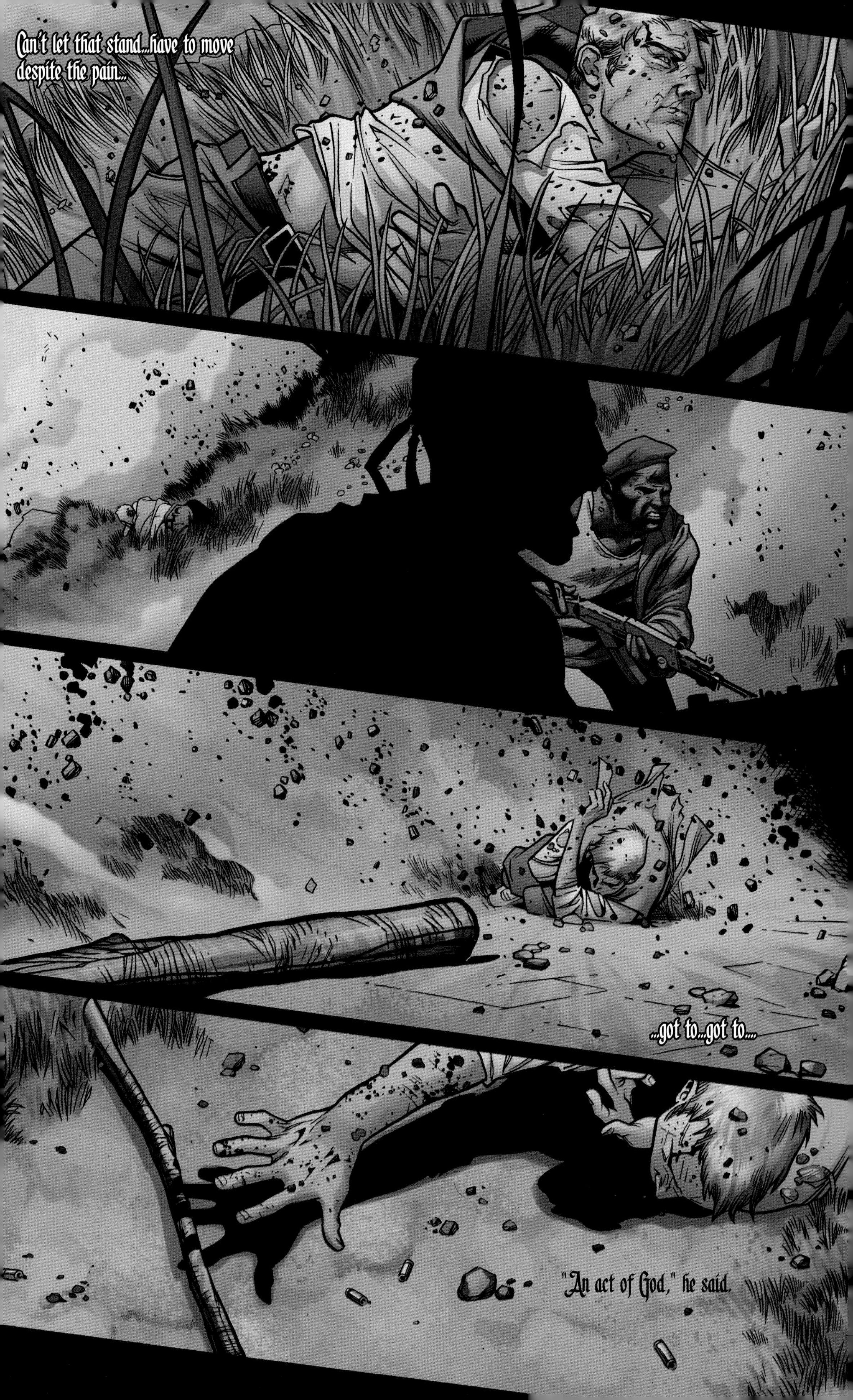
Can't let that stand...have to move despite the pain...
...got to...got to....
"An act of God," he said.

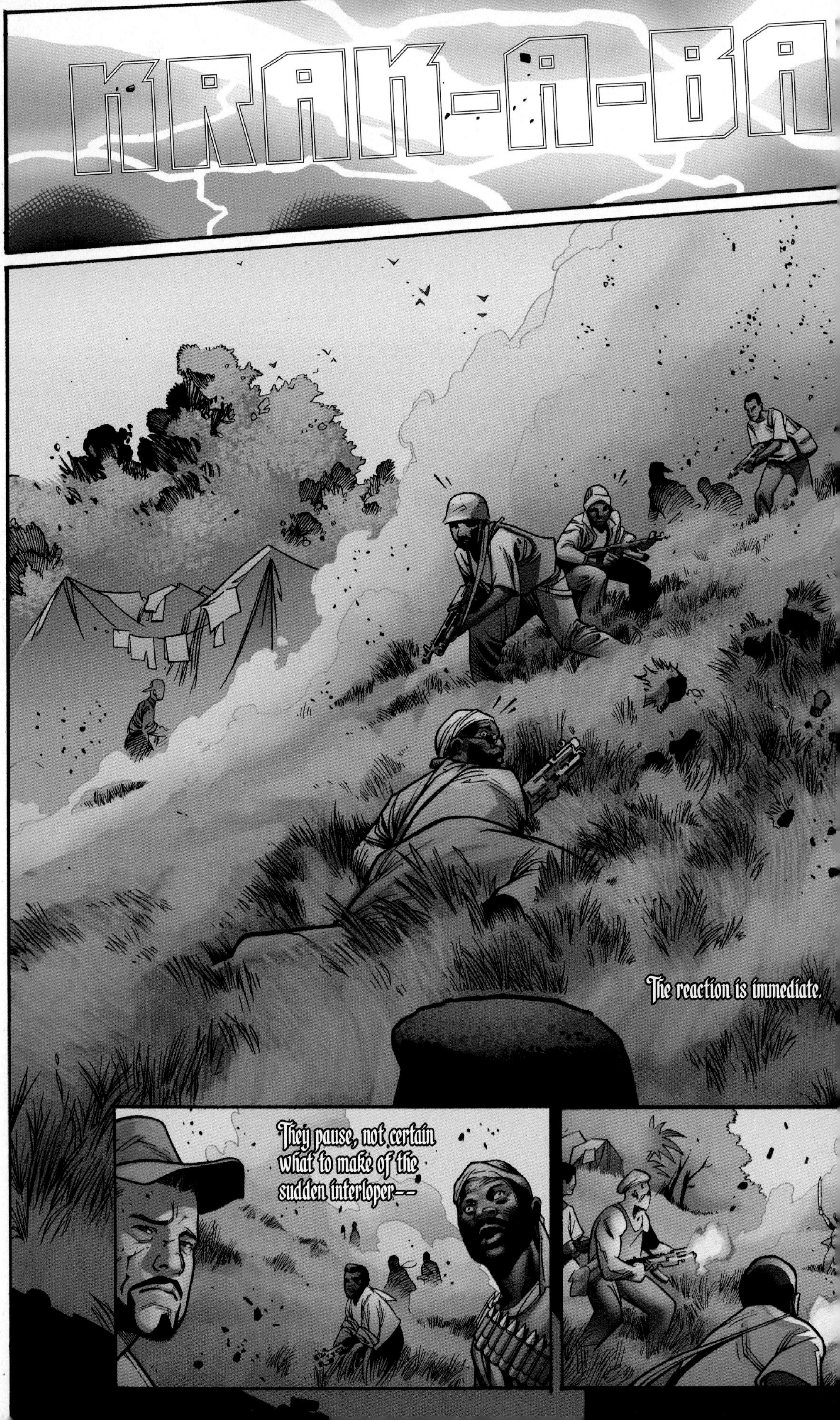
KRAK-A-BA
The reaction is immediate.
They pause, not certain what to make of the sudden interloper--

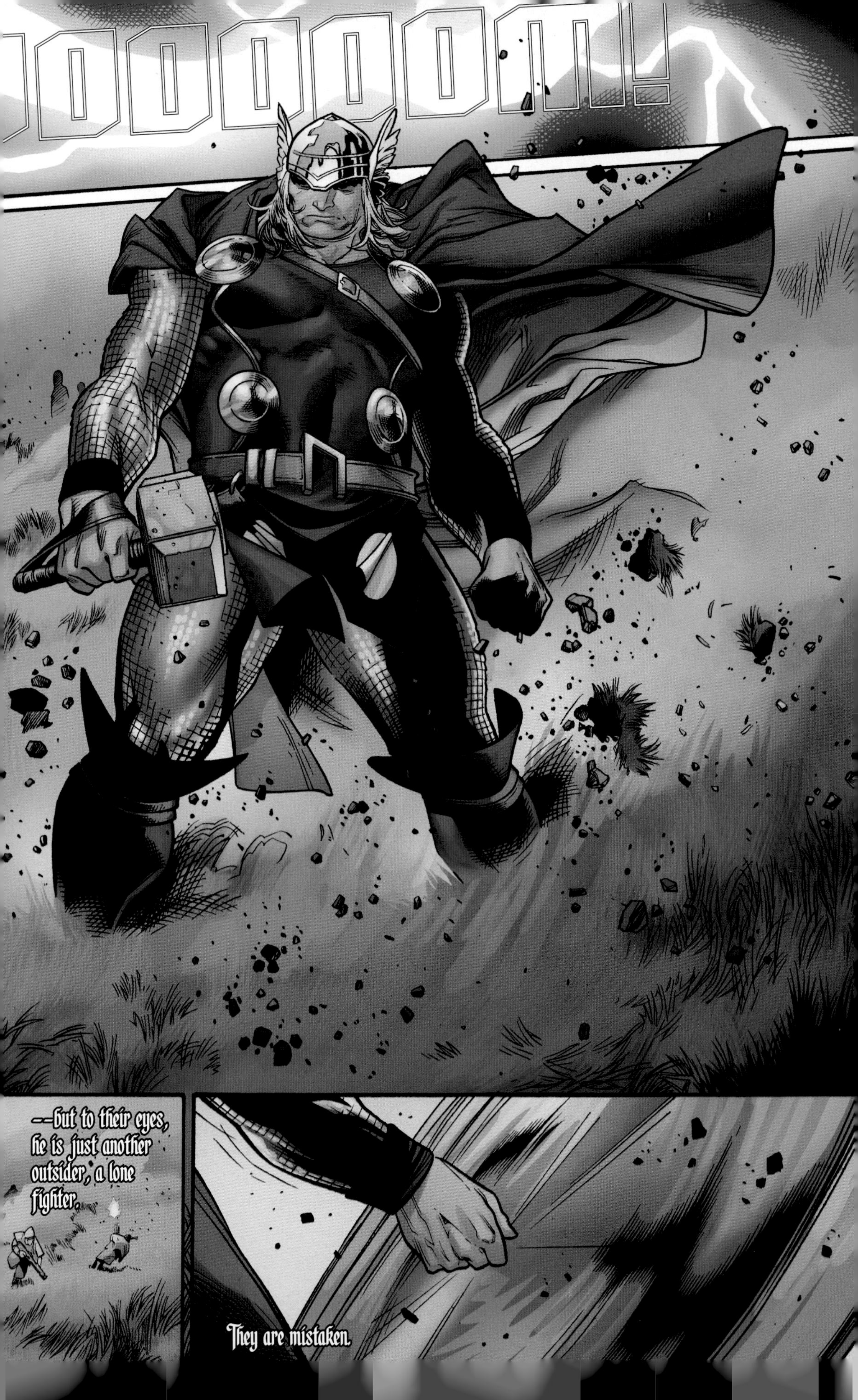

OOOOOM!
--but to their eyes, he is just another outsider, a lone fighter.
They are mistaken.

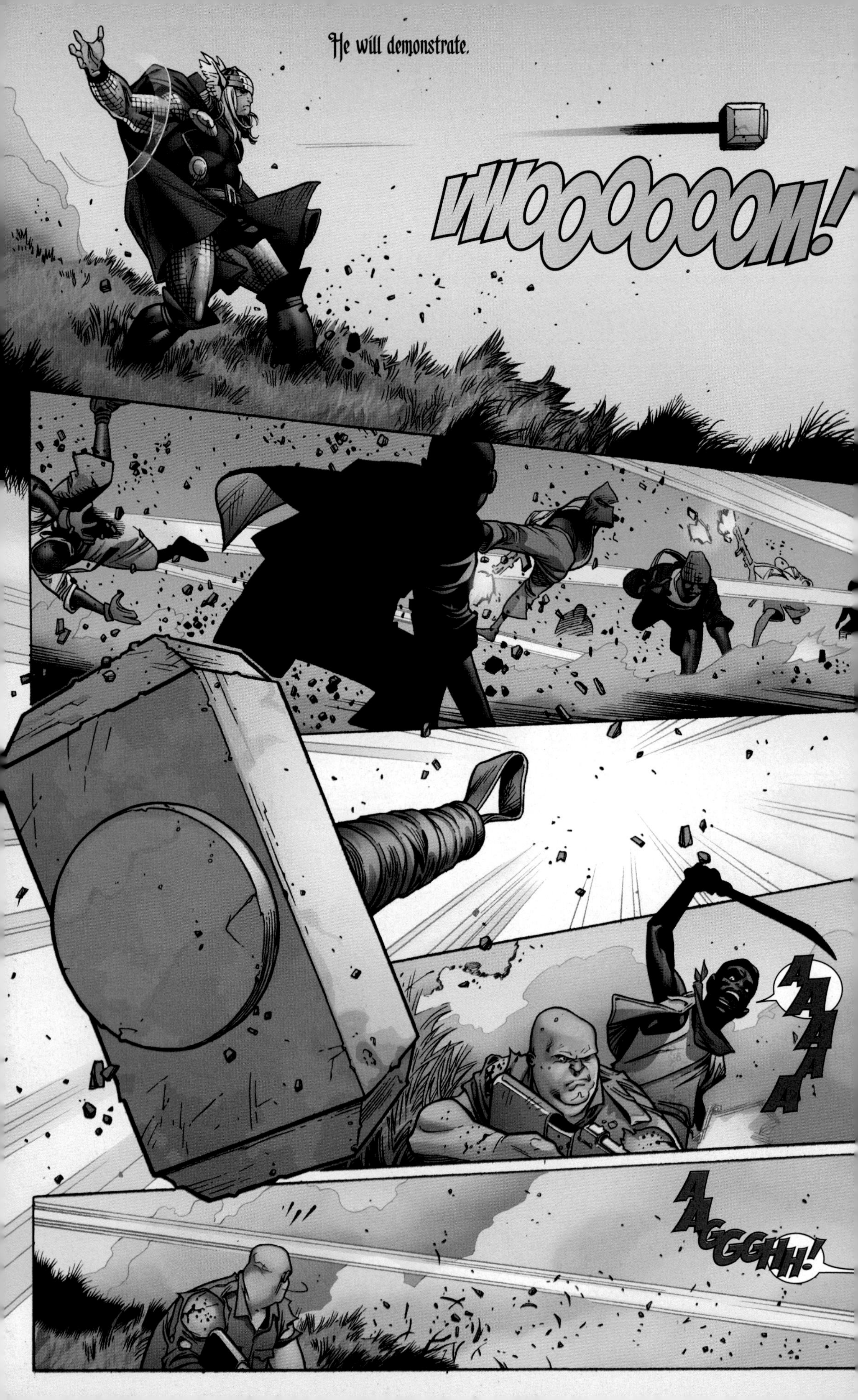
He will demonstrate.
VWOOOOOOM!
AAAAA
AAGGGHH!

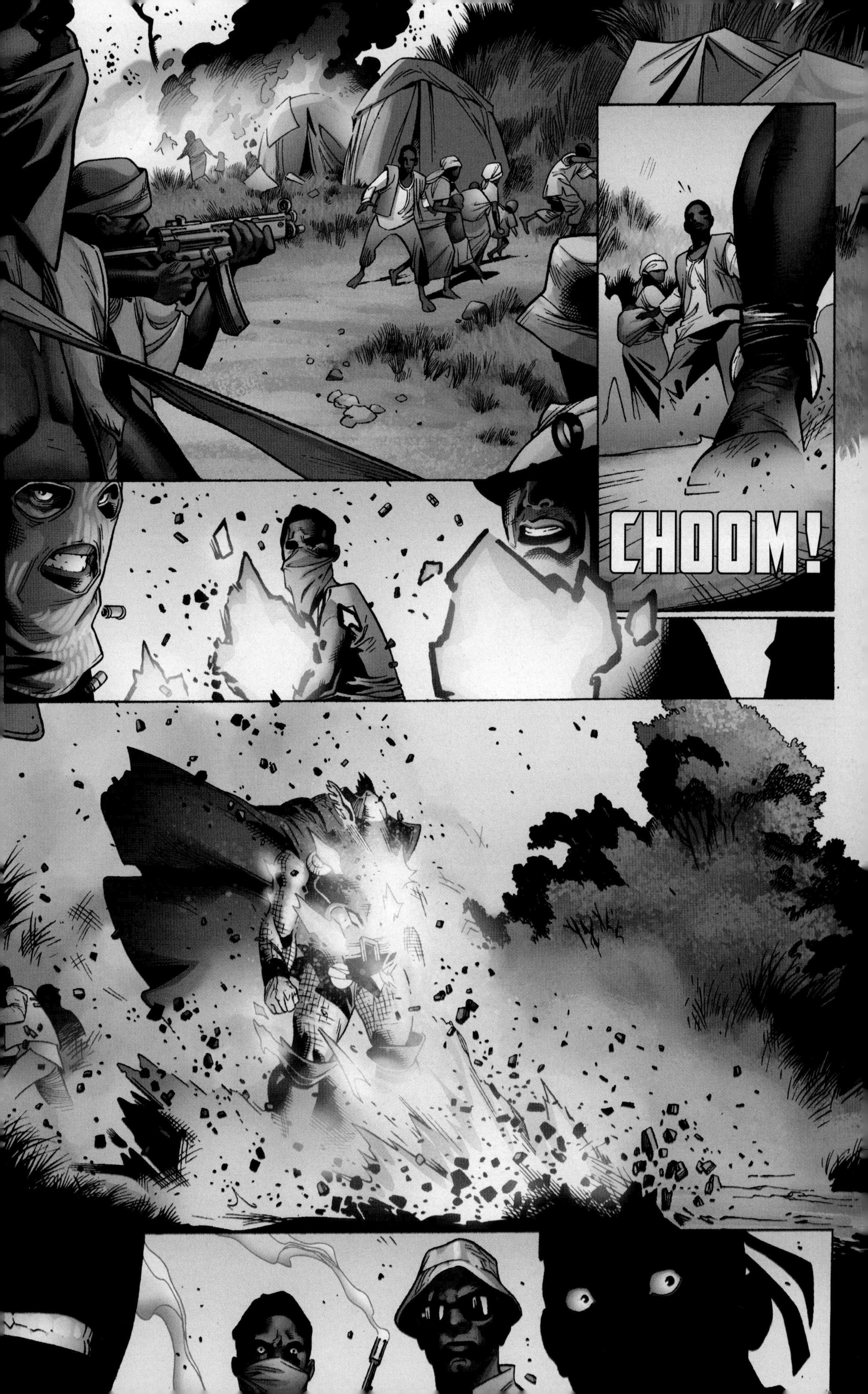
CHOOM!

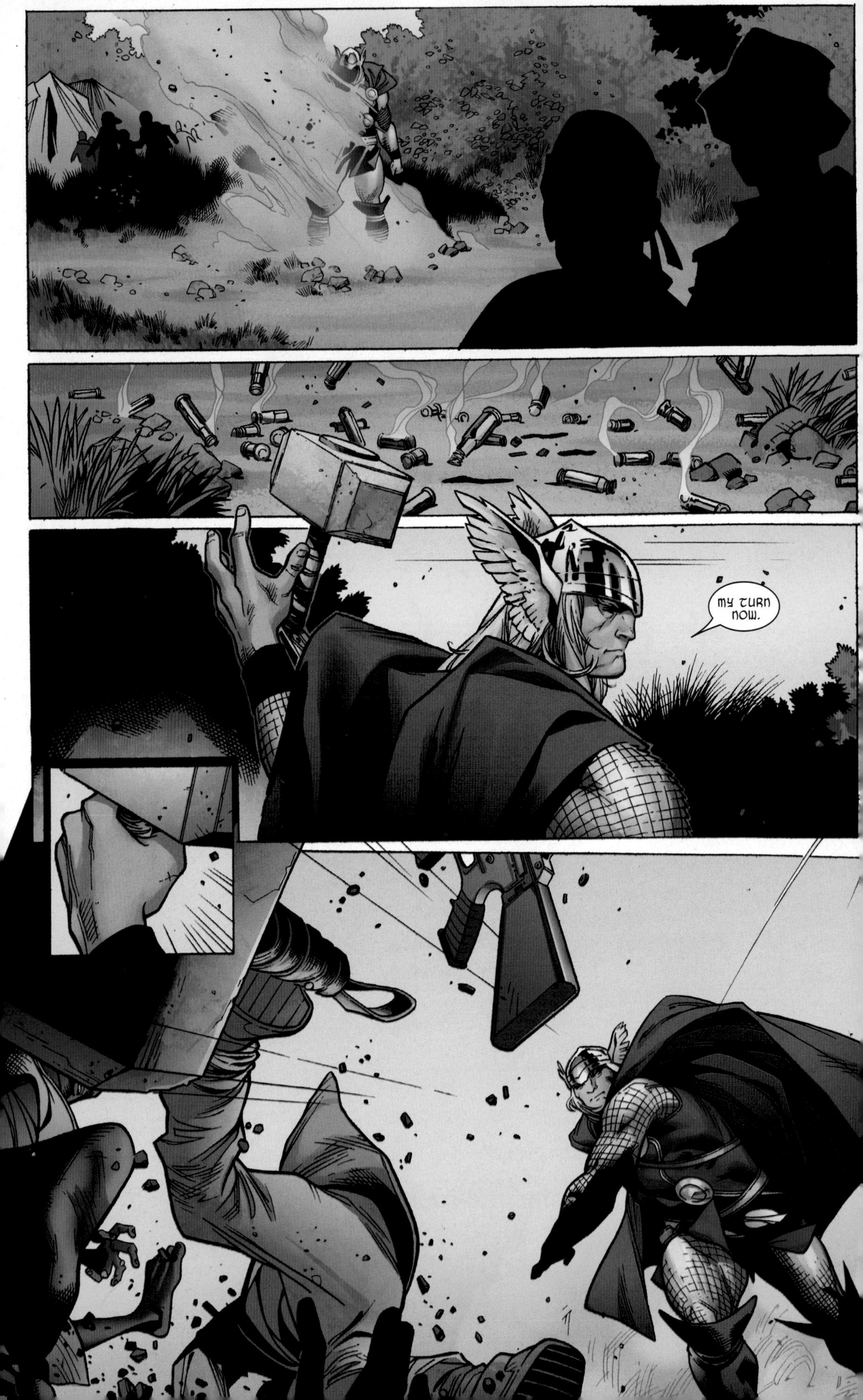
MY TURN NOW.

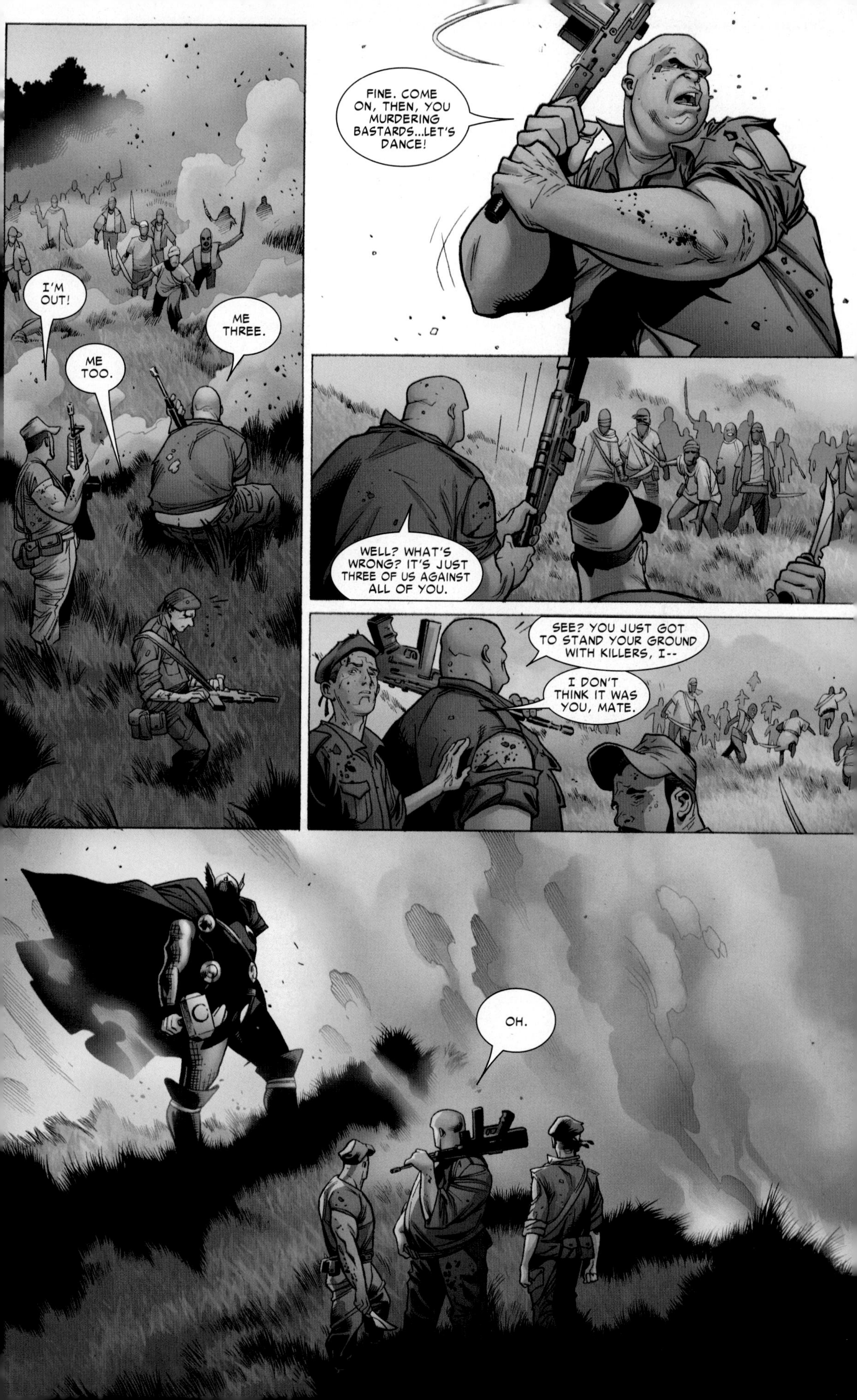
FINE. COME ON, THEN, YOU MURDERING BASTARDS...LET'S DANCE!
I'M OUT!
ME TOO.
ME THREE.
WELL? WHAT'S WRONG? IT'S JUST THREE OF US AGAINST ALL OF YOU.
SEE? YOU JUST GOT TO STAND YOUR GROUND WITH KILLERS, I--
I DON'T THINK IT WAS YOU, MATE.
OH.

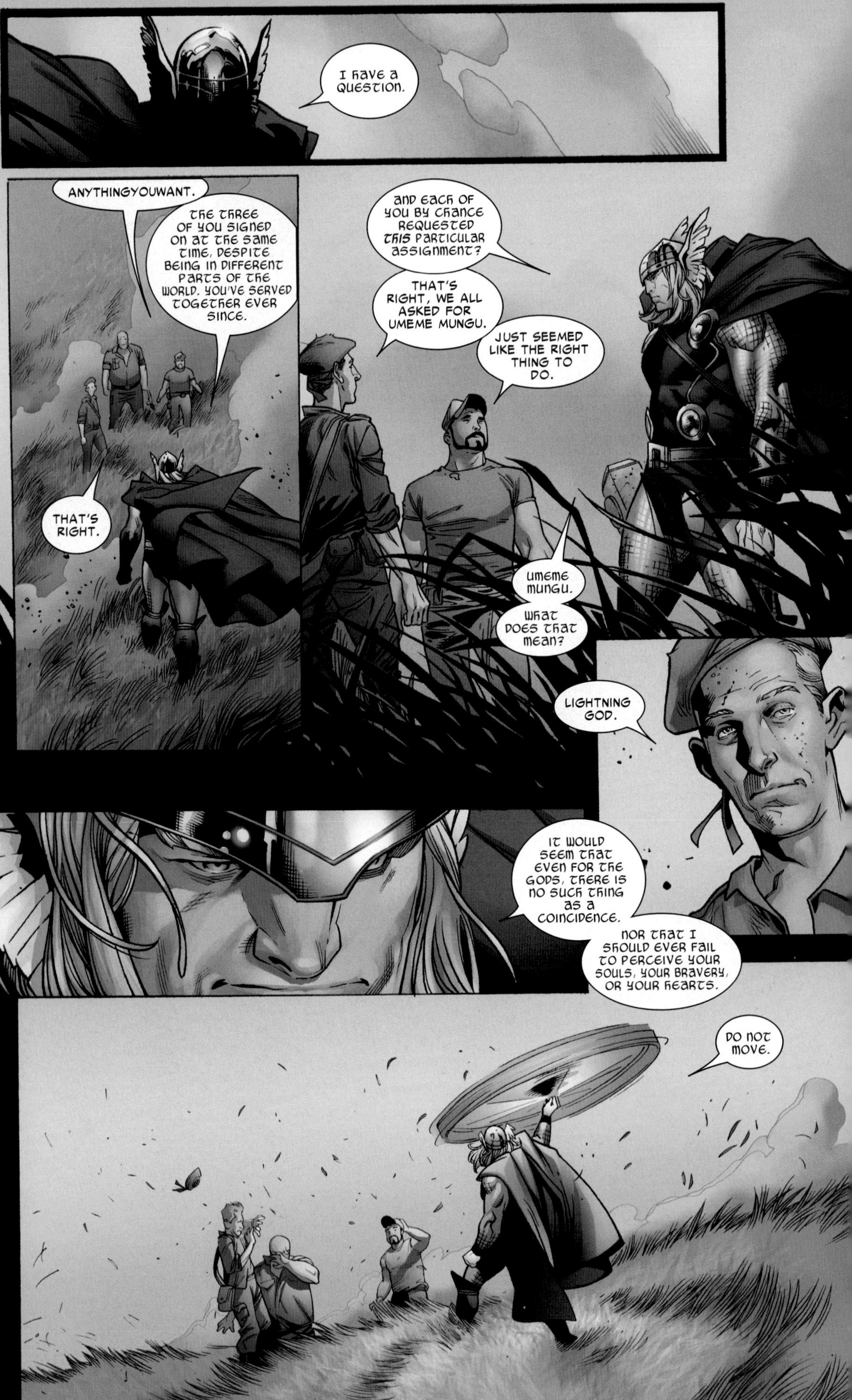
I HAVE A QUESTION.
ANYTHINGYOUWANT.
THE THREE OF YOU SIGNED ON AT THE SAME TIME, DESPITE BEING IN DIFFERENT PARTS OF THE WORLD. YOU'VE SERVED TOGETHER EVER SINCE.
THAT'S RIGHT.
AND EACH OF YOU BY CHANCE REQUESTED THIS PARTICULAR ASSIGNMENT?
THAT'S RIGHT, WE ALL ASKED FOR UMEME MUNGU.
JUST SEEMED LIKE THE RIGHT THING TO DO.
UMEME MUNGU.
WHAT DOES THAT MEAN?
LIGHTNING GOD.
IT WOULD SEEM THAT EVEN FOR THE GODS, THERE IS NO SUCH THING AS A COINCIDENCE.
NOR THAT I SHOULD EVER FAIL TO PERCEIVE YOUR SOULS, YOUR BRAVERY, OR YOUR HEARTS.
DO NOT MOVE.

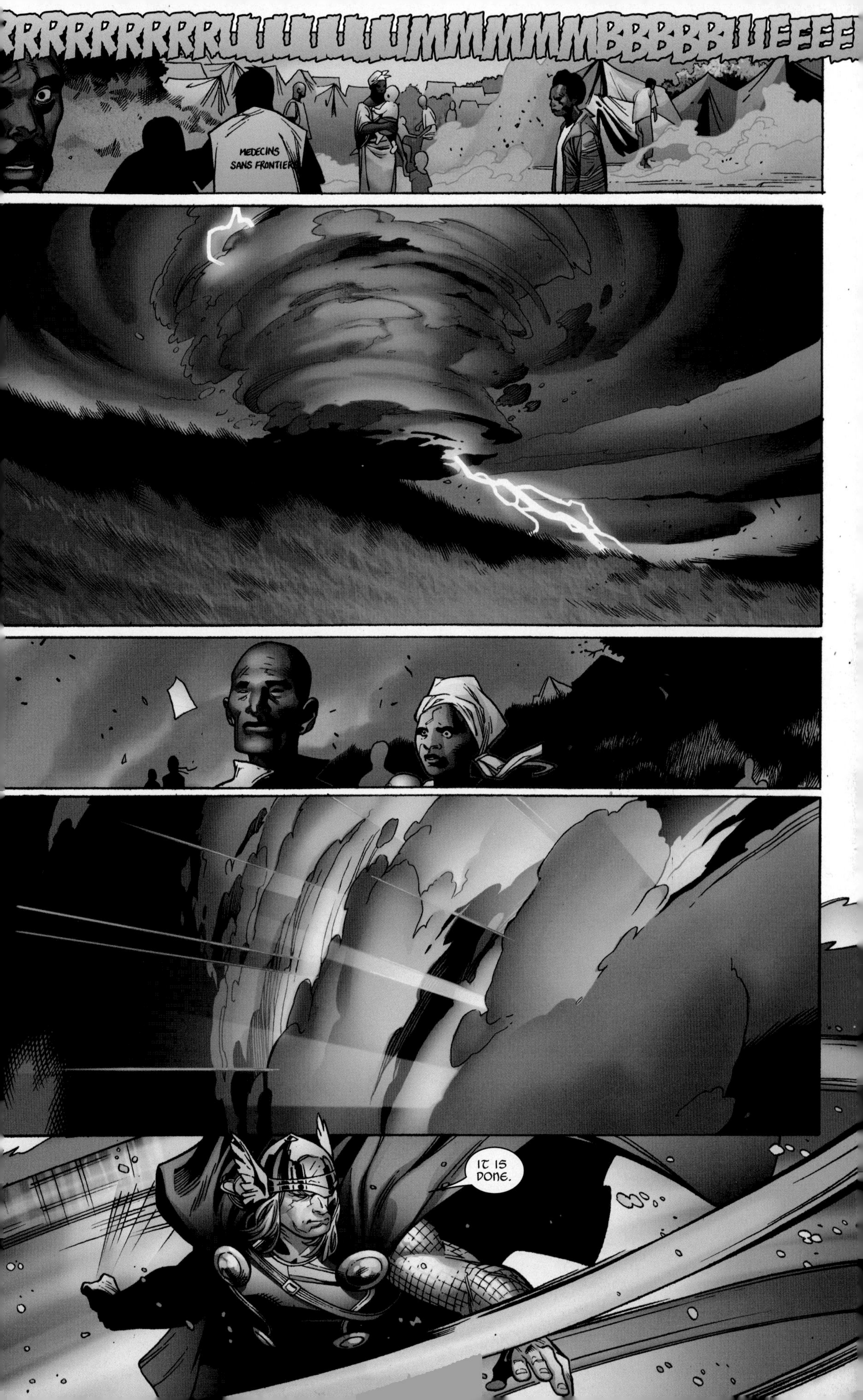
RRRRRRRRRRUUUUUUMMMMMMBBBBBLLEEEE
MEDECINS SANS FRONTIERES
IT IS DONE.

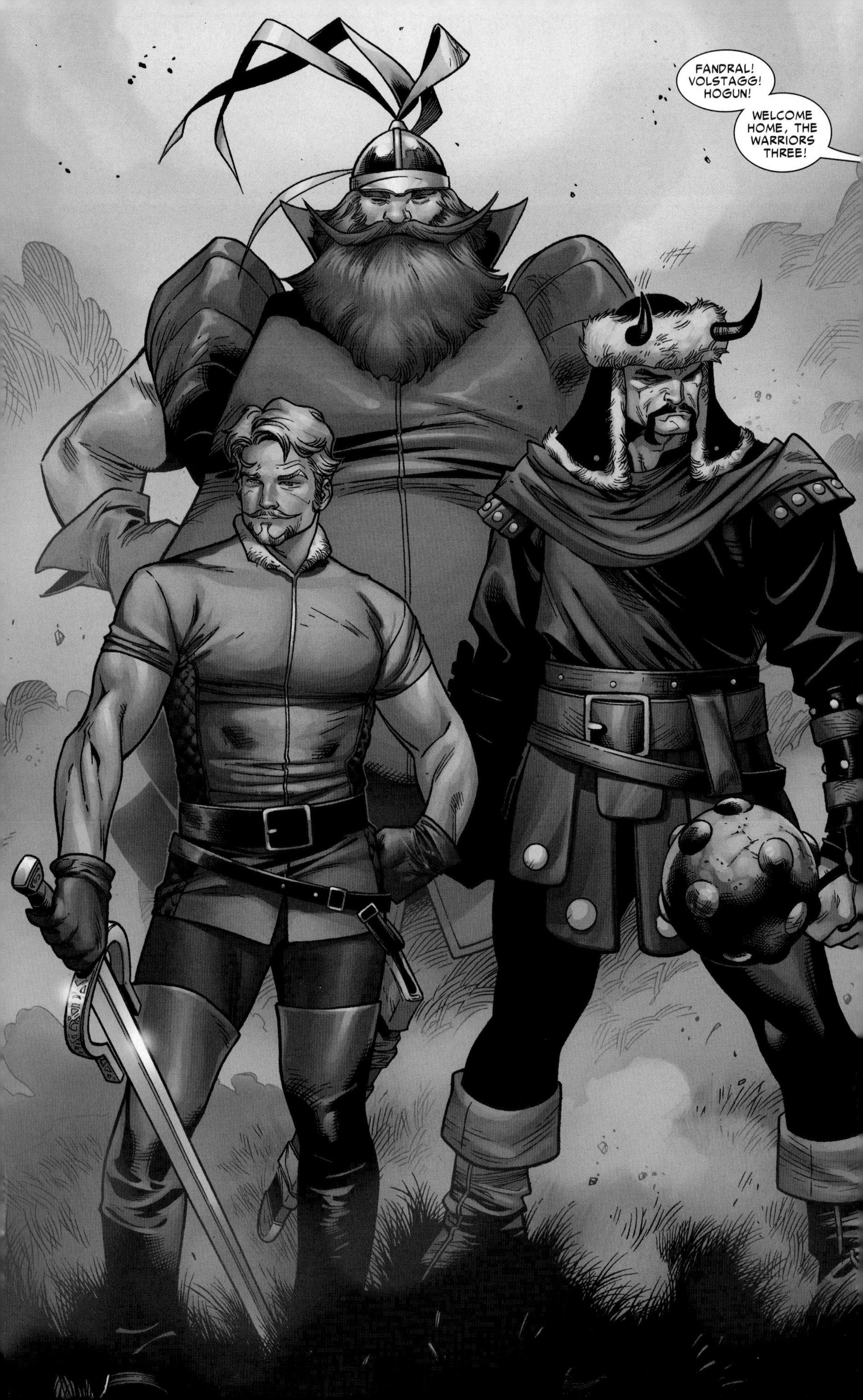
FANDRAL! VOLSTAGG! HOGUN!
WELCOME HOME, THE WARRIORS THREE!

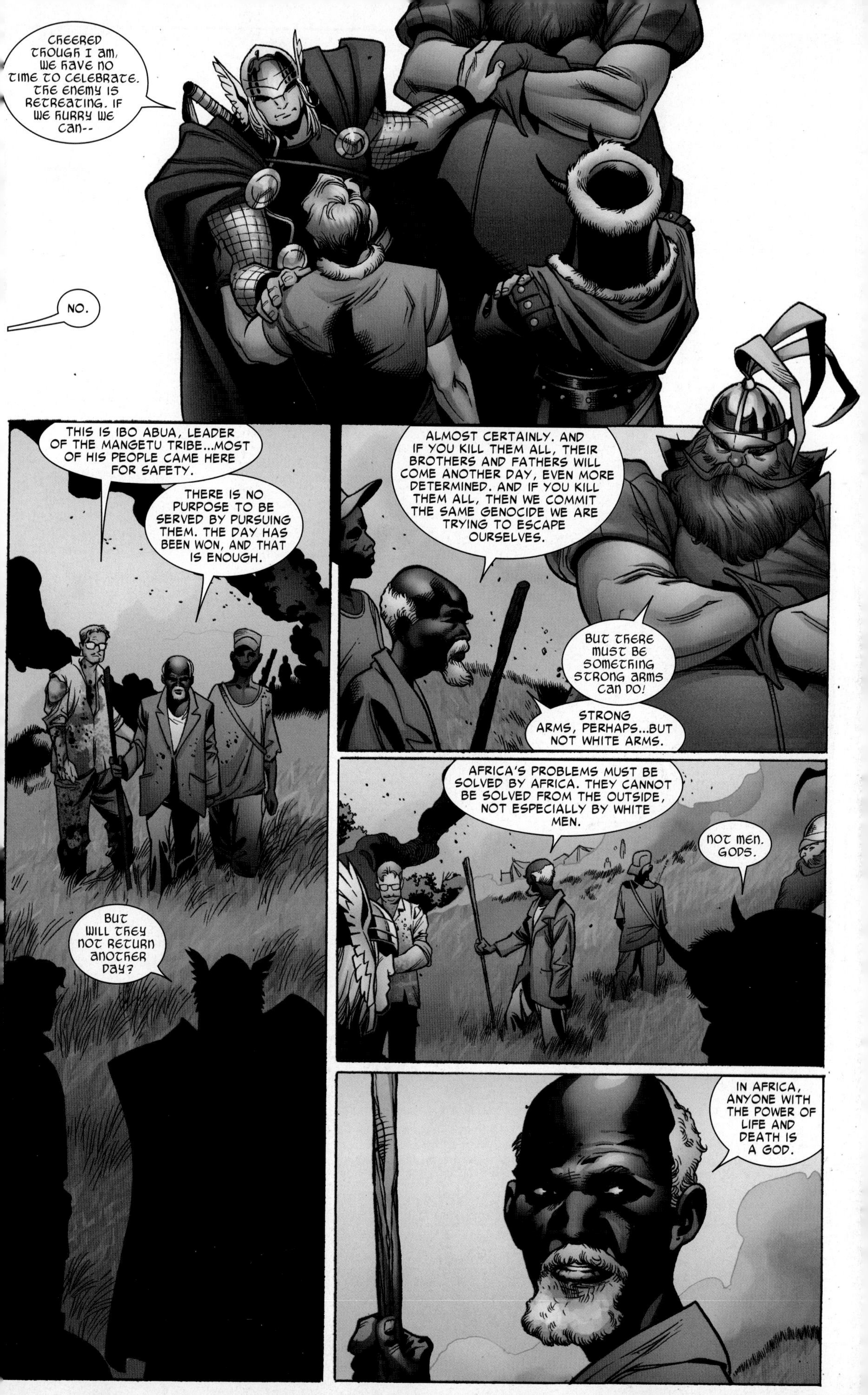
CHEERED THOUGH I AM, WE HAVE NO TIME TO CELEBRATE. THE ENEMY IS RETREATING. IF WE HURRY WE CAN--
NO.
THIS IS IBO ABUA, LEADER OF THE MANGETU TRIBE...MOST OF HIS PEOPLE CAME HERE FOR SAFETY.
THERE IS NO PURPOSE TO BE SERVED BY PURSUING THEM. THE DAY HAS BEEN WON, AND THAT IS ENOUGH.
BUT WILL THEY NOT RETURN ANOTHER DAY?
ALMOST CERTAINLY. AND IF YOU KILL THEM ALL, THEIR BROTHERS AND FATHERS WILL COME ANOTHER DAY, EVEN MORE DETERMINED. AND IF YOU KILL THEM ALL, THEN WE COMMIT THE SAME GENOCIDE WE ARE TRYING TO ESCAPE OURSELVES.
BUT THERE MUST BE SOMETHING STRONG ARMS CAN DO!
STRONG ARMS, PERHAPS...BUT NOT WHITE ARMS.
AFRICA'S PROBLEMS MUST BE SOLVED BY AFRICA. THEY CANNOT BE SOLVED FROM THE OUTSIDE, NOT ESPECIALLY BY WHITE MEN.
NOT MEN. GODS.
IN AFRICA, ANYONE WITH THE POWER OF LIFE AND DEATH IS A GOD.

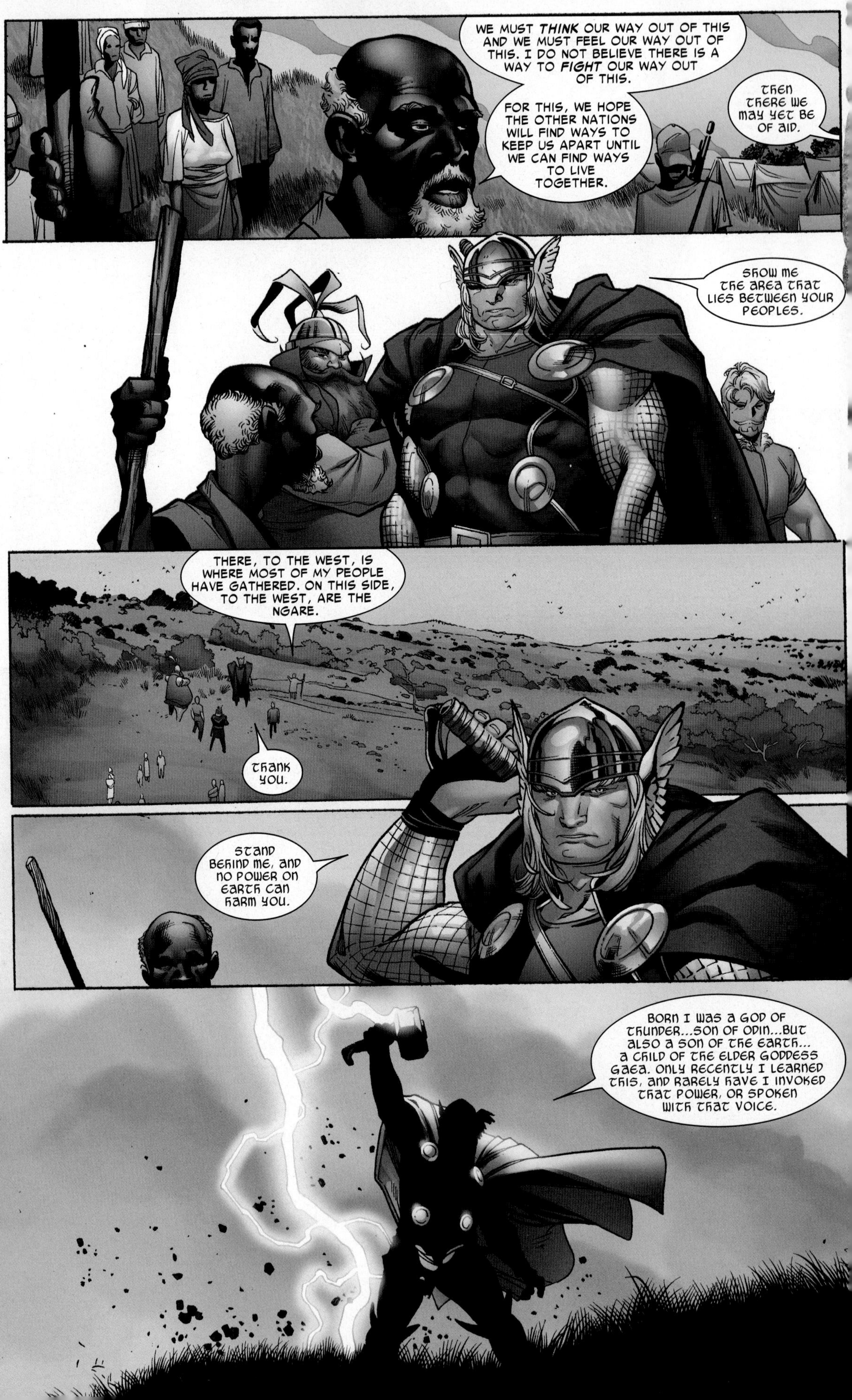
WE MUST THINK OUR WAY OUT OF THIS AND WE MUST FEEL OUR WAY OUT OF THIS. I DO NOT BELIEVE THERE IS A WAY TO FIGHT OUR WAY OUT OF THIS.
FOR THIS, WE HOPE THE OTHER NATIONS WILL FIND WAYS TO KEEP US APART UNTIL WE CAN FIND WAYS TO LIVE TOGETHER.
THEN THERE WE MAY YET BE OF AID.
SHOW ME THE AREA THAT LIES BETWEEN YOUR PEOPLES.
THERE, TO THE WEST, IS WHERE MOST OF MY PEOPLE HAVE GATHERED. ON THIS SIDE, TO THE WEST, ARE THE NGARE.
THANK YOU.
STAND BEHIND ME, AND NO POWER ON EARTH CAN HARM YOU.
BORN I WAS A GOD OF THUNDER...SON OF ODIN...BUT ALSO A SON OF THE EARTH... A CHILD OF THE ELDER GODDESS GAEA. ONLY RECENTLY I LEARNED THIS, AND RARELY HAVE I INVOKED THAT POWER, OR SPOKEN WITH THAT VOICE.

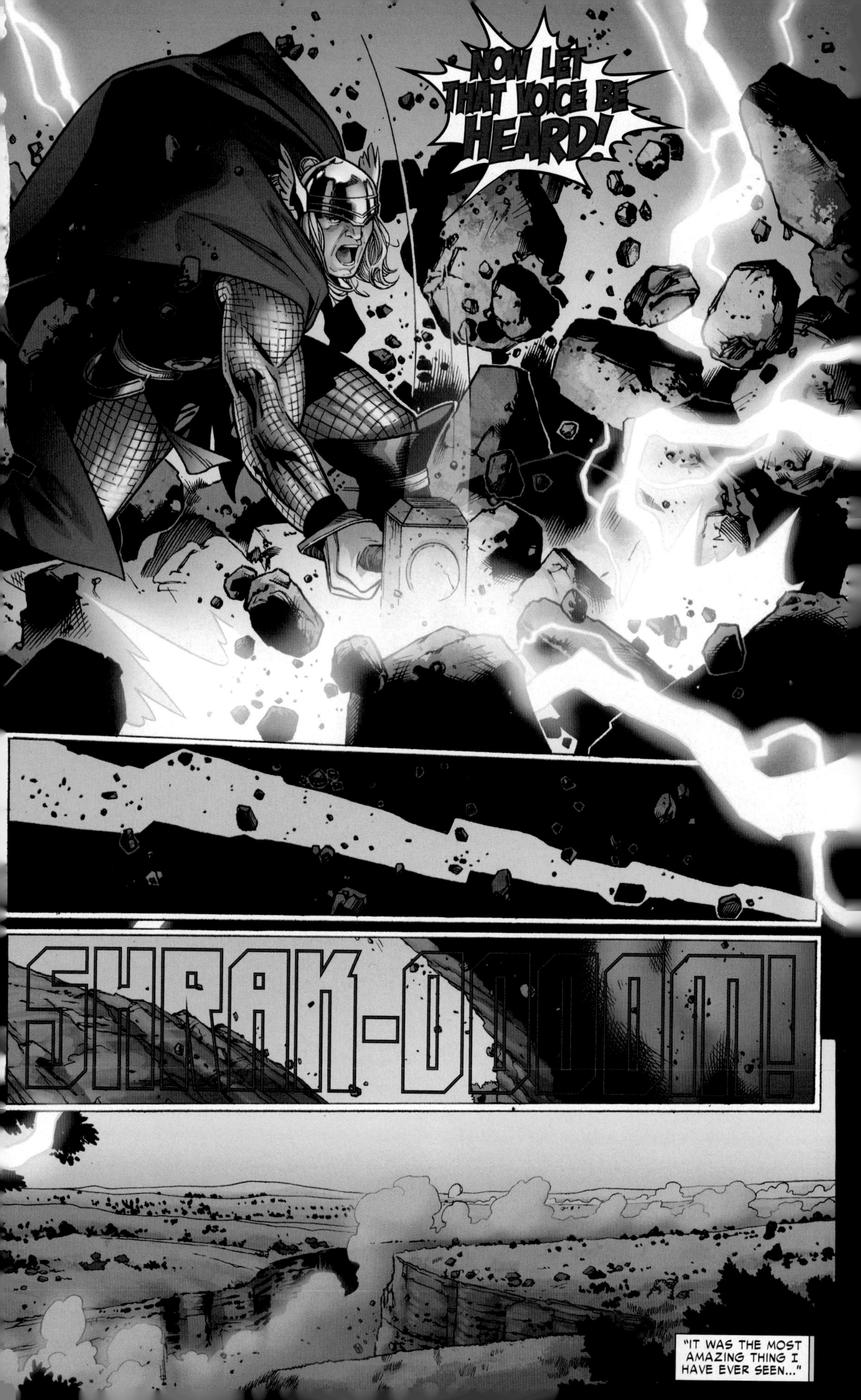
NOW LET THAT VOICE BE HEARD!
SHRAK-OOOOM!
"IT WAS THE MOST AMAZING THING I HAVE EVER SEEN..."

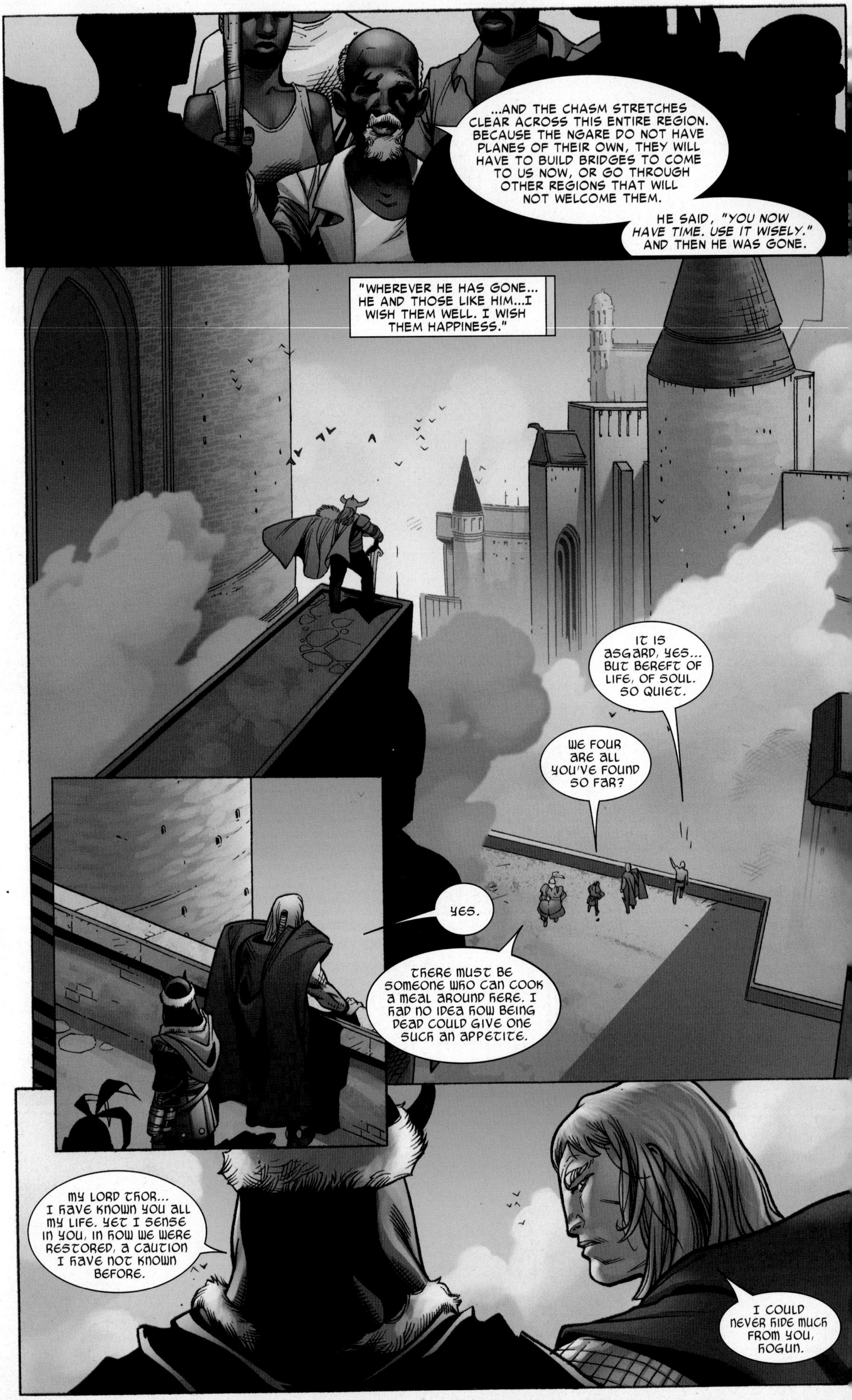
...AND THE CHASM STRETCHES CLEAR ACROSS THIS ENTIRE REGION. BECAUSE THE NGARE DO NOT HAVE PLANES OF THEIR OWN, THEY WILL HAVE TO BUILD BRIDGES TO COME TO US NOW, OR GO THROUGH OTHER REGIONS THAT WILL NOT WELCOME THEM.
HE SAID, "YOU NOW HAVE TIME. USE IT WISELY." AND THEN HE WAS GONE.
"WHEREVER HE HAS GONE... HE AND THOSE LIKE HIM...I WISH THEM WELL. I WISH THEM HAPPINESS."
IT IS ASGARD, YES... BUT BEREFT OF LIFE, OF SOUL. SO QUIET.
WE FOUR ARE ALL YOU'VE FOUND SO FAR?
YES.
THERE MUST BE SOMEONE WHO CAN COOK A MEAL AROUND HERE. I HAD NO IDEA HOW BEING DEAD COULD GIVE ONE SUCH AN APPETITE.
MY LORD THOR... I HAVE KNOWN YOU ALL MY LIFE. YET I SENSE IN YOU, IN HOW WE WERE RESTORED, A CAUTION I HAVE NOT KNOWN BEFORE.
I COULD NEVER HIDE MUCH FROM YOU, HOGUN.

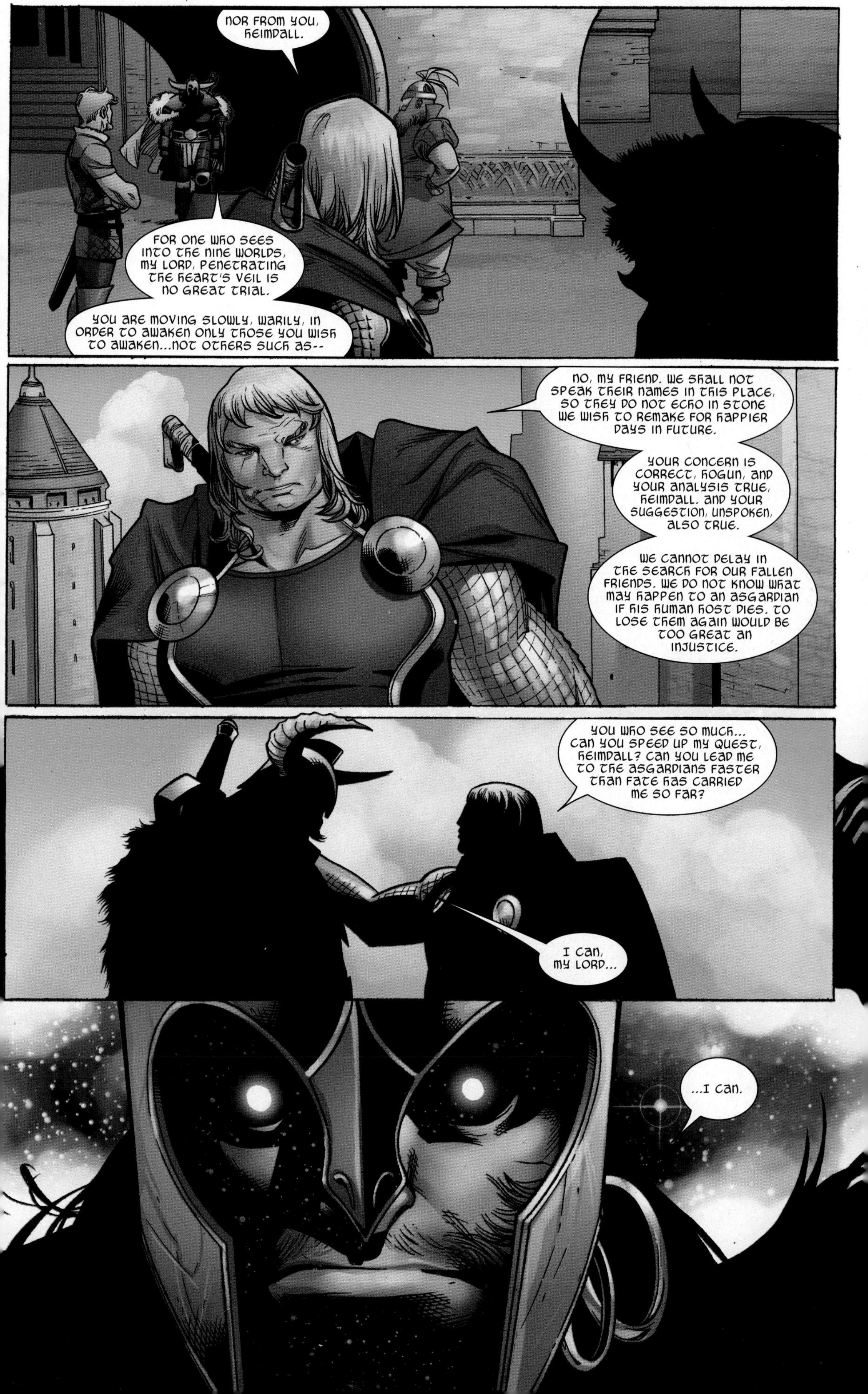
NOR FROM YOU, HEIMDALL.
FOR ONE WHO SEES INTO THE NINE WORLDS, MY LORD, PENETRATING THE HEART'S VEIL IS NO GREAT TRIAL.
YOU ARE MOVING SLOWLY, WARILY, IN ORDER TO AWAKEN ONLY THOSE YOU WISH TO AWAKEN...NOT OTHERS SUCH AS--
NO, MY FRIEND. WE SHALL NOT SPEAK THEIR NAMES IN THIS PLACE, SO THEY DO NOT ECHO IN STONE WE WISH TO REMAKE FOR HAPPIER DAYS IN FUTURE.
YOUR CONCERN IS CORRECT, HOGUN, AND YOUR ANALYSIS TRUE, HEIMDALL. AND YOUR SUGGESTION, UNSPOKEN, ALSO TRUE.
WE CANNOT DELAY IN THE SEARCH FOR OUR FALLEN FRIENDS. WE DO NOT KNOW WHAT MAY HAPPEN TO AN ASGARDIAN IF HIS HUMAN HOST DIES. TO LOSE THEM AGAIN WOULD BE TOO GREAT AN INJUSTICE.
YOU WHO SEE SO MUCH... CAN YOU SPEED UP MY QUEST, HEIMDALL? CAN YOU LEAD ME TO THE ASGARDIANS FASTER THAN FATE HAS CARRIED ME SO FAR?
I CAN, MY LORD...
...I CAN.

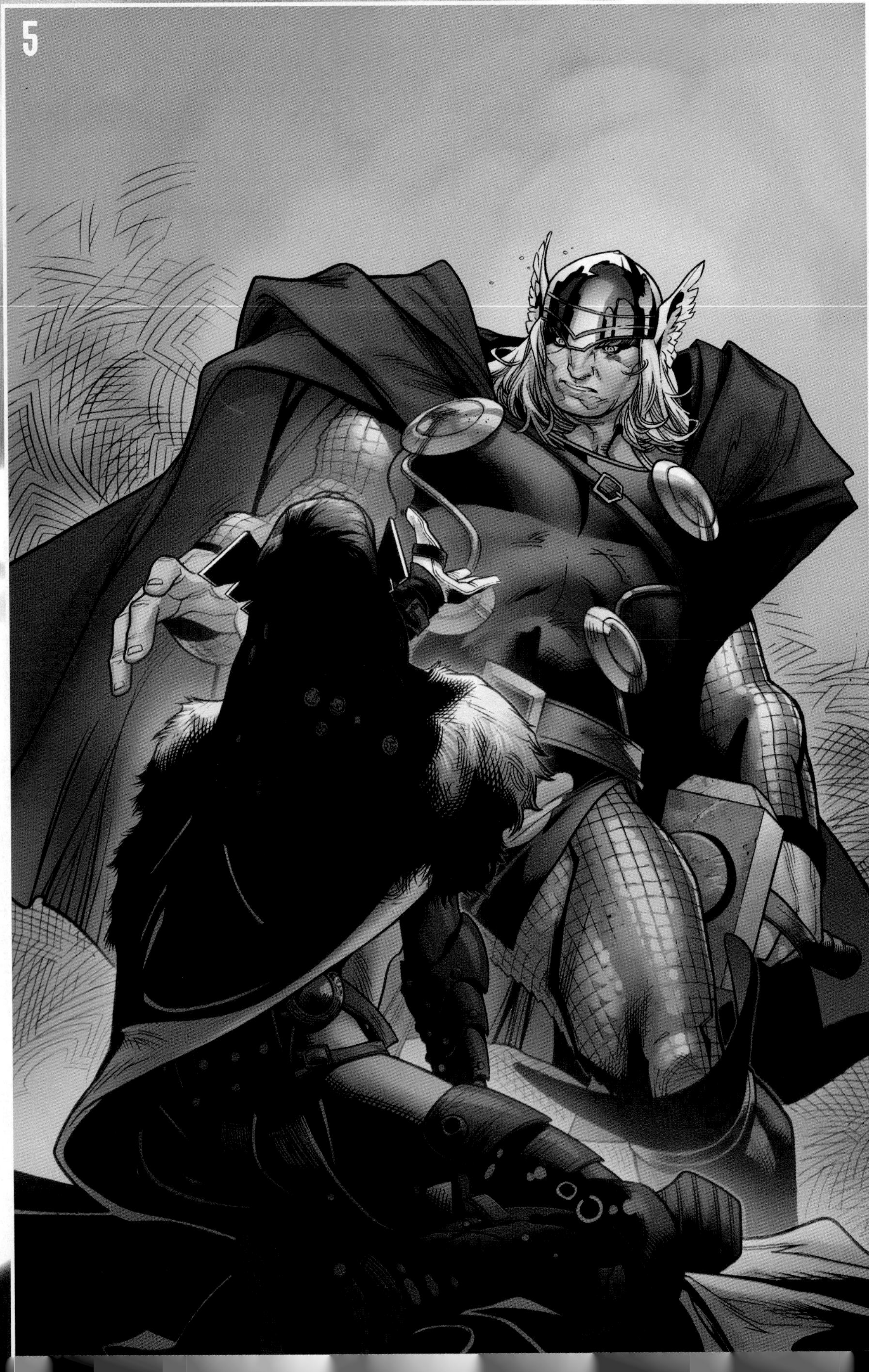
5

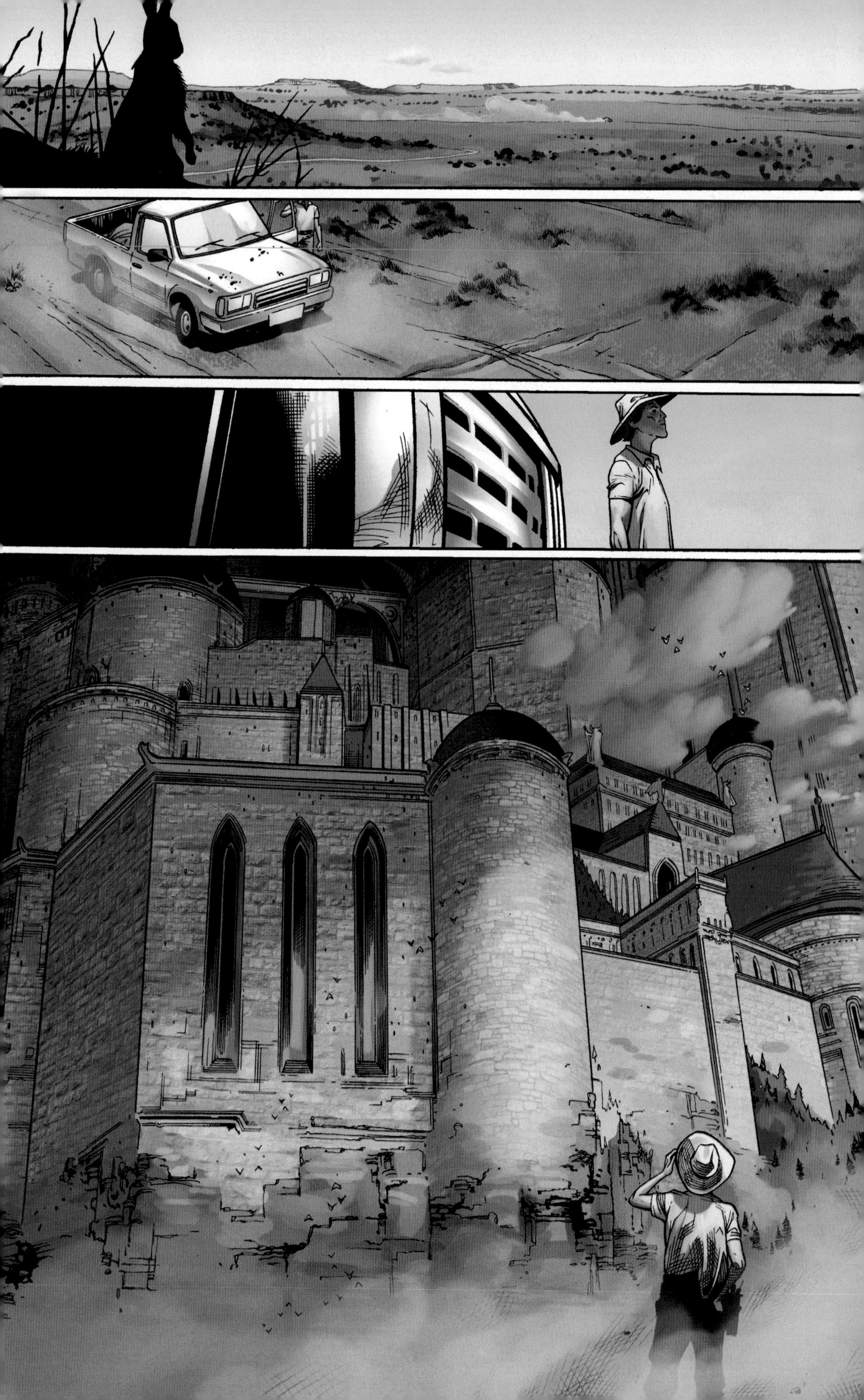

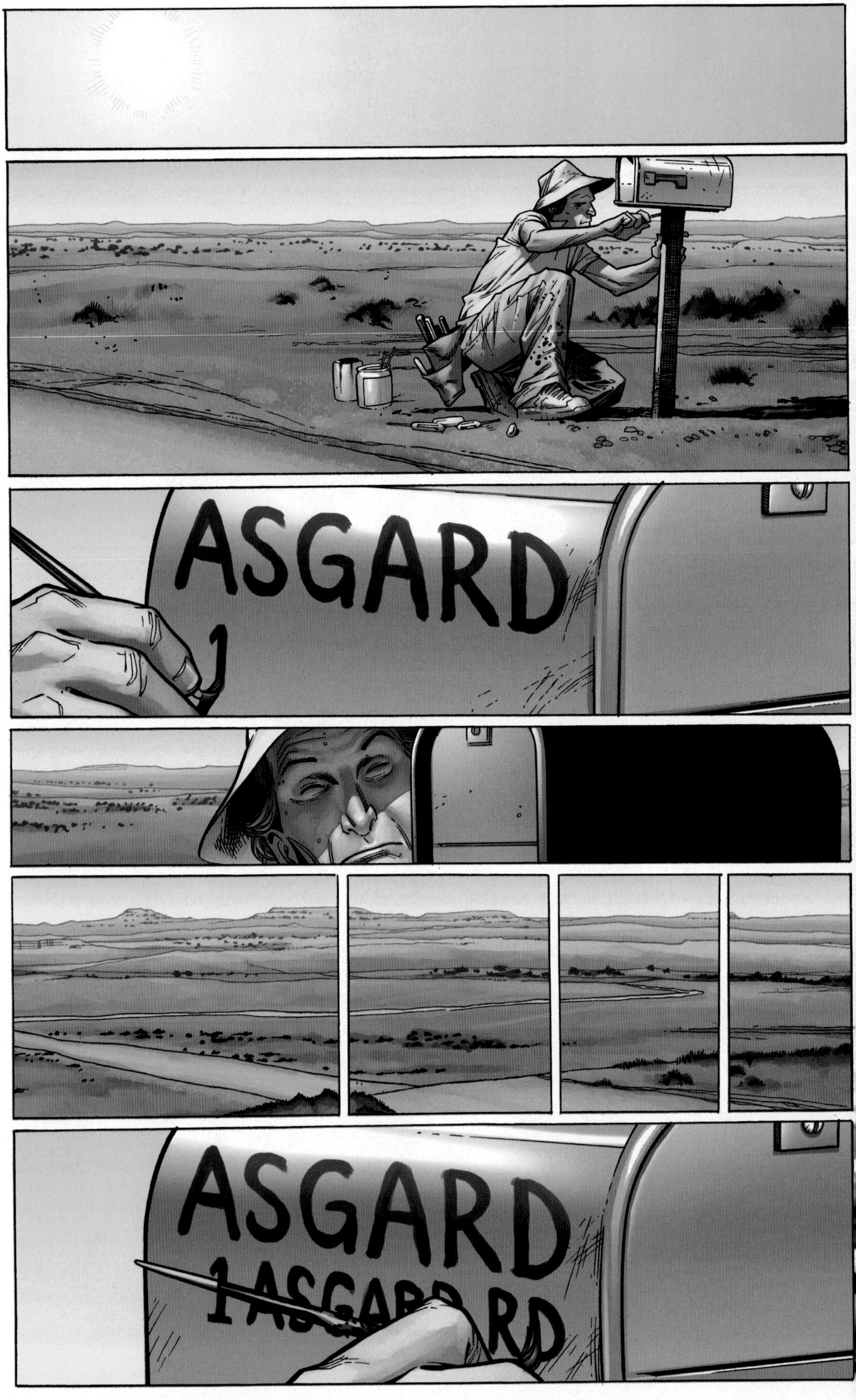
ASGARD
1
ASGARD
RD

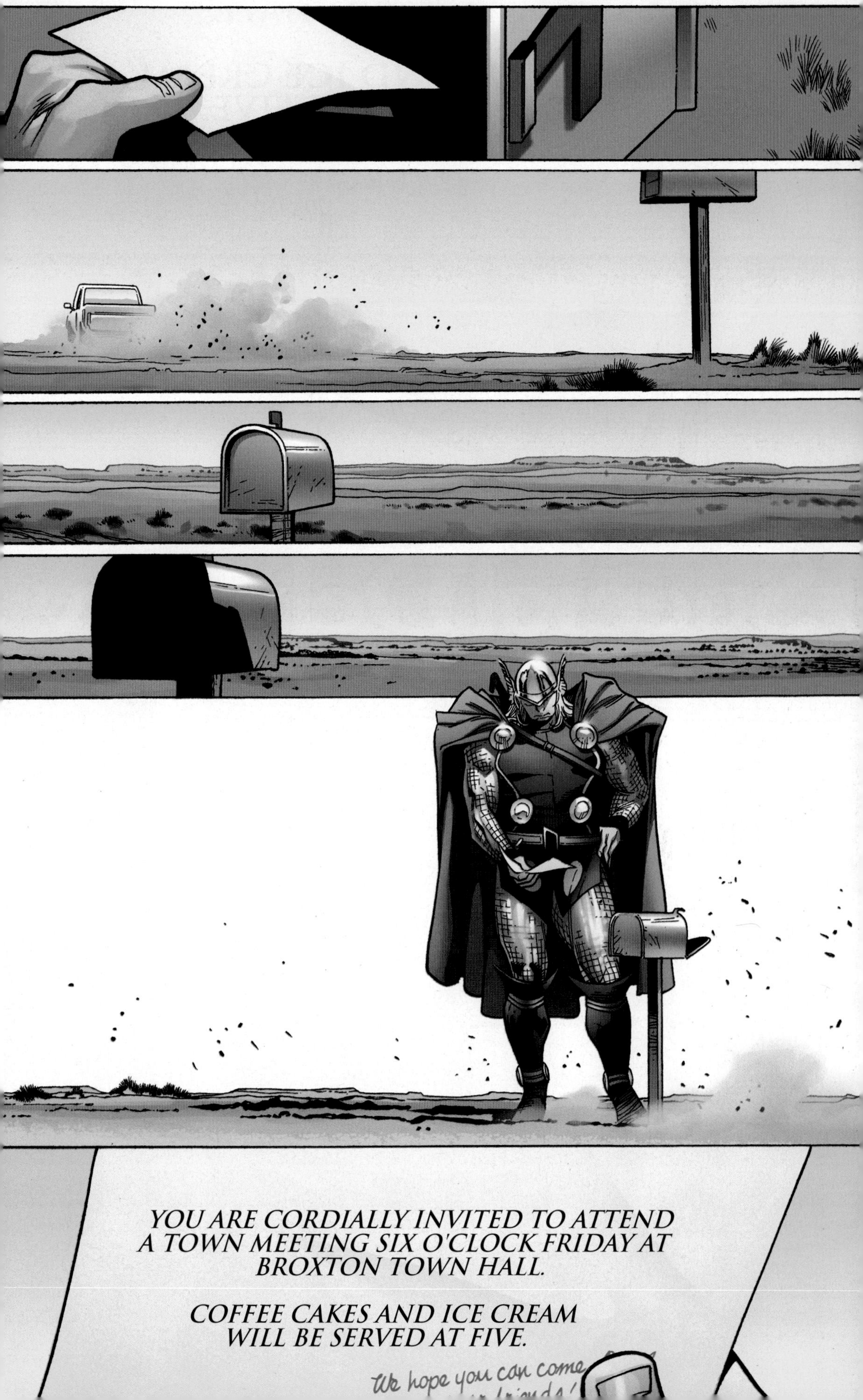
YOU ARE CORDIALLY INVITED TO ATTEND A TOWN MEETING SIX O'CLOCK FRIDAY AT BROXTON TOWN HALL.
COFFEE CAKES AND ICE CREAM WILL BE SERVED AT FIVE.
We hope you can come

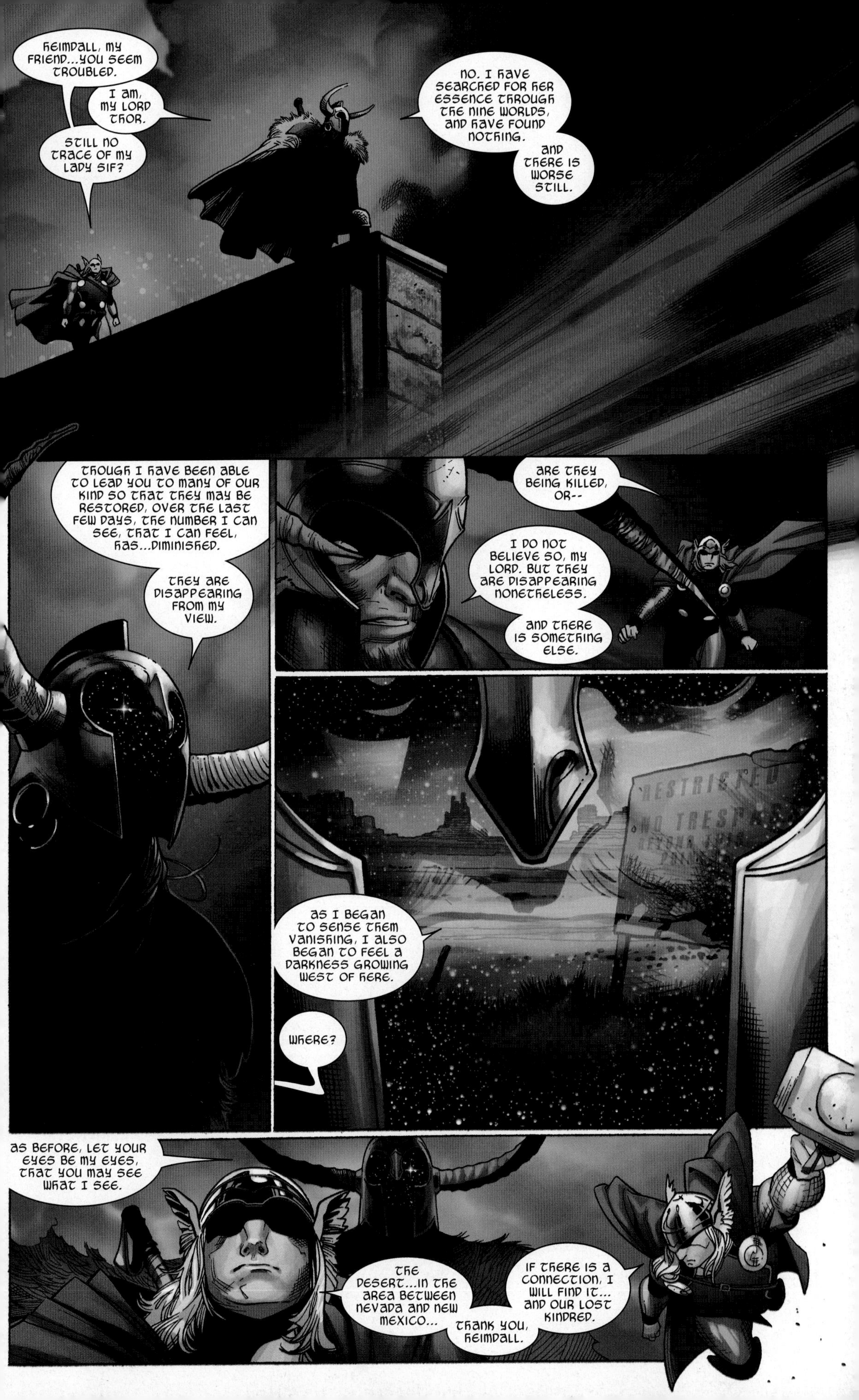
HEIMDALL, MY FRIEND...YOU SEEM TROUBLED.
I AM, MY LORD THOR.
STILL NO TRACE OF MY LADY SIF?
NO. I HAVE SEARCHED FOR HER ESSENCE THROUGH THE NINE WORLDS, AND HAVE FOUND NOTHING.
AND THERE IS WORSE STILL.
THOUGH I HAVE BEEN ABLE TO LEAD YOU TO MANY OF OUR KIND SO THAT THEY MAY BE RESTORED, OVER THE LAST FEW DAYS, THE NUMBER I CAN SEE, THAT I CAN FEEL, HAS...DIMINISHED.
THEY ARE DISAPPEARING FROM MY VIEW.
ARE THEY BEING KILLED, OR--
I DO NOT BELIEVE SO, MY LORD. BUT THEY ARE DISAPPEARING NONETHELESS.
AND THERE IS SOMETHING ELSE.
AS I BEGAN TO SENSE THEM VANISHING, I ALSO BEGAN TO FEEL A DARKNESS GROWING WEST OF HERE.
WHERE?
AS BEFORE, LET YOUR EYES BE MY EYES, THAT YOU MAY SEE WHAT I SEE.
THE DESERT...IN THE AREA BETWEEN NEVADA AND NEW MEXICO...
THANK YOU, HEIMDALL.
IF THERE IS A CONNECTION, I WILL FIND IT... AND OUR LOST KINDRED.

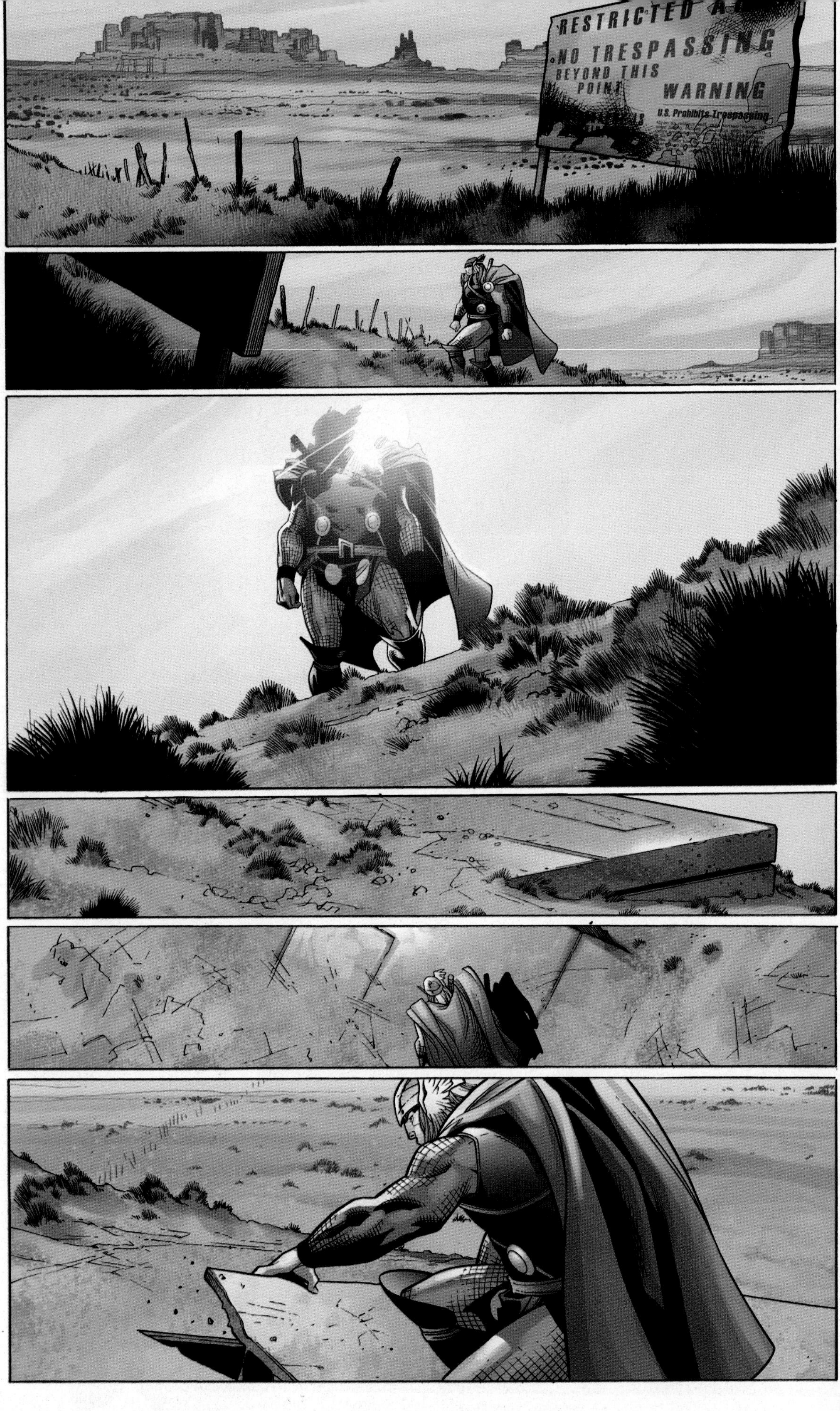
RESTRICTED
NO TRESPASSING
BEYOND THIS
POINT
WARNING
U.S. Prohibits Trespassing

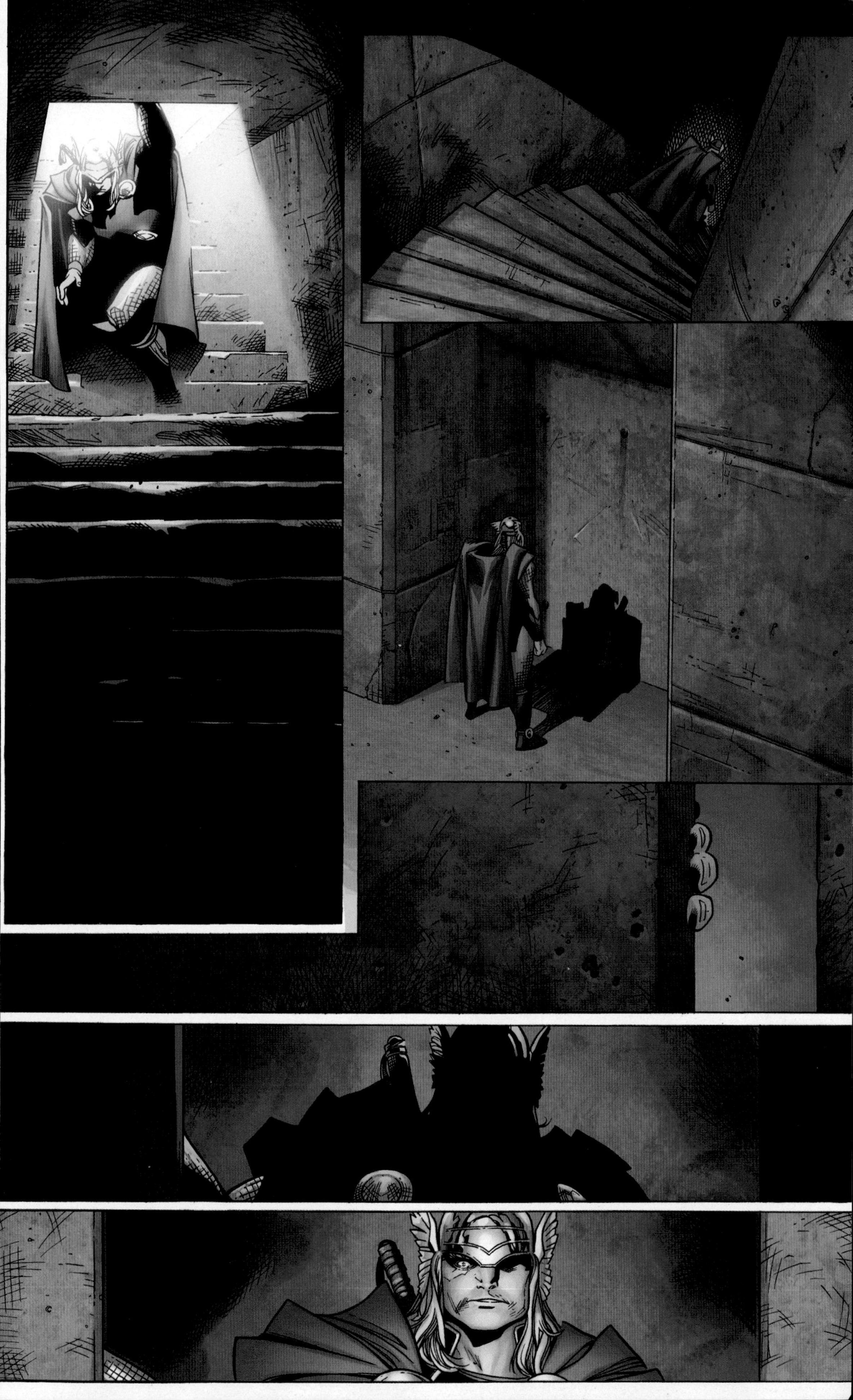

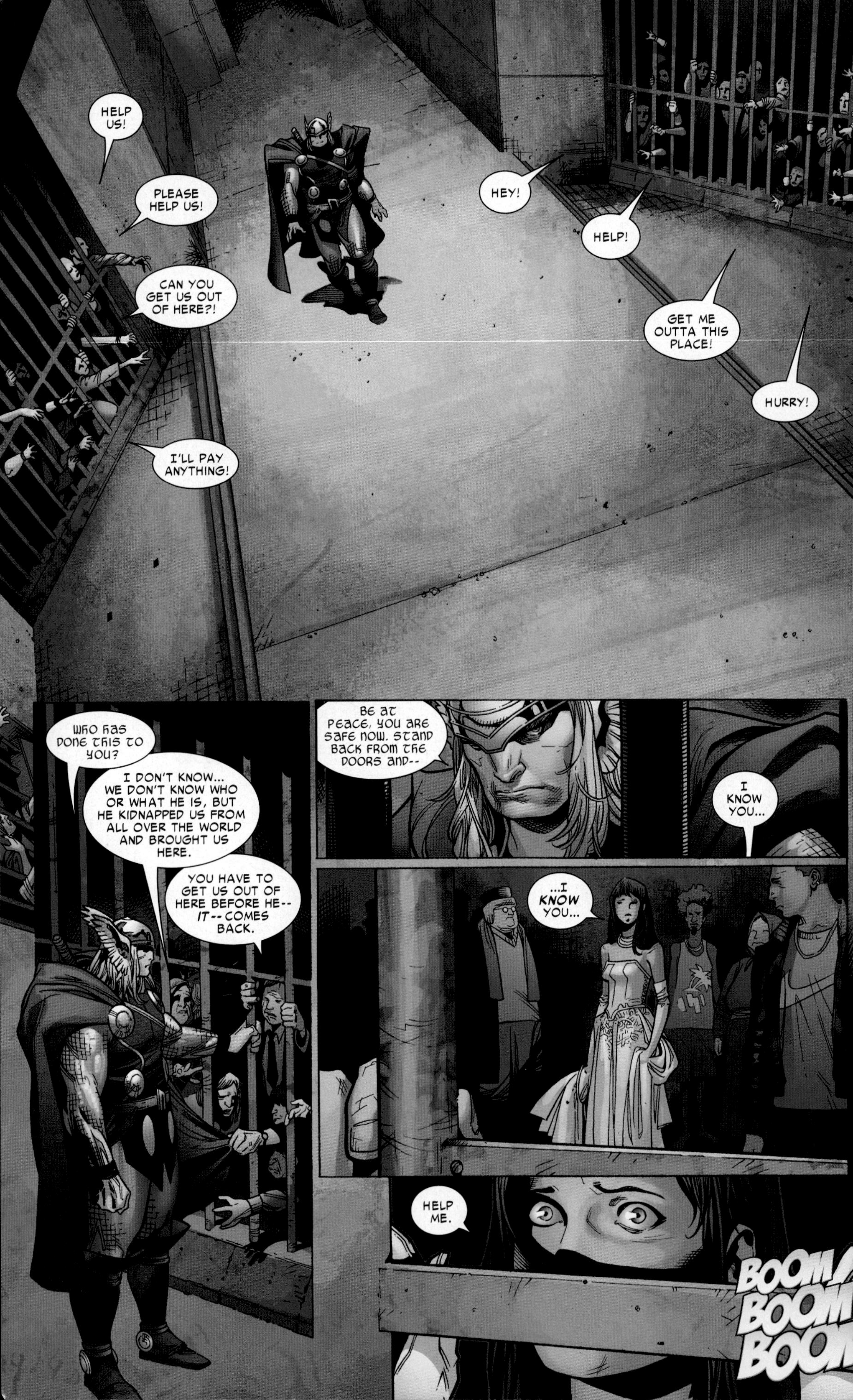

HELP US!
PLEASE HELP US!
CAN YOU GET US OUT OF HERE?!
I'LL PAY ANYTHING!
HEY!
HELP!
GET ME OUTTA THIS PLACE!
HURRY!
WHO HAS DONE THIS TO YOU?
I DON'T KNOW... WE DON'T KNOW WHO OR WHAT HE IS, BUT HE KIDNAPPED US FROM ALL OVER THE WORLD AND BROUGHT US HERE.
YOU HAVE TO GET US OUT OF HERE BEFORE HE-- *IT*-- COMES BACK.
BE AT PEACE, YOU ARE SAFE NOW. STAND BACK FROM THE DOORS AND--
I KNOW YOU...
...I **KNOW** YOU...
HELP ME.
BOOM BOOM BOOM

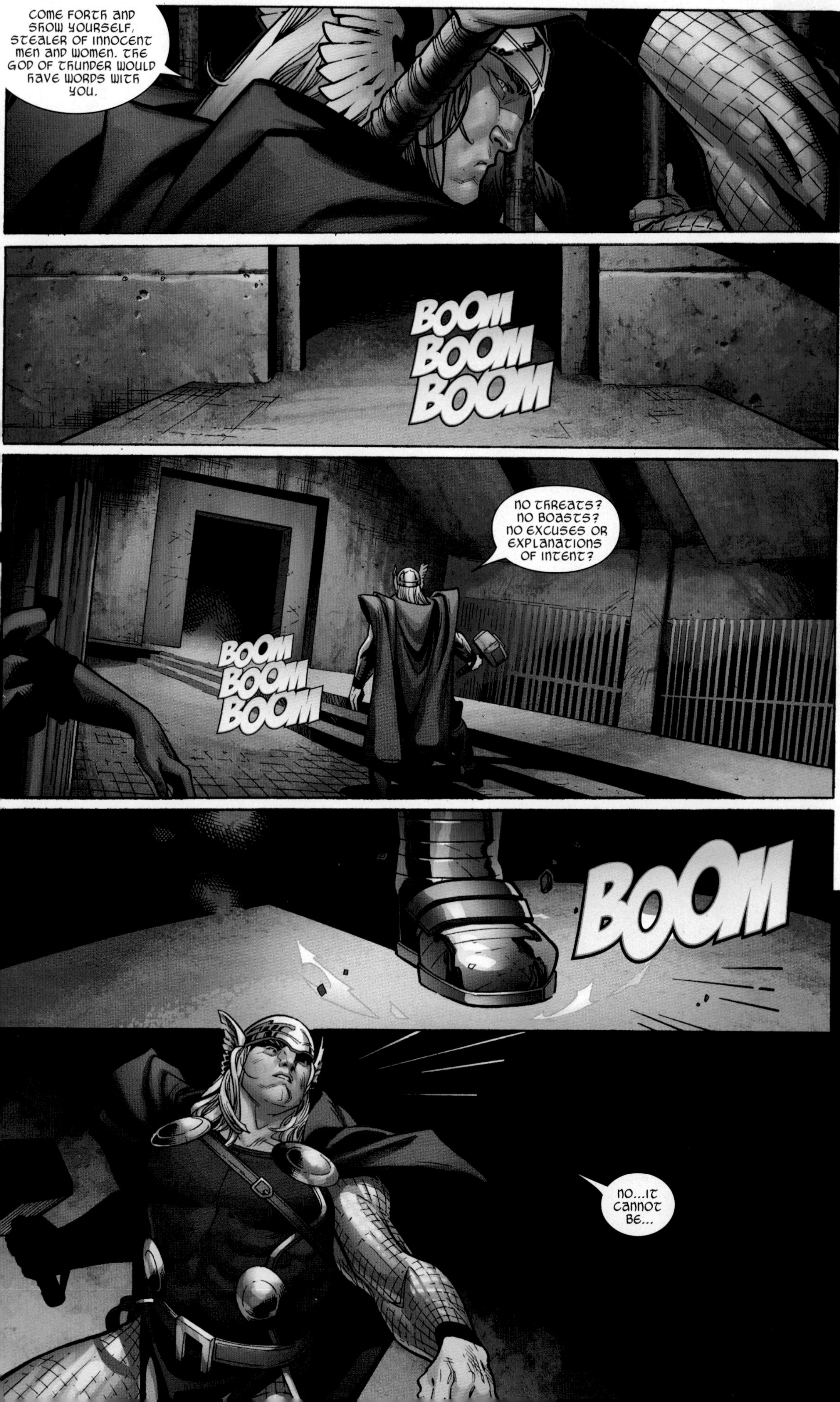
COME FORTH AND SHOW YOURSELF, STEALER OF INNOCENT MEN AND WOMEN. THE GOD OF THUNDER WOULD HAVE WORDS WITH YOU.
BOOM BOOM BOOM
NO THREATS? NO BOASTS? NO EXCUSES OR EXPLANATIONS OF INTENT?
BOOM BOOM BOOM
BOOM
NO...IT CANNOT BE...

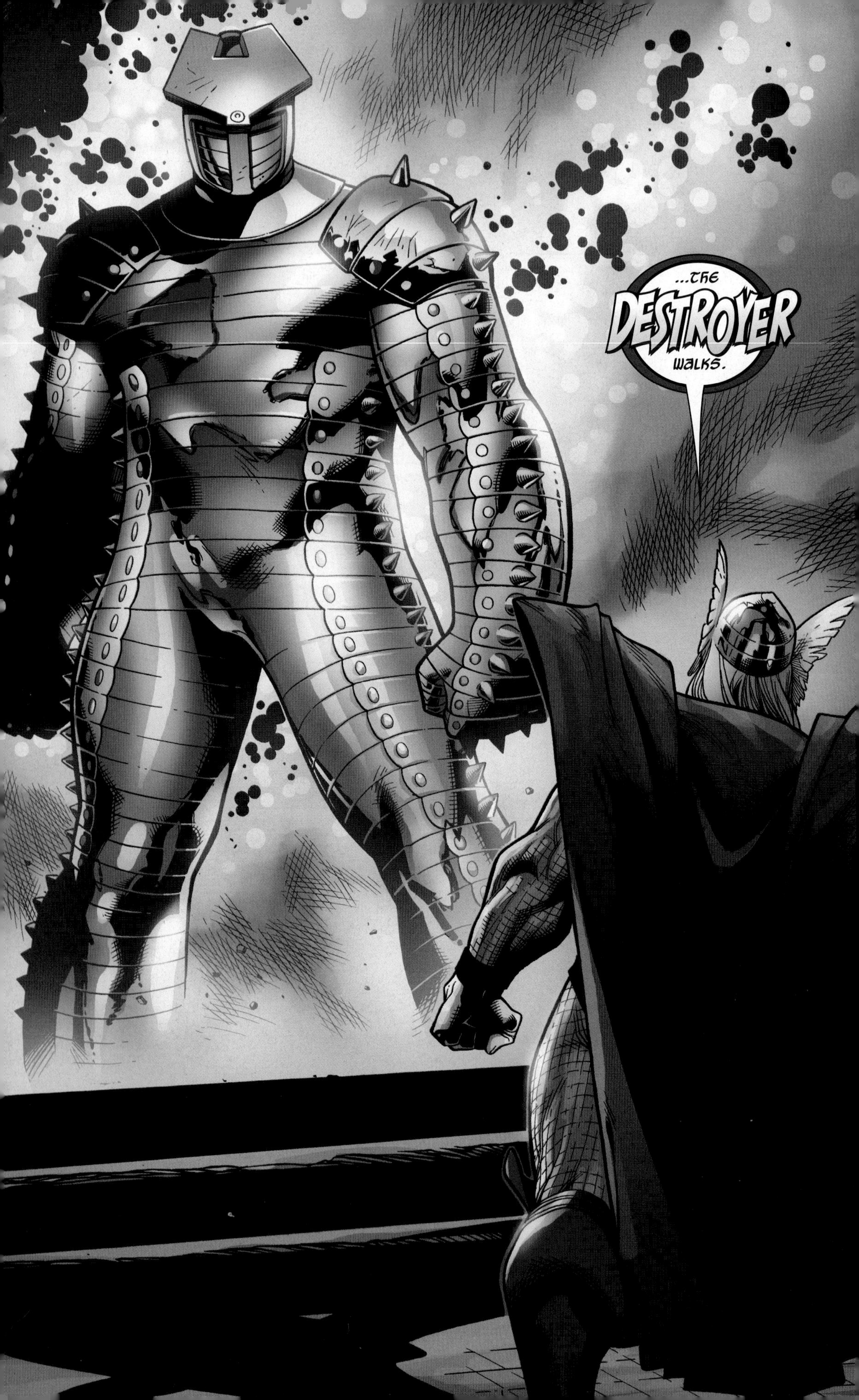
...THE DESTROYER WALKS.

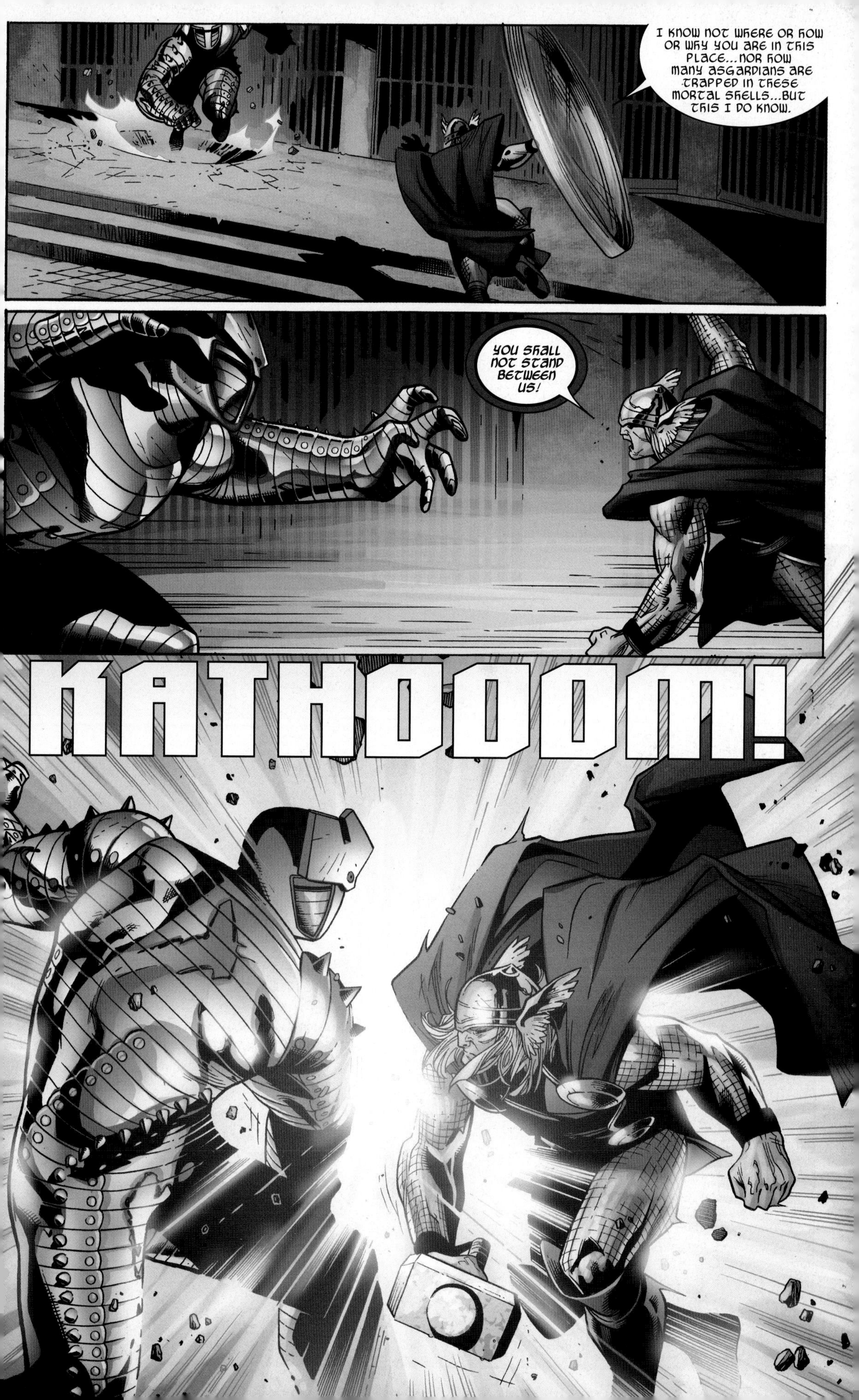
I KNOW NOT WHERE OR HOW OR WHY YOU ARE IN THIS PLACE... NOR HOW MANY ASGARDIANS ARE TRAPPED IN THESE MORTAL SHELLS... BUT THIS I DO KNOW.
YOU SHALL NOT STAND BETWEEN US!
KATHOOOM!

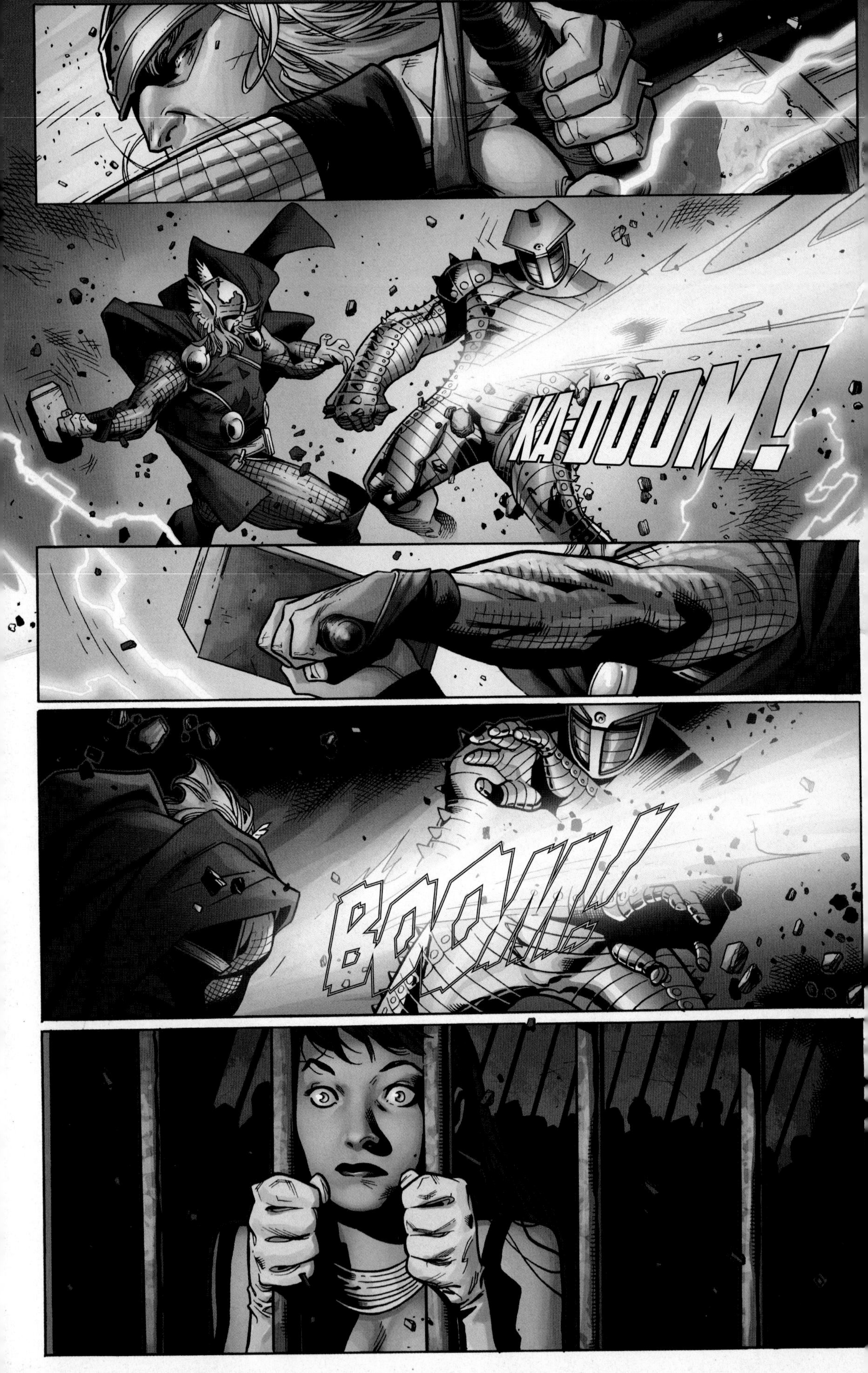
KA-DOOM!
BOOM!

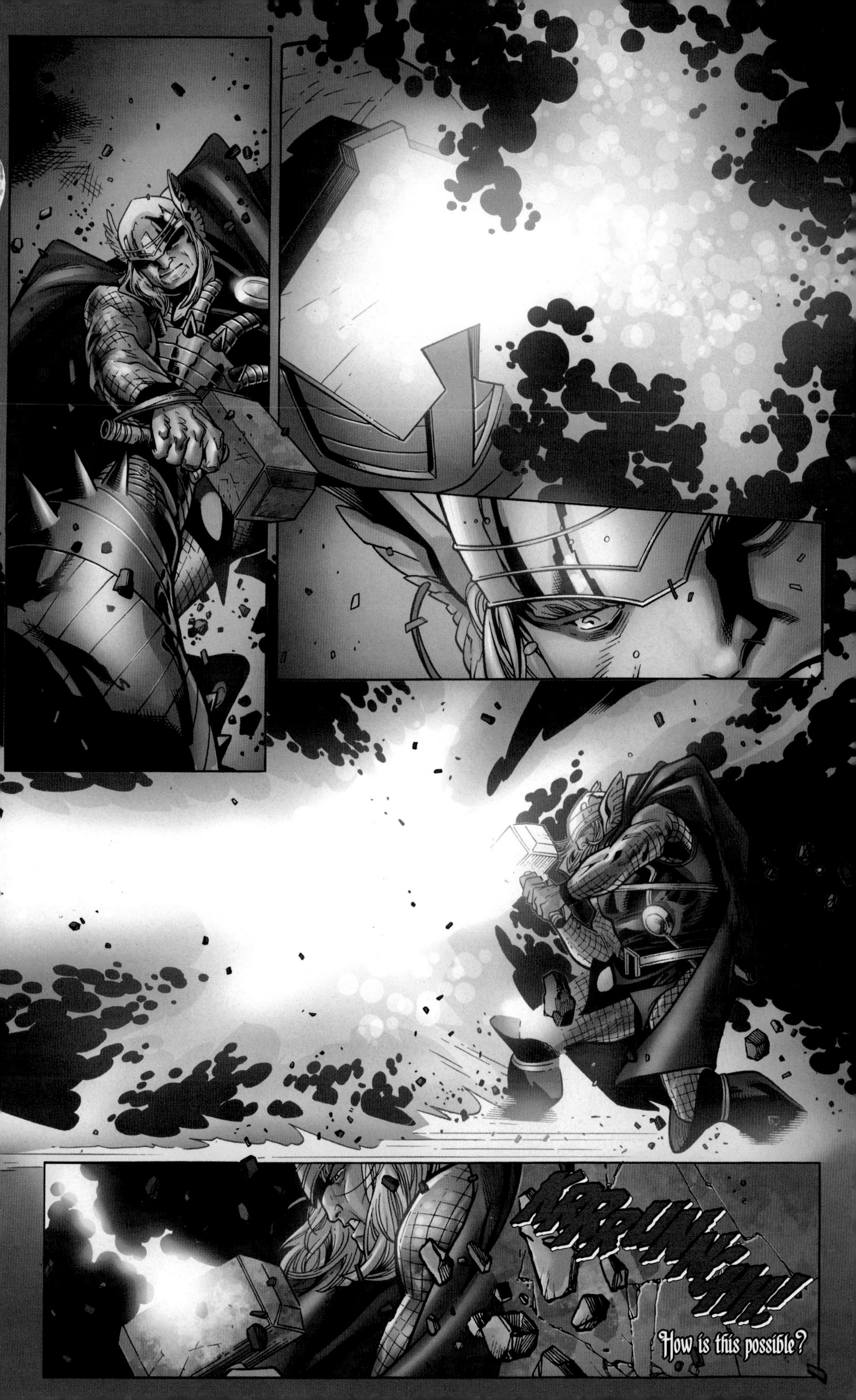
KRRRUNNNNK!
How is this possible?

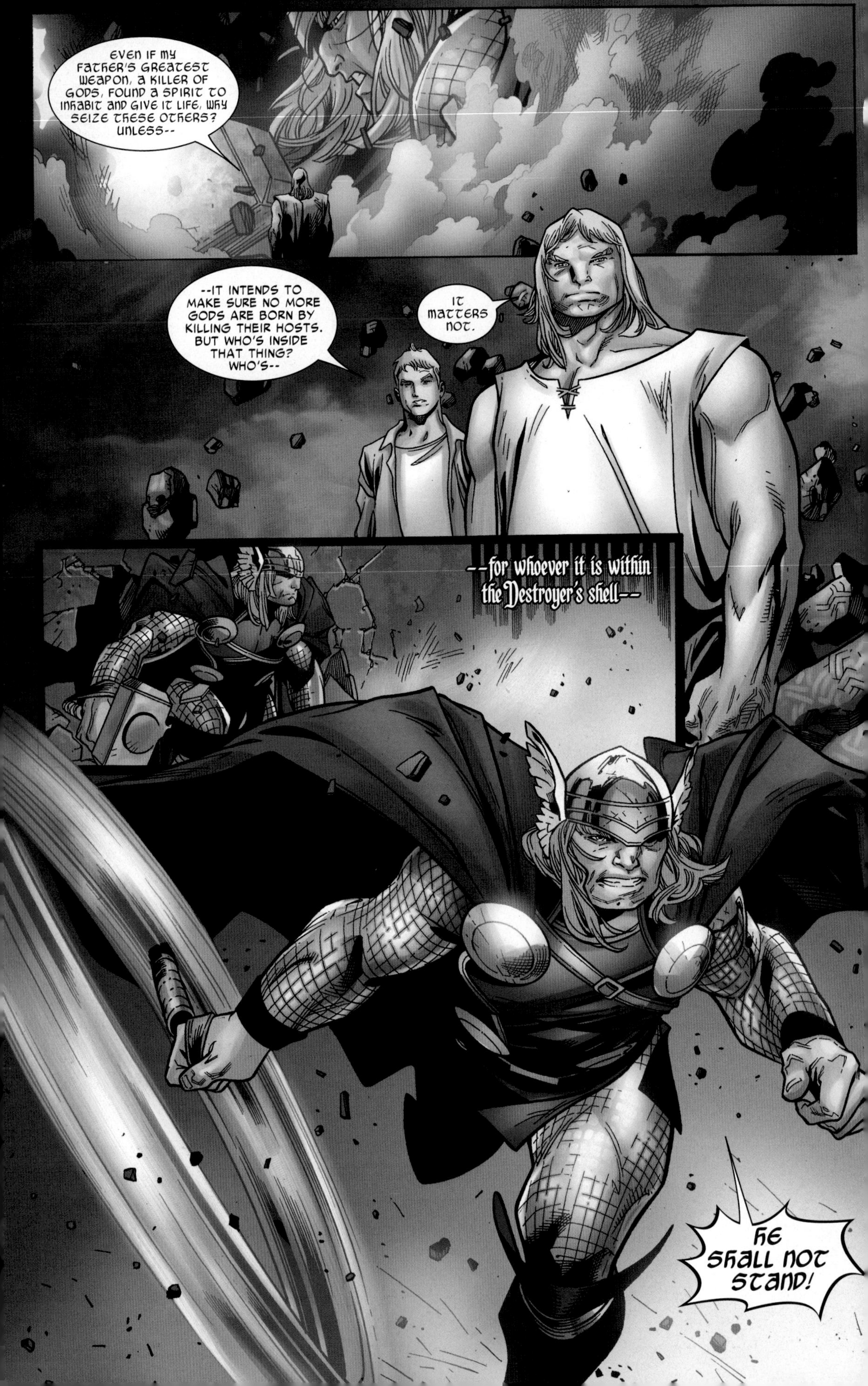
EVEN IF MY FATHER'S GREATEST WEAPON, A KILLER OF GODS, FOUND A SPIRIT TO INHABIT AND GIVE IT LIFE, WHY SEIZE THESE OTHERS? UNLESS--
--IT INTENDS TO MAKE SURE NO MORE GODS ARE BORN BY KILLING THEIR HOSTS. BUT WHO'S INSIDE THAT THING? WHO'S--
IT MATTERS NOT.
--for whoever it is within the Destroyer's shell--
HE SHALL NOT STAND!

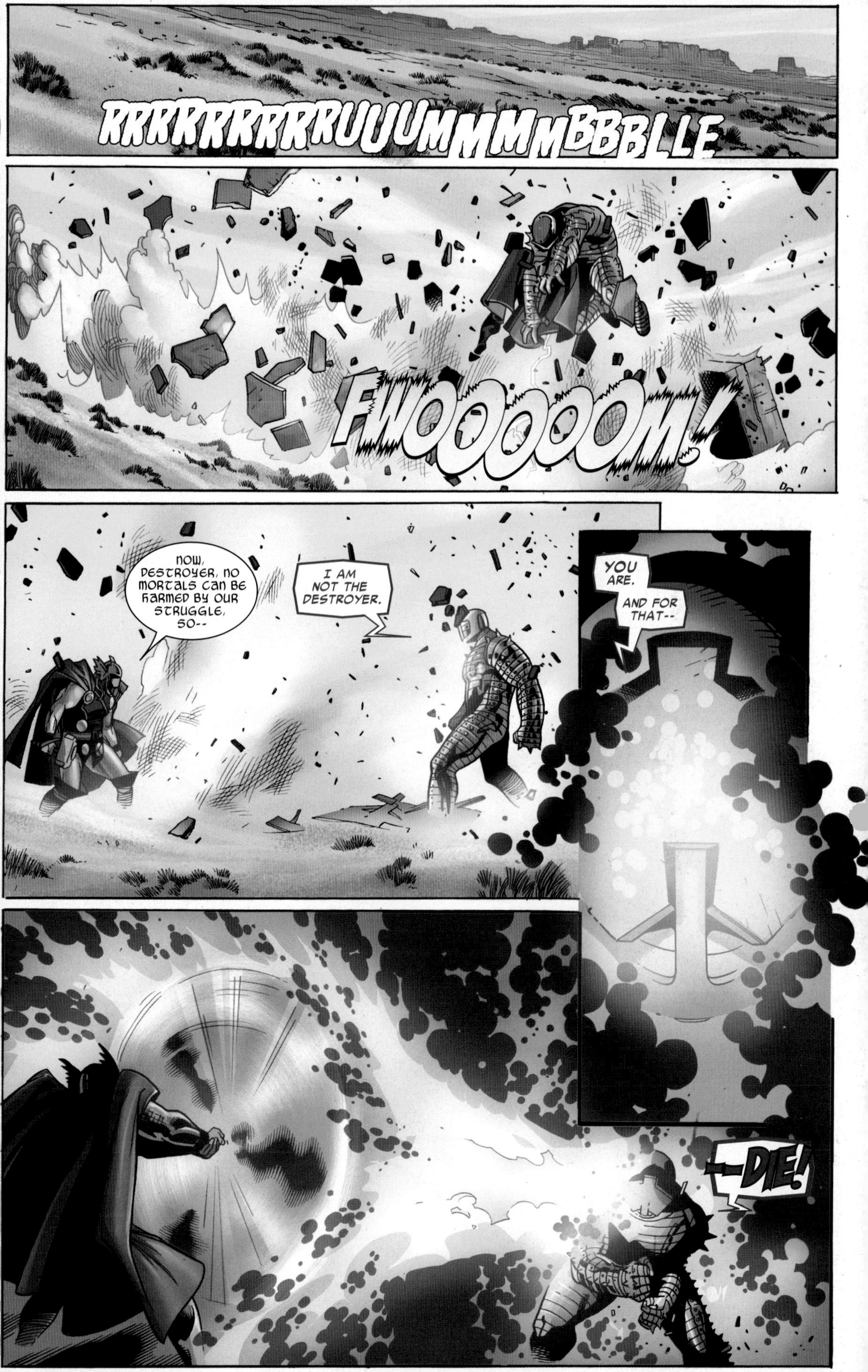
RRRRRRRRRRRUUUUMMMMBBBLLE
FWOOOOOOM!
NOW, DESTROYER, NO MORTALS CAN BE HARMED BY OUR STRUGGLE, SO--
I AM NOT THE DESTROYER.
YOU ARE.
AND FOR THAT--
--DIE!

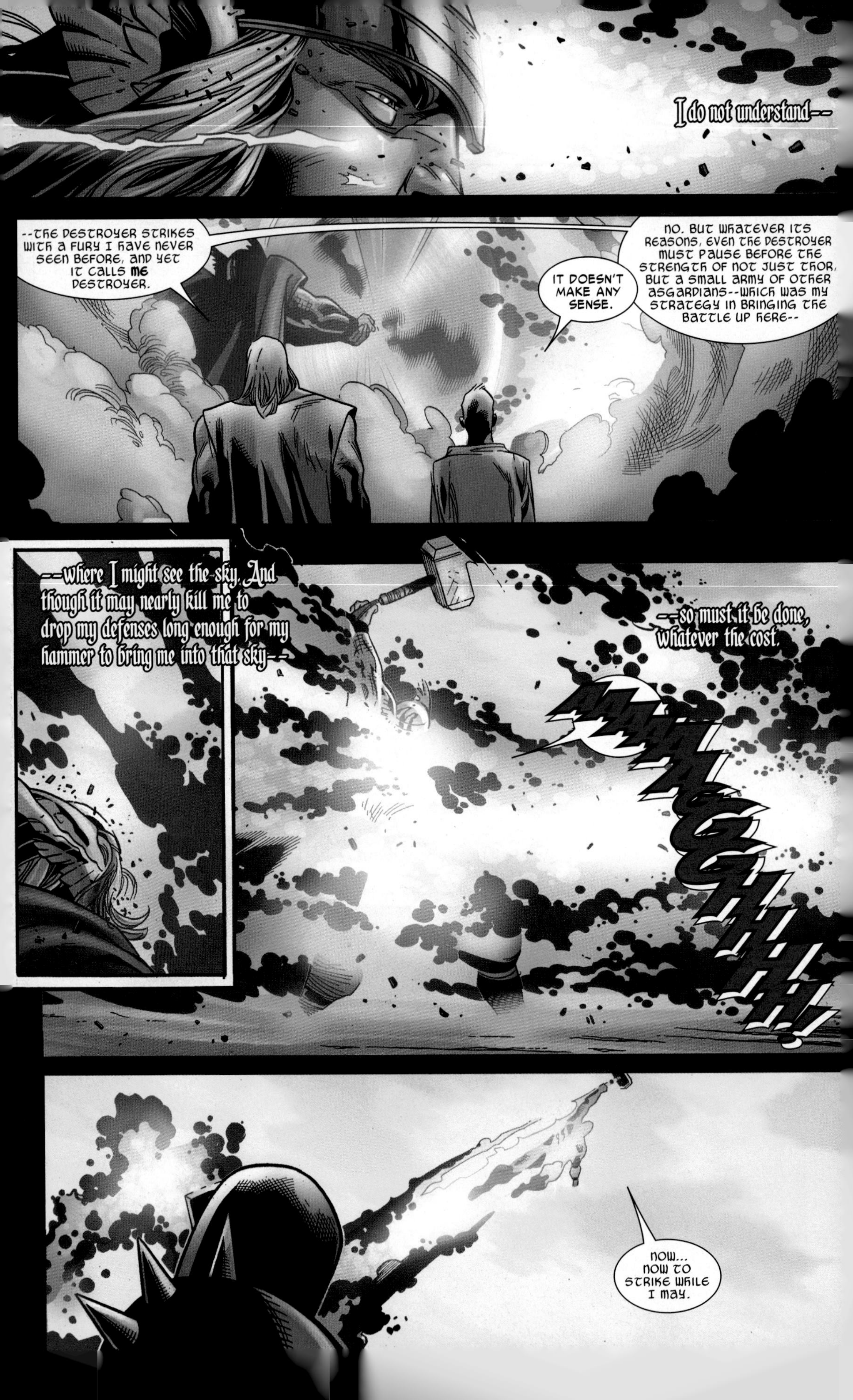
I do not understand--
--THE DESTROYER STRIKES WITH A FURY I HAVE NEVER SEEN BEFORE, AND YET IT CALLS ME DESTROYER.
IT DOESN'T MAKE ANY SENSE.
NO. BUT WHATEVER ITS REASONS, EVEN THE DESTROYER MUST PAUSE BEFORE THE STRENGTH OF NOT JUST THOR, BUT A SMALL ARMY OF OTHER ASGARDIANS--WHICH WAS MY STRATEGY IN BRINGING THE BATTLE UP HERE--
--where I might see the sky. And though it may nearly kill me to drop my defenses long enough for my hammer to bring me into that sky--
--so must it be done, whatever the cost.
NOW... NOW TO STRIKE WHILE I MAY.

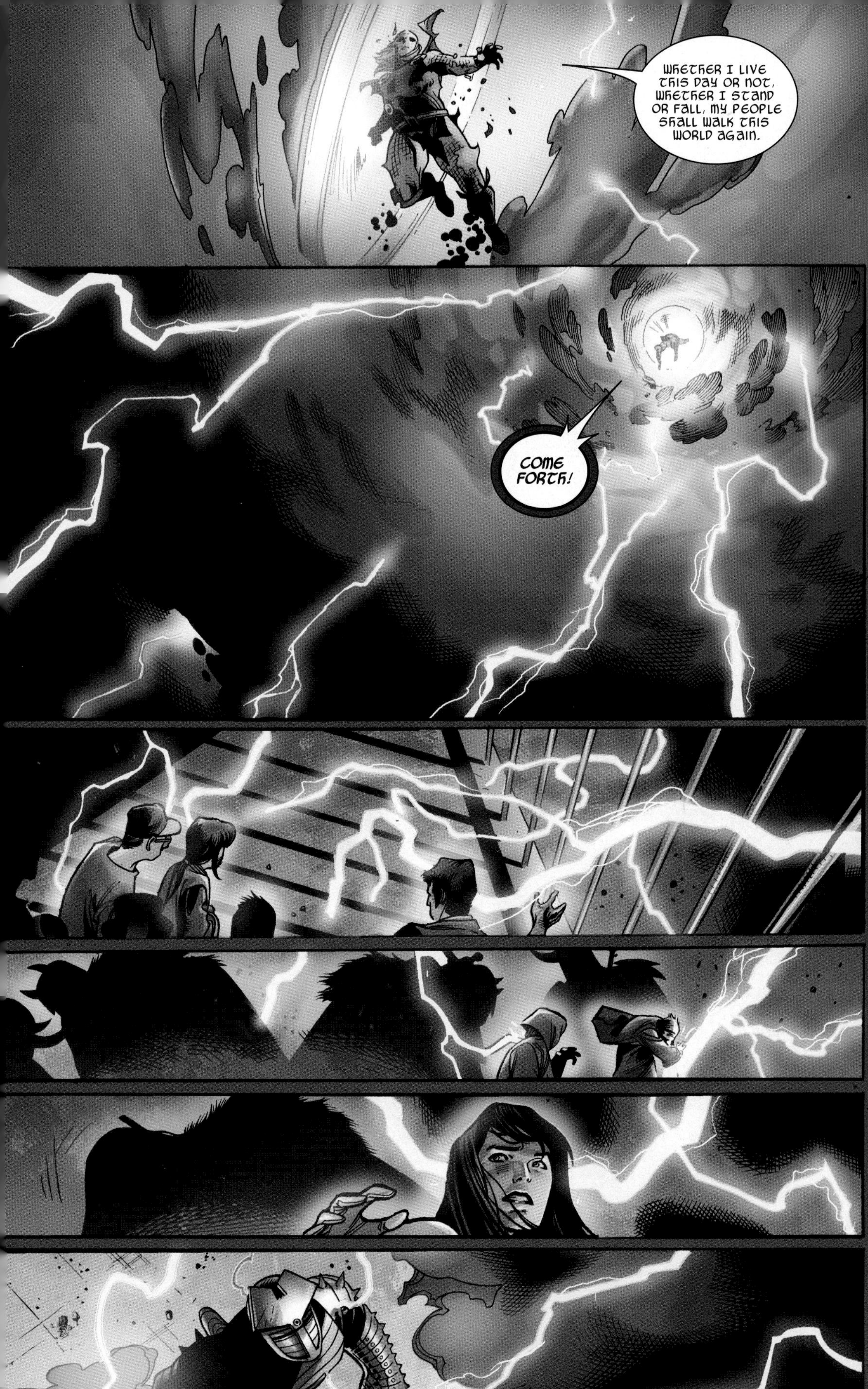
WHETHER I LIVE THIS DAY OR NOT, WHETHER I STAND OR FALL, MY PEOPLE SHALL WALK THIS WORLD AGAIN.
COME FORTH!

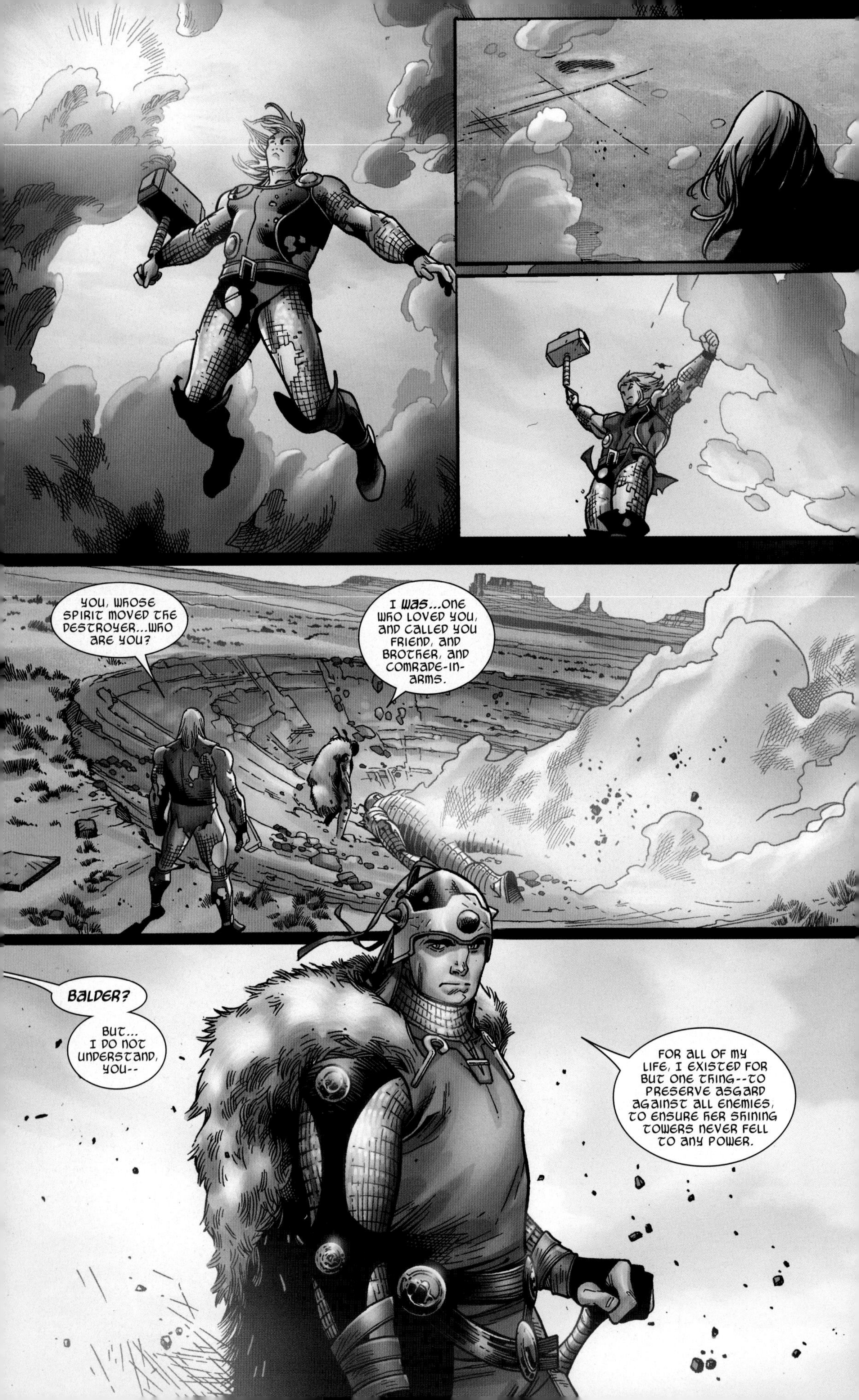
YOU, WHOSE SPIRIT MOVED THE DESTROYER...WHO ARE YOU?
I WAS...ONE WHO LOVED YOU, AND CALLED YOU FRIEND, AND BROTHER, AND COMRADE-IN-ARMS.
BALDER?
BUT... I DO NOT UNDERSTAND, YOU--
FOR ALL OF MY LIFE, I EXISTED FOR BUT ONE THING--TO PRESERVE ASGARD AGAINST ALL ENEMIES, TO ENSURE HER SHINING TOWERS NEVER FELL TO ANY POWER.

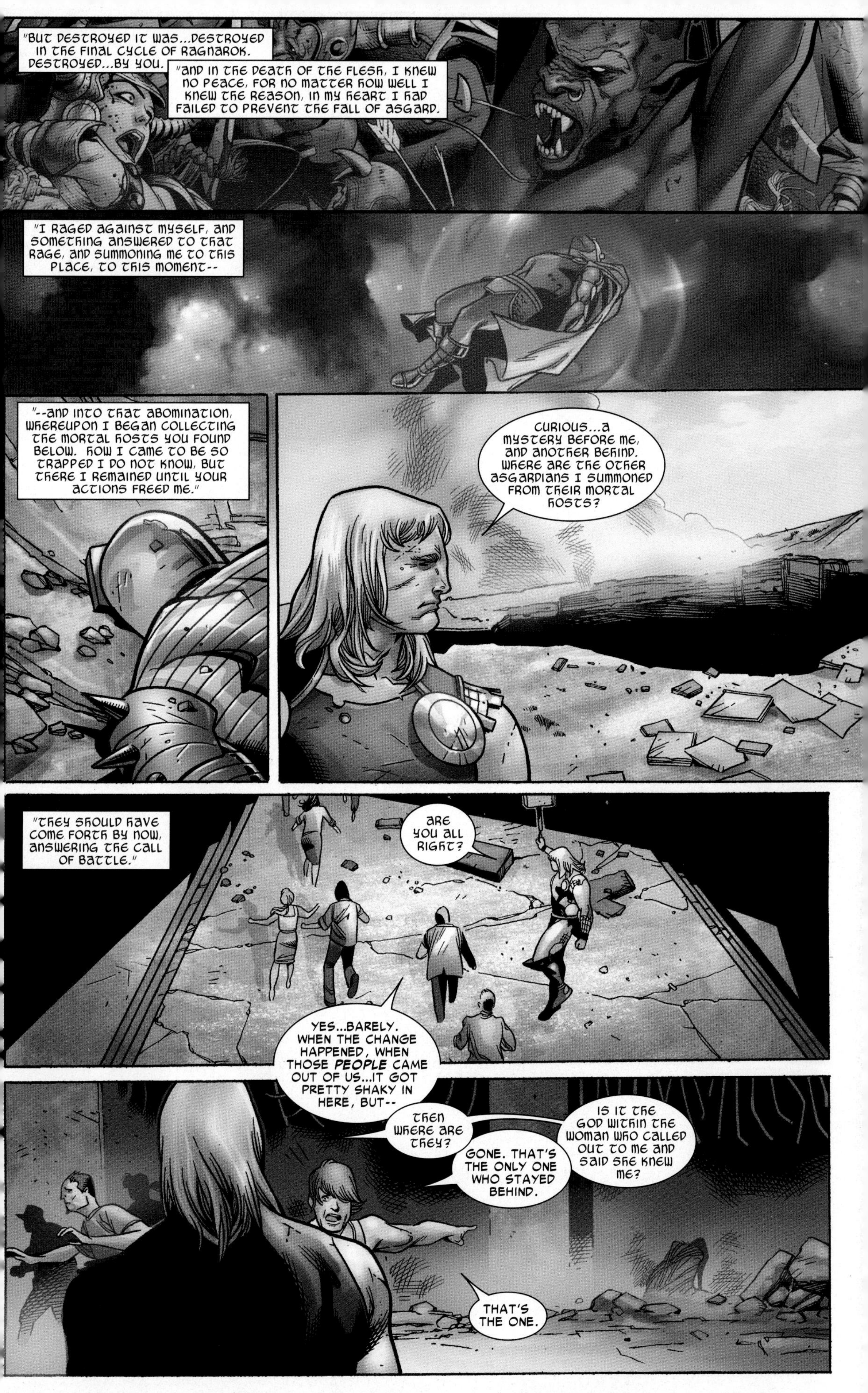
"BUT DESTROYED IT WAS...DESTROYED IN THE FINAL CYCLE OF RAGNAROK. DESTROYED...BY YOU.
"AND IN THE DEATH OF THE FLESH, I KNEW NO PEACE, FOR NO MATTER HOW WELL I KNEW THE REASON, IN MY HEART I HAD FAILED TO PREVENT THE FALL OF ASGARD.
"I RAGED AGAINST MYSELF, AND SOMETHING ANSWERED TO THAT RAGE, AND SUMMONING ME TO THIS PLACE, TO THIS MOMENT--
"--AND INTO THAT ABOMINATION, WHEREUPON I BEGAN COLLECTING THE MORTAL HOSTS YOU FOUND BELOW. HOW I CAME TO BE SO TRAPPED I DO NOT KNOW, BUT THERE I REMAINED UNTIL YOUR ACTIONS FREED ME."
CURIOUS...A MYSTERY BEFORE ME, AND ANOTHER BEHIND. WHERE ARE THE OTHER ASGARDIANS I SUMMONED FROM THEIR MORTAL HOSTS?
"THEY SHOULD HAVE COME FORTH BY NOW, ANSWERING THE CALL OF BATTLE."
ARE YOU ALL RIGHT?
YES...BARELY. WHEN THE CHANGE HAPPENED, WHEN THOSE PEOPLE CAME OUT OF US...IT GOT PRETTY SHAKY IN HERE, BUT--
THEN WHERE ARE THEY?
GONE. THAT'S THE ONLY ONE WHO STAYED BEHIND.
IS IT THE GOD WITHIN THE WOMAN WHO CALLED OUT TO ME AND SAID SHE KNEW ME?
THAT'S THE ONE.

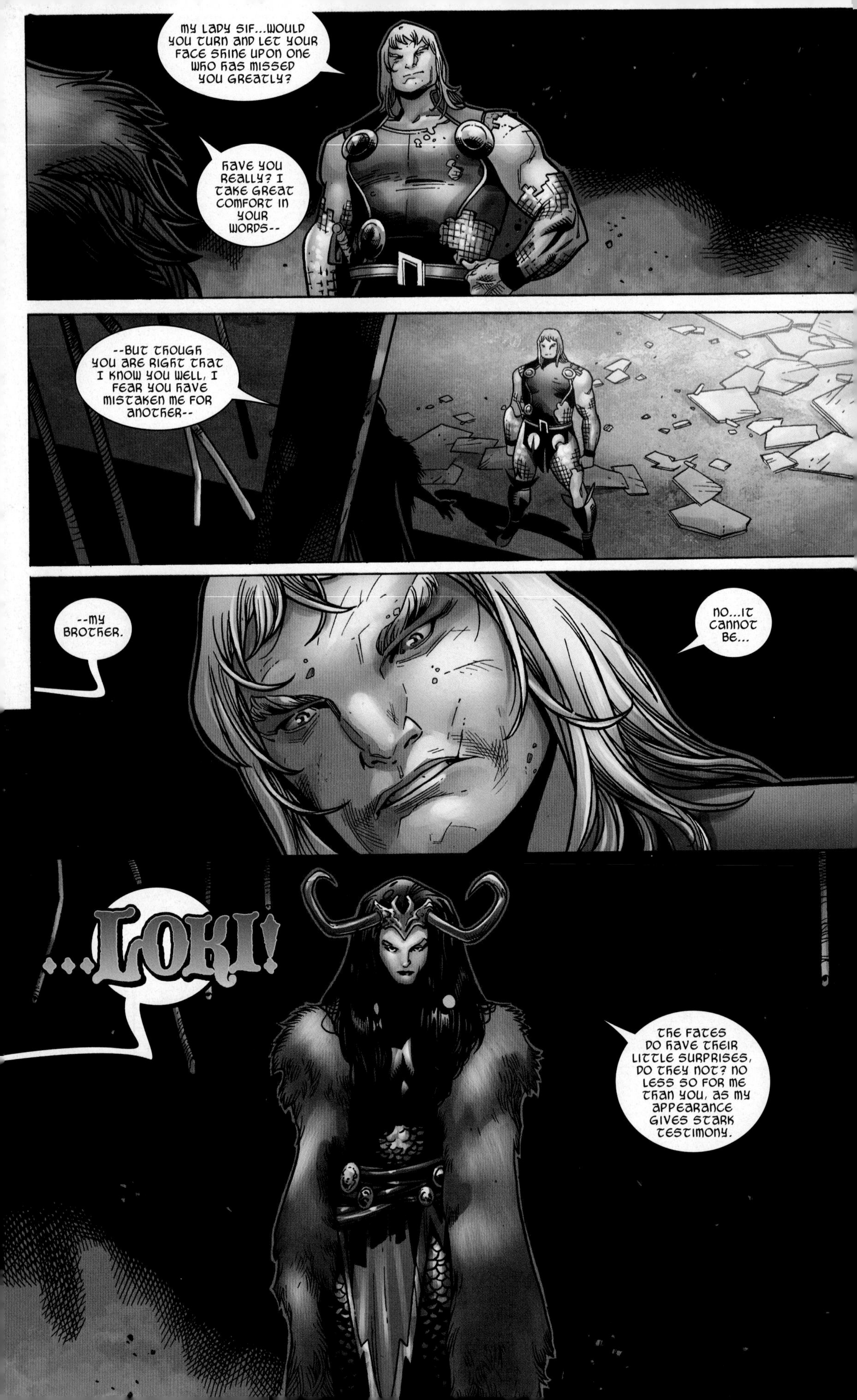
MY LADY SIF...WOULD YOU TURN AND LET YOUR FACE SHINE UPON ONE WHO HAS MISSED YOU GREATLY?
HAVE YOU REALLY? I TAKE GREAT COMFORT IN YOUR WORDS--
--BUT THOUGH YOU ARE RIGHT THAT I KNOW YOU WELL, I FEAR YOU HAVE MISTAKEN ME FOR ANOTHER--
--MY BROTHER.
NO...IT CANNOT BE...
...LOKI!
THE FATES DO HAVE THEIR LITTLE SURPRISES, DO THEY NOT? NO LESS SO FOR ME THAN YOU, AS MY APPEARANCE GIVES STARK TESTIMONY.

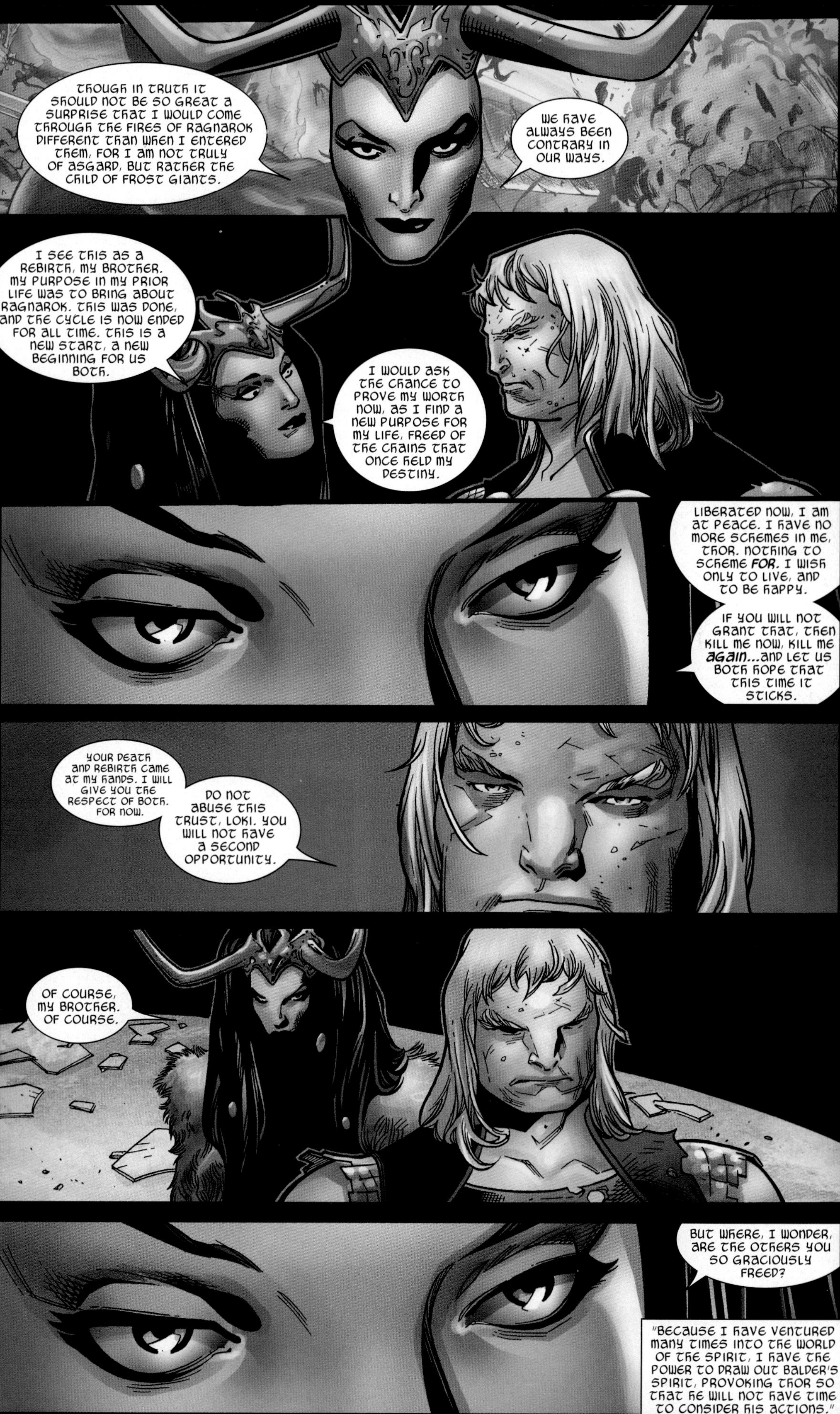
THOUGH IN TRUTH IT SHOULD NOT BE SO GREAT A SURPRISE THAT I WOULD COME THROUGH THE FIRES OF RAGNAROK DIFFERENT THAN WHEN I ENTERED THEM, FOR I AM NOT TRULY OF ASGARD, BUT RATHER THE CHILD OF FROST GIANTS.
WE HAVE ALWAYS BEEN CONTRARY IN OUR WAYS.
I SEE THIS AS A REBIRTH, MY BROTHER. MY PURPOSE IN MY PRIOR LIFE WAS TO BRING ABOUT RAGNAROK. THIS WAS DONE, AND THE CYCLE IS NOW ENDED FOR ALL TIME. THIS IS A NEW START, A NEW BEGINNING FOR US BOTH.
I WOULD ASK THE CHANCE TO PROVE MY WORTH NOW, AS I FIND A NEW PURPOSE FOR MY LIFE, FREED OF THE CHAINS THAT ONCE HELD MY DESTINY.
LIBERATED NOW, I AM AT PEACE. I HAVE NO MORE SCHEMES IN ME, THOR. NOTHING TO SCHEME **FOR**. I WISH ONLY TO LIVE, AND TO BE HAPPY.
IF YOU WILL NOT GRANT THAT, THEN KILL ME NOW, KILL ME **AGAIN**...AND LET US BOTH HOPE THAT THIS TIME IT STICKS.
YOUR DEATH AND REBIRTH CAME AT MY HANDS. I WILL GIVE YOU THE RESPECT OF BOTH. FOR NOW.
DO NOT ABUSE THIS TRUST, LOKI. YOU WILL NOT HAVE A SECOND OPPORTUNITY.
OF COURSE, MY BROTHER. OF COURSE.
BUT WHERE, I WONDER, ARE THE OTHERS YOU SO GRACIOUSLY FREED?
"BECAUSE I HAVE VENTURED MANY TIMES INTO THE WORLD OF THE SPIRIT, I HAVE THE POWER TO DRAW OUT BALDER'S SPIRIT, PROVOKING THOR SO THAT HE WILL NOT HAVE TIME TO CONSIDER HIS ACTIONS."

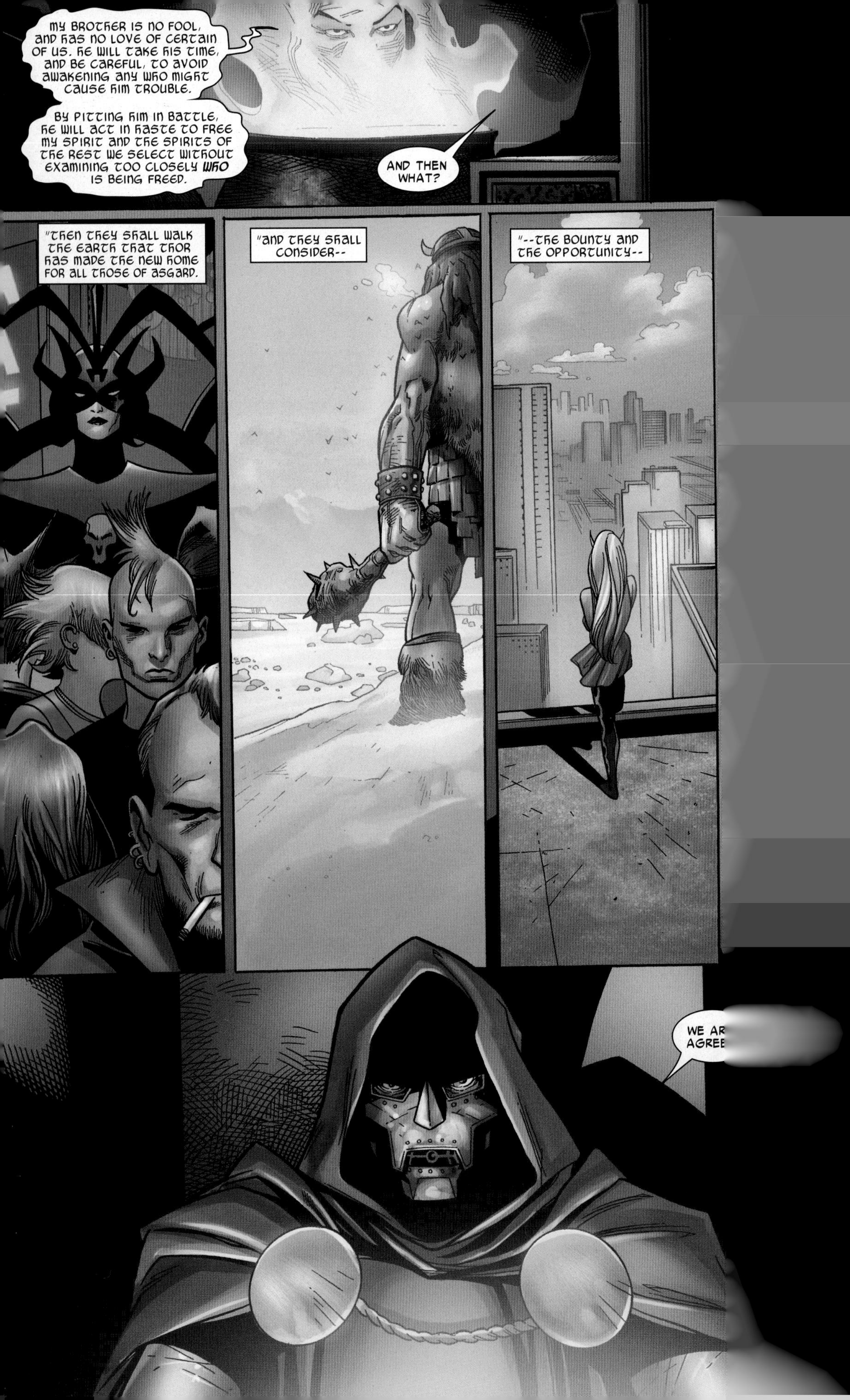
MY BROTHER IS NO FOOL, AND HAS NO LOVE OF CERTAIN OF US. HE WILL TAKE HIS TIME, AND BE CAREFUL, TO AVOID AWAKENING ANY WHO MIGHT CAUSE HIM TROUBLE.
BY PITTING HIM IN BATTLE, HE WILL ACT IN HASTE TO FREE MY SPIRIT AND THE SPIRITS OF THE REST WE SELECT WITHOUT EXAMINING TOO CLOSELY WHO IS BEING FREED.
AND THEN WHAT?
"THEN THEY SHALL WALK THE EARTH THAT THOR HAS MADE THE NEW HOME FOR ALL THOSE OF ASGARD.
"AND THEY SHALL CONSIDER--
"--THE BOUNTY AND THE OPPORTUNITY--
WE AR
AGREE

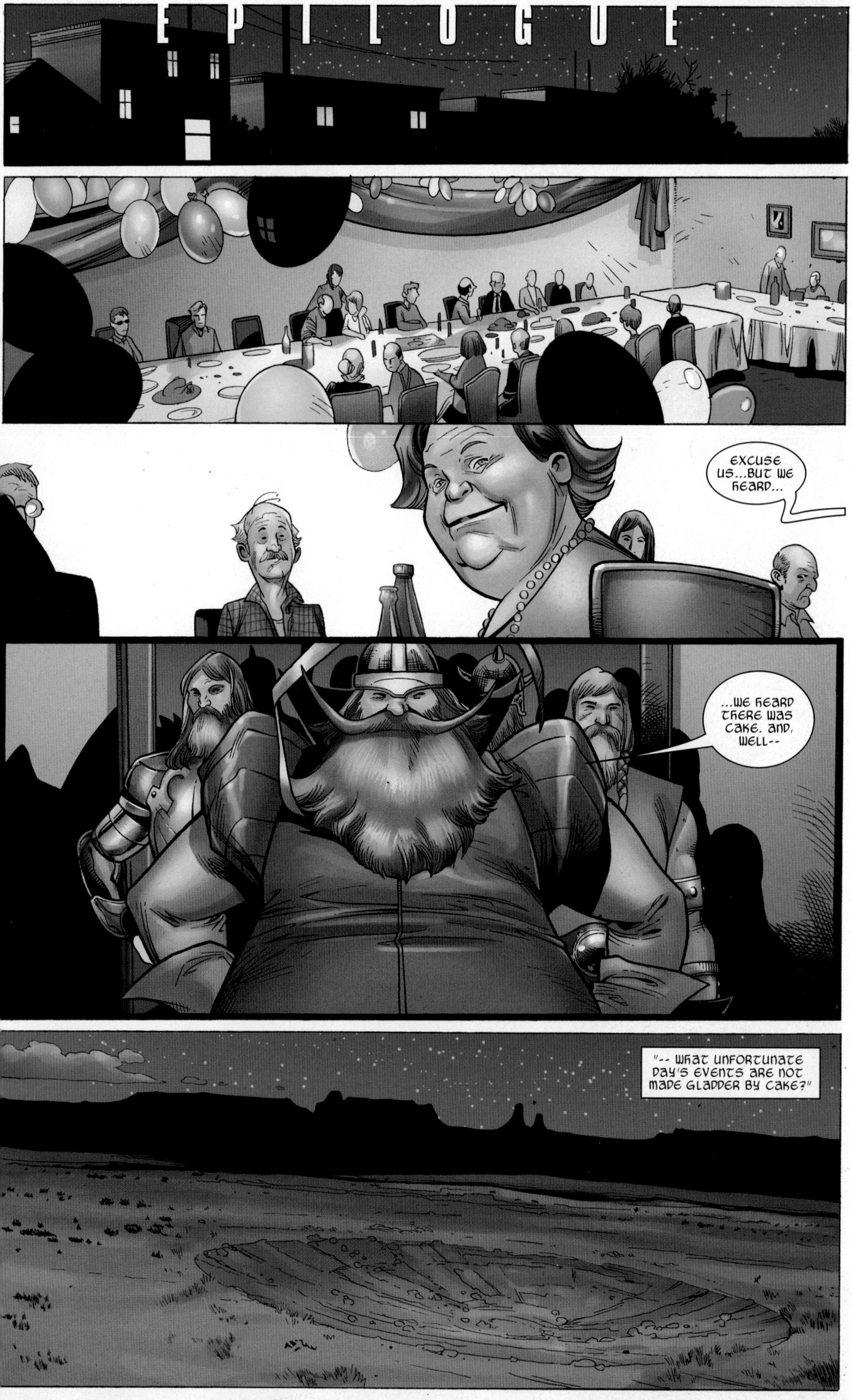
EPILOGUE
EXCUSE US...BUT WE HEARD...
...WE HEARD THERE WAS CAKE. AND, WELL--
"-- WHAT UNFORTUNATE DAY'S EVENTS ARE NOT MADE GLADDER BY CAKE?"

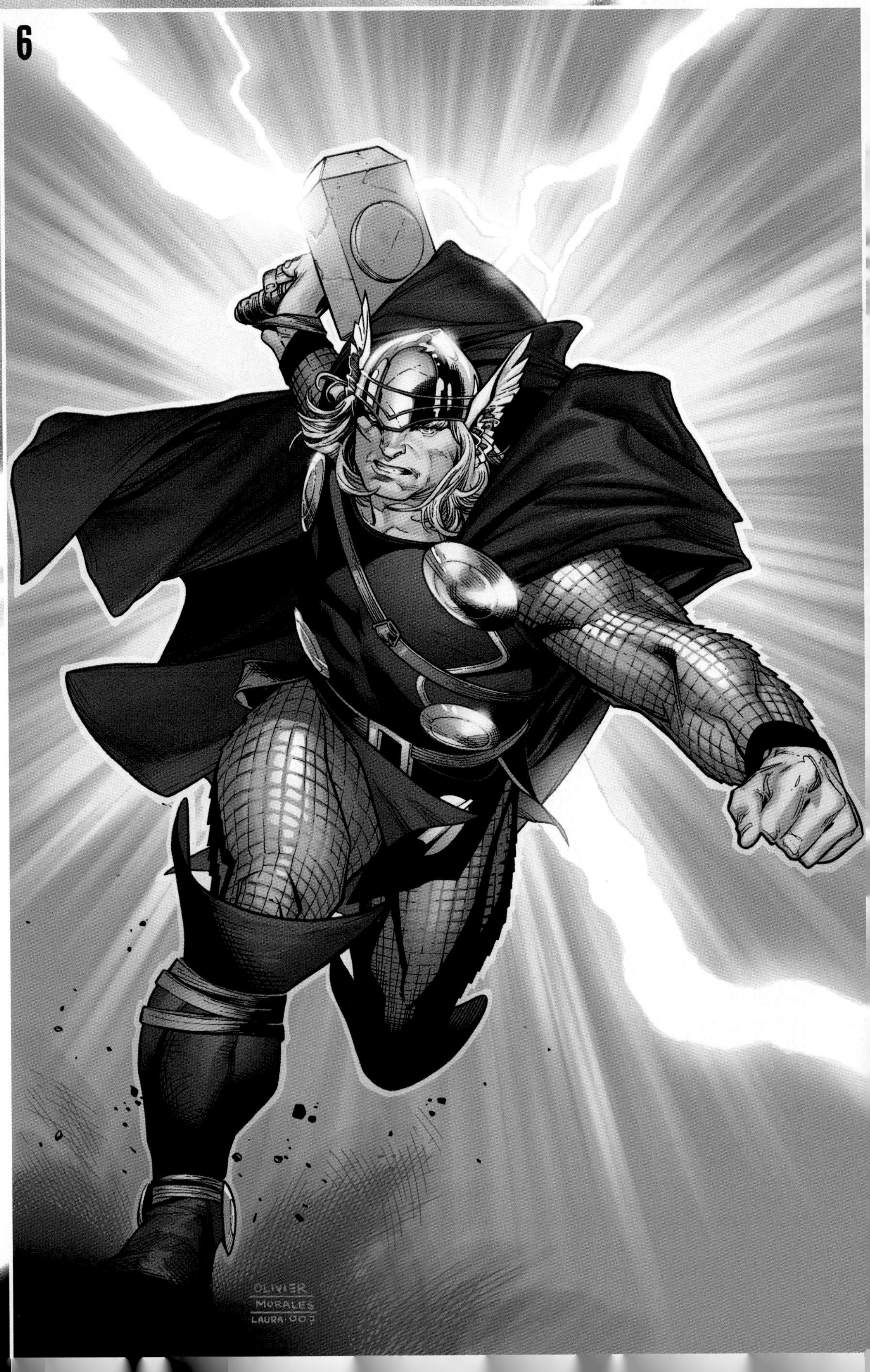
6
OLIVIER
MORALES
LAURA·007

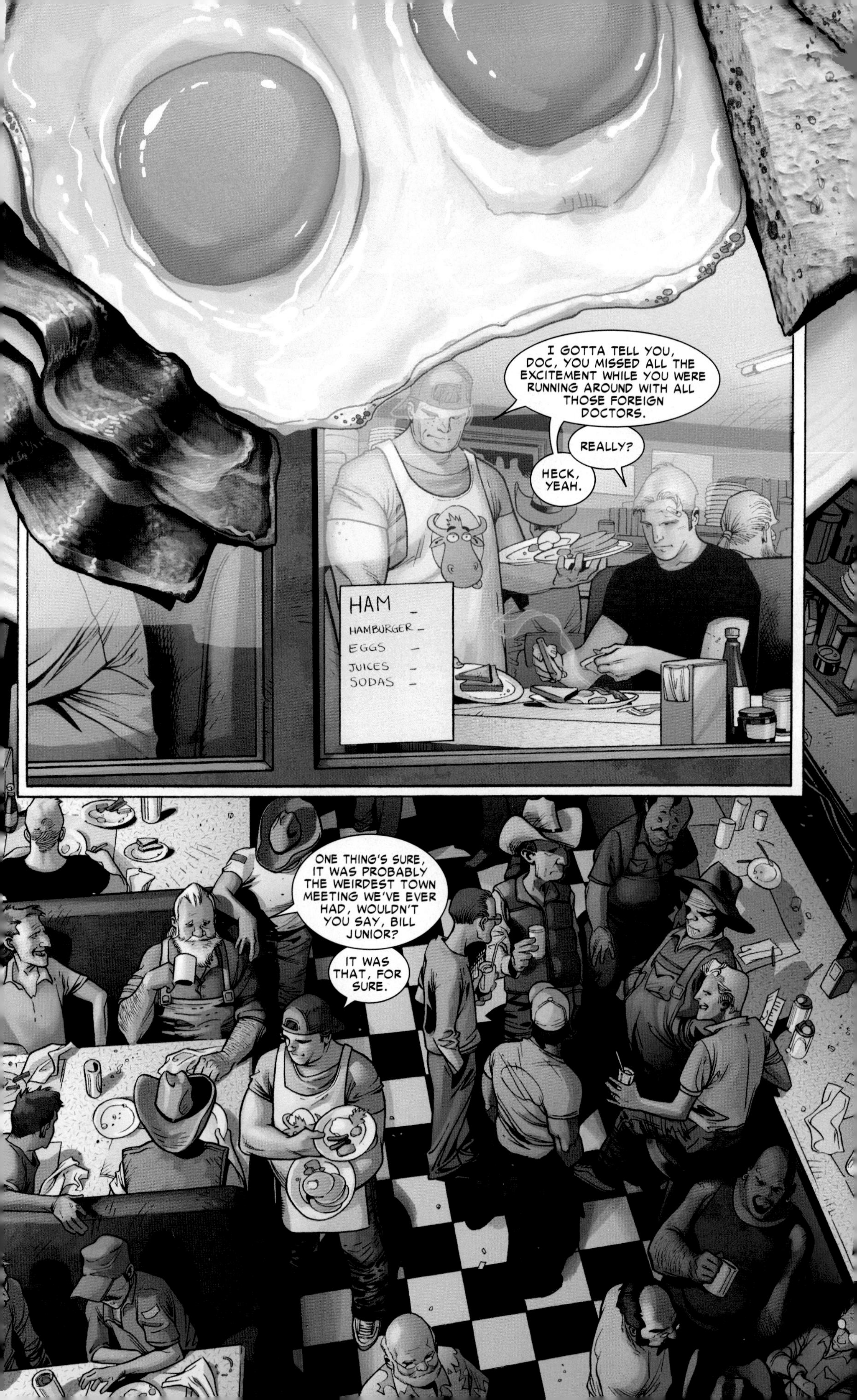
I GOTTA TELL YOU, DOC, YOU MISSED ALL THE EXCITEMENT WHILE YOU WERE RUNNING AROUND WITH ALL THOSE FOREIGN DOCTORS.
REALLY?
HECK, YEAH.
HAM
HAMBURGER
EGGS
JUICES
SODAS
ONE THING'S SURE, IT WAS PROBABLY THE WEIRDEST TOWN MEETING WE'VE EVER HAD, WOULDN'T YOU SAY, BILL JUNIOR?
IT WAS THAT, FOR SURE.

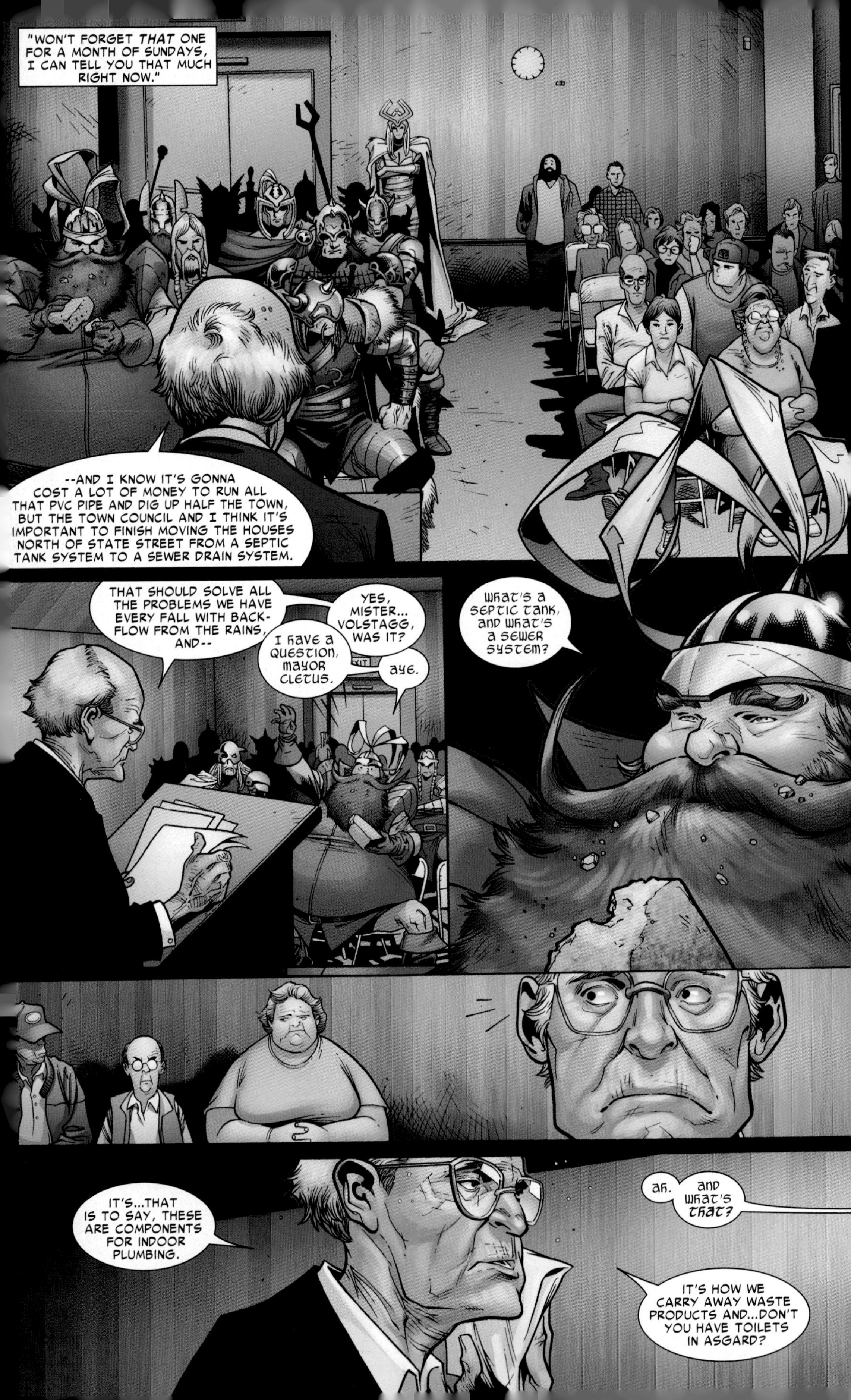
"WON'T FORGET THAT ONE FOR A MONTH OF SUNDAYS, I CAN TELL YOU THAT MUCH RIGHT NOW."
--AND I KNOW IT'S GONNA COST A LOT OF MONEY TO RUN ALL THAT PVC PIPE AND DIG UP HALF THE TOWN, BUT THE TOWN COUNCIL AND I THINK IT'S IMPORTANT TO FINISH MOVING THE HOUSES NORTH OF STATE STREET FROM A SEPTIC TANK SYSTEM TO A SEWER DRAIN SYSTEM.
THAT SHOULD SOLVE ALL THE PROBLEMS WE HAVE EVERY FALL WITH BACK-FLOW FROM THE RAINS, AND--
I HAVE A QUESTION, MAYOR CLETUS.
YES, MISTER... VOLSTAGG, WAS IT?
AYE.
WHAT'S A SEPTIC TANK, AND WHAT'S A SEWER SYSTEM?
IT'S...THAT IS TO SAY, THESE ARE COMPONENTS FOR INDOOR PLUMBING.
AH. AND WHAT'S THAT?
IT'S HOW WE CARRY AWAY WASTE PRODUCTS AND...DON'T YOU HAVE TOILETS IN ASGARD?

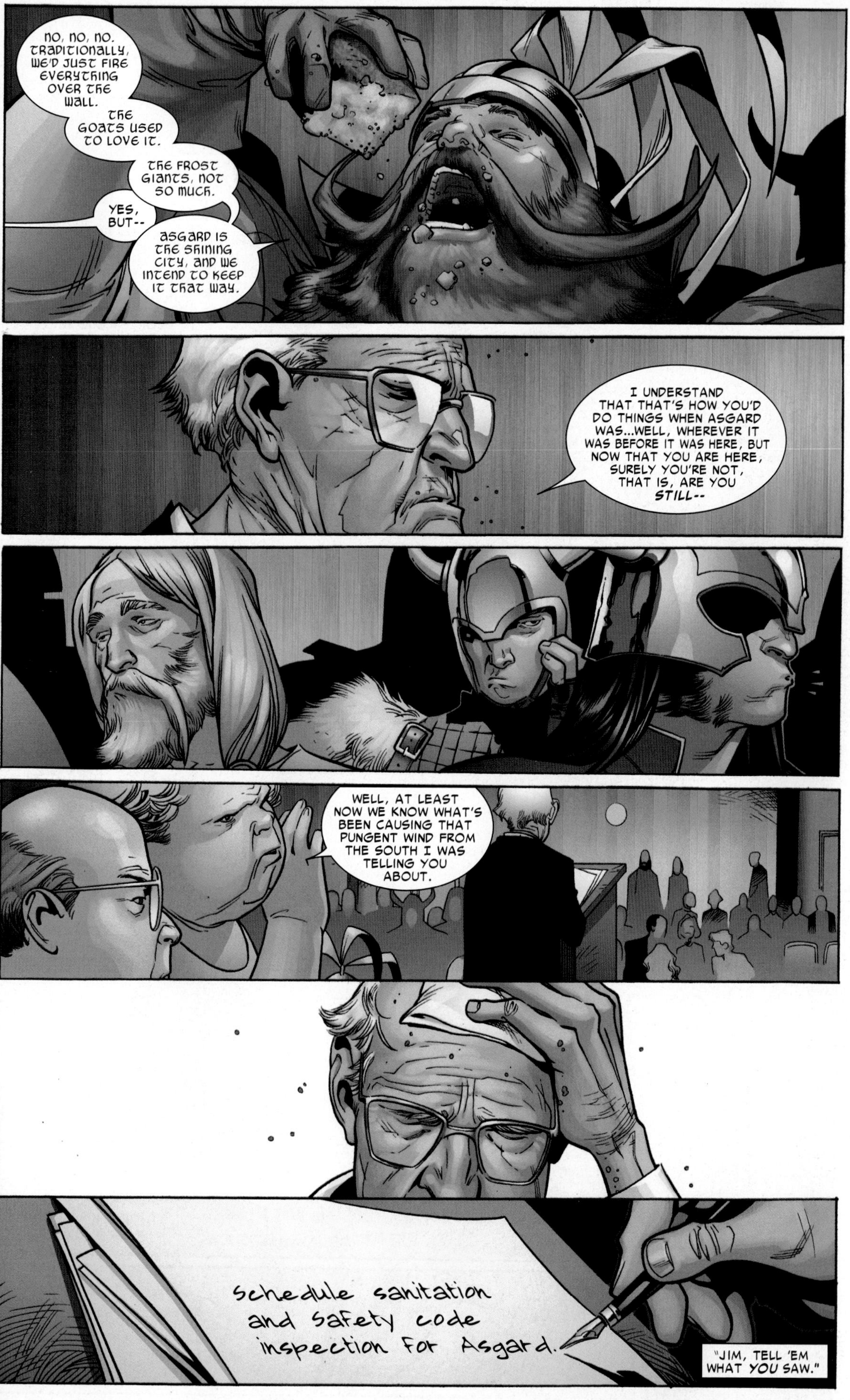
NO, NO, NO. TRADITIONALLY, WE'D JUST FIRE EVERYTHING OVER THE WALL.
THE GOATS USED TO LOVE IT.
THE FROST GIANTS, NOT SO MUCH.
YES, BUT--
ASGARD IS THE SHINING CITY, AND WE INTEND TO KEEP IT THAT WAY.
I UNDERSTAND THAT THAT'S HOW YOU'D DO THINGS WHEN ASGARD WAS...WELL, WHEREVER IT WAS BEFORE IT WAS HERE, BUT NOW THAT YOU ARE HERE, SURELY YOU'RE NOT, THAT IS, ARE YOU STILL--
WELL, AT LEAST NOW WE KNOW WHAT'S BEEN CAUSING THAT PUNGENT WIND FROM THE SOUTH I WAS TELLING YOU ABOUT.
Schedule sanitation and safety code inspection for Asgard.
"JIM, TELL 'EM WHAT YOU SAW."

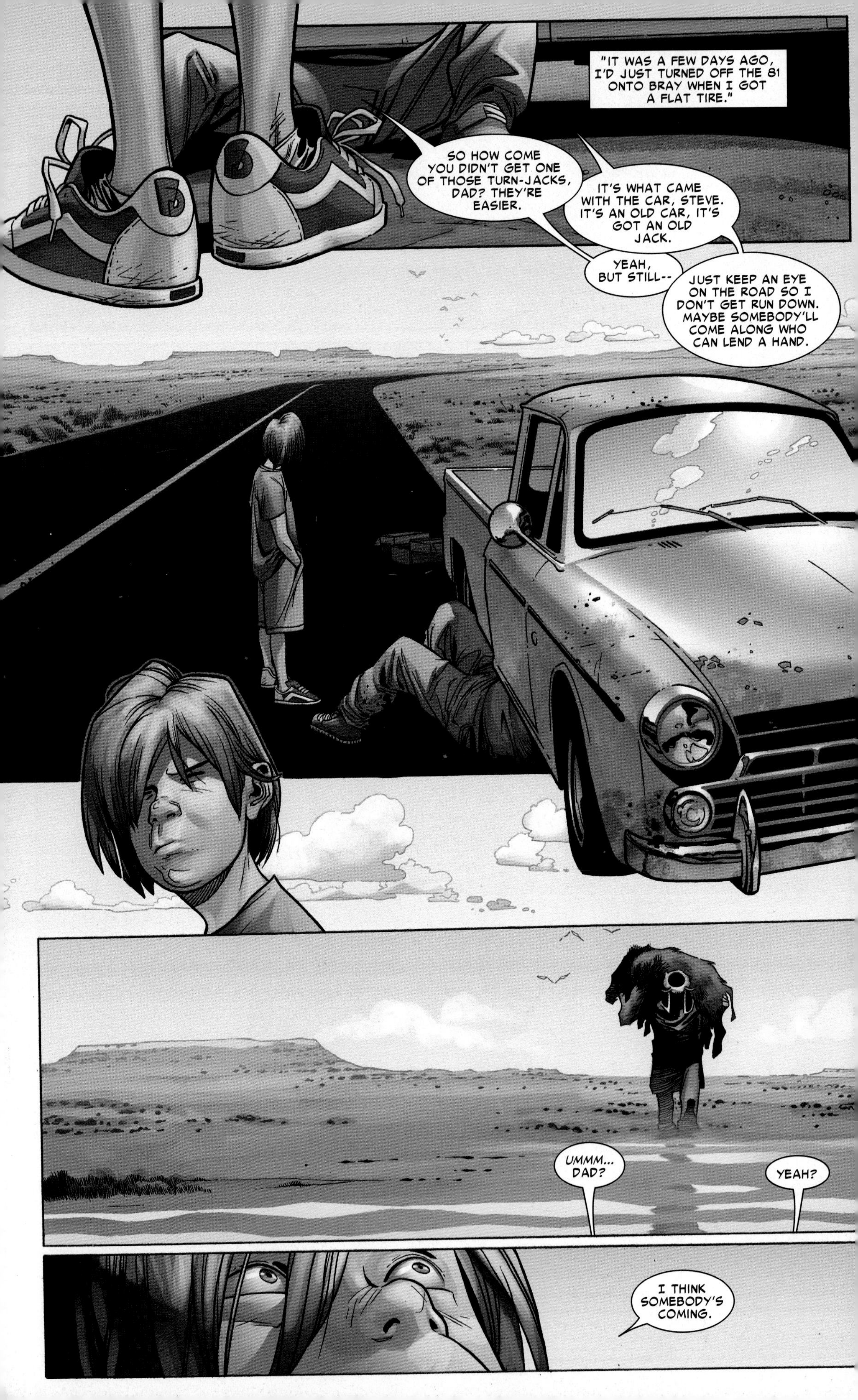
"IT WAS A FEW DAYS AGO, I'D JUST TURNED OFF THE 81 ONTO BRAY WHEN I GOT A FLAT TIRE."
SO HOW COME YOU DIDN'T GET ONE OF THOSE TURN-JACKS, DAD? THEY'RE EASIER.
IT'S WHAT CAME WITH THE CAR, STEVE. IT'S AN OLD CAR, IT'S GOT AN OLD JACK.
YEAH, BUT STILL--
JUST KEEP AN EYE ON THE ROAD SO I DON'T GET RUN DOWN. MAYBE SOMEBODY'LL COME ALONG WHO CAN LEND A HAND.
UMMM... DAD?
YEAH?
I THINK SOMEBODY'S COMING.

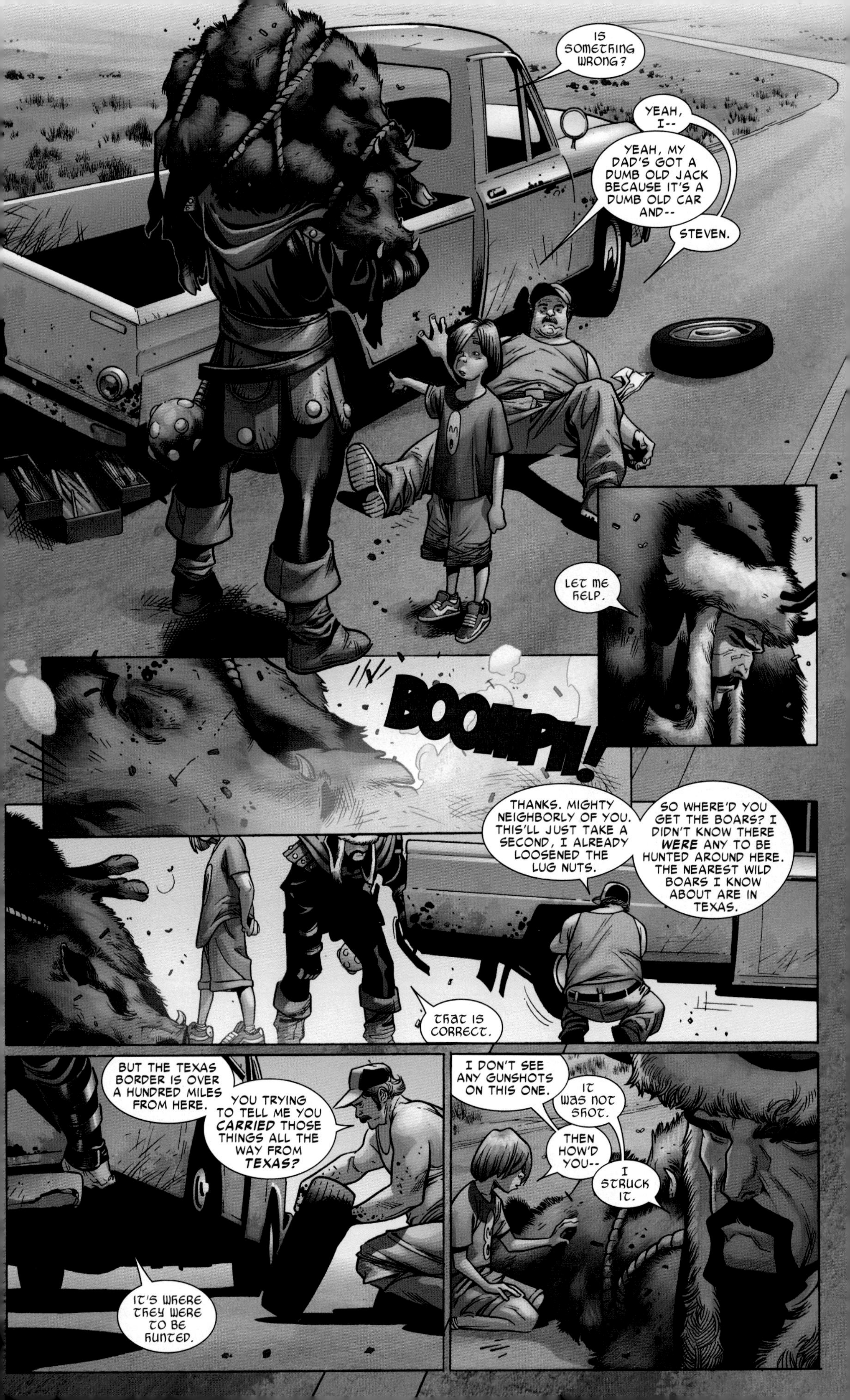
IS SOMETHING WRONG?
YEAH, I--
YEAH, MY DAD'S GOT A DUMB OLD JACK BECAUSE IT'S A DUMB OLD CAR AND--
STEVEN.
LET ME HELP.
BOOMPH!
THANKS. MIGHTY NEIGHBORLY OF YOU. THIS'LL JUST TAKE A SECOND, I ALREADY LOOSENED THE LUG NUTS.
SO WHERE'D YOU GET THE BOARS? I DIDN'T KNOW THERE WERE ANY TO BE HUNTED AROUND HERE. THE NEAREST WILD BOARS I KNOW ABOUT ARE IN TEXAS.
THAT IS CORRECT.
BUT THE TEXAS BORDER IS OVER A HUNDRED MILES FROM HERE.
YOU TRYING TO TELL ME YOU CARRIED THOSE THINGS ALL THE WAY FROM TEXAS?
IT'S WHERE THEY WERE TO BE HUNTED.
I DON'T SEE ANY GUNSHOTS ON THIS ONE.
IT WAS NOT SHOT.
THEN HOW'D YOU--
I STRUCK IT.

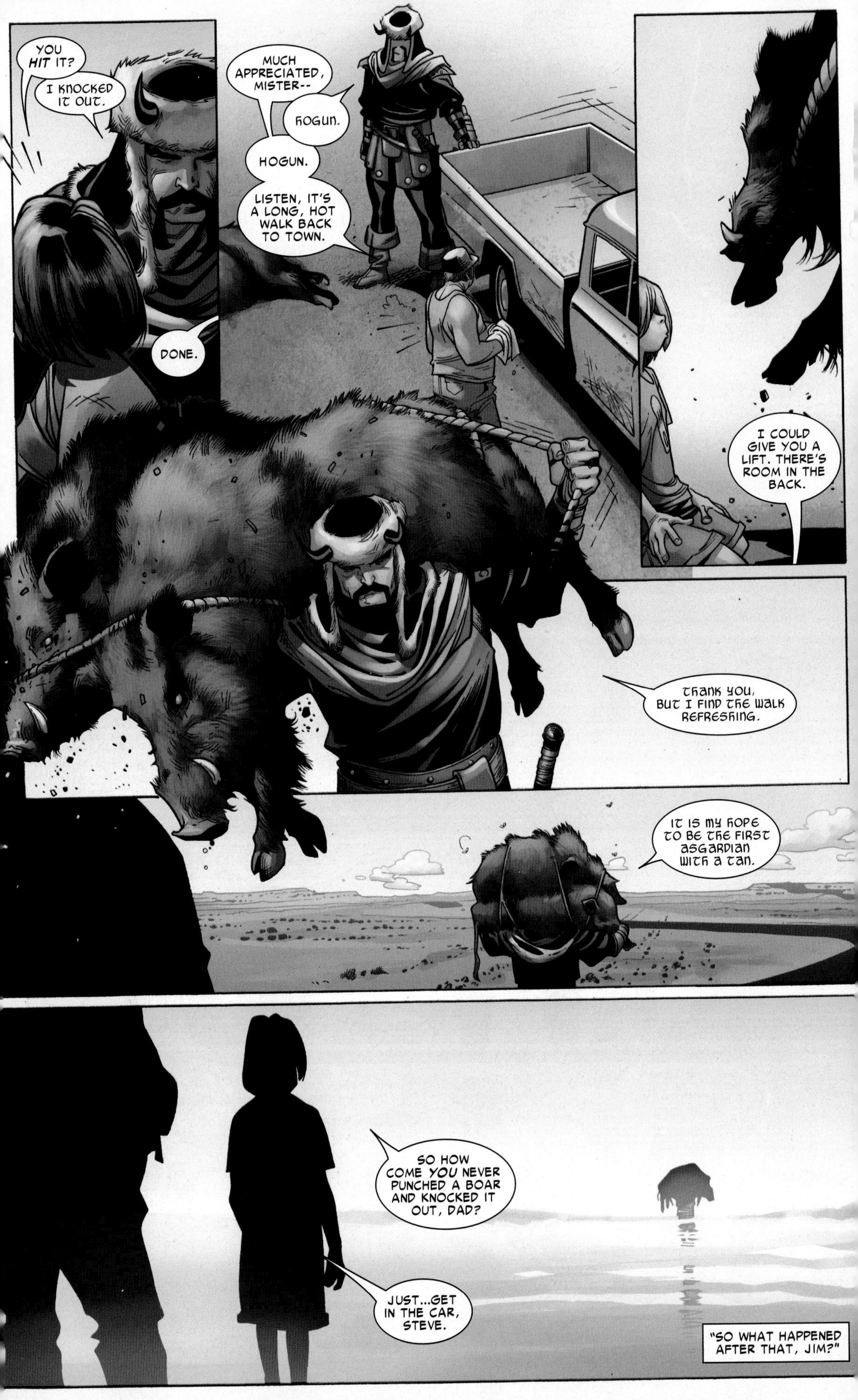
YOU HIT IT?
I KNOCKED IT OUT.
MUCH APPRECIATED, MISTER--
HOGUN.
HOGUN.
LISTEN, IT'S A LONG, HOT WALK BACK TO TOWN.
DONE.
I COULD GIVE YOU A LIFT. THERE'S ROOM IN THE BACK.
THANK YOU, BUT I FIND THE WALK REFRESHING.
IT IS MY HOPE TO BE THE FIRST ASGARDIAN WITH A TAN.
SO HOW COME YOU NEVER PUNCHED A BOAR AND KNOCKED IT OUT, DAD?
JUST...GET IN THE CAR, STEVE.
"SO WHAT HAPPENED AFTER THAT, JIM?"

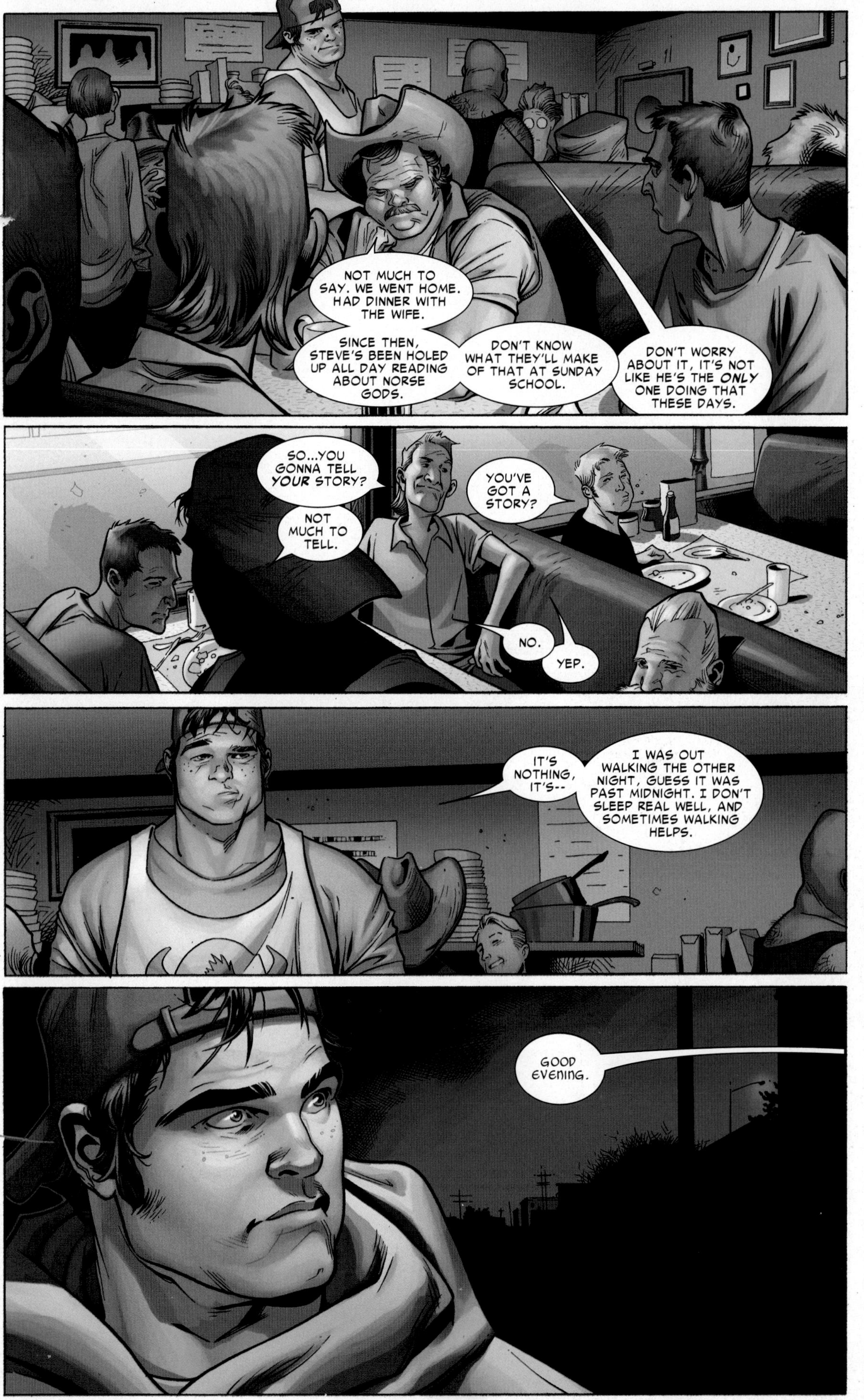
NOT MUCH TO SAY. WE WENT HOME. HAD DINNER WITH THE WIFE.
SINCE THEN, STEVE'S BEEN HOLED UP ALL DAY READING ABOUT NORSE GODS.
DON'T KNOW WHAT THEY'LL MAKE OF THAT AT SUNDAY SCHOOL.
DON'T WORRY ABOUT IT, IT'S NOT LIKE HE'S THE ONLY ONE DOING THAT THESE DAYS.
SO...YOU GONNA TELL YOUR STORY?
YOU'VE GOT A STORY?
NOT MUCH TO TELL.
NO.
YEP.
IT'S NOTHING, IT'S--
I WAS OUT WALKING THE OTHER NIGHT, GUESS IT WAS PAST MIDNIGHT. I DON'T SLEEP REAL WELL, AND SOMETIMES WALKING HELPS.
GOOD EVENING.

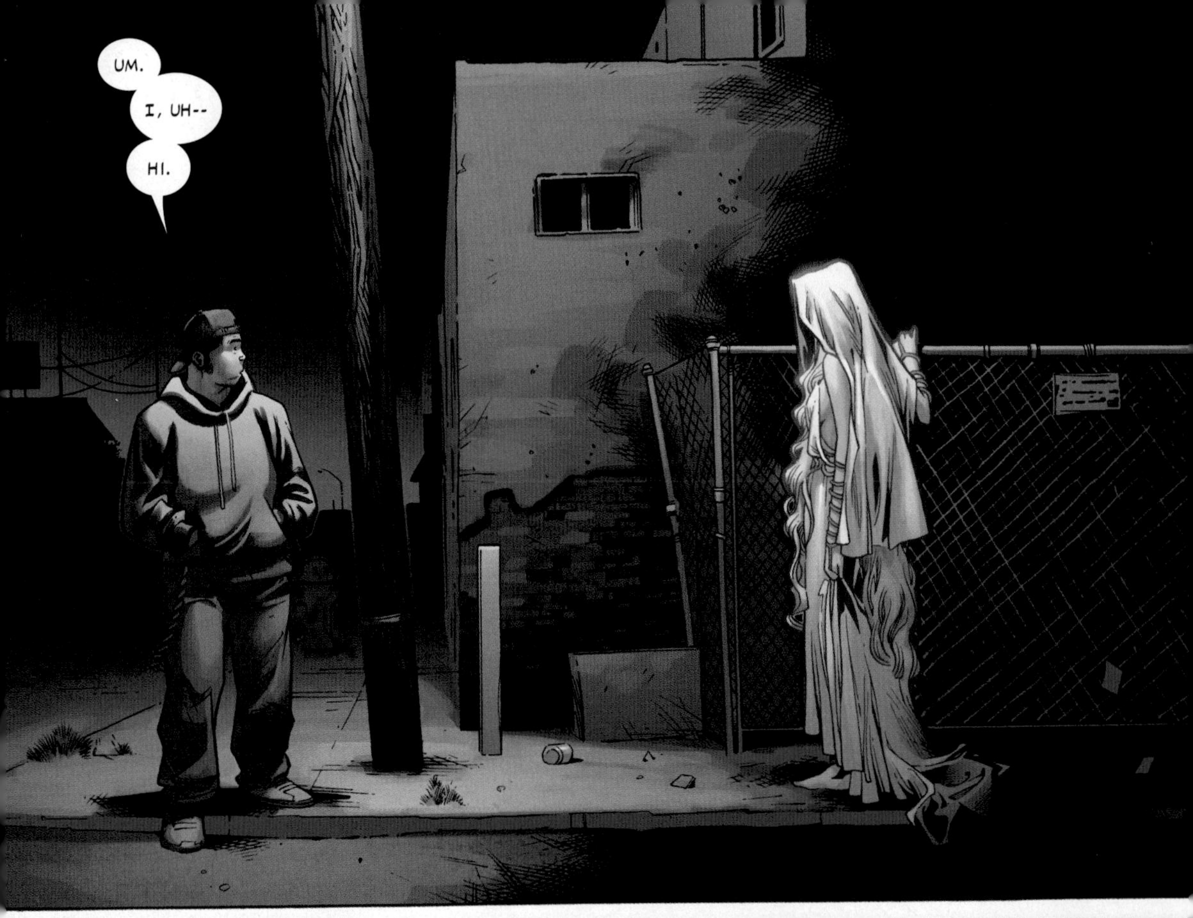
UM.
I, UH--
HI.

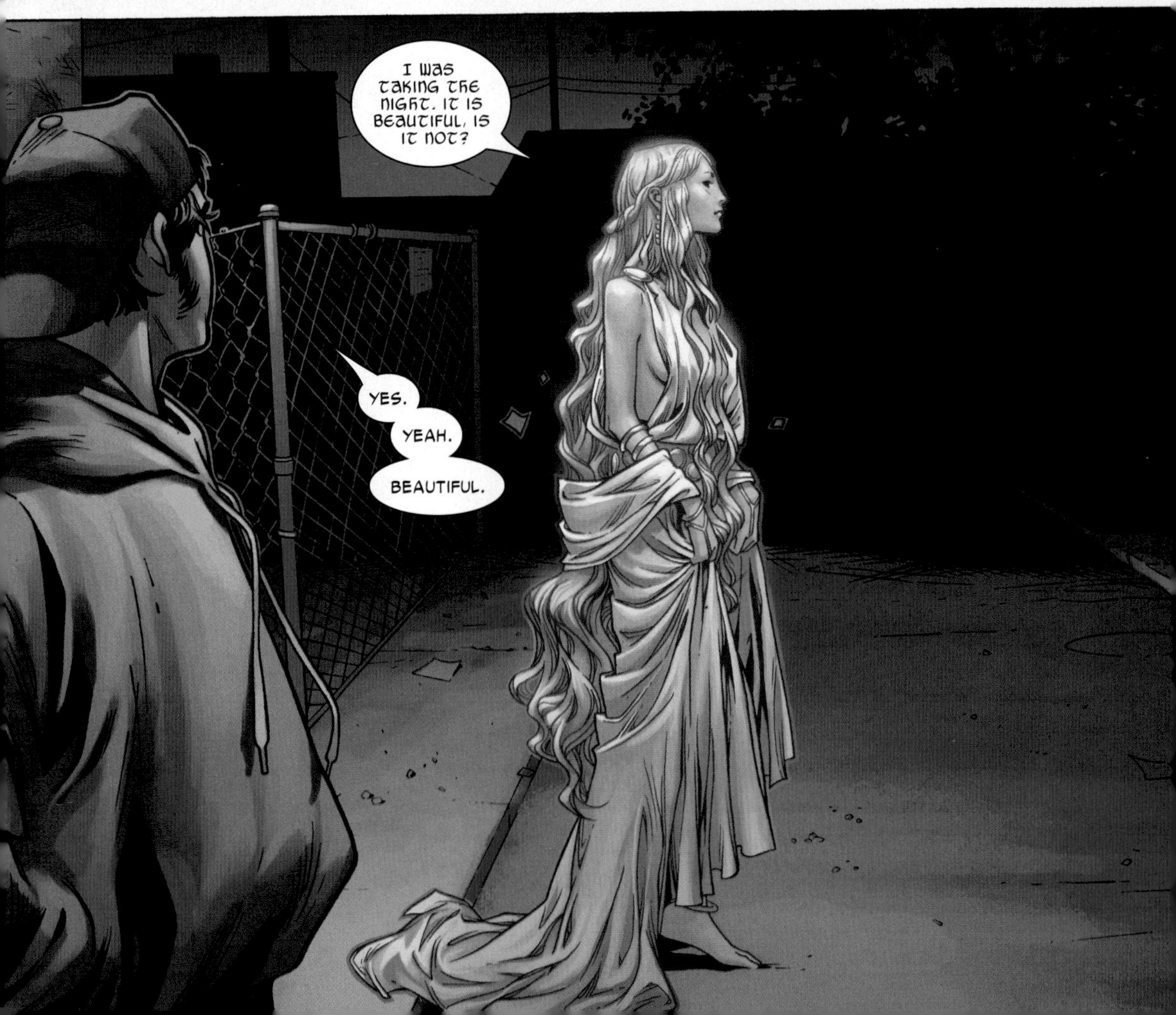
I WAS TAKING THE NIGHT. IT IS BEAUTIFUL, IS IT NOT?
YES.
YEAH.
BEAUTIFUL.

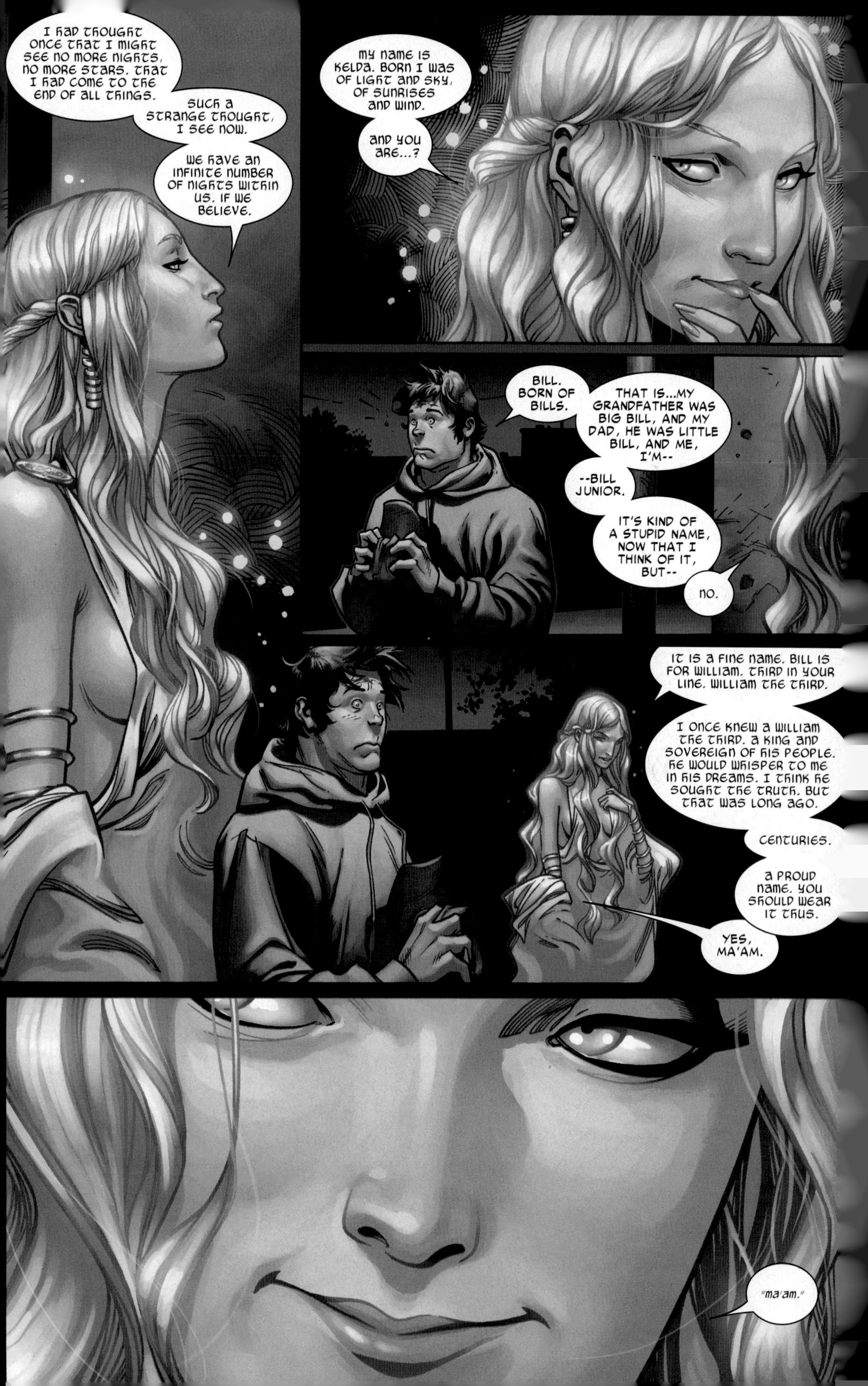
I HAD THOUGHT ONCE THAT I MIGHT SEE NO MORE NIGHTS, NO MORE STARS. THAT I HAD COME TO THE END OF ALL THINGS.
SUCH A STRANGE THOUGHT, I SEE NOW.
WE HAVE AN INFINITE NUMBER OF NIGHTS WITHIN US. IF WE BELIEVE.
MY NAME IS KELDA. BORN I WAS OF LIGHT AND SKY, OF SUNRISES AND WIND.
AND YOU ARE...?
BILL. BORN OF BILLS.
THAT IS...MY GRANDFATHER WAS BIG BILL, AND MY DAD, HE WAS LITTLE BILL, AND ME, I'M--
--BILL JUNIOR.
IT'S KIND OF A STUPID NAME, NOW THAT I THINK OF IT, BUT--
NO.
IT IS A FINE NAME. BILL IS FOR WILLIAM. THIRD IN YOUR LINE. WILLIAM THE THIRD.
I ONCE KNEW A WILLIAM THE THIRD. A KING AND SOVEREIGN OF HIS PEOPLE. HE WOULD WHISPER TO ME IN HIS DREAMS. I THINK HE SOUGHT THE TRUTH. BUT THAT WAS LONG AGO.
CENTURIES.
A PROUD NAME. YOU SHOULD WEAR IT THUS.
YES, MA'AM.
"MA'AM."

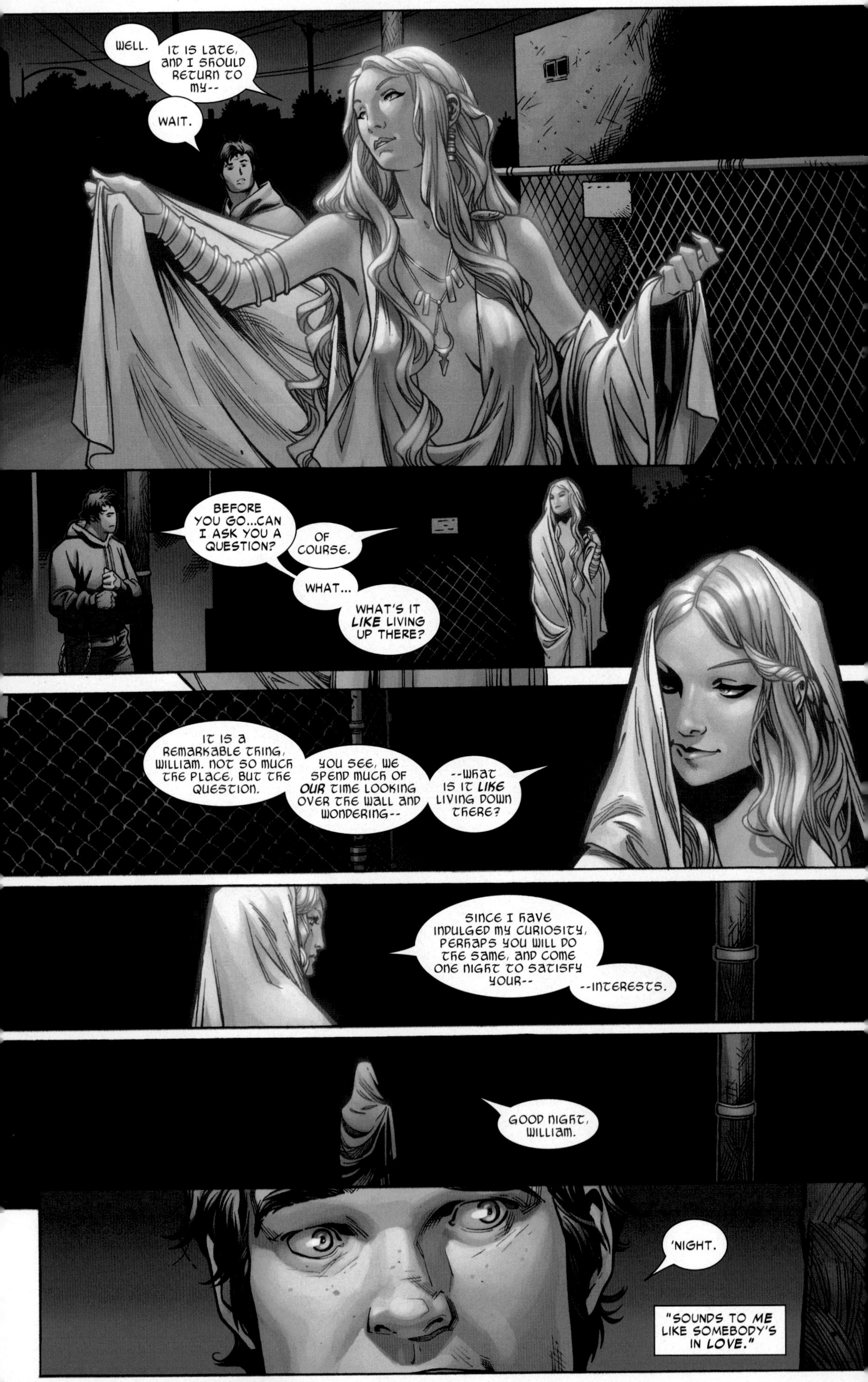
WELL.
IT IS LATE, AND I SHOULD RETURN TO MY--
WAIT.
BEFORE YOU GO...CAN I ASK YOU A QUESTION?
OF COURSE.
WHAT...
WHAT'S IT LIKE LIVING UP THERE?
IT IS A REMARKABLE THING, WILLIAM. NOT SO MUCH THE PLACE, BUT THE QUESTION.
YOU SEE, WE SPEND MUCH OF OUR TIME LOOKING OVER THE WALL AND WONDERING--
--WHAT IS IT LIKE LIVING DOWN THERE?
SINCE I HAVE INDULGED MY CURIOSITY, PERHAPS YOU WILL DO THE SAME, AND COME ONE NIGHT TO SATISFY YOUR--
--INTERESTS.
GOOD NIGHT, WILLIAM.
'NIGHT.
"SOUNDS TO ME LIKE SOMEBODY'S IN LOVE."

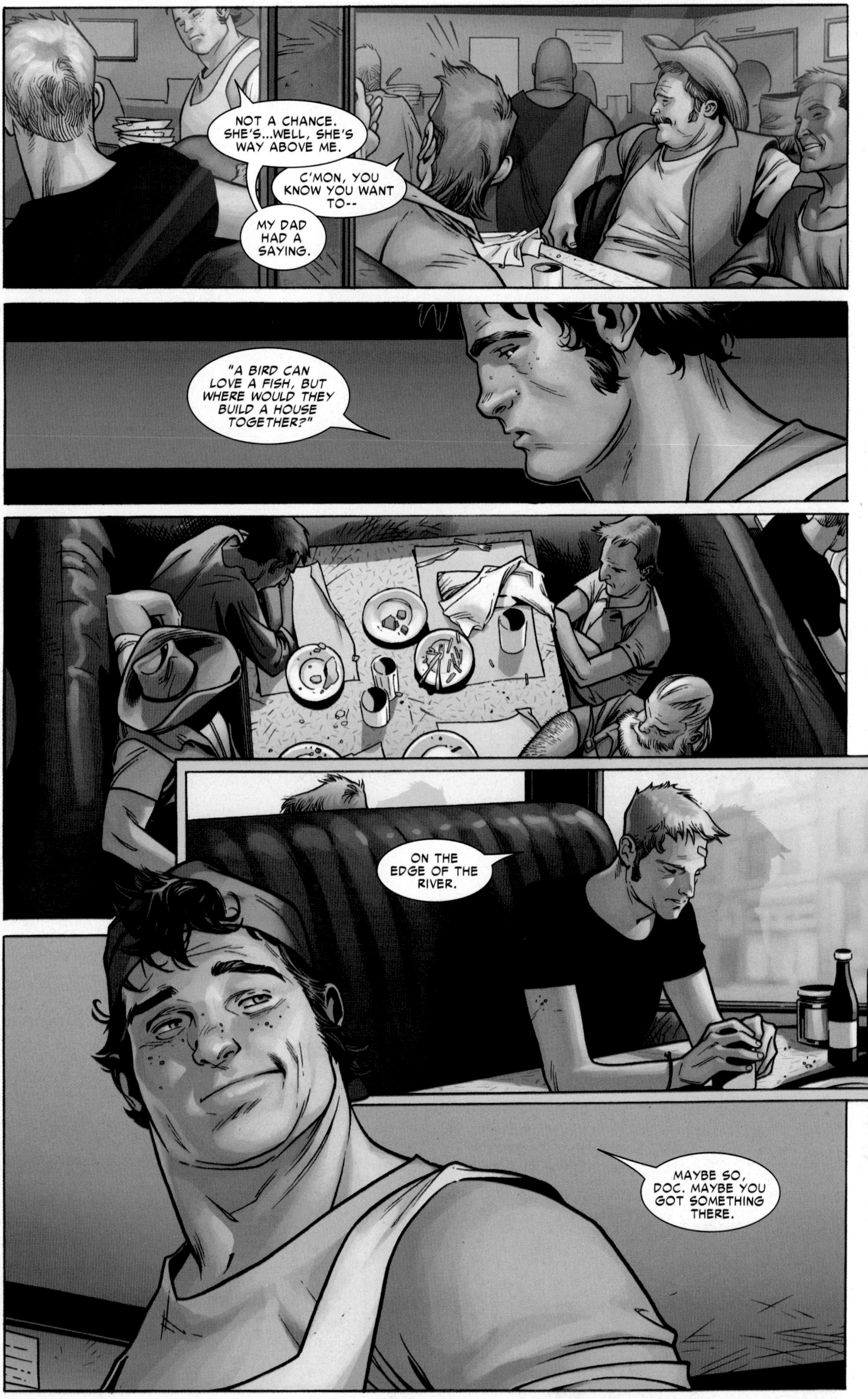
NOT A CHANCE. SHE'S...WELL, SHE'S WAY ABOVE ME.
C'MON, YOU KNOW YOU WANT TO--
MY DAD HAD A SAYING.
"A BIRD CAN LOVE A FISH, BUT WHERE WOULD THEY BUILD A HOUSE TOGETHER?"
ON THE EDGE OF THE RIVER.
MAYBE SO, DOC. MAYBE YOU GOT SOMETHING THERE.

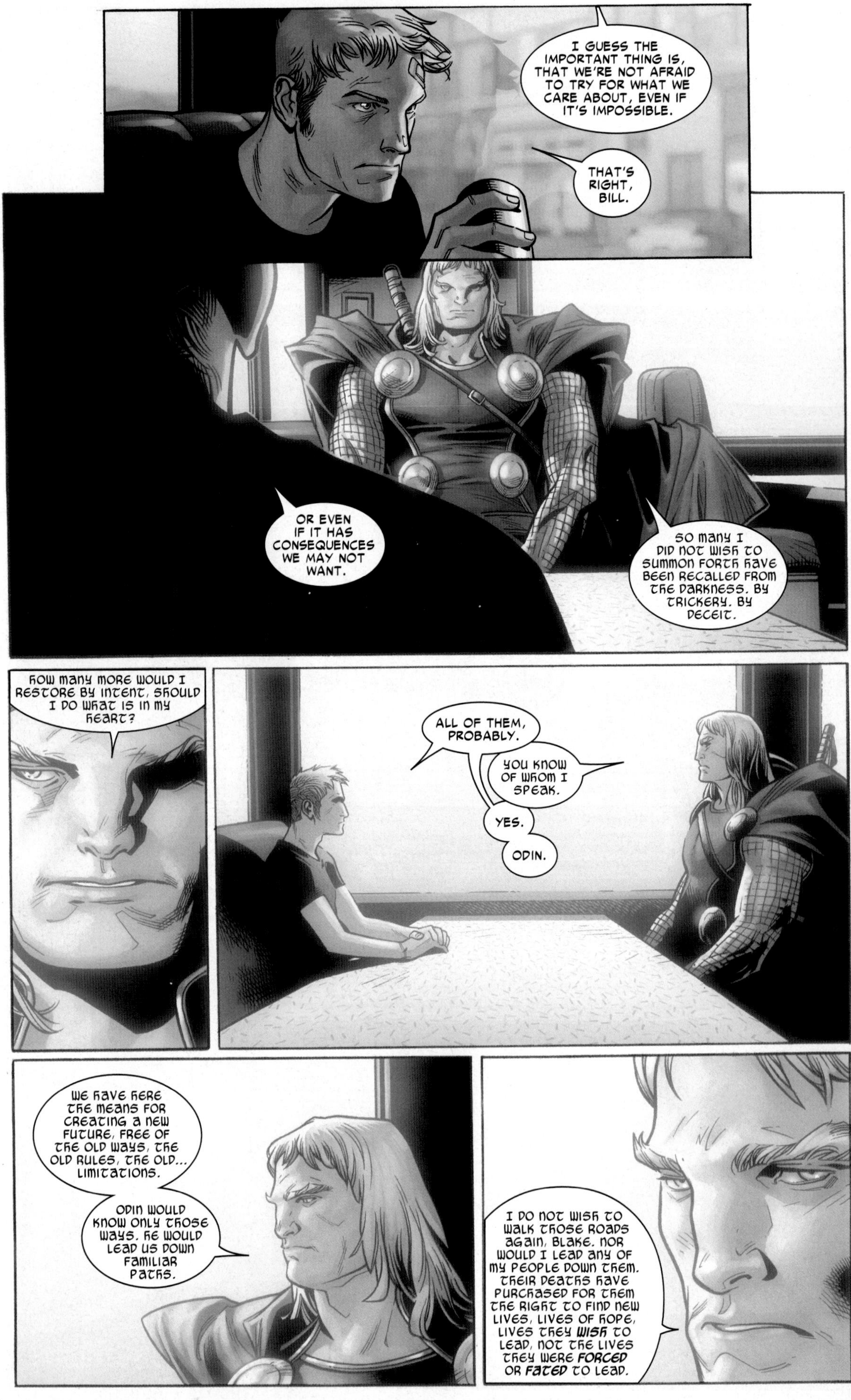
I GUESS THE IMPORTANT THING IS, THAT WE'RE NOT AFRAID TO TRY FOR WHAT WE CARE ABOUT, EVEN IF IT'S IMPOSSIBLE.
THAT'S RIGHT, BILL.
OR EVEN IF IT HAS CONSEQUENCES WE MAY NOT WANT.
SO MANY I DID NOT WISH TO SUMMON FORTH HAVE BEEN RECALLED FROM THE DARKNESS. BY TRICKERY. BY DECEIT.
HOW MANY MORE WOULD I RESTORE BY INTENT, SHOULD I DO WHAT IS IN MY HEART?
ALL OF THEM, PROBABLY.
YOU KNOW OF WHOM I SPEAK.
YES.
ODIN.
WE HAVE HERE THE MEANS FOR CREATING A NEW FUTURE, FREE OF THE OLD WAYS, THE OLD RULES, THE OLD... LIMITATIONS.
ODIN WOULD KNOW ONLY THOSE WAYS. HE WOULD LEAD US DOWN FAMILIAR PATHS.
I DO NOT WISH TO WALK THOSE ROADS AGAIN, BLAKE. NOR WOULD I LEAD ANY OF MY PEOPLE DOWN THEM. THEIR DEATHS HAVE PURCHASED FOR THEM THE RIGHT TO FIND NEW LIVES, LIVES OF HOPE, LIVES THEY WISH TO LEAD, NOT THE LIVES THEY WERE FORCED OR FATED TO LEAD.

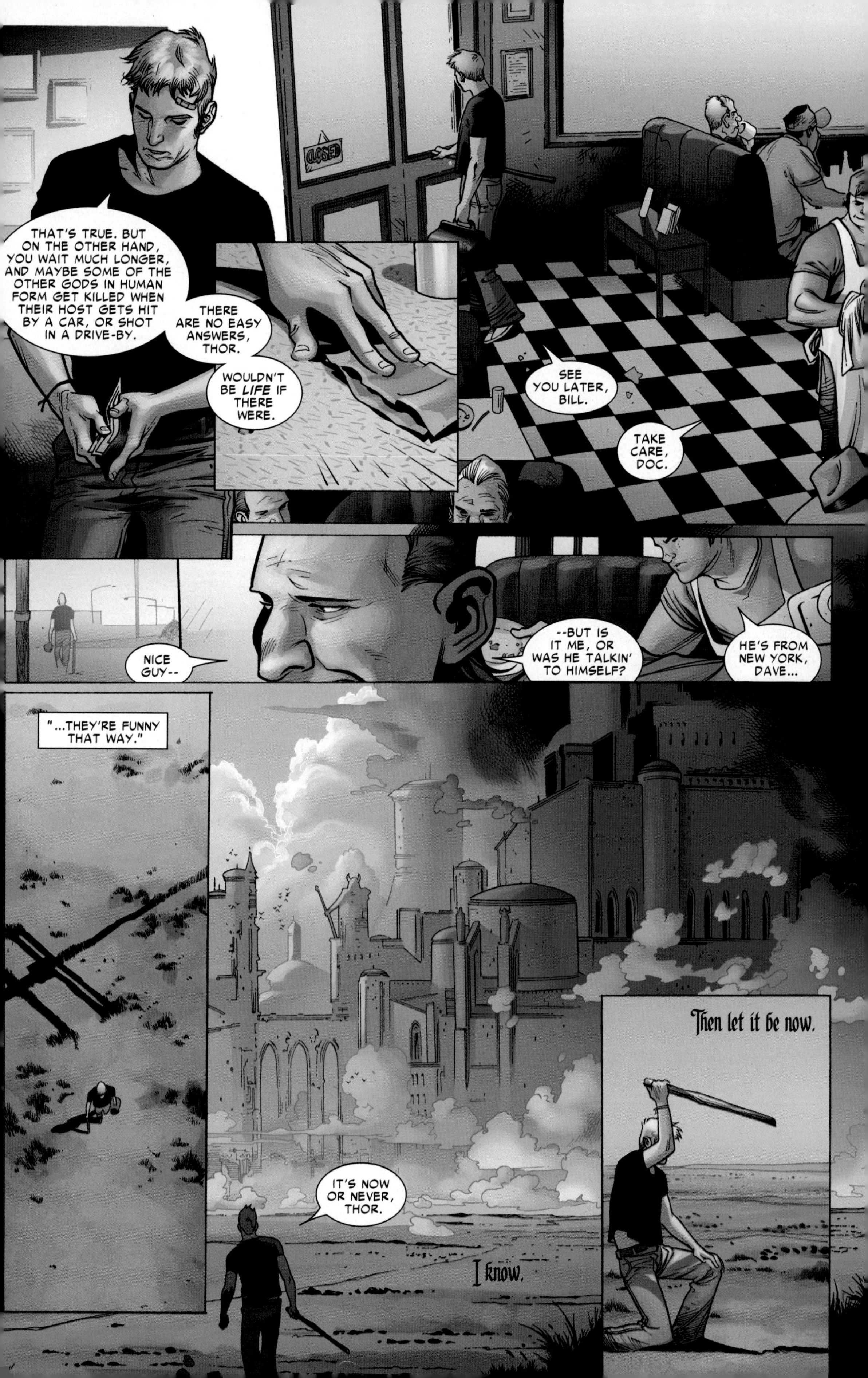
THAT'S TRUE. BUT ON THE OTHER HAND, YOU WAIT MUCH LONGER, AND MAYBE SOME OF THE OTHER GODS IN HUMAN FORM GET KILLED WHEN THEIR HOST GETS HIT BY A CAR, OR SHOT IN A DRIVE-BY.
THERE ARE NO EASY ANSWERS, THOR.
WOULDN'T BE *LIFE* IF THERE WERE.
CLOSED
SEE YOU LATER, BILL.
TAKE CARE, DOC.
NICE GUY--
--BUT IS IT ME, OR WAS HE TALKIN' TO HIMSELF?
HE'S FROM NEW YORK, DAVE...
"...THEY'RE FUNNY THAT WAY."
IT'S NOW OR NEVER, THOR.
I know.
Then let it be now.

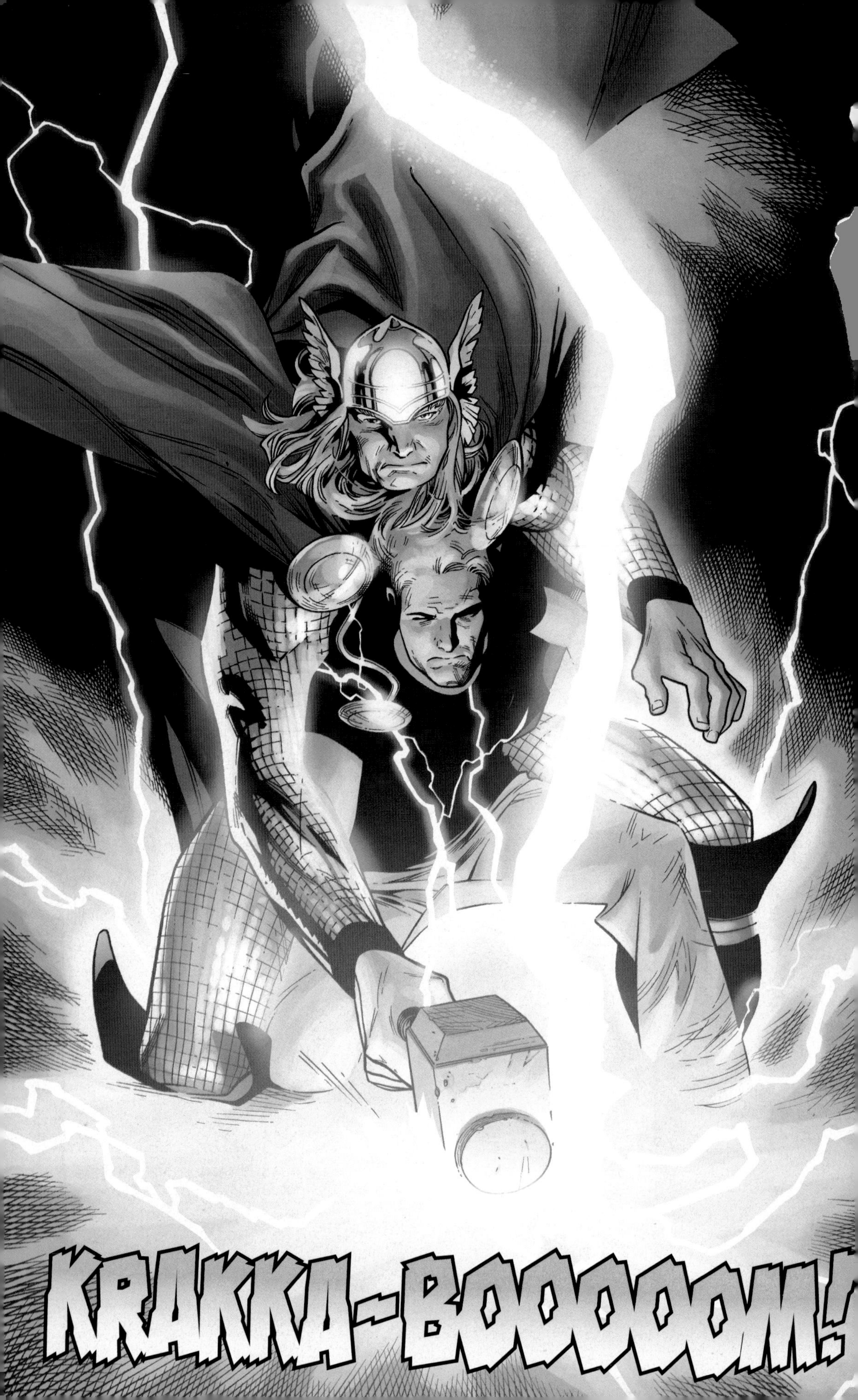
KRAKKA-BOOOOOM!

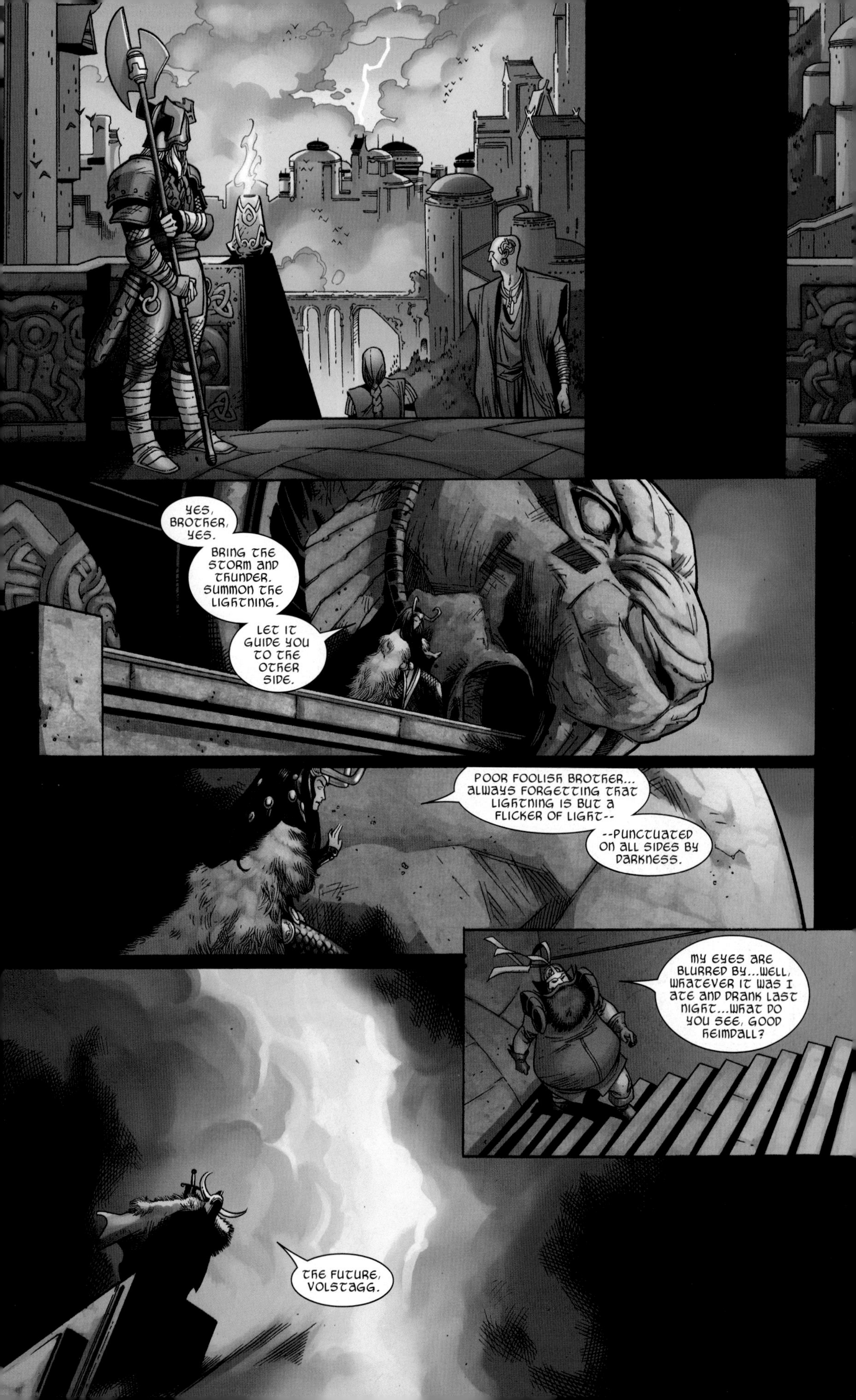
YES, BROTHER, YES.
BRING THE STORM AND THUNDER. SUMMON THE LIGHTNING.
LET IT GUIDE YOU TO THE OTHER SIDE.
POOR FOOLISH BROTHER... ALWAYS FORGETTING THAT LIGHTNING IS BUT A FLICKER OF LIGHT--
--PUNCTUATED ON ALL SIDES BY DARKNESS.
MY EYES ARE BLURRED BY...WELL, WHATEVER IT WAS I ATE AND DRANK LAST NIGHT...WHAT DO YOU SEE, GOOD HEIMDALL?
THE FUTURE, VOLSTAGG.

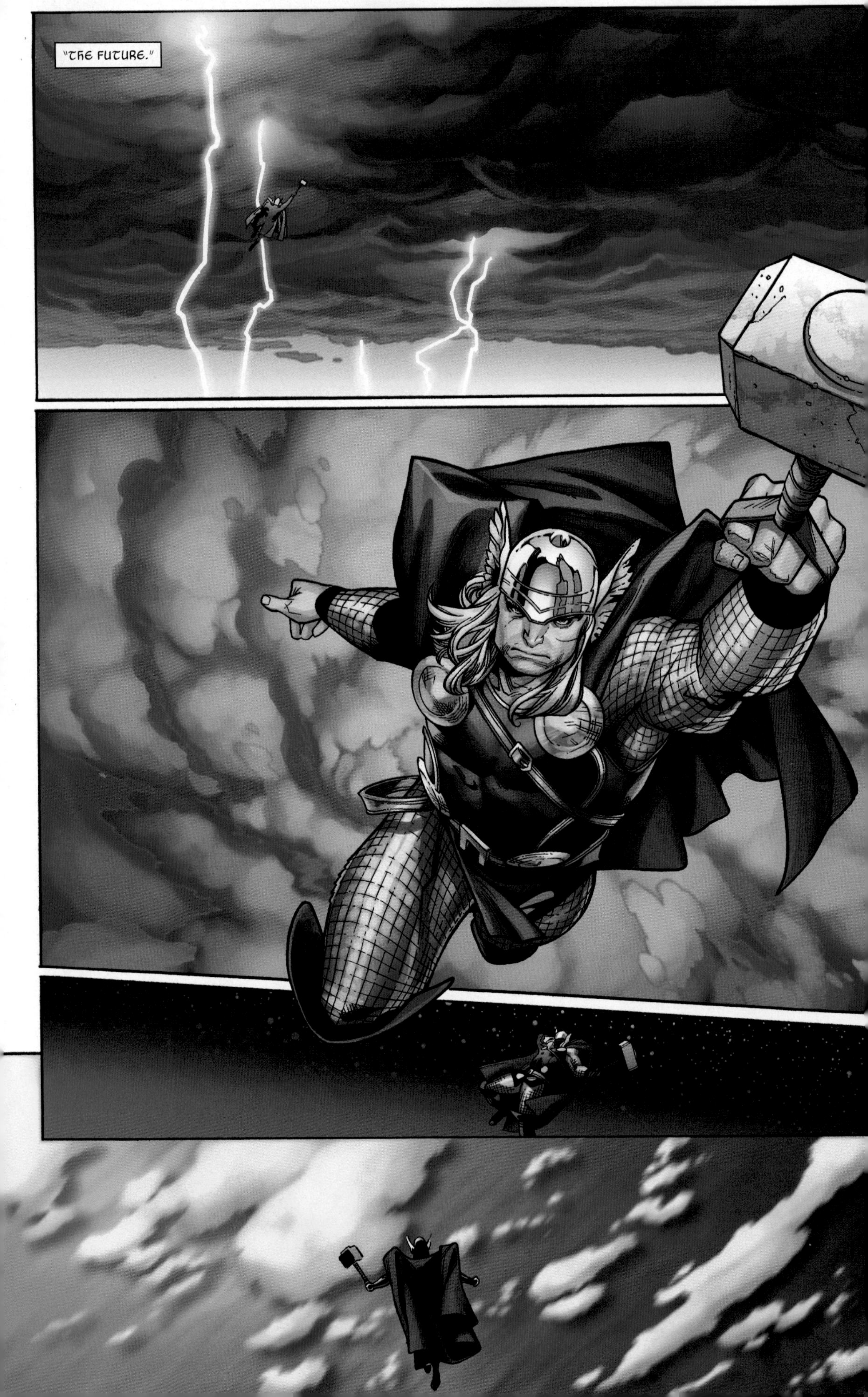
"THE FUTURE."

I do not know if I
can do this, Blake.

I do not know if I can
*survive* doing this.

I do not know the consequences,
whatever and whoever may be
summoned forth...whether I
will live or die in the effort.

I know only that
I must try.

If I should fall, find Sif.
Tell her I love her. Tell
her...tell her...

...that I fell loving her above all
risk, all danger, all consequence.

Tell her goodbye.

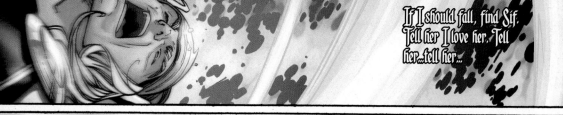

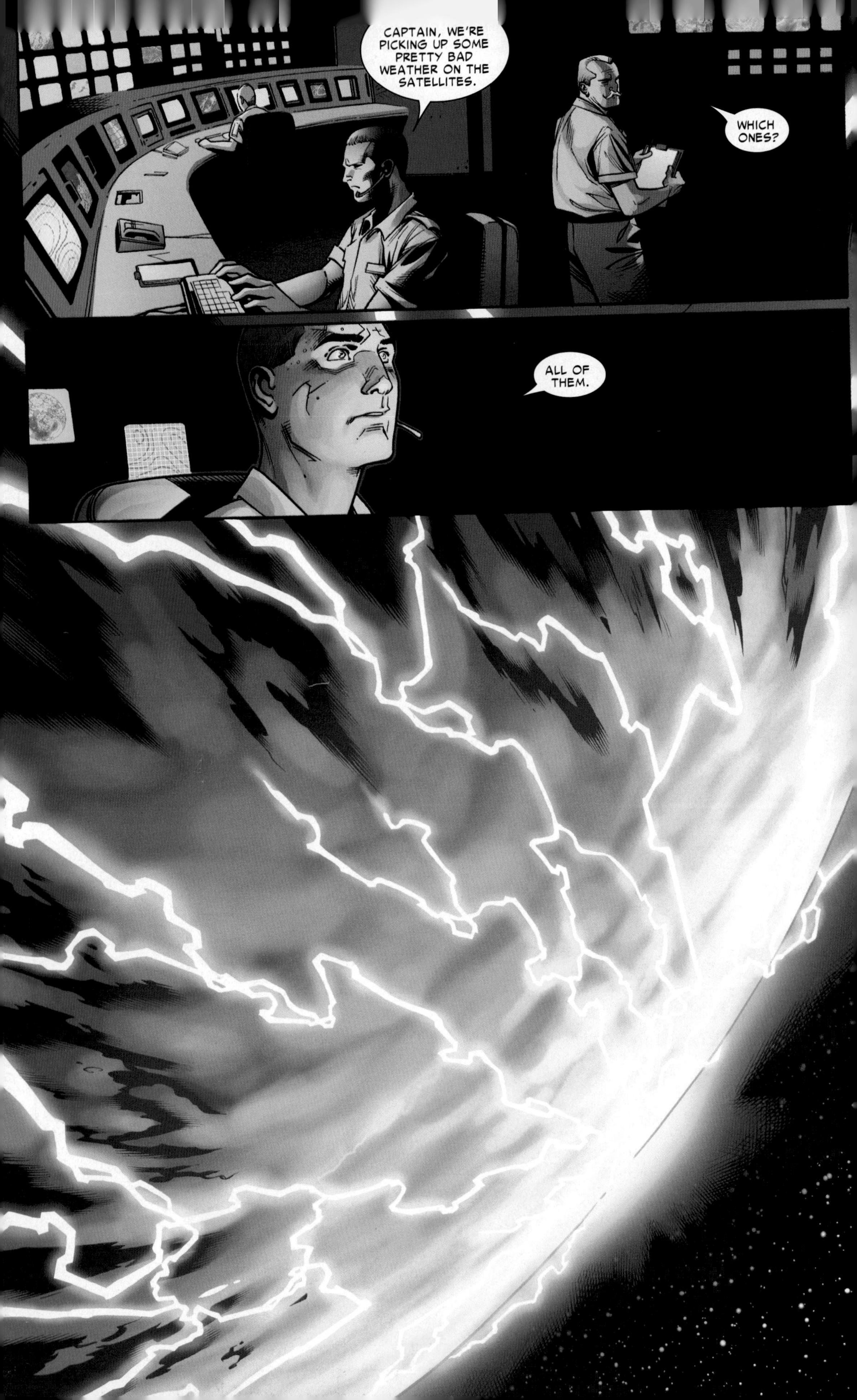
CAPTAIN, WE'RE PICKING UP SOME PRETTY BAD WEATHER ON THE SATELLITES.
WHICH ONES?
ALL OF THEM.

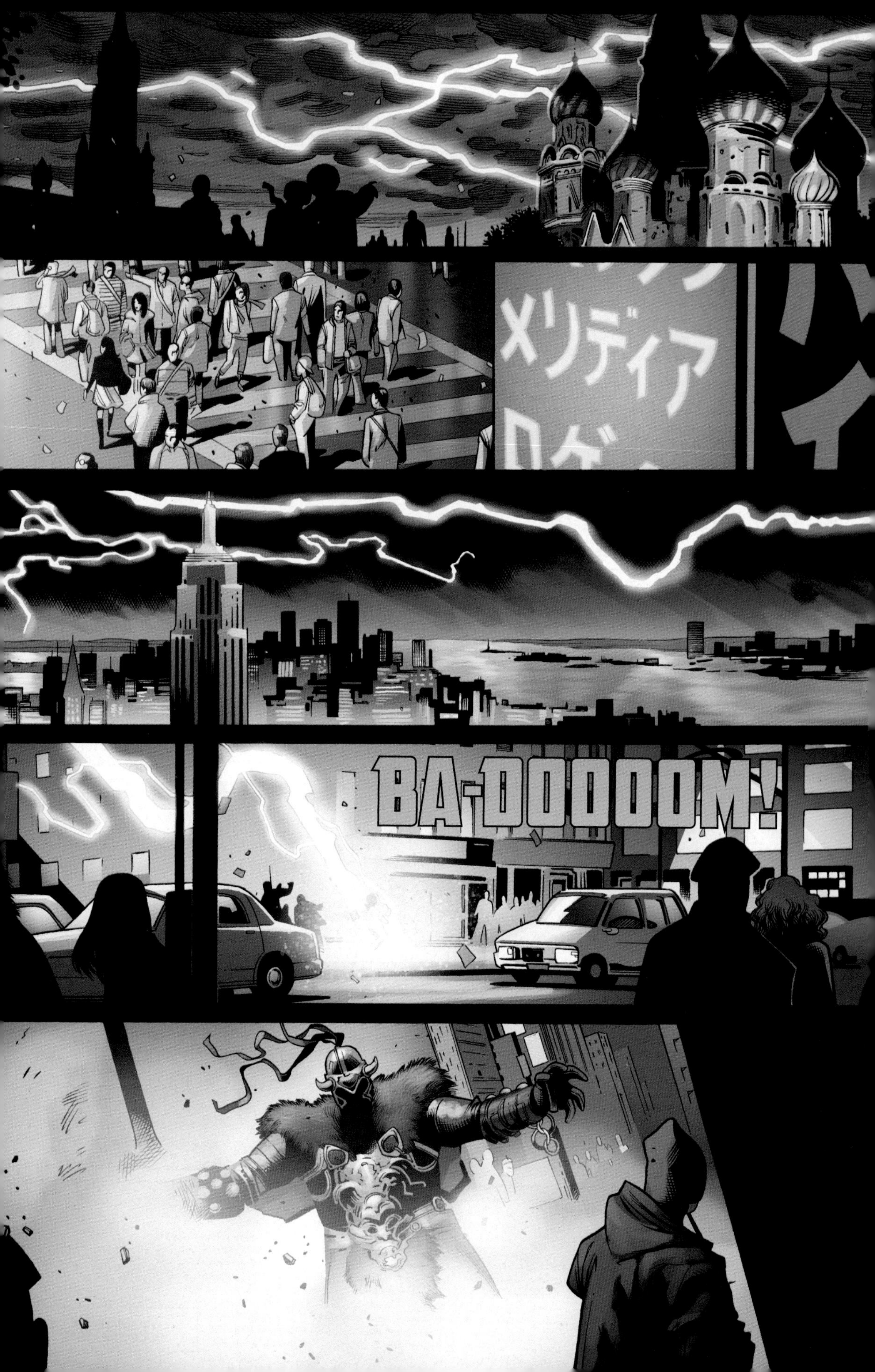
メリディア
BA-DOOOOOM!

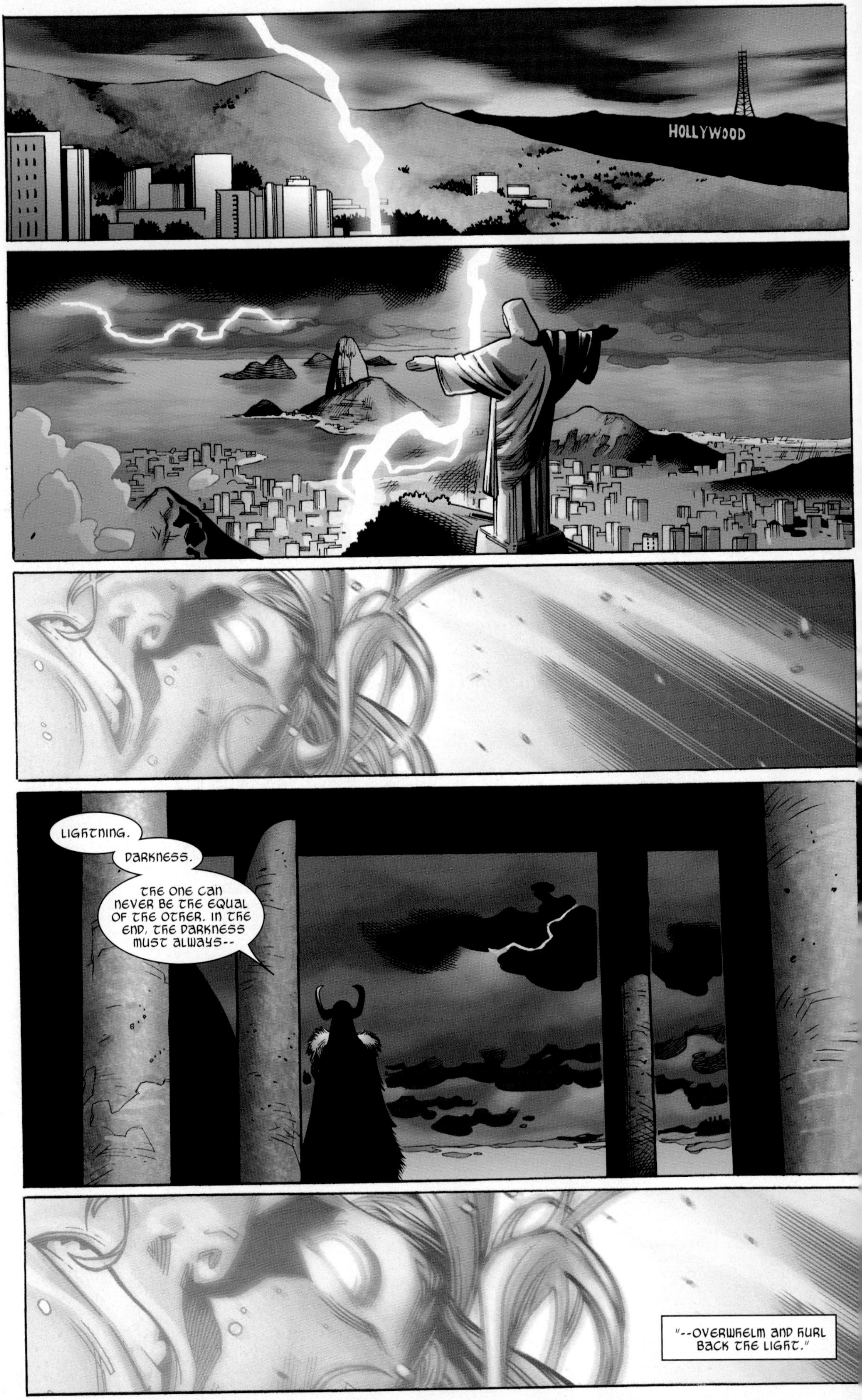
HOLLYWOOD
LIGHTNING.
DARKNESS.
THE ONE CAN NEVER BE THE EQUAL OF THE OTHER. IN THE END, THE DARKNESS MUST ALWAYS--
"--OVERWHELM AND HURL BACK THE LIGHT."

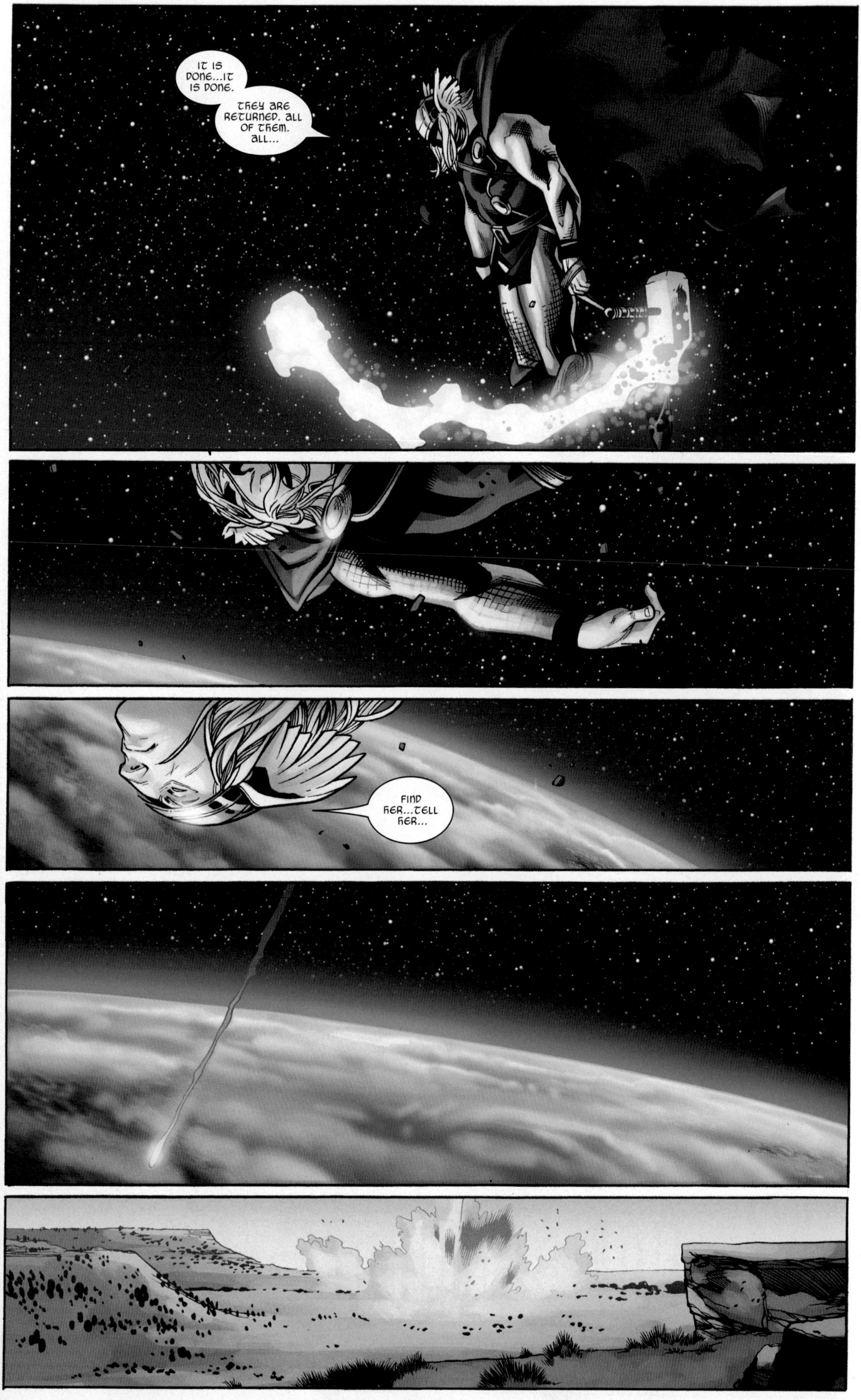
IT IS DONE...IT IS DONE.
THEY ARE RETURNED. ALL OF THEM. ALL...
FIND HER...TELL HER...

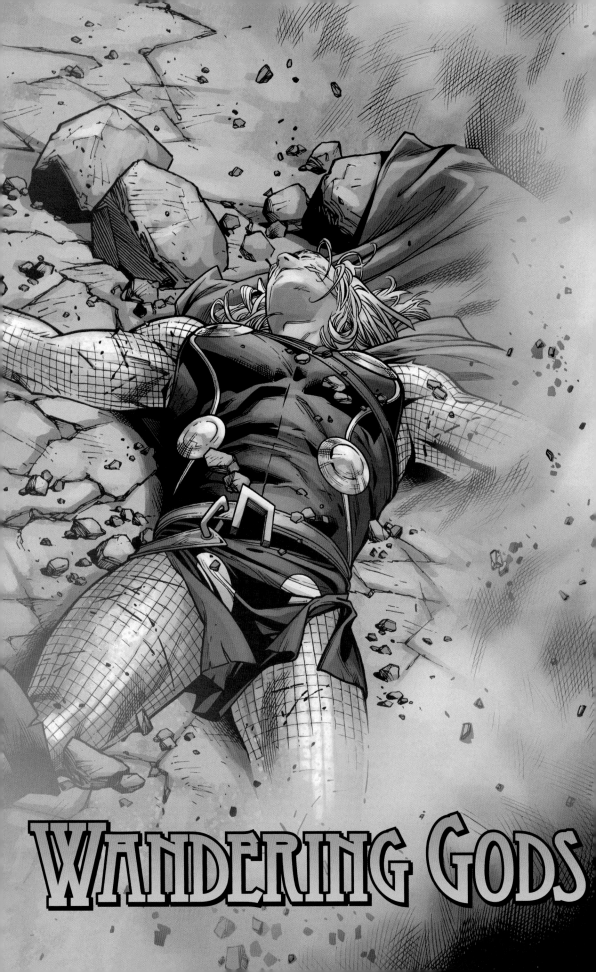

# WANDERING GODS

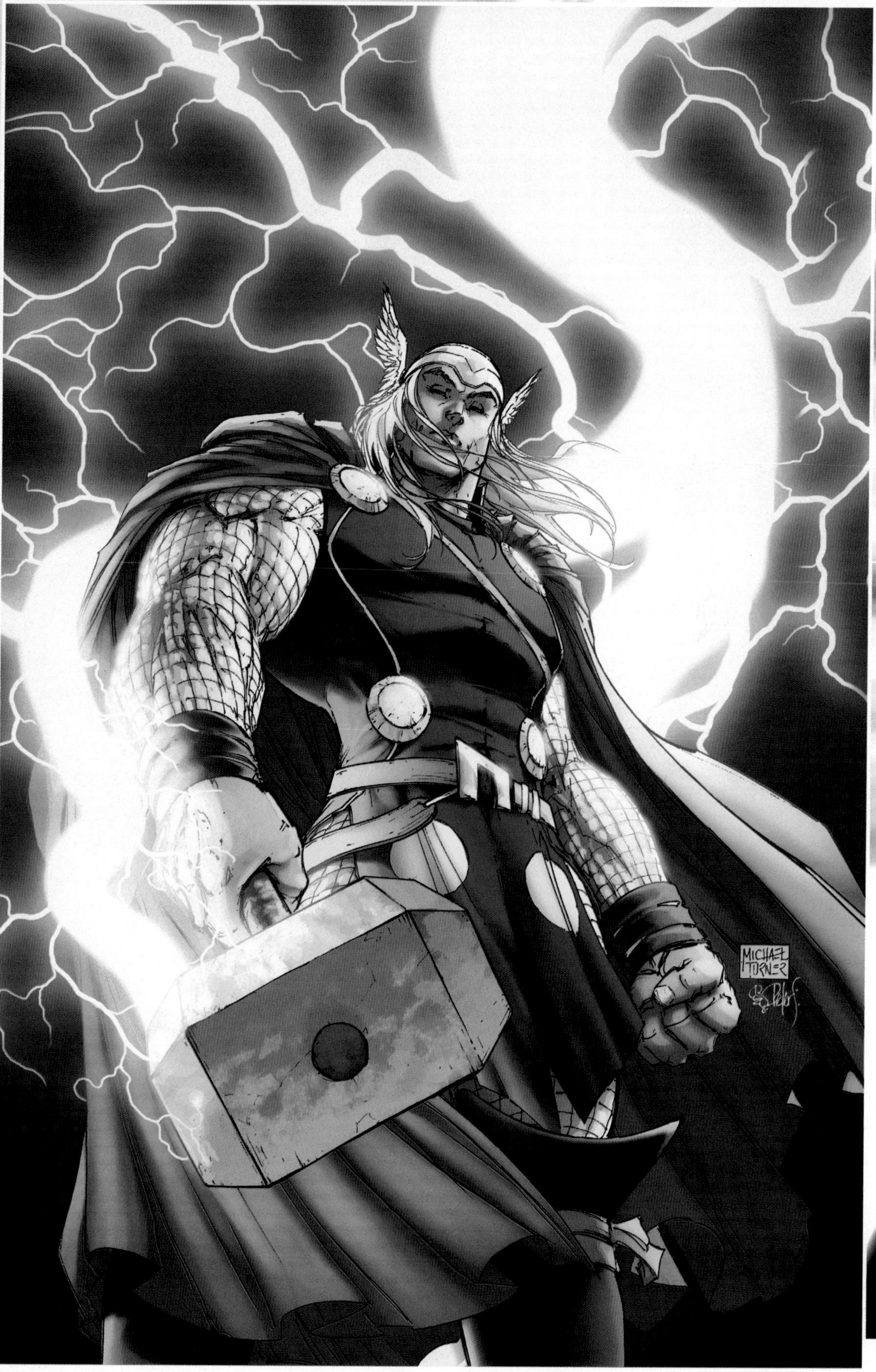
MICHAEL
TURNER

**THOR #1 VARIANT BY MICHAEL TURNER**

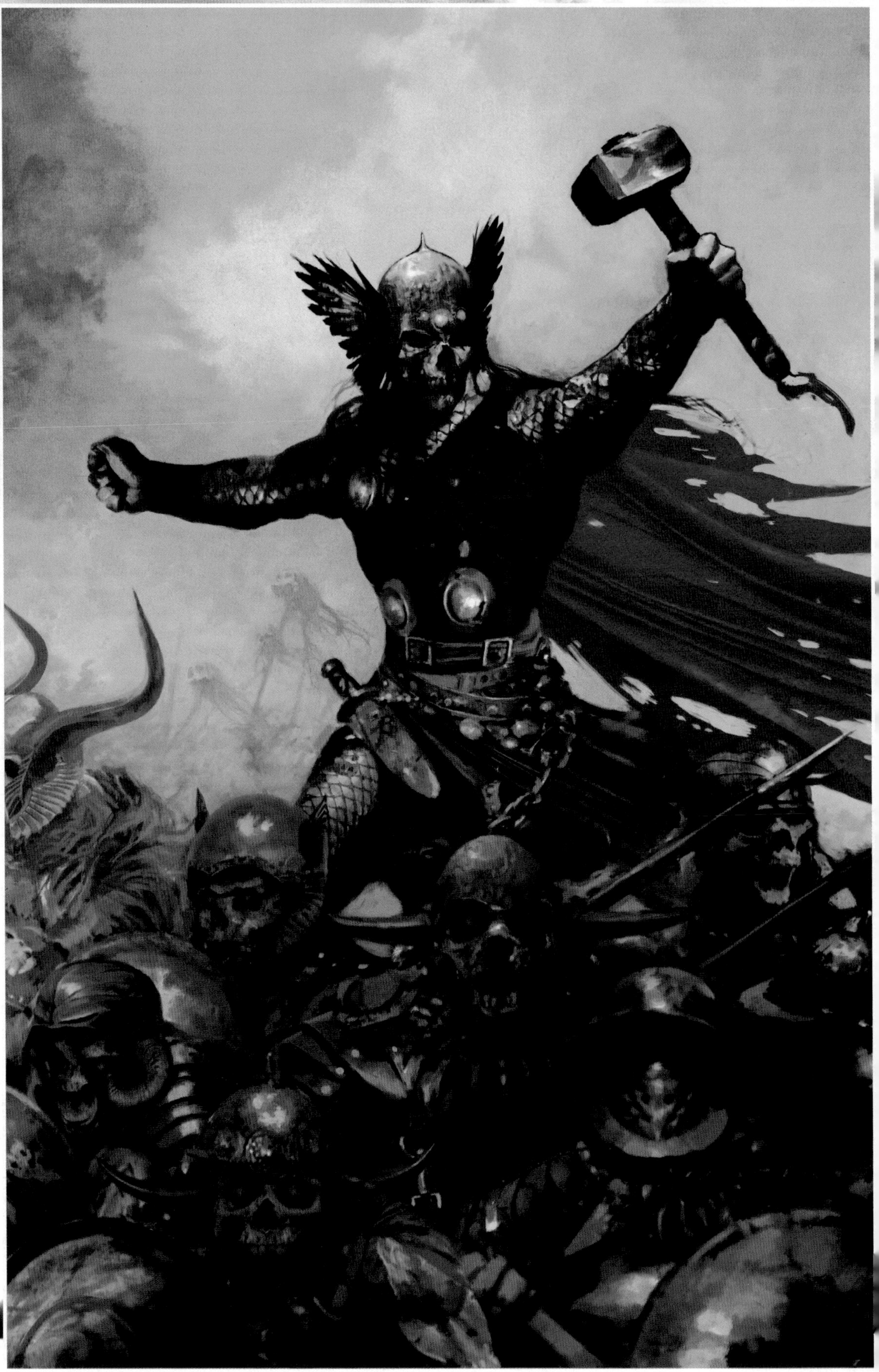

**THOR #1 ZOMBIE VARIANT BY ARTHUR SUYDAM**

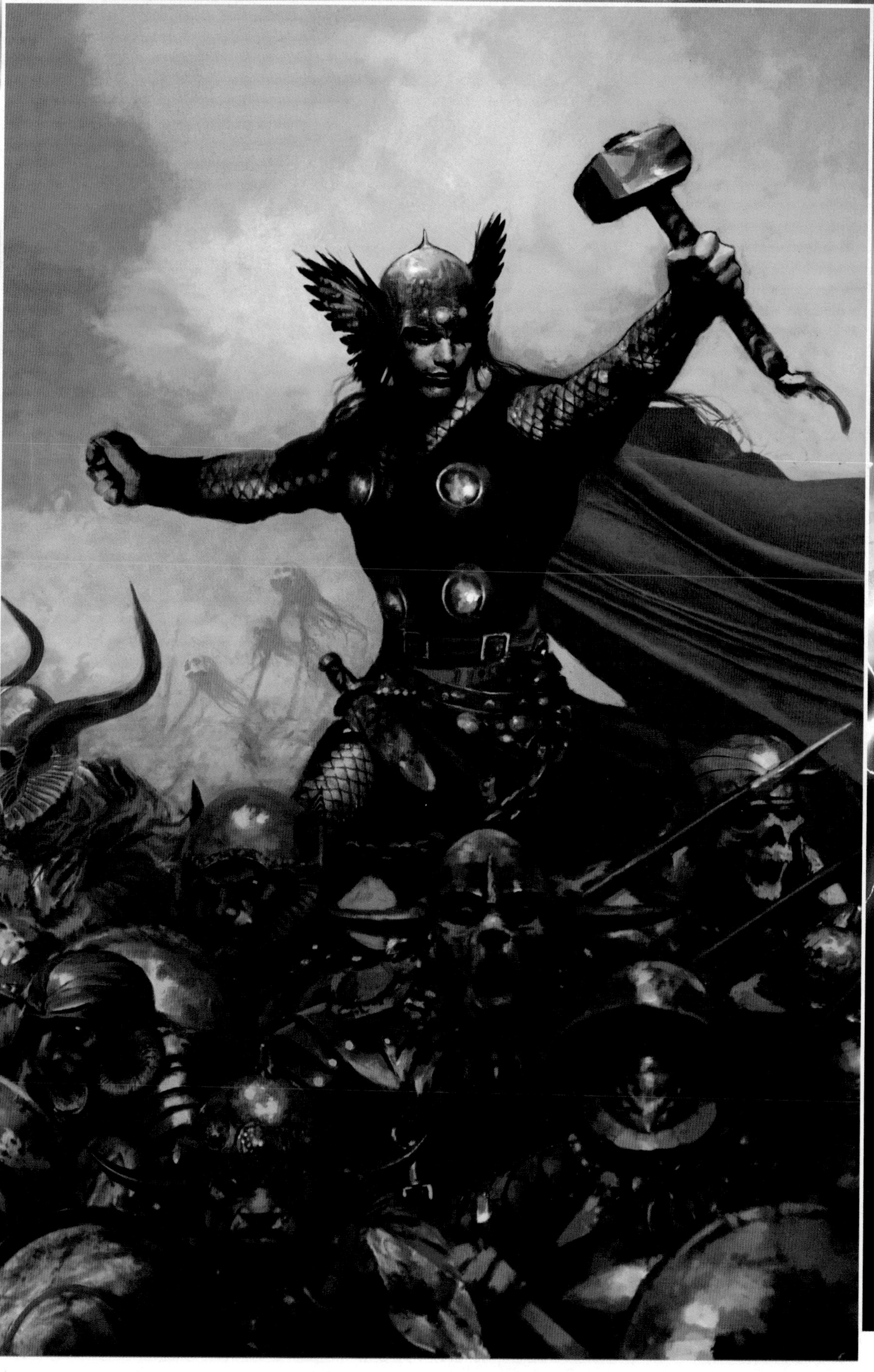

THOR #1 VARIANT BY ARTHUR SUYDAM

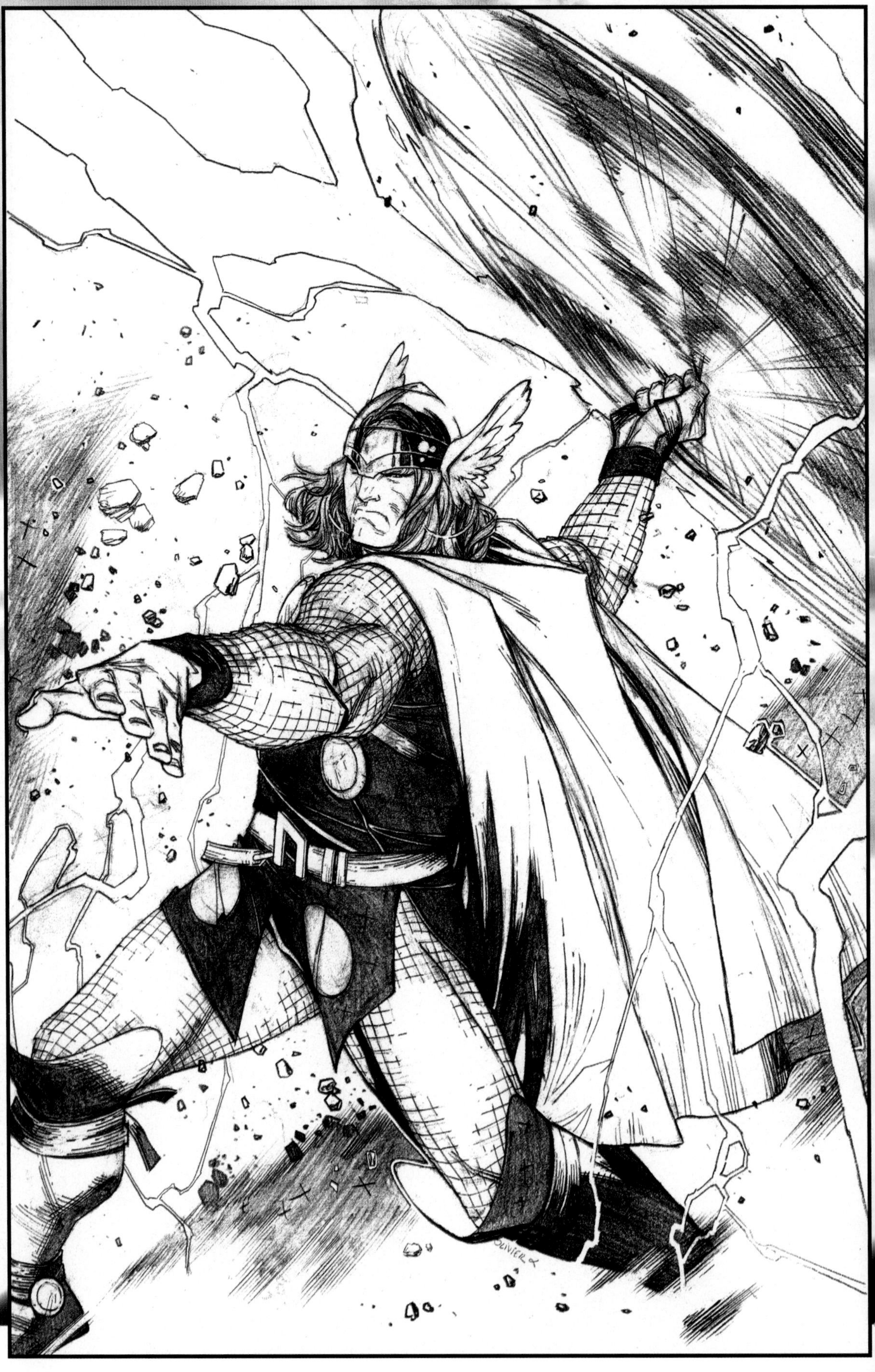

**THOR #1 SKETCH VARIANT BY OLIVIER COIPEL**

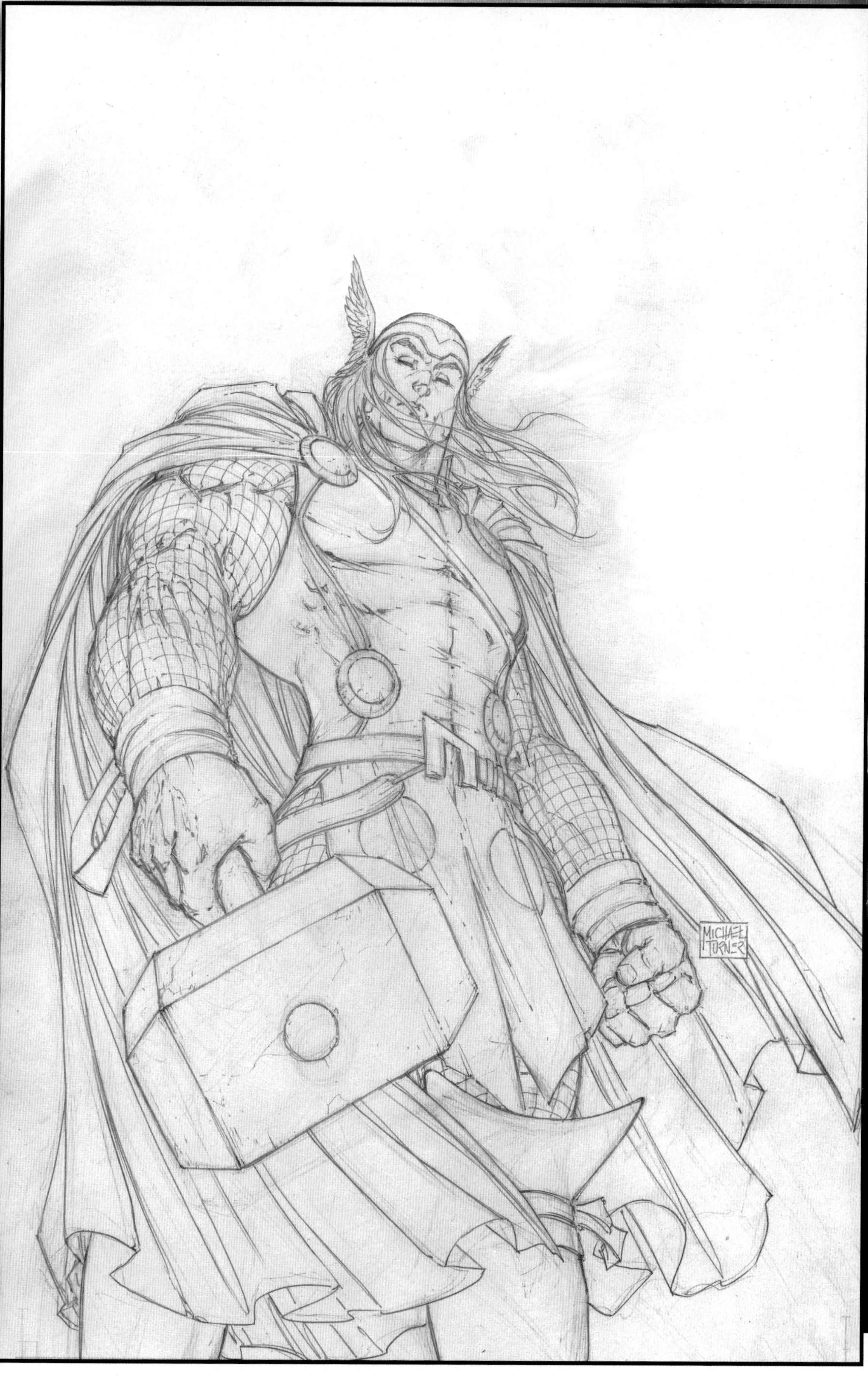
MICHAEL TURNER

**THOR #1 3RD PRINTING SKETCH VARIANT BY MICHAEL TURNER**

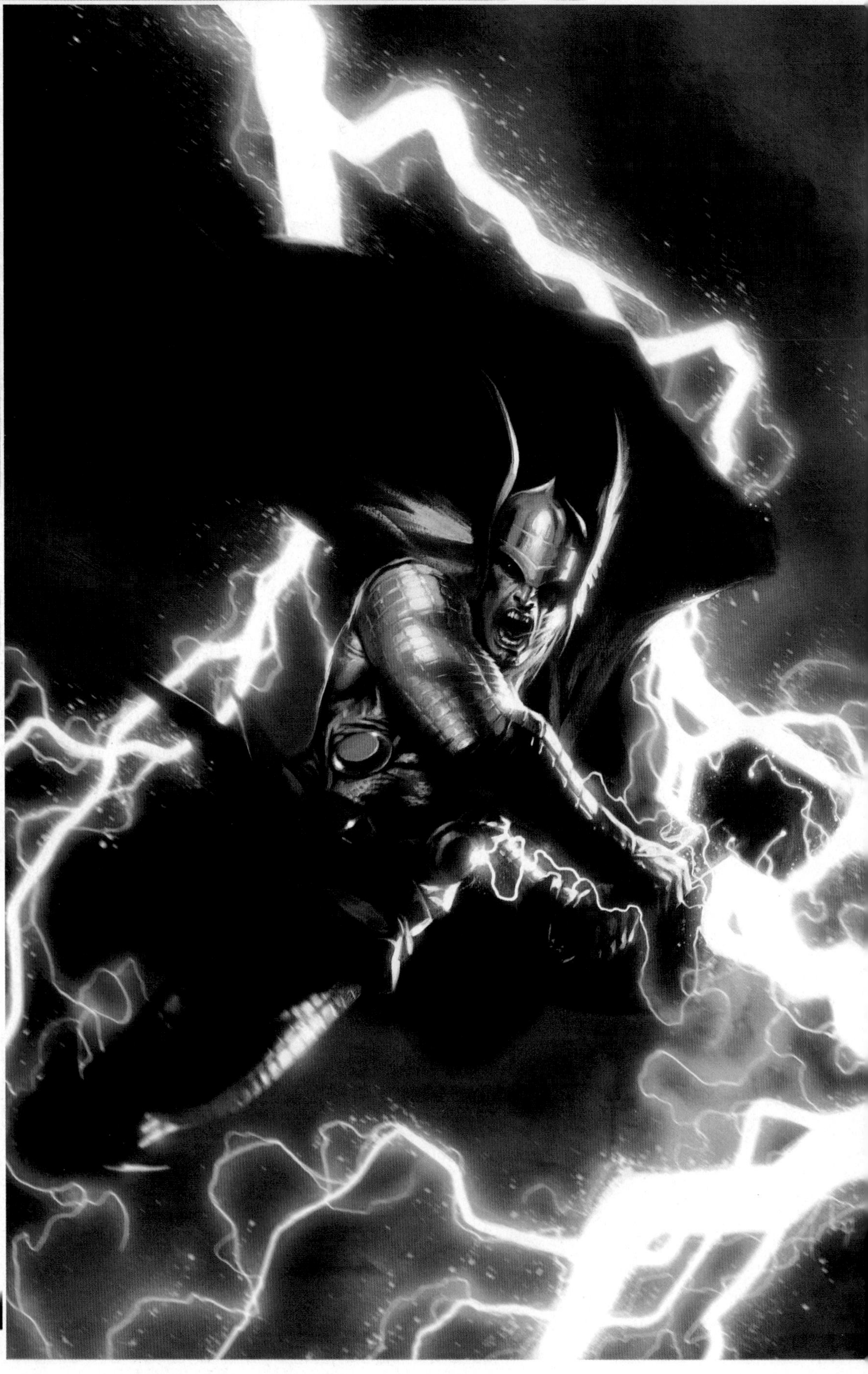

THOR #2 VARIANT BY GABRIELE DELL'OTTO

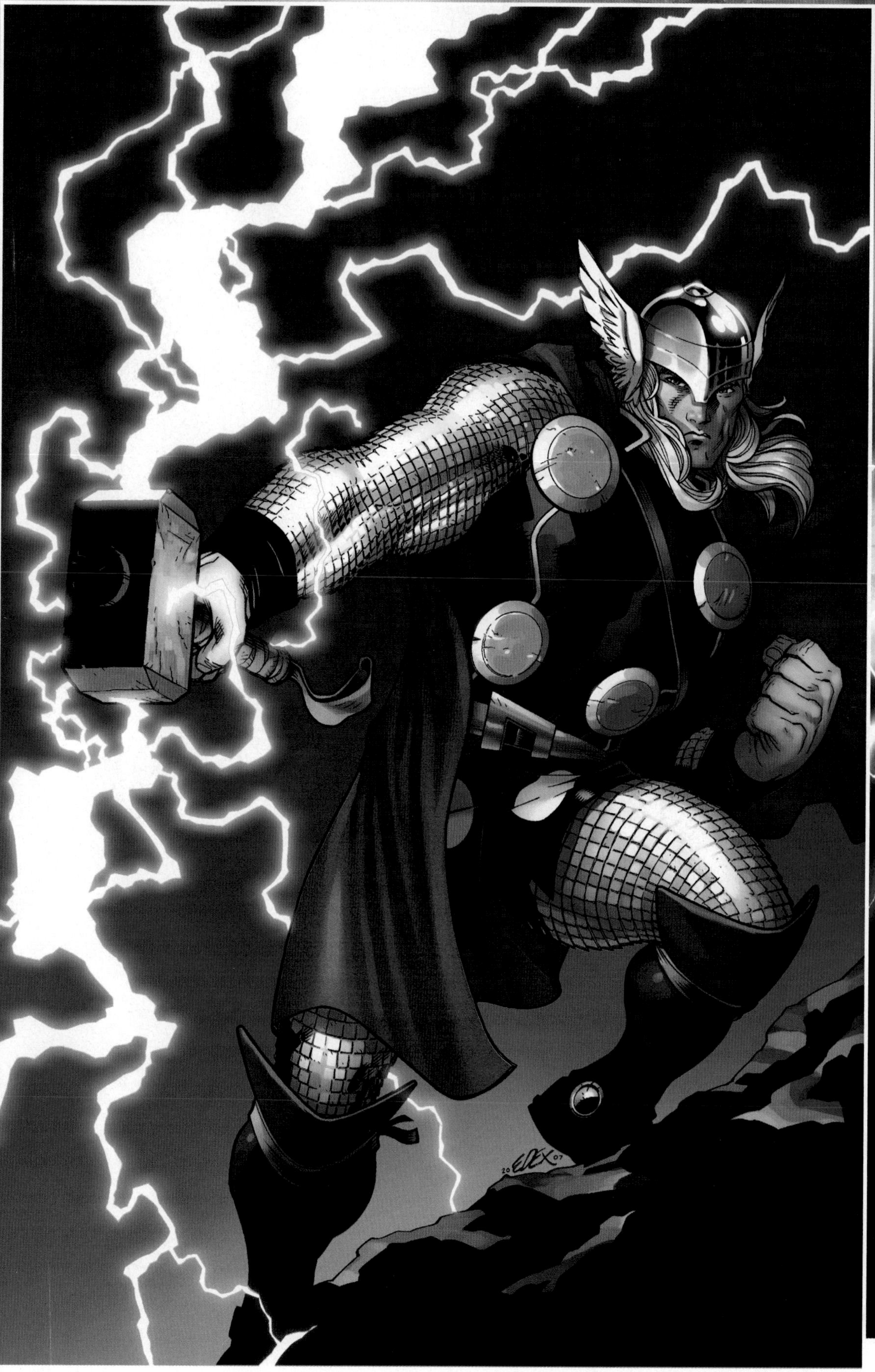

**THOR #3 VARIANT BY ED MCGUINNESS**

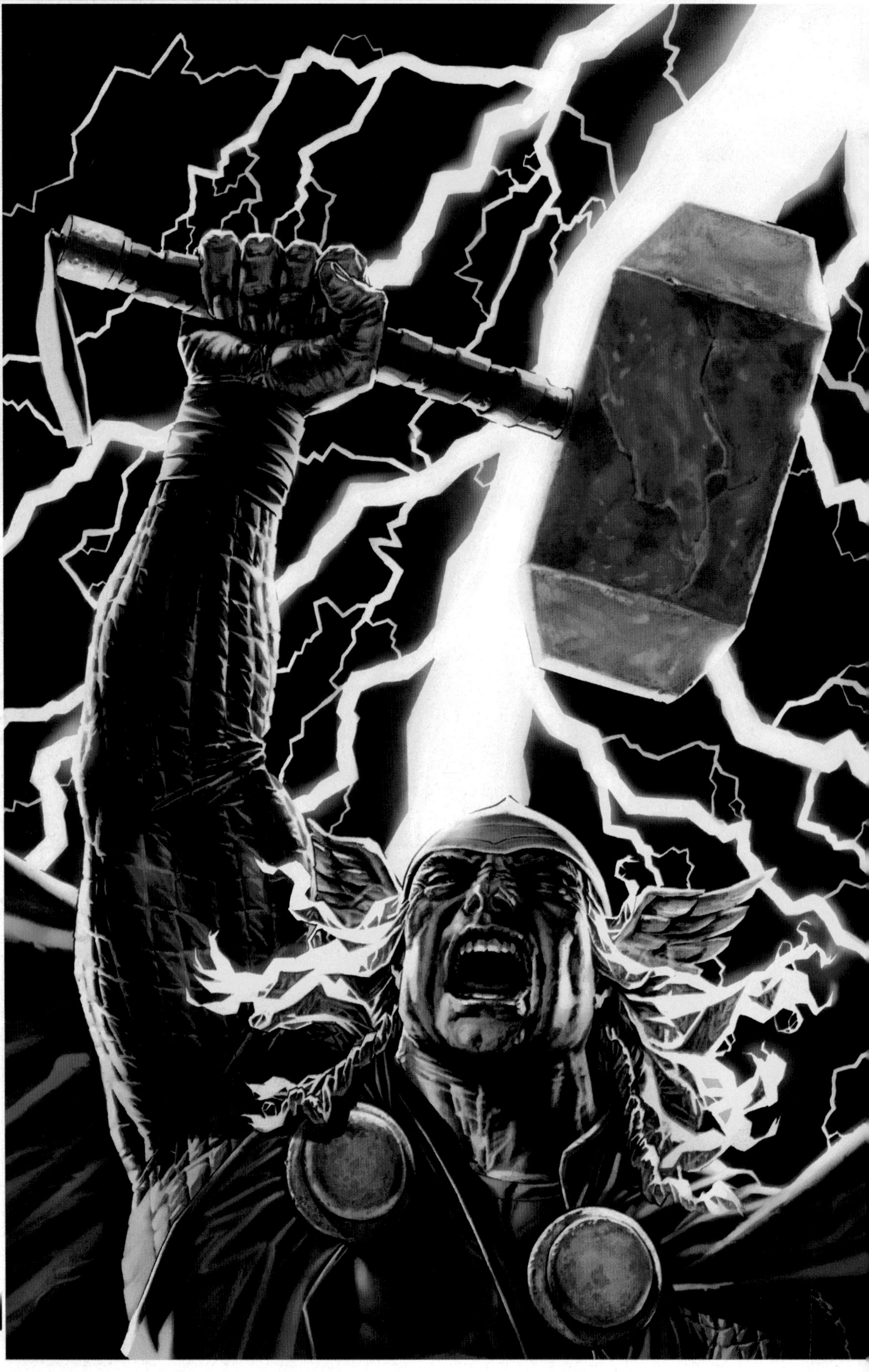

THOR #4 VARIANT BY LEE BERMEJO

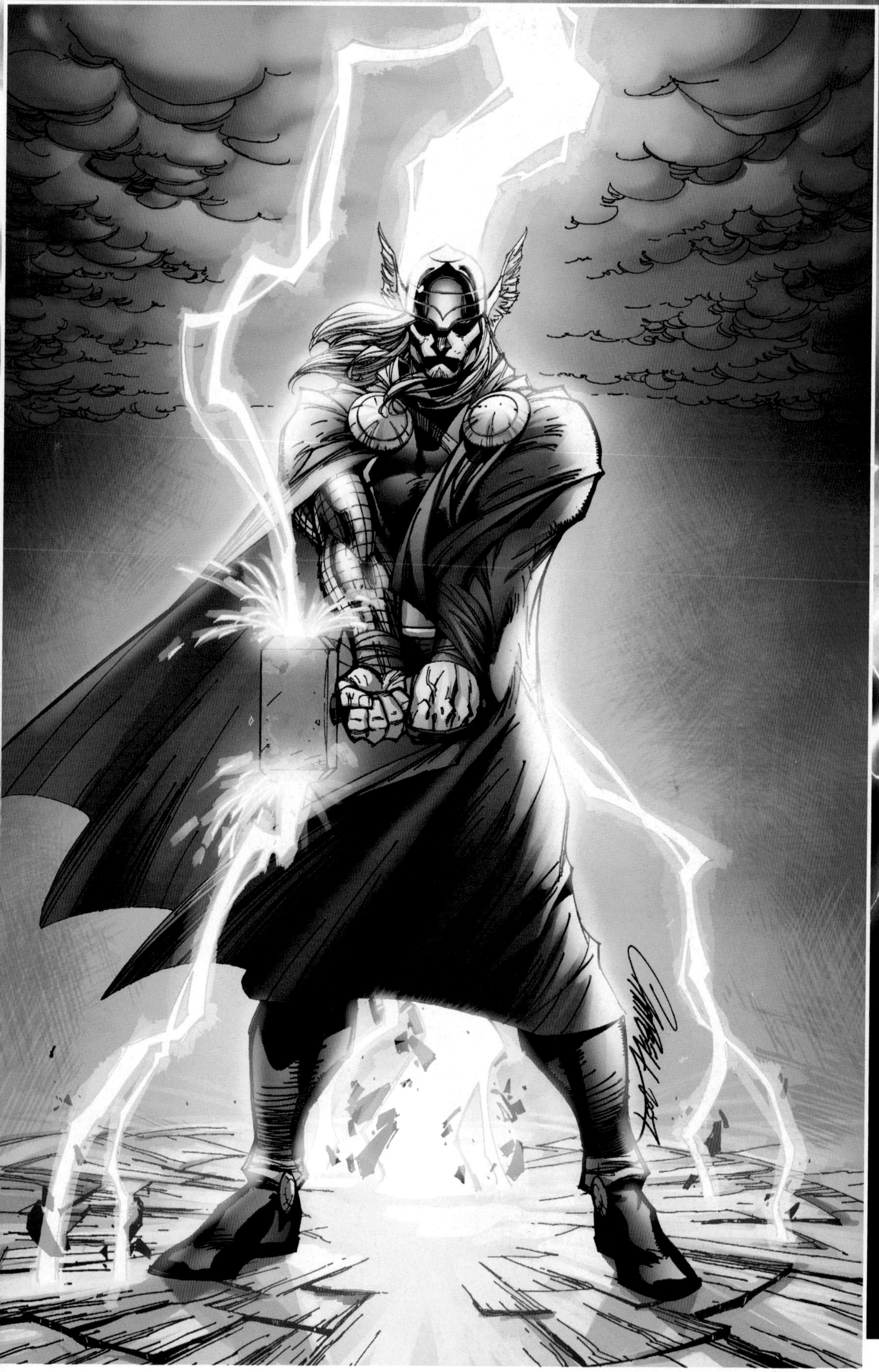

THOR #5 VARIANT BY J. SCOTT CAMPBELL

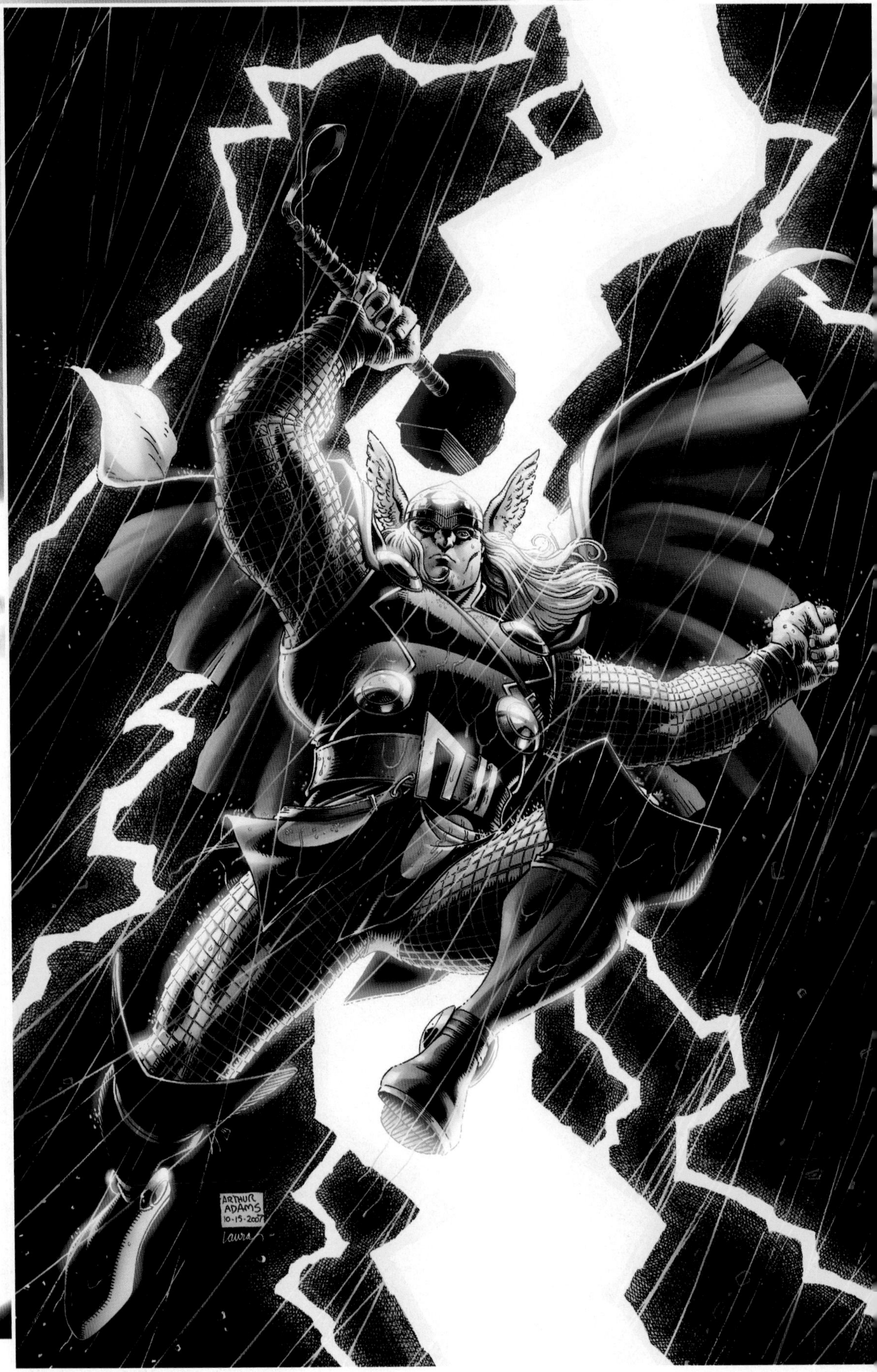
ARTHUR ADAMS 10-15-2007
Laura

**THOR #6 VARIANT BY ARTHUR ADAMS**

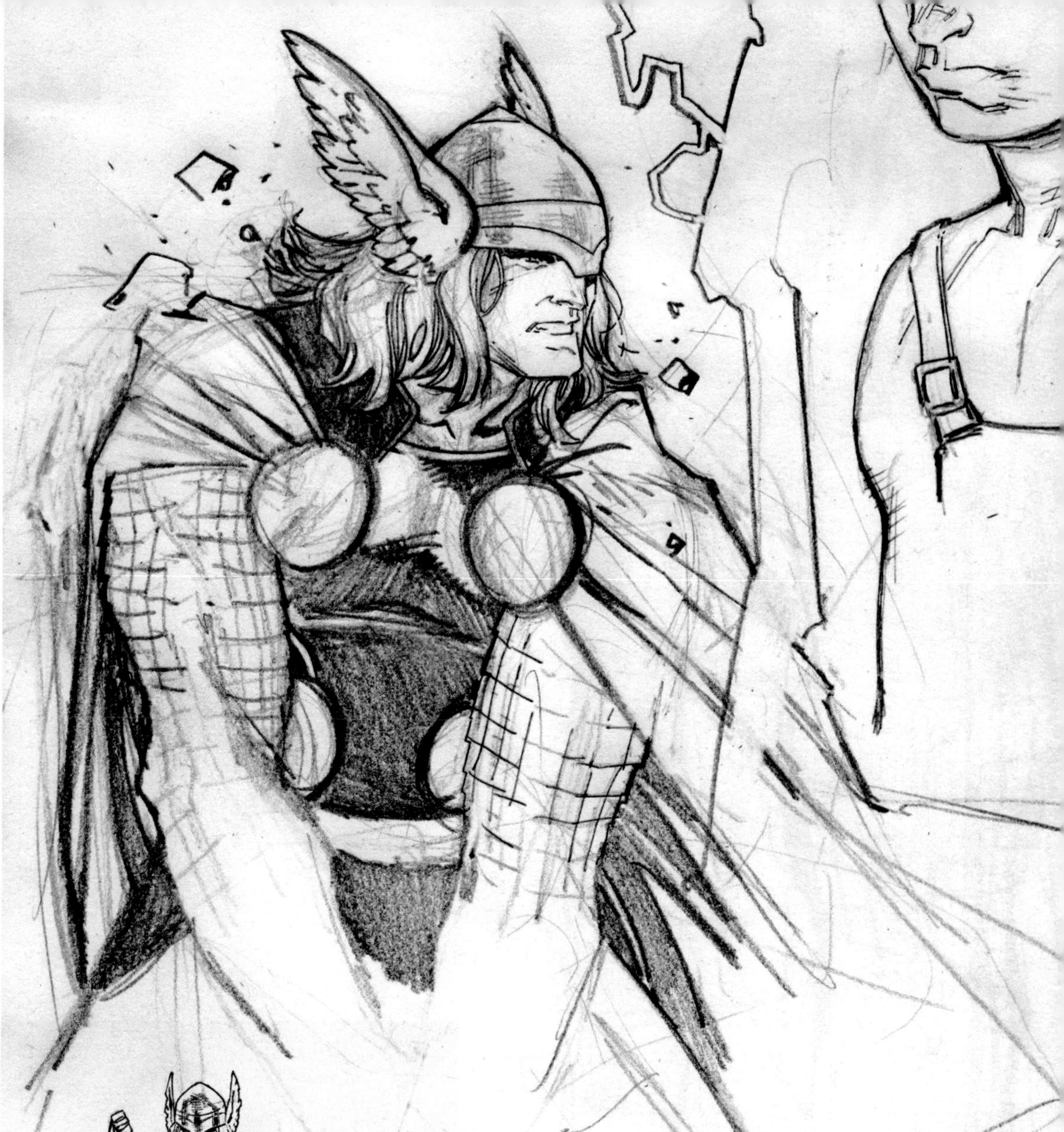

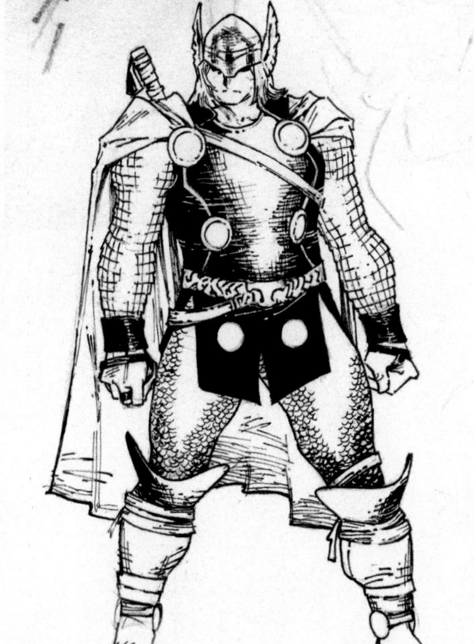

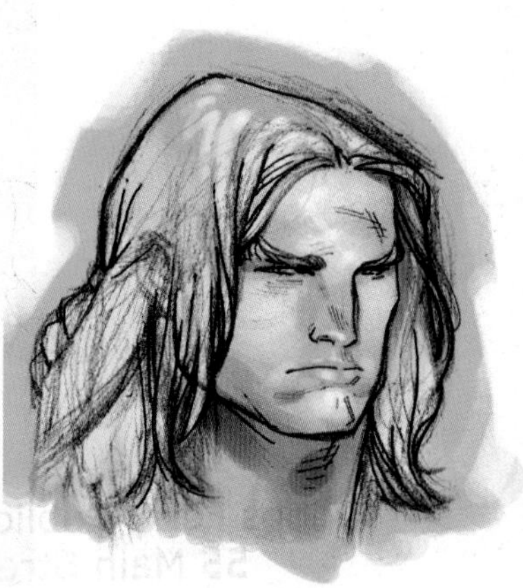

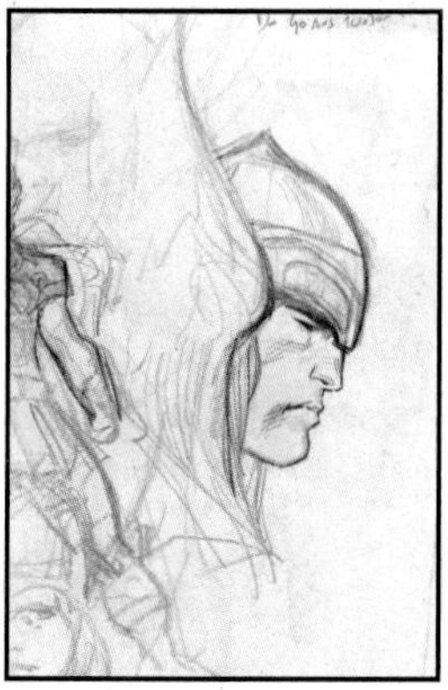

THOR DESIGNS BY OLIVIER COIPEL

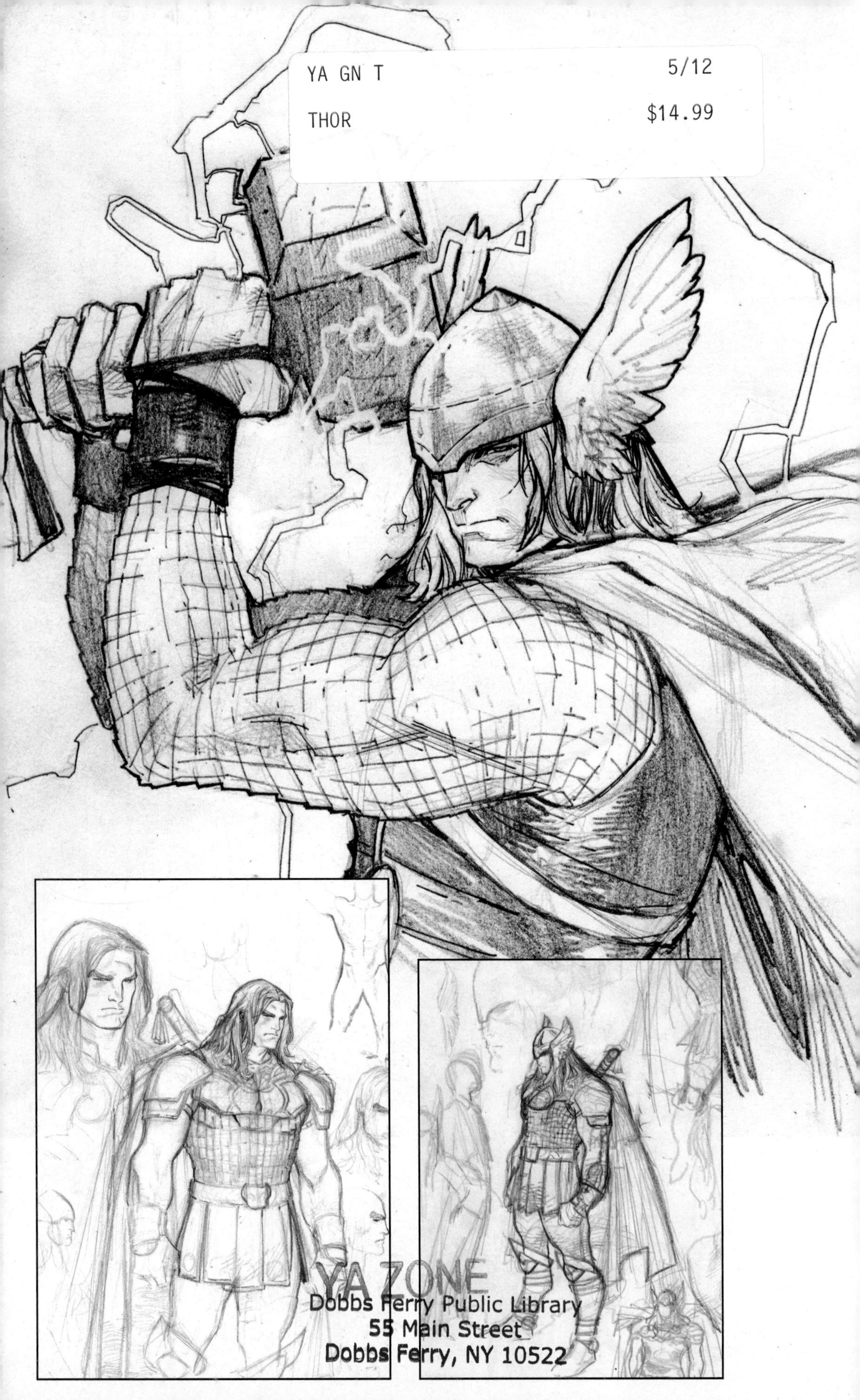